MAKING MUSIC AND HAVING A BLAST!

MUSIC FOR LIFE

MAKING MUSIC AND HAVING A
Blast!

A Guide for All Music Students

BONNIE BLANCHARD
WITH
CYNTHIA BLANCHARD ACREE

Indiana University Press
Bloomington and Indianapolis

This book is a publication of

Indiana University Press
601 North Morton Street
Bloomington, IN 47404-3797 USA

www.iupress.indiana.edu

Telephone orders	800-842-6796
Fax orders	812-855-7931
Orders by e-mail	iuporder@indiana.edu

All chapter illustrations by Kathryn Cunningham

Library of Congress Cataloging-in-Publication Data

Blanchard, Bonnie.
  Making music and having a blast! : a guide for all music students / Bonnie
Blanchard ; with Cynthia Blanchard Acree.
    p. cm.
  Includes bibliographical references and index.
  ISBN 978-0-253-22135-3 (pbk : alk. paper) — ISBN 978-0-253-35379-5
(cl : alk. paper) 1. Music—Instruction and study. I. Acree, Cynthia
Blanchard. II. Title.
  MT1.B6523 2009
  780.71—dc22
                                    2009009970

1 2 3 4 5   14 13 12 11 10 09

*To the wonderful music students I have had the
privilege of teaching, including my two sons.
May music enrich your lives forever.*

Music can change the world because it can change people.

Bono, activist and lead singer of the rock band U2

CONTENTS

Preface: The Long, Winding, and Exciting Road to Becoming a Musician   xi

Acknowledgments   xv

Introduction   xvii

PART ONE · GETTING OFF TO A GOOD START   1

1. Tips and Tricks for Fast Success   3
2. The Surprising Truth about Talent   8
3. The Top Mistake New Musicians Can Make   12
4. How to Persuade Your Parents to Buy You an Instrument   20
5. Where and How to Buy Your Instrument   29

PART TWO · GETTING THE MOST FROM YOUR LESSONS   41

6. Are Private Lessons for You?   43
7. Finding the Perfect Teacher   50
8. How to Be a Great Student   59
9. Is It Time to Change Teachers?   62
10. Singers: You Are the Instrument   67

PART THREE · USING PRACTICE TIPS FOR FASTER RESULTS   77

11. The Attitude of Success   79
12. Get in Gear with Goals   82
13. How to Fit Practice into Your Already Busy Life   90
14. Quit Wasting Your Practice Time   98
15. Shake Up Your Practice Routine   114

PART FOUR · SOLVING THE MYSTERY OF MUSIC THEORY   123

16. Note Names on the Piano, Sharps and Flats, and the Chromatic Scale   125
17. Major Scales and Key Signatures   132
18. Intervals   139
19. Minor Scales   148
20. Chords and Arpeggios   153
21. Chord Inversions, Figured Bass, and Cadences   161

PART FIVE · TUNE IN TO CLASSICAL MUSIC   169

22. The Middle Ages and the Renaissance   171
23. The Baroque and Classical Periods   177
24. The Romantic Period   183
25. The Contemporary Period   187
26. Why Listen to Classical Music?   191
27. Hey, Listen to This!   198

PART SIX · BECOMING A SKILLED MUSICIAN   211

28. Learn the Tricks to Become a Confident Sight-Reader   213
29. Intonation: You *Can* Learn to Play in Tune   218
30. Musicality: The Difference between Playing and Typing   223
31. How to Memorize without Having a Brain Freeze   238

PART SEVEN · PERFORMING WITH CONFIDENCE   245

32. Put Concerts and Contests into Perspective   247
33. Conquer Your Fear Factor   252
34. Ace the Audition   266

PART EIGHT · AVOIDING STUMBLING BLOCKS ALONG THE WAY   275

35. Finding the Middle Ground: A Guide for Frustrated Students and Their "Helpful" Parents   277
36. Student to Student: Advice from Teens   285
37. Brace Yourself for Braces   289
38. Help! I Want to Quit   293
39. Thorny Questions from Students: You're Not Alone!   309
40. Is All This Hard Work Worth It?   324

PART NINE · MAKING BEAUTIFUL MUSIC TOGETHER   333

41. Have Fun and Make Friends When You Play Music Together   335

42. What Can I Do If I'm Bored in Band or Orchestra?   346

43. Concert Etiquette, or Dude! When Do I Clap?   348

PART TEN · DECIDING IF A MUSIC CAREER   355
IS RIGHT FOR YOU

44. So You Want to Be a Music Major?   357

45. Choosing a College or Conservatory   364

46. Getting into the School of Your Dreams   375

47. Preparing for the College or Professional Orchestra Audition   386

48. Music Professions: Ways to Live by What You Love   396

49. Life as a Professional Musician: Is It for You?   407

50. Lessons about Life You Can Learn from Professional Musicians   411

Appendix A. Music Theory Review   415

Appendix B. The Musical Periods   421

Glossary of Musical Terms   423

Reading, Browsing, Watching, Listening: A List of References   431

Index   439

PREFACE

The Long, Winding, and Exciting Road to Becoming a Musician

Welcome! My name is Bonnie Blanchard. I've been a freelance musician and private music teacher for 35 years. I'm also the author of the Music for Life series. The first book in this series is *Making Music and Enriching Lives: A Guide for All Music Teachers*. You're reading the second book, dedicated to students ranging in age from teens to adults, and in experience from beginners to college graduates starting music careers. Adult students returning to music, or playing for the first time, will also benefit from my practical tips and advice on the challenges all musicians share.

I've taught music for many years, yet memories of my days as a middle school beginner and a struggling college music major remain vivid today. My introduction to the world of music began at age 12. Every Tuesday after school I trudged up the long flight of wooden stairs to the second-floor apartment of Mrs. Shell, my elderly piano teacher.

Mrs. Shell never took the time to teach me how to read notes and rhythms and to understand music theory. She preferred the more "efficient" method of giving me all the answers. The tedious process of writing in the names of every note and then circling every sharp and flat in my music book with her red pencil took nearly half of every lesson. And then she made my job even easier—by playing each new piece for me. Once I knew how each piece sounded, I breezed through them, never needing to learn the difference between a half-note and a quarter-note.

It wasn't that I worried much about improving my playing anyway. Why would I? My "helpful" teacher never held recitals and was the only person who ever heard me play. Besides, no matter how much I practiced (and most weeks I didn't!), she told me my playing was "wonderful!" Her praise boosted my ego and gave me the warped idea that I was so naturally gifted I didn't need to practice. I was convinced only stupid or untalented people had to practice. Did I ever get that one wrong! After nearly two years of no practice and no progress, I finally made the connection and realized that being stuck in beginner books was no fun at all. I loved music but hated my playing. At age 14, it was time for me to trade in my red pencil habit.

My next piano teacher was also nice but not without her own quirks. She assigned me more challenging pieces, but when she discovered I was a better singer than pianist, our roles changed. Now *she* played the piano at my lessons while I stood behind her and sang. We became a popular duo at her ladies' club functions. But while my singing skills improved, my piano skills did not. As a freshman in high school, I quit my second attempt at piano lessons.

Over the next two years I continued to sing in my school choral groups, but gave up on finding the right piano teacher. Then one day I passed by a store window with a big sign advertising piano lessons. The lessons were close to my house and reasonably priced. I arrived at my first lesson and met my new teacher, a middle-aged man wearing his hair in a ponytail. "What kind of music did you play with your old teacher?" he asked me. "Classical music," I said. He frowned. "You hated that kind of music, right? Wouldn't you rather play pop music and jazz?" That was my first and last lesson with him.

Two more years passed with no piano lessons. Now I was a freshman at the University of Washington in Seattle. The happiest part of my school day was attending my chorale class with a select group of 40 talented singers. Singing high-quality music with this tight-knit group motivated me to become a music major. I had only one problem, one *big* problem. To be accepted, I needed to audition on both voice and piano. Singing in choirs had prepared me a little for the voice audition. But the piano audition? Yikes! Not only were my meager piano skills rusty, but what piece could I quickly prepare to impress the jury? A friend came to my rescue and taught me the Mozart fantasia she had learned at her own lessons. I practiced hard and somehow passed the piano audition.

My first piano lesson at the University of Washington quickly exposed the huge gaps in my skills. When my world-famous teacher asked me to play my scales, I said, "I don't know what a scale is." He almost fell off his chair. That poor man had to build my knowledge and technique from the ground up. I passed the voice audition and was thrilled to be accepted as a voice student with a piano minor. I was now officially a music major! My new life in music had begun.

Having always been an "outsider" looking in, I was now a full-fledged member of the music community, studying music theory and history, singing in the choir, and taking voice and piano lessons. Yet something was missing: a longtime desire to play the flute, an instrument that had captured my heart at an early age. Growing up in a small town with parents who placed little value on music, I'd never had the opportunity to learn to play the flute. Now at age 19, the time was right.

I bought an old beginner flute and finally found a teacher who taught me the mechanics of the flute and coached me on music history and theory. She generously gave me two free flute lessons a week. After two years, her husband even taught me to play violin. I practiced hard and learned fast, and I later studied viola and guitar, too. My eyes opened to all that the thrilling world of music offered. I was home at last!

Despite my newfound joy, the road to becoming a musician was stressful, too. As a late bloomer, I had a lot of catching up to do. I struggled in music classes. I didn't know chords or intervals and hadn't even heard of famous composers or great masterpieces. Did I ever feel dumb! I sat in the back of the theory class hoping the teacher wouldn't call on me or at least would assign homework in C major. Even though I tried hard, starting as a beginner on every instrument sometimes overwhelmed me. I felt worlds behind the other students, who all had more experience and better playing skills. Taking five lessons a week and preparing for them, studying for my other classes, living on my own, working three days a week, and singing in a church choir made my life a little crazy. But it was all worth it. I've had a rewarding career as a professional musician playing in chamber music groups and teaching a full studio of dedicated flute students.

Music is what I do, what I love, and who I am.

I began my musical "journey" in middle school. If only I knew *then* what I know *now,* after teaching hundreds of students and learning from my struggles and those of my sons. I wrote this book to help you avoid the common pitfalls and frustrations of learning to sing or play an instrument. Within these pages, you'll find amazing, easy-to-apply tips and tricks to playing better faster, and having a lot more fun. Whether you're a middle-school student playing in your first band or orchestra, a teen picking up an instrument for the first time, or a young adult considering college and career choices, this book addresses your unique challenges. Adult amateurs and music professionals will also find tips to expand their knowledge and enjoyment. No matter what your skill level, *Making Music and Having a Blast!* will become a handy reference on many topics. Please read on to learn how this book can guide you along the fastest route to the exciting world of musicianship.

ACKNOWLEDGMENTS

Writing a book is always a group project, with only the authors getting credit. The ideas, tips, and tricks drawn from my 35 years of teaching are mine, but this book is not mine alone.

At the top of the list is my sister, Cynthia Acree, an author and writing coach. Day after day, she brought more life, organization, creativity, and knowledge to these pages. Without her, neither this nor the first book in the Music for Life series, *Making Music and Enriching Lives: A Guide for All Music Teachers,* would exist. Writing and publishing books takes more time and energy than I ever imagined. Cindy shared my vision of helping music teachers and students become happier and more successful, and she kept me on track. Thank you, Cliff and the boys, for sharing her while she hibernated with the computer to write. I know you won't miss those daily volleys of "Please turn down the TV!" versus "You're *always* on the computer!" She'll reopen the Acree Bakery soon.

Jim Sutton, my wise and ultraprofessional literary agent, has been a driving force behind both Music for Life books. A highly respected author, agent, and editor, Jim's days are filled with work and many projects, all more significant than ours. Yet, starting with Cindy more than 12 years ago, he has always found time to counsel and support us. Jim cared not only about the success of our books but also about our success in life. Thank you, Jim, for your ideas, direction, humor, and passion for our projects. Your faith in us has been the inspiration we needed to do our best.

With Jim Sutton's help, I found Indiana University Press, the perfect publisher for the Music for Life series. Sponsoring editor Jane Behnken shared my excitement for this book and offered helpful suggestions. The team at Indiana University Press, including Miki Bird, managing editor, Elaine Durham Otto, copy editor, and Kate Matthen, assistant sales manager, worked hard to create and promote my books. I look forward to working with you for years to come.

Nancy Zylstra, my former college roommate and internationally known singing coach, contributed valuable information for the chapter devoted to singers. It's reassuring to know that readers have the latest advice on how to protect their singing voices.

I love teaching and love my students. Knowing and working with so many wonderful students has been the inspiration for my books. Throughout this book, you'll find contributions from both current and former music students who generously shared their stories and advice to help other music students succeed. My flute students Simon Berry and Lydia Walsh, two bright, brutally honest 16-year-olds, told me their opinions of every page. They often hit the delete key—especially after reading my "lame" jokes. I finally let them write their own chapter, which *I* got to edit. Payback time! My friend and former student Margie Byers also read some chapters and added her own twist. Drawing on the ideas of many has strengthened this book.

Spell-check doesn't catch every mistake. A perfectionist in both music and grammar, my friend and accompanist, Mary Kay Wilson, does. She read many versions of these chapters and patiently endured my whining about working so hard on this book.

I also want to thank my friends and music associates who have supported both of my books, including Hal Ott, Carolyn Nussbaum, Cathy Miller, Steve West, and Donna Shin. Of course, I could never leave out my personal support group, the many friends who encouraged me during the writing process.

By the time you're finished writing a book-length manuscript, you've written through enough stages and revisions to nearly memorize the book, making it almost impossible to proofread accurately. Our brilliant friend and supporter Melinda Bargreen offered to read the final manuscript from beginning to end. Thank you, Melinda, for making this book factual, readable, and grammatically correct. I can relax, knowing these chapters have met your high standards.

Finally, thank you to my husband, Don, and our sons, Scott and Kyle. Sorry the computer is right beside the TV. Sorry I can't concentrate when the TV is on. Sorry you have only seen the back of my head for months. I'll make it up to you with homemade cinnamon bread and chocolate chip cookies.

INTRODUCTION

Every musician has special needs, from beginners looking for a good teacher to experienced singers or players ready to choose a college or shift their music careers into the fast lane. What do *you* want to know? Would you be happy to never again worry about stage fright? Do you want to learn the easiest ways to memorize, play musically, and sight-read? Do you want to learn your music faster and get out of the practice room sooner? Are you having trouble getting along with your parents, music teacher, or other music students? Do you hate practicing or have a hard time fitting it into your busy schedule? Do you want an easy way to learn music history and music theory? Do you wonder if you have what it takes to become a professional musician? If you answered yes to any of these questions, this is the book for you. Although it may take you time to read, *Making Music and Having a Blast!* will save you time and trouble in the long run. No matter what you want to know, you'll find tools to solve your problems and stories to inspire you. Singers, this book is for you, too. Even though you'll read the word *playing* more often than *singing, all* of these tips and tricks apply equally to you.

Making Music and Having a Blast! is divided into 10 sections. Each chapter targets specific topics and is full of ideas you can use right away. You can read the book straight through or skip to chapters you're most interested in. Throughout the book, I've also included firsthand accounts of experiences from students who have had their own share of struggles and triumphs. When you're done reading, hang on to this book! In a few months you might find yourself heading to a new chapter! Here's a quick tour of what you'll find inside:

Part 1. Getting Off to a Good Start

    Whether you're a beginning student or have a few years of playing experience, part 1 gives you a solid foundation in music. You'll learn:

    • Tips and tricks for fast success.

- What talent can and can't do for you.
- The top mistake new music students make.
- How to persuade your parents to buy you an instrument.
- Where and how to find a quality instrument for a good price.

Part 2. Getting the Most from Your Lessons

In this section you'll learn:

- What music lessons can do for you.
- How to find the "perfect" teacher.
- Ways to be a great student.
- The best way to switch teachers without hurting feelings.
- Why singers and instrumentalists need to use the same techniques to improve.

Part 3. Using Practice Tips for Faster Results

The tips in this section will show you how to spend less time practicing and more time playing. You'll quit dreading practice when you learn:

- Steps to build confidence in yourself.
- How to make your work count with goals.
- Ways to fit practice into your busy day.
- How to practice smarter and faster.
- Why practice can make the difference between improving and quitting.
- What to do if you're sick of practicing.
- Ways to practice differently and not be bored.

Part 4. Solving the Mystery of Music Theory

This workbook will walk you through the basics of music theory. Why learn boring scales and music theory? Because once you understand the "rules" of music, you will have a solid foundation in music, a good start in your college music courses, and the music theory skills you need to become a more intelligent and independent player. You'll feel you have your own tutor when you learn how to:

- Recognize intervals by sight and sound.
- Memorize major and minor scales and key signatures.
- Build major, minor, augmented, and diminished chords.
- Analyze chords and realize figured bass.

Part 5. Tune In to Classical Music

How can listening to classical music make you a better player? Why should anyone be interested in the lives of dead composers? Why should you listen to all genres of music? In this part you'll learn:

- Where to start listening if you don't really know or like classical music.
- How to make classical music part of your daily life.
- How music changed through time.
- The characteristics and composers of the major musical periods.
- What music to choose to start your listening library.

Part 6. Becoming a Skilled Musician

Sure you can finger the notes on your instrument, but are you really
making music? Part 6 shows you how to learn music faster and
more accurately, how to play those notes musically and in tune,
and how to memorize them. In this section you'll learn how to:

- Scan the music to sight-read it right the first time.
- Use music theory, dynamics, articulation, and
      more to make music come alive.
- Hear yourself and play in tune.
- Memorize pieces and know what to do if you have a brain freeze.

Part 7. Performing with Confidence

Have you ever felt a little weak at the knees before a contest or audition?
Most players have! In this section, we'll meet that challenge with a step-
by-step method to prepare your music and your performance. You'll
learn how to calm negative thoughts or emotions that can interfere
with performing your best. And perhaps most important, you'll learn
how to put concerts and contests into perspective. Believe it or not,
you'll live! You'll look forward to your performances when you know:

- How to prepare for a performance, starting from
      the moment you receive the piece.
- What to do in the weeks, hours, minutes, and
      even seconds before you perform.
- The power of positive self-talk.
- How to connect with your audience and put them at ease.
- How to survive if you mess up.
- What being a winner really means.

Part 8. Avoiding Stumbling Blocks along the Way

In this section we'll turn our attention to the inevitable bend in the road.
Our "advice column" chapter will teach you how to smooth conflicts
with your parents, your teachers, and other music students. Students will
give you insider advice. You'll know you're not alone when you learn:

- How to ask your parents to support your play-
      ing or quit pressuring you to excel.
- Strategies for dealing with jealousy.
- Steps to take if you feel like quitting.
- Tips from kids to help you survive playing through braces.
- How other students handled the ups and downs of learning music.
- How learning music helps you in other areas of your life.

Part 9. Making Beautiful Music Together

Music is like a delicious meal; it's better when shared with friends. Part
9 shows you how to act on the stage or in the audience. It includes:

- The fun and benefits of playing in band, or-
      chestra, choir, or chamber groups.

- The basics of getting a group started and running rehearsals.
- What to do if you're bored in band or orchestra without driving your director crazy.
- The not-so-subtle differences between how to act at a classical concert and a rock concert.

Part 10. Deciding If a Music Career Is Right for You

You'll learn straight answers to the realities of life as a musician and whether you have what it takes:

- The one and only reason to become a music major.
- When and how to prepare to be accepted as a music major.
- How to compare colleges and conservatories.
- Solid ways to boost your chances of being accepted to the school of your dreams.
- Many ways to make music your profession.
- The realities of the job market.
- What life is like as a professional musician.
- How to be a successful musician and a happy person.

Handy Reference Section

Do you want to learn more about your instrument, music genre, or professional organizations? Look here for helpful books, magazines, websites, and other resources. This section is organized in categories to make it easier for you to find information on your particular interests. This is the section you'll turn to again and again when you need to know:

- Rhythm information
- Tempo markings
- Key signatures
- Musical periods and composers
- Musical terms
- What resources are available for reading, listening, and more

Whew! As you can see, *Making Music and Having a Blast!* has the tools and advice you need. Ready to get started? Let's go.

PART ONE

GETTING OFF TO A
GOOD START

ONE

Tips and Tricks for Fast Success

Before you dive into the hundreds of tips and tricks in the following chapters, I want to give you a few quick suggestions to help you get on the right track. If I only had five minutes to give advice to new and experienced musicians, here's what I'd say.

1. PLAY A DECENT INSTRUMENT

If you play a tin can, your playing will sound like a tin can! Your parents may say they'll only buy you a good instrument when you play better, but tell them it's hard to improve when you're fighting your instrument. A good instrument allows you to sound better and play faster. Playing a good instrument will inspire you to practice more and can be a solid investment over the long run.

2. GET THE BASICS RIGHT

Use proper fingering from the beginning. Learn the right way before the wrong way becomes a habit. On single line instruments, such as the flute, make sure you're not making up fingering. If you do, you'll have a devil of a time trying to unlearn your fingering habits. Pay special attention to the fingering in piano music and the positions on string instruments. If you play it a different way every time, your brain will get confused and your playing will never sound polished.

Learn how music works, not just how to play some pieces. Sure, it's great to wow your family and friends with lots of black notes. But much more important than playing one impressive piece is knowing the basics that can be applied to all pieces. Use scales and études to work on technique before you need it in real music. Your audience will thank you if you work out the tricky parts before you attempt the big piece. Learn music theory, scales and arpeggios, the rules of musicality, and how to sight-read. These building blocks of music will enable you to become an independent learner (you don't really want your teacher to live with you, do you?) and a well-rounded musician, not just a parrot who can play a few songs well.

Watch your posture. Moving your body correctly not only makes you look better but helps you play better. You might get away with playing with bad posture and position now, but it will catch up with you when the music gets harder. When you're older, holding your body and your instrument in the wrong position can make playing painful instead of fun.

3. TAKE LESSONS FROM A GOOD TEACHER

Here again your parents may want you to play on your own for a while or reach a certain level to prove that you like your instrument, you'll practice, and you'll stick with it. But learning wrong on your own can be worse than not learning at all. It's much easier to teach beginning students who have never touched their instrument than ones who learned by themselves or in a school program with little individual help.

What's so great about having a teacher? Imagine never going to school and just learning math and English on your own. Not very efficient, huh? A teacher helps you learn faster, and the sooner you learn, the sooner you'll have fun. A teacher saves you lots of time fixing mistakes. A teacher has a plan for you and knows what music you need to learn to improve. And a teacher keeps you interested and practicing. Without a teacher's help, you may get bogged down with problems that have simple solutions. Perhaps most important of all, a teacher can become a good friend, role model, and mentor through your sometimes rocky teen years.

If you already have a teacher, are you progressing quickly and having fun? Does your teacher help you fulfill your potential? Even if your music is only a hobby, get a good teacher who motivates you.

4. MAKE PRACTICING A DAILY HABIT

Imagine the team's reaction if your high school basketball coach told them, "Team, we've got a tough season coming up, and we're going to need to work hard to make it to the finals. Every Monday we'll meet in the gym for a one-hour lecture on how to play basketball. Don't worry about practicing. You'll improve just by listening to my lecture." Would this team make the playoffs?

Whether you're learning to play a sport or a musical instrument, you can't gain the skill you need in a one-hour weekly lesson; the real learning happens *between* lessons. It's simple: the more you practice, the better you'll get. If you don't practice regularly, you'll never get anywhere and may be tempted to give up playing. But when you play well, you can choose more interesting music, have more playing opportunities, and play in fun ensembles—not to mention that wonderful feeling of accomplishment you'll have.

How do you get in the habit of practicing? By scheduling a regular and convenient practice time in a place without distractions—no, not in front of the TV! Start with short sessions, then build your stamina to longer ones. Use a metronome and a tuner. (They never lie.) And find a teacher who cares if you're

prepared. You will be extra motivated to practice and improve because you
won't want to let your teacher down.

5. PRACTICE THE RIGHT WAY

Putting in hours of grueling practicing every day isn't necessary if you practice the right way. Practicing is like digging a hole. If you keep making the same mistakes over and over, you are digging your hole in the wrong place, and the hole just gets deeper. When you finally realize your mistake, it takes a lot longer to fill up that hole and start a new one than it would to just dig the hole in the right place the first time.

Practice in bite-sized pieces, or you'll choke on the whole piece. Focus on one small section (even a measure) at a time. Don't just play through the whole piece—that's playing, not practicing. Listen to each note under a microscope and make sure it's played right before it's played fast. Trust me on this one. Slow practice means fast progress.

6. LET YOUR PARENTS HELP YOU

I can already hear you groaning. You may sometimes think of your parents as annoying intrusions, but with their support you'll progress faster. If you're a beginner, invite your parents to come to your lessons. Work with them to set up a practice spot and schedule. Ask your parents to supervise your practice or be available if you need help. It doesn't matter if your parents are musically knowledgeable or not. It's their investment in your success that counts, not whether they also know how to play the instrument. You may even get them to set up a reward system for you for careful (and uncomplaining) practice.

On the other hand, don't become too dependent on your parents' help. When you're older and more experienced, ask them to let you be more independent. Music is for you. You're in control of how much effort you put in. It may have been your parents' idea for you to play an instrument and take lessons, but if you're only continuing because you're forced, you'll end up hating music and may quit just to spite your parents. Be open to this wonderful opportunity called music and give it a try. You may be surprised how much you grow to like it and that your parents were right all along.

7. WORK HARD AND SET GOALS

Think you don't have enough talent to improve? Think again. The best musicians aren't born, they're made. Yes, even the great musical geniuses studied, practiced, and set goals. You can bet that "musical genius" who sits in first chair in band or orchestra is the one who practices the most.

Now is the time to set some goals. Decide what you want to accomplish and start small. Your short-term goal might be to play your favorite piece or be able to perform in public without fainting. Your long-term goal might be to keep up with your peers, get into an elite ensemble, win a contest, or become a professional. Those huge goals may seem a long way from where you are now, but setting small goals along the way will guide you toward the big ones. Be sure to write down your specific goals. Doing so helps your brain go into a whole new mode to help your goals become reality. Believe in yourself, and don't let anyone talk you out of your dreams.

8. ENJOY YOUR PLAYING

Whether you're practicing scales or struggling with tricky rhythms and memorizing, keep in mind that all your hard work now will pay off for years to come. But what about now? Music should be fun while you're learning it, too. Balance pushing yourself with giving yourself a break. When you've worked hard, reward yourself by playing something easy, something you really enjoy, or something you've already mastered. Join your school music group or play with your friends. You don't always have to focus on preparing for a lesson or performance. Play for the fun of it.

9. COMMIT TO HANGING IN THERE WHEN THE GOING GETS ROUGH

Music is like life. Some things don't turn out the way you had hoped, and other good things will surprise you. Your reaction is up to you. You lose the competition, the person seated ahead of you in band or orchestra isn't as good as you but gets all the solos, or you don't get accepted to the college of your choice. You can choose to feel sad, mad, or motivated to try harder next time. Music is a tough business, and if you want to make it a career, you'll be better off learning to deal positively with your disappointments starting now.

Be patient. Some of the best players have had a slow start. Expect moments of frustration; that's what learning is all about. Don't even think about quitting until you've made a commitment to stick with it for six months or you've had the joy of accomplishing something you never thought possible and the fun of playing a great piece.

Take an occasional break to rejuvenate. Don't beat yourself up when you feel as if you're not making any progress. Just think back to the last few months to see how far you've come and congratulate yourself. Treat yourself as you would your best friend. You're worth it!

10. REALIZE IT'S NOT JUST ABOUT THE MUSIC

One of my longtime students, Ana, stopped by to see me before heading to college. "When I first came for lessons," she told me, "I thought I was just going to learn about the flute. But I learned about life, too." She was right. Music teaches you how to work hard, how to play well with others, how to accept disappointment, and so much more. You'll be surprised how music will affect what you do and who you are. Being a musician is one of the most rewarding things in life.

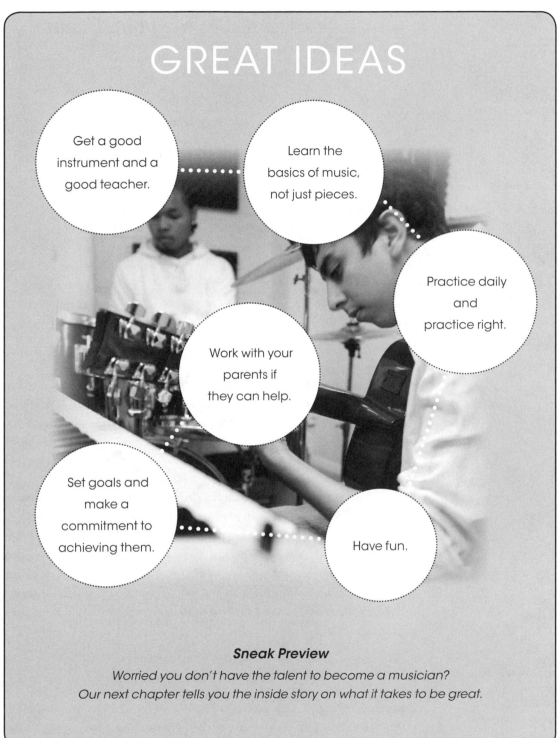

GREAT IDEAS

Get a good instrument and a good teacher.

Learn the basics of music, not just pieces.

Practice daily and practice right.

Work with your parents if they can help.

Set goals and make a commitment to achieving them.

Have fun.

Sneak Preview

Worried you don't have the talent to become a musician?
Our next chapter tells you the inside story on what it takes to be great.

TWO

The Surprising Truth about Talent

Many people think they don't have musical ability. They say things like, "Me sing? I can't even carry a tune" or "I'm way too uncoordinated to play an instrument." Guess what? They're wrong. Thanks to our DNA, virtually all people have musical intelligence. It's part of our genetic blueprint. With rare exception, we're all born with some musical talent. Think you are tone-deaf? If you can recognize your friends' voices on the phone or recognize the accents of speakers from different regions, then you have a good ear.

WHAT IS MUSICAL TALENT?

When I perform with my flute/violin/guitar jazz trio, I feel so untalented. Lonnie and Paul are so good at improvisation and playing in the jazz style, while I struggle to turn my Baroque style into improv and try to remember the modes and jazz licks. But when I play classical favorites with my Silverwood Quartet, I sometimes feel very accomplished. I play piano and flute, and I sing; I lead the ensemble, and we make beautiful music together.

Am I talented? That depends on the situation. I'm talented in some areas and not in others, just as I'm pretty talented in learning languages or music but not so great in math. Having perfect pitch, being able to play by ear, improvise, play or sing in tune, develop a beautiful sound, memorize easily, compose, sight-read, learn new pieces quickly, or play musically are all facets of talent. Some lucky musicians have them all, but most of us are skilled at some things and not at others. Don't think you're not a talented musician because you're not good at everything.

DO YOU HAVE TO SHOW EXCEPTIONAL TALENT TO PLAY AN INSTRUMENT?

If you look for signs of musical talent before giving children lessons, many children will miss out. Do you have to have innate talent to play golf? To win at chess or board games? To become a teacher or a doctor? Would you teach a child math only if he or she showed exceptional ability in math? Should only the very talented play music while the rest become just listeners? No. There's room for everyone to enjoy and create music. You'll never know how much talent you have unless you try.

IS EVERYONE BORN WITH THE SAME AMOUNT OF TALENT?

Josh was a "natural" musician. The first time he picked up his clarinet, he got a strong sound, his hand position was great, he easily learned to read music, had a great sense of rhythm, and played musically from the start. Things didn't go so smoothly for Emma. Every step of learning the clarinet was a struggle. She couldn't get a sound for more than a month, then she couldn't hold a note for longer than 10 seconds. Her tone was wispy, and her hand position was awkward. She struggled to read and to count, and she learned the rules of musicality one by one. Nothing came easily to her. She sounded like a beginner for a long time.

Were Josh and Emma born with the same amount of talent? I believe that every child has the ability to be a musician, but I don't believe that every child is born with the same abilities. This musical intelligence is like other intelligence. You may notice some kids in your class who learn math easier than others, and because they are innately good at math, they like it and want to do more. Kids who learn music easily will love music and want to practice and perform, and that may make them seem even more talented.

Who will become the best musician, Josh or Emma? You can't tell from my descriptions. Those who become good musicians aren't necessarily the ones who seem the most talented. The best musicians are the ones who want it the most. It's not what you are born with that matters most but what you do with your innate abilities.

LACK OF TALENT OR LACK OF OPPORTUNITY?

For most people, the problem isn't lack of talent. The real problem is lack of opportunity, training, and the encouragement we need to develop the talents we are born with. Take superstar golf pro Tiger Woods, for example. At 21 he became the youngest winner of the U.S. Masters tournament. No doubt he was born with athletic ability, but he also had passion for his sport and a dad who devoted himself to developing his son's talent. Would he have broken as many records if his father hadn't put a golf club in his hands before he could walk? What if his dad hadn't coached him, trained him to be mentally tough, and encouraged him every step of the way? We'll never know, because Tiger Woods grew up with the perfect combination of talent, training, and encouragement.

"But my parents didn't give me lessons when I was 3, and they never even took me to a concert," you whine. So you weren't as lucky as Tiger Woods. But don't let that be an excuse. You can make your own opportunities now.

DO ALL MUSICIANS SHOW TALENT AT AN EARLY AGE?

Some, like Mozart, are born musicians. When you were 3, you were probably playing with blocks. But Mozart was already picking out melodies on the keyboard, and by age 5 he was composing short pieces that his father wrote down. Makes you feel a little inadequate, right? Well, don't feel bad. Not all great musicians are prodigies like Mozart. Beethoven's dad tried to push him to be like Mozart (so he could become famous and make money for him), but it didn't work because Beethoven's talents developed more slowly. He didn't become an established composer until he was in his thirties. See, you've still got time!

THE TROUBLE WITH TALENT

People born with extra talent get a head start on the rest of us, and at first doors may open easily for them. They zoom past others without even trying—and that's where their troubles can start. Knowing they have an edge, talented people are often tempted to coast by on their abilities. When they do, their head start quickly evaporates. Talent may get you noticed, but it won't keep you ahead. Why? *Because hard work beats talent when talent doesn't work hard.* Hard work and repetition are multipliers of talent. They allow people with average talent to become wildly successful. And without hard work, people with tons of talent can fade into the woodwork.

◀)) *Ron Patterson, professor of violin at the University of Washington, explains talent and hard work to his students this way: "Everyone is born with some sprinkles (talent). Some people have more sprinkles than others. But sprinkles are not good without cake (knowledge and technique, which are the products of hard work). If you have all sprinkles and no cake, you're all fluff. If you have all cake and no sprinkles, you're boring. Cake and a few sprinkles are better than all sprinkles and a little cake. Take the talent you were born with and build a solid foundation. If you want to be a good musician, you need your sprinkles and your cake, too."*

◀)) *Fourteen-year-old Andy, who plays violin and guitar, agrees. "I think I'm talented because I've tried many instruments. My parents never tried any instruments, and they think I'm creative. Working hard is just as important as being talented. If someone works hard, they can achieve everything someone with natural talent can do. The hardworking person tries harder, and it means more to them to play an instrument."*

HOW TO BE A VIRTUOSO

I fear not the man who has practiced 10,000 kicks once,
but I fear the man who has practiced one kick 10,000 times.
—Bruce Lee, American actor and martial artist (1940–73)

The key to extraordinary success is committing to years of intense practice. Research shows that to become a real expert at anything, whether it's swinging a golf club, playing the violin, or even trading stocks on Wall Street, people need to rack up about 10,000 hours of practice. By the time Tiger Woods won that championship, he had accumulated at least 10,000 hours of intense practice in the 19 years since he had started playing. Many times he didn't feel like heading out to the golf course, but he did. If he had said, "I'm out of here!" instead of "Let's go!" he would just be another good golfer. Being successful means that some days you have to practice even when you don't feel like it. That's what makes someone great. Being born with talent can make it easier, but it's the hours of deliberate practice that make you a star.

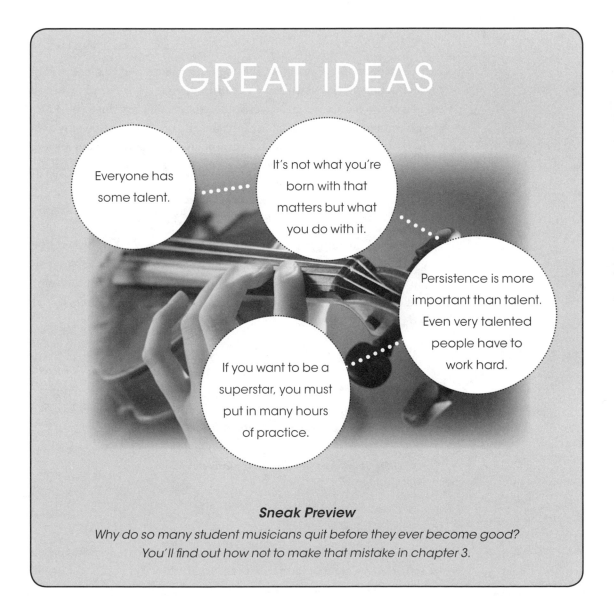

GREAT IDEAS

Everyone has some talent.

It's not what you're born with that matters but what you do with it.

Persistence is more important than talent. Even very talented people have to work hard.

If you want to be a superstar, you must put in many hours of practice.

Sneak Preview

Why do so many student musicians quit before they ever become good? You'll find out how not to make that mistake in chapter 3.

THREE

The Top Mistake New Musicians Can Make

I love making and sharing music. There's nothing like it. But let's face it. Playing an instrument can sometimes be confusing, tiring, boring, and frustrating. Many new musicians start out excited, thinking they're going to be skilled players without much time or effort, and then give up in frustration only a few months later. Learning to play an instrument doesn't offer the instant rewards of rapid-fire electronic games, and it takes time to get used to the demands of a good teacher and the practice load.

THE FRUSTRATION FACTOR

Even experienced musicians feel frustrated at times (make that *many* times). After the fiftieth repetition of the "impossible measure," I've felt like throwing my flute out the window—except it's too expensive! It's even harder for beginners like 14-year-old Janna, who doesn't have a track record of success to fall back on.

"When I started learning to play the flute," Janna says, "I couldn't have been more excited. I expected to work hard and practice. My mom and I spent countless hours hunched over the Tune a Day *book trying to figure out easy quarter-note rhythms and key signatures. Two months went by, and I was still struggling with rhythms and getting a decent tone. I really began to question whether flute was right for me. I enjoyed the challenge of working for something rewarding, but dissecting music every day wasn't exactly what I had in mind."*

Do Struggles Signal Defeat?

Even naturally talented musicians aren't great from day one. Successful people see setbacks as temporary and say, "I can handle this." Less confident people doubt themselves and say, "I'll never be any good. Why even try?" Most people have the talent to play an instrument, but those who don't have a vision of the future and who lack confidence in their abilities more often make the biggest mistake new musicians can make: *They give up their music before they give it a chance.*

Is Learning to Play Not What You Expected?

Were you surprised by the amount of effort and practice it takes to play an instrument? Simon, aged 16, understands.

> *"When you hear someone play a beautiful song, you want to play like that, too. But trying to get those sounds as a beginner is like giving someone from 4,000 years ago a laptop and expecting them to use it. It's not that easy." Simon offers this advice to beginners tempted to give up too soon: "At the very least, keep going until you can play through some fun, easy pieces. Then you'll know how it feels to make music." Lucy can relate. She took private flute lessons from sixth through eleventh grade and played only in high school band. "You read about how playing flute changed this person's life or gave that person a whole new look on the world. My story is different. I wasn't such a good student. I didn't try my hardest, and I let bad habits eat me alive. I'm so glad I play music, but it hasn't always been easy."*

Some beginners struggle to get a decent sound.

> *Kianna, 11, started flute lessons after taking piano for three years. "Flute was harder to learn than piano because of the way you have to form your lips to get a decent sound," she recalls. "I got really frustrated and discouraged when I couldn't make a good sound and thought about quitting. Then I remembered how I went through that hard stage when I learned to play piano. I kept going, and it got fun. My teacher encouraged me to keep trying."*

Even those kids who sail through the basics may have a hard time when the going gets tough.

> *Keleah felt overwhelmed when she moved from a child-sized harp to a full-sized one. "When I went from a 5-pound lever harp to a 79-pound pedal harp, it was hard to adjust. I loved the levers and wanted to stay with them forever. Soon I realized the pedals were more efficient, and I'm still learning how to use them." Keleah knows a lot of people get discouraged a few months after they start playing. "After you get past the beginning stage and it gets more difficult, there's probably a time when everyone feels like quitting. It's harder because you have to practice more, and you can feel discouraged learning new techniques and rhythms. But when you pass that stage, it becomes fun to play."*

Ninth-grader Andy has played violin, guitar, and now trombone. "The trombone was easy to learn at first," he says. "Then it got harder learning new slide positions and hitting high notes. My only help was in band, and our class was so big I thought the teacher couldn't help me. I wanted to give up. But our teacher knew every instrument, and she worked with me and made me feel I could do it."

Like Babies, All Musicians Start Out Wobbly

We live in a quick-fix society. Most people want instant answers and instant success. Most people, that is, except babies. Have you watched a video of yourself learning to walk? Your first baby steps often ended in a crash, but that didn't stop you. You didn't dwell on those failures or doubt your abilities. You jumped up and tried again. To do well in music, you need that same drive to keep working, even when you struggle.

Fourth-grader Yulan played violin from age 4 to 6 before she moved on to the piano. "When I started taking music lessons, I was nervous because I like to succeed on the first try. But that's not how it works with music. I did great at first, and then I had a lull when things started getting harder. I'd get frustrated and stop listening to my teacher. When she tried to explain something to me, all I could think was that I can't do this! It's too hard. But now I've learned that if you get discouraged easily, you won't learn anything."

Model the Masters

Even top performers struggle as they sharpen their skills. Do they waste time feeling defeated and wondering if they'll ever get it? No. Instead, they remember the hundreds of times they felt discouraged learning new techniques and pushed through until they mastered them. Remember Janna hunching over her *Tune a Day* book? She persisted and is now happy she did.

"Boy, am I glad I kept pushing myself through the initial struggle," Janna says. "Now seven years later I'm enjoying my high school and youth symphony orchestras and the solo and ensemble opportunities I've had. The joy and work ethic that you can get from playing an instrument outweighs all of the work and exertion. I want to remind frustrated beginners that getting started is always the toughest part. Once you get into it, the fruits of your labor will show. If you keep practicing, your progress will serve as your momentum to continue working hard. Having to carefully count out the lengths of notes won't last forever."

PRACTICE PRIORITIES

Players who don't devote enough time to daily practice often get discouraged by their slow progress.

Thirteen-year-old Sarah had trouble making practice a priority and never made it to her second year of lessons. "I don't really want to quit, but piano keeps going to the back of the list. When I have time, I'm too tired or I forget to do it."

Without enough practice, students stuck at the beginner stage just quit.

Yulan struggled to get into the practice habit. "At first, I wasn't serious about playing. I'd practice just 15 minutes and then go on the computer. Because I didn't practice much, my lessons weren't great. When I learned how to practice, it helped me stick with it. Now I like to perform, and I enjoy the attention that being a good musician brings because people know my talent."

Eighteen-year-old Joe used to play trumpet. "I enjoyed playing the trumpet, but never wanted to commit to it. I practiced now and then, but it was a struggle. Then it became a vicious circle of no practice, not sounding good, and then not wanting to practice. I didn't make playing music a huge part of my life. When I see other kids who really practice and really enjoy it, I feel a little jealous."

Janna offers these hints for getting into your instrument: "Keep a regular practice schedule and follow through even on days it doesn't sound like fun. This will get you used to the daily grind that a musical instrument requires. Don't hesitate to get help as often as you need it, especially in the first few months when everything is confusing and you're not in a good practice routine. I had to be told when to practice, and some days I dreaded it even more than doing homework. I remember the day when I looked forward to practicing as a welcome break from homework. Then I knew how much music meant to me."

If you're having trouble fitting in practice, there's help for you in chapter 13, "How to Fit Practice into Your Already Busy Life." If you still dread your practice sessions or have a hard time getting everything accomplished, chapter 14, "Quit Wasting Your Practice Time," and chapter 15, "Shake Up Your Practice Routine," will teach you how to make your practice sessions more efficient and more fun.

What You See Now Is *Not* What You Get

Katy started taking lessons with me in fourth grade and played like a beginner for almost three years. I reviewed techniques and demonstrated them for her so many times I felt like tearing my hair out. Then one day she entered a contest, and her motivation caught on fire. The gorgeous sounds of the advanced players and the cool pieces they played inspired her to work hard to play as well as they did. She practiced faithfully, steadily improved, and three years later won a scholarship to a major conservatory, where she is now happily practicing.

When students first arrive in my studio, I find it hard to envision that these raw beginners may someday win contests and play with the symphony—until I remember how far my experienced students have come. I imagine each new student as a treasure box, and with my teaching and their practicing we'll discover the real musician inside.

If you're still struggling to get a decent tone or read music, it may be hard to imagine being a skilled, happy musician one day. My son Scott remembers struggling to learn beginning piano songs.

🔊

> *"Each new song seemed too hard, and I didn't believe I could do it. My mom knew better. Every time I complained about a song being too hard, she wrote 'NCD' (Never Can Do) at the top of the page. Six months later she had me look back at all those easy pieces I thought were too hard to ever play. I began to see that what seems hard today will be easy tomorrow if you practice."*

Getting Good Takes Time

Try not to lose heart when your progress seems slow or your lessons seem hard. Learning music may be the most complicated thing you're learning right now, and that includes the math and science you're learning at school. Just like learning math or science, it takes years to build up your skills. You wouldn't expect to be doing calculus after just five years of grade school math, and you shouldn't expect to be a concert artist until you've had many years of lessons and practice.

DOUBLE CHECK YOUR MOTIVATION

Why do you sing or play an instrument? Because your parents wanted you to? Because it might make you smarter or help you get into a good college? For all the friends you'll make? Those might be good reasons, but do you know the best reason to study music? The joy you get from creating it!

🔊

> *Trevor played in his middle school band for two years, and he listens to music all the time. "Making music is different," he says. He's right. Making music, called* active *music, stimulates your brain in different ways from passive listening. Trevor agrees. "The difference between listening to music and playing music is like the difference between watching sports on TV and actually playing them. It's a lot more fun to play, because you meet new people and you're part of a team." He adds with a grin, "In band you get to go on trips and goof off on the bus while other kids are still in school."*

🔊

> *Selina, 15, started playing in fifth grade. "Playing an instrument is fun because you get to play music you've heard other people play or heard only on the radio. Now I am the person who plays that piece."*

Anna, a graduating senior who has played since she was 10, says most teens aren't that patient. "Most kids think they'll pick up an instrument and instantly find their passion. When it doesn't happen, it's hard for them to cope with the work and time it takes to play well enough to enjoy it. Learning to play and even learning to enjoy it is a gradual process. I fell in love with music at summer music camp. For others it might be going to a concert and loving the music. But for most people it takes time, and you might not even be aware you're getting hooked. Then one day you look back and see how far you've come."

Is learning music all hard work? No! Learning to play shouldn't be on par with having your wisdom teeth pulled. "Music is not supposed to be hard work and drudgery," says Simon. "You're supposed to be enjoying yourself."

FIND YOUR BEST INSTRUMENT AND MUSIC

Playing the instrument you love can make all the difference.

Sam tried several instruments before finding his best match. "My parents signed me up for piano lessons in second grade. In fourth grade, I quit piano to play sax. I liked sax, but then in fifth grade I discovered the sound of the French horn and really liked that. If you don't love the sound of your instrument, what you play, and the level you can reach, then you should quit or find a better instrument."

Twelve-year-old Kurt tried clarinet for a year, but knew it wasn't for him. "I played clarinet first, but wanted to do jazz, so I quit. I didn't want to play alto sax, because it's so common. Now I'm the only one in my band who plays tenor sax."

Play a Good Instrument

Is your piano a clunker? Do you have to press the keys on your wind instrument extra hard just to keep them from leaking? Anyone gets discouraged playing an instrument that doesn't respond well.

Kurt can vouch for that. "I felt like quitting when I started sounding horrible on the tenor sax," he says. "I thought it was me until we took my sax into the shop and I found out the problem was the sax. What a relief!"

Play the Right Music

Eighteen-year-old Andrew says music has something for everyone; you just need to look in the right places. "There has to be an instrument and type of music you'll enjoy. I don't believe people when they say 'music is not for me.'

There's jazz, classical, rap, hip-hop, country, rock, and rhythm and blues. With all these choices and so many more, I believe every person can find some type of music and some instrument to enjoy."

GIVE IT SIX MONTHS (OR EVEN A YEAR)

If you've been playing an instrument for a while and aren't sure if music is for you, ride it out for a few more months. I recommend you keep playing for at least six months before you give up—even when you feel like breaking your instrument over the nearest chair. If you've practiced consistently, by the half-year mark you'll have experienced some of the rewards of your music adventure. If you're seriously thinking about quitting, please read chapter 38, "Help! I Want to Quit," before making that big decision.

What separates the musician who makes it from the one who gives up? Determination. Don't quit at the first sign of a struggle. Sometimes the time you're about to give up is almost the time for things to come together. Are you willing to push through your struggles for a future reward? Accept the fact that learning to play an instrument is a long journey. Be proud of each small success and enjoy the trip.

GREAT IDEAS

It takes time to get good and it takes time to have fun.

Even top performers once played like you do.

Everyone gets discouraged sometimes.

Choose music that you enjoy.

Stick with it until you can play some fun pieces.

Sneak Preview

Playing a good instrument can make all the difference in how you sound and how much you want to practice. But how do you persuade your parents to buy you a new instrument? See the next chapter for our great tips. They'll never know what hit them!

The Top Mistake New Musicians Can Make

FOUR

How to Persuade Your Parents to Buy You an Instrument

Every time you take your instrument out of the case or sit down at the piano, you sigh. "I hate the sound of this old thing, and I know I could play so much better on a new instrument." But every time you talk to your parents about buying a new instrument, they sigh, too. "You've learned fine on this instrument, and a new one would cost so much money." But playing on a bad instrument is like driving a tricycle in the Indy 500. It just won't do what you need it to do. How can you make your parents understand why having a good instrument is so important and convince them that it's worth the money?

The beginning of this chapter has scenarios taken from real-life situations concerning the decision to purchase a new instrument. You may recognize your situation below and use it for discussion with your parents.

Q: *Noah's parents have an old clunker piano that's been in the family for years. Noah wants a new piano, but his parents don't see the point, because this piano is playable. What advantage would a better piano have?*
A: Old clunkers make you sound like an old clunker. The action of the keys makes it impossible to repeat notes, so you're limited in speed. Old clunkers don't stay in tune long, and some are not worth fixing. It's hard to play softly and delicately on an old clunker and sometimes it's hard to play loudly, too. But worst of all, if the action is too easy, you get used to a percussive sound, and even when you change pianos, you'll think that's the norm.

Q: *Justin is 8 and has been playing for three years on a half-size cello. It's time for him to move up to a three-quarter size. Would it be okay for him to continue on the half size until he's big enough to play a full-size instrument?*
A: Justin needs to move up progressively in size. Playing on an instrument that's too small will give him bad posture and position habits. But Justin's parents should not sink a lot of money into an instrument that is less than full size; they should just rent or get a loaner three-quarter-size cello.

Q: *Emily's mom used to play the oboe when she was young. She found her old instrument in the attic and thought Emily should play it, because they already owned the oboe. Should Emily have more say in which instrument she chooses?*

A: When asked how they chose their instrument, professionals have a range of answers from "I always loved the sound" to "My grandfather had one in the attic." If Emily likes the sound of the oboe, she should give it a try, but if she has her heart set on another instrument, she'll be more dedicated to the instrument she herself chooses.

Q: *Lori has been playing a beginner student violin for three years. Now that she's in seventh grade, her teacher has recommended a better instrument. Lori and her parents are sure Lori will continue playing through high school and probably through college. Should they buy an intermediate violin or bite the bullet and get her a very good instrument now?*

A: This is a tough one. On one hand, an excellent instrument will allow Lori to maximize her practice and talent. The price of good instruments is going up, so the violin purchased today will cost less than one of the same quality purchased in five years. On the other hand, Lori herself will have changed as a player and may not like the violin she got as a seventh grader. She also may not be mature enough to handle the responsibility of taking care of such an expensive instrument. If she gets an intermediate instrument now, it can be the instrument she takes to school when she moves up to a better one. Lori's parents can always sell the intermediate violin to offset the cost of the expensive one when Lori is ready for it.

Q: *Cathy plays an intermediate flute. She wants a new instrument, but her parents can't afford it. Is there anything that can help?*

A: Cathy should try out new headjoints with her present flute. The cost of a new headjoint is about one-sixth of a quality flute. Headjoints make the most difference in the tone, and so this is a cost-effective option. Other wind instruments may have similar alternatives to replacing the entire instrument.

Q: *Patrick found a clarinet with a good sound made by a very obscure instrument company. Is it wise for him to buy this clarinet?*

A: If Patrick is thrilled with the clarinet and intends to play it for a long time, it might be a good option. On the other hand, the famous companies usually offer a higher level of design and may back up their work if something goes wrong. Another thing to consider is the resale value of a standard-make clarinet.

Q: *Maggie wants to buy a new flute. Is there any reason for her to keep her old flute, or should she sell it to help pay for the new flute?*

A: If Maggie's flute is not worth very much, keeping it might be the best option. It's convenient to have a "junker flute" to take to camp, play outside in marching band, and use when the new one is at the repair shop. But if selling the old one will help her get a better flute, it would be the wise decision.

Q: Nick's middle school band teacher recommends the same brand of instrument for all the clarinetists. This brand has been around for a long time and is a very basic model at a very basic price. Should Nick's parents just follow the teacher's recommendation or investigate other options, too?

A: Nick's band teacher may like this particular brand because of its cost or its reliability, but that doesn't necessarily mean it's the best instrument for Nick. Nick and his parents should go to a couple of music stores and try out different makes and models to see if there is a better fit for his sound and their budget.

Q: Steven has been playing the same trombone for years. Steven is very advanced, and the trombone is just a beginner's model, but Steven still sounds pretty darn good on it. Should he move up to a more expensive instrument?

A: Why throw money away when you don't need to? If Steven sounds good and is "competitive" with his peers, he should stick to the instrument he already owns.

Q: Eleven-year-old Eric has a rental saxophone. Periodically his parents take it in to be fixed because of Eric's rough treatment of the instrument. Should they wait to buy an instrument until Eric is more careful?

A: Most rental policies offer free repairs and tune-ups, so Eric should wait to buy an instrument until he can be more responsible with his saxophone.

Q: Amber is auditioning for the local youth orchestra. She's playing on a beginner violin. Will it make that much difference to play a more expensive instrument if she is just in the orchestra?

A: Amber may not win the audition if she is playing on a bad instrument. It's easier to play well on a good instrument and so much more fun, too!

Q: Brett's parents want to buy him an electronic keyboard instead of a piano to practice on. They found one that's a great deal and comes with so many cool sounds; you sure can't sound like a fire engine or a choir on a regular piano. Is there any reason to invest in a real piano?

A: Although the keyboard simulates a real piano, it is not a real piano. It's what many teachers call "a piano-shaped object." The only keyboards that may in some way resemble real pianos have as many keys as the regular piano, with fully weighted keys to simulate the touch on a piano. They also have a "sampler," which means the sound of a real piano was recorded. But one of these "super model" keyboards can still be fairly expensive. If Brett is entranced with the different sounds a keyboard can make, his parents can buy him a cheap one to fool around on.

Q: It's time for Juliet to get a new cello. Although Juliet's parents know nothing about music, can they still help in her decision?

A: Juliet's teacher should always be asked for input when choosing a new instrument, but her parents may be surprised at how well they can differentiate between cellos that Juliet tries. They should be part of the listening team. Since they're paying for the instrument, they should be part of the process.

Q: *Susan is playing the same flute her mom played 30 years ago in grade school. Is it still just as good today?*
A: The flute world has exploded with new makers, new models, new metals, new tuning, new added keys, and other features. Mom's old flute might be just fine for the first year or two, but when Susan is more advanced, the new flutes can provide so much more. Flute technology has improved over the years, so the flute that was originally expensive 25 years ago may not be as good as a student beginner model made today. On the other hand, if Mom's old flute is a good one, it may be just fine for Susan for many years.

Q: *Lucy's parents read Consumer Reports and are astute shoppers. They have researched clarinets and feel they have found the perfect instrument for their price range. Should they trust their judgment and buy the clarinet out of a catalog?*
A: Buying a new instrument is not like buying a new car. Lucy's parents need help. There are more variables to consider that need the professional opinion of a musician. Does this particular instrument have a good tone? Does it need a lot of repair work? Does it have any additional features? Ask Lucy's school or private music teacher for advice on what she needs from her clarinet, then let Lucy try out some clarinets to find the best match.

Q: *Allison's younger brother just got a new trumpet for $800. Her parents said they would spend the same amount of money on Allison's new cello. Is that fair?*
A: Not all instruments are created equal. Strings in general are much more expensive than other instruments. To buy Allison an instrument equal in quality to her brother's trumpet, they will have to spend more money. Just be grateful she doesn't play the harp!

Q: *Christopher's parents put a $2,000 limit on the purchase of a new oboe. The oboes in that price range don't sound dramatically better than the one he has. Should he wait to purchase a new instrument or buy one now so he can sound better for his upcoming auditions?*
A: Not every $2,000 oboe is better than every $1,000 one. If the change in sound is not dramatic, Christopher's parents should hold off on buying a new oboe or let him try more expensive oboes for a future purchase to see if he finds one that makes a huge difference.

Q: *Kyle wants to play the French horn, so his aunt loaned him her old instrument. The only problem is that the instrument looks like it has been hit by a truck and sounds like it, too. Is it okay to play on it until Kyle gets more advanced and needs a better instrument?*

A: If you are going to teach someone to drive a car, why have them practice on roller skates? Although you hate to look a gift horse in the mouth, playing a bad instrument can be so discouraging that Kyle may want to quit before he improves. He may also learn bad technique on a bad instrument and have to start over when he gets a good one. Take the French horn to an instrument repair shop and see if it is worth fixing.

Q: *Karen wants to go to summer music camp and get a new clarinet. Her parents only have enough money for one or the other. Which should she choose?*
A: In the long run, Karen will advance more with a new instrument than a summer camp experience. Perhaps it is possible for Karen to earn a scholarship to the music camp or to get a part-time job that would help finance this experience. She also could look at the possibility of a summer camp close to home that wouldn't cost as much as a higher-priced resident camp.

Q: *Jeff's parents were astounded at the price of a new violin. How could it cost as much as a small car? Though Jeff says he wants to be a professional musician when he grows up, what if he changes his mind and all the money is wasted?*
A: Although the violin has a steep price tag, Jeff's parents should consider it an investment in Jeff's future as it will help him become a better musician and offer him opportunities he could not reach with a cheap violin. He will need a quality instrument to be competitive. And on the off chance that Jeff's plans change, unlike the car whose value drops the minute it is driven off the dealer's lot, the more expensive the instrument, the more its value will hold or increase with time.

Q: *Colleen has been playing the piano for years, but she is bored with the same routine. Would having an electric piano give her a boost?*
A: An electric piano is no substitute for a real piano, but it can be tons of fun and add to learning. Playing scales sounding like a choir, a flute, or orchestra can ease the boredom. Perhaps the keyboard will open up Colleen's interest in other kinds of music, such as jazz. Keyboards come in all price ranges, so give it a try.

Q: *Evan is playing on an old trombone but wants to audition next year for the music program at the university. Should he wait for the teacher at the university to help him decide on a new trombone or buy one now?*
A: Evan may not be accepted into the program without a quality instrument. Follow his teacher's advice on whether to buy a trombone now. Maybe he could borrow or rent a higher quality instrument for the audition.

Q: *Carolyn can't decide whether to get a new viola or a new bow. What will improve her sound the most?*
A: If there is money for an instrument, buy the instrument. But if she has a horrible bow and only several hundred dollars, then go for the bow. Usually the bow should be 20 percent of the cost of the instrument.

Q: *Tim just got a great new trumpet, but his parents are worried about him bringing it to school. Should he use his old instrument at school and keep the good one at home?*

A: Tim's decision may depend on the security at the school and Tim's own level of responsibility. If he is a careful kid, and the trumpet can be locked up when not in use, then perhaps he should bring the good instrument to school. Would his trumpet be safer kept in his locker? If not, perhaps he could just bring the new trumpet on days where there is a contest or concert. Either way, Tim's parents need to insure the trumpet through their homeowners' insurance.

Q: *Peter's interest in the guitar has been lagging. He blames his lack of practice on his poor instrument. Will a new guitar give him the jump start he needs?*

A: A new instrument can be inspirational, but if Peter is not really interested in guitar, it will probably not be enough. Peter needs to make a commitment before his parents spend more money.

Q: *Katelyn is an excellent flute player with an eye to becoming a music major. Now she wants to buy a piccolo, too. Should she just stick to the flute until she knows her future plans?*

A: Serious players need to know all variations of their instrument. Flute players who play piccolo are more in demand, as are oboists who play English horn, and clarinetists and saxophonists who play more than one variation of their instrument. If money is a problem, perhaps Katelyn can borrow a school piccolo or rent one.

Q: *Hannah plays piano and now wants to switch to harp. Her parents blanched when they learned the cost of a new harp. Is it really worth all that money?*

A: Harps don't lose their value if treated carefully; in fact, they go up in value every year. But if Hannah's parents aren't sure of her commitment, they should consider the option of renting. Starting on a lever harp (one without pedals) is a good beginning. Rentals for lever harps are about half of that for pedal harps, and some companies allow the rental fees to be deducted from the purchase price. Harps are priced differently according to size and carving, gold, and so forth, so when buying, Hannah could go for the basic model. If she finds a secondhand harp, it would be wise to have a reputable harp technician check it over.

Q: *Anna is in ninth grade but plays oboe like a college music major. Should her parents invest in a professional instrument now or wait until she matures?*

A: The instrument should match the person, not the age. Anna needs an instrument that matures with her. Years of advancement could be lost if she is hobbled by an inferior instrument.

Q: *Becca longs for a grand piano, but her parents don't see the reason to upgrade. Is a grand worth the grand price?*

A: Becca can learn everything she needs to know on a quality upright, so there is no need to buy a grand except for the joy of the sound, the thrill of the touch, and the inspiration a grand brings. As with other instruments, the better the piano, the more its value will appreciate.

Q: *Andy's friend Matt got a new bassoon that he loves. Andy's parents want to buy him a new bassoon for his birthday, and they thought they would get one like Matt's. Should they surprise Andy with the bassoon or wait until he can try out some instruments on his own?*

A: Although Matt's bassoon may be perfect for Matt, it may not be perfect for Andy. Andy's parents should wrap up a gift card telling Andy about the bassoon and then go shopping with him.

Q: *Ian sounds pretty good on his middle-grade trumpet, but he's dissatisfied with some aspects of his tone. He feels it is "cheating" to buy a new instrument and that he should fix his tone himself with hard work and practice before he buys a higher level trumpet. Is it cheating to depend on an instrument for good tone?*

A: A new instrument won't solve all of Ian's problems. He may be able to improve 0–50 percent on his own, but a quality instrument could help him improve even more.

Q: *Heather has only been playing the violin for a year, but she has fallen in love with it. She practices without being asked and loves everything about music. She is only in second grade. Should she move up to an intermediate instrument now?*

A: If Heather is responsible and treats her violin with care, she should get a better violin. Keep in mind, though, that at that age she is playing on a small instrument. Good ones are hard to find and will probably still not be able to produce the tone she'll get when she's ready for a larger instrument. Heather's parents should wait to invest a lot of money until she graduates to a full-size violin.

Q: *Tom plays trombone in the marching band. He doesn't want to take private lessons, and he doesn't practice his band music, but he enjoys the fun of the band. Should he get a new trombone of the same level as the rest of the kids to keep up in band?*

A: Buying a new instrument is a big commitment from parents and should also demand a big commitment from Tom. If he just plays casually, then he only needs a trombone that's good enough to play in the band.

Q: *Alana wants a new flute now. The annual flute fair where representatives from the different flute makers showcase their wares is not for six months. Should Alana buy a flute out of a catalog or a local store or wait until the fair?*

A: There is a real advantage to trying out many makes of flutes and being able to play the exact instrument you buy. Many times, although two instruments have the very same specs, they sound different. Alana should be patient, knowing that she has a good chance of getting the flute of her dreams at the flute fair.

Now that you've seen a variety of scenarios and solutions, it's time for the big talk with your parents. If you've talked to your teacher and done your homework about what to buy and where to buy it, you're ready. Sit down calmly with them and listen to their side, too. You'll have a better chance of having a discussion rather than an argument. Most parents are willing to sacrifice for their child if they feel their child is deserving, so this is the time to tell them what music means to you. Don't tell them you want a new instrument because everyone else has one or that they owe you because of all your practicing. Speak from your heart. If you love it and are committed to practicing, they'll want to support you. Include these reasons to bolster your case:

With a new instrument:
- You'll sound better.
- It will be much easier to play.
- You'll have even more incentive to practice.
- You'll spend less time at the repair shop.
- Your instrument will retain its value and can be more easily sold or traded in.
- You'll have the recognition and reward for years of practice and hard work.
- You'll love and appreciate your parents (even more!) forever.

Show your parents the value of a new instrument.
- Have your teacher demonstrate on your present instrument and a good one (and plead your case).
- Rent an instrument to see if it's better.
- Convince them it is an investment.

Zoë's parents ended up paying more than was in their original budget, but she has proven to them it was worth it. "When I had to get a new flute, I sucked up to my parents big time. I practiced hard, showing them I was dedicated and that a new flute would be put to good use. I kept on bringing up the topic about a new flute, and I was really nice to them."

A good instrument can make all the difference, but it can't improve your playing if it just sits in the case.

Show your parents your commitment.
- Promise to make a commitment to stick with lessons and do your best.
- Put some of your own money toward the cost.

- Practice without being told.
- Practice when they're around.
- Practice a lot.
- Play for grandma and grandpa. (They may even kick in some money.)

If the money's just not in the budget this year or they're not sure you will "stick with it," then take a deep breath. "No" today doesn't mean "no" forever.

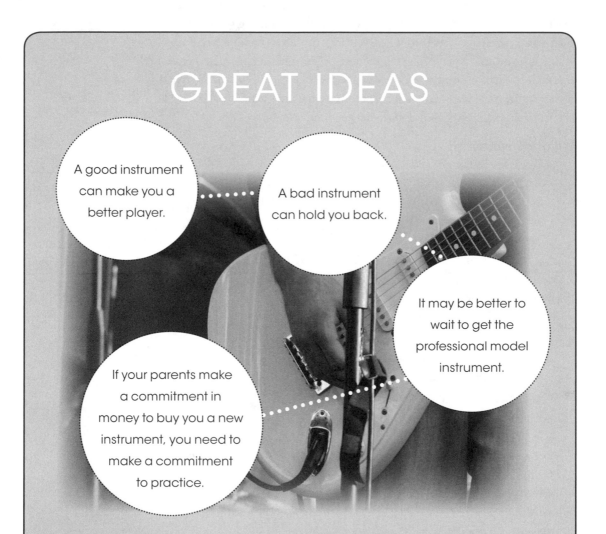

GREAT IDEAS

A good instrument can make you a better player.

A bad instrument can hold you back.

It may be better to wait to get the professional model instrument.

If your parents make a commitment in money to buy you a new instrument, you need to make a commitment to practice.

Sneak Preview

If you're one of the lucky ones who's persuaded your parents to buy you a new instrument, our next chapter will help you. What kind? How much to spend? Where to look? Let's get your search started.

FIVE

Where and How to Buy Your Instrument

If you're renting your instrument and want to buy one, or if you've persuaded your parents to buy you a new instrument, this chapter is for you. If you've never bought an instrument, you probably have lots of questions about the process. Is a brand name important? Should you buy new or used? Is it better to rent or buy? Before you jump in the car, become an educated consumer by visiting local music stores and going online.

SEEK ADVICE FROM PROFESSIONALS

Talk to your school's music teacher, band director, or orchestra instructor. They'll have practical information about a variety of instruments and what it takes to play them well. Ask your teacher and advanced students about their favorite makes and models and where to shop. Your teachers may even have students who are selling used instruments.

Ask around to find other families who recently purchased instruments. They'll have firsthand advice about where to go and where not to go. In the process they'll have met musicians and retailers they trust.

NEW AND USED INSTRUMENTS

It's sure fun to be the first to play on a shiny new instrument. It's also fun to have the one-year warranty that goes with it. Another plus is being able to order an instrument entirely to your own specifications. Do you want this kind of metal? That extra key? But as with everything, the more perks, the higher the price.

Buying a used instrument can save lots of money. Many instruments have not changed much over the years, so if you don't need all the new bells and whistles, especially when you are a beginner, used can be the way to go. Know what the instrument originally sold for, what repairs it has had, and what it would sell for now. The more expensive the instrument, the more it will retain its value. Many string instruments increase in value, and the really old ones are the most expensive. (Just don't have any illusions about finding a Stradivarius in someone's attic!) Many instrument stores will carry both new and used.

It may be hard to tell if an old instrument is good or if it just needs a tune-up. I've had students who thought they couldn't play, only to find out it was the instrument, not them. (What a relief. It's a lot easier to fix an instrument than a person.) Ask to take the instrument to a repair person for an evaluation. You may find the $500 clarinet needs $500 worth of work and is not such a great bargain after all, or you may find a used trombone that sells for $1,000 when the same model new costs $1,300. Do your research.

Linda gave her childhood flute to her daughter, Kianna, when she started lessons. "My old flute had been fine for me when I was young, so my fifth-grade daughter brought it to her first lesson. The old flute her teacher named "the tin can" forced Kianna to work harder to learn. She had a terrible time getting a good tone and holding out long notes. I never thought about how bad my flute was because that's all I had ever played.

"When we bought Kianna a new flute, she just blossomed. It was an amazing difference! I felt bad about how she suffered on the old one. When she got her new flute, it was like someone who has never sung a note suddenly opening her mouth and singing soaring high notes. A good instrument has motivated Kianna to practice more, and it's so much more fun."

BUDGET CONSIDERATIONS

First, decide your price range. Or more precisely, ask your parents what they can afford. Stretch your budget by looking in places like eBay, craigslist, newspaper classified ads, yard sales, and local musical instrument stores. But when you're buying from someone other than a reputable dealer or someone you know and trust, you're taking more of a chance. Stores sometimes have sellout or inventory reduction sales to reduce their stock of old instruments before they restock new ones. School music departments often keep a small inventory of instruments for students to borrow, especially the more expensive ones like tubas.

It's rarely a good idea to pay for a large purchase over many months or years on a credit card, but perhaps you can charge the instrument and pay it off fairly quickly. Ask the store if they have a layaway program.

Keep in mind that the cost of the instrument is just the beginning. You'll also need to budget for maintenance, replacement, and lesson costs. Instruments are no different than other retail purchases: you get what you pay for. Don't look for the cheapest instrument. Cheap instruments may need costly repairs that will offset any price savings. They will also sound bad and make learning harder.

RESEARCH BRANDS, MODELS, PRICE RANGES

Use the internet as a fun and easy way to narrow your selection of instruments. You'll find consumer product reviews, pricing information, and recommendations from experienced players and instrument teachers. You can search for player blogs on the sites of associations or societies for your instrument and on other online music communities. See the list of references at the back of this book.

When shopping for string instruments, there are many makers. Some may not be well known but may have an excellent product. You need the help of a professional to be the judge.

Check music retailer and manufacturer websites and local music stores to learn what new models are available in your price range. Most sort their instruments by playing level and also offer buying information. Has the model you're considering been replaced by a new, better model? Is the newer model essentially the same as the old but commands a higher price? Compare prices of the same model instrument at different retailers with websites like Discountmore.com and pricegrabber.com. Do any of these stores or websites have any sales or special offers?

> *Kianna, age 12, tells her side of the story playing her mom's flute. "The flute I started on was Mom's when she was a girl. I was very confused about how much to roll in or out. We finally discovered that I was too rolled out. I found the correct position when I rolled in a little bit, and it helped a ton. But I was still having a lot of trouble. One day my teacher discovered the real reason I was having so much trouble. It was my flute. She recommended renting a better quality used flute. So right after my lesson we went to the music store and looked for a flute to rent. The first one I tried was miraculous. I could hold notes longer, and it actually made it fun. And I took off from there."*

WHERE DO I LOOK?

Reputable music stores in your area offer a chance to try out an instrument, and they're handy when you need your instrument repaired. They will usually offer you a loaner during that time. It's also a good thing to support your local economy. The disadvantage is that the small store may not carry many makes or upper-level instruments, and unless you play guitar, their staff may not be that knowledgeable.

If you deal with a larger instrument store, they may lend you a couple of instruments to try for a week and may also have used instruments. Don't be afraid to ask lots of questions of the staff. That's their job. Stores that specialize in your particular instrument are guaranteed to have a wider selection and more knowledgeable staff.

Seek the advice of instrument repair professionals. They'll know which instruments are brought in more often for repair, where their customers buy their instruments, and what stores back up their warranties. They'll often sell instruments when customers decide to trade up rather than repair, and they may also have clients who have instruments for sale. Your local yellow pages should list music stores, dealers of used instruments, and repair shops.

Wal-Mart and similar big box stores may offer cheap instruments, but again you get what you pay for: a cheap instrument and no customer service. Once these instruments break, it's not worth it to repair them. But if that's all your budget can afford, it may be better than nothing, though it's probably wiser to rent a better instrument.

You can sometimes get surprisingly good deals in pawn shops and in newspaper ads if you know what you want and have the time and patience to keep looking and asking the right questions. You have more bargaining power when you deal with an individual.

INTERNET BUYER BEWARE

What you'll miss out on with internet purchases is not seeing, hearing, feeling, or trying the instrument in person. It's a smart idea to visit your local music store and try out a similar instrument. You may have your heart set on that gorgeous rose gold–toned instrument, but what if it feels too heavy for you to handle? Even if the one in the store is identical to the model you saw on eBay, you're still taking risks when you purchase sight unseen. Instruments are like cars, and every once in a while a good car company produces a lemon. You also don't know for sure that the instrument you saw on your computer is the same one that could arrive on your doorstep.

Instruments at bargain prices abound on the internet, but you need to know what you're doing. As in so many areas in life, most of the people are honest and a few are not.

Before you consider buying:
- Check the seller's ID history to see how long they've been in business and how often they've changed their eBay name.
- What is their feedback rating? Even if the rating is in the mid-90s or higher, read all the negatives for the past three to six months.
- Is there a trend with negatives? Sometimes a good seller gets sloppy with quality control, packing, or shipping speed.
- Require the seller to give you the serial number, history, and specifications of the instrument.
- Ask about their return policy, but remember, even if you can return it in 30 days, it will be a hassle to pack and ship.
- Are you planning to be the first bidder on an instrument that is priced unbelievably low? Buyers beware. Chances are the people who aren't bidding have noticed something you haven't. Unless it's only the first or second day of bidding, stay away from terrific deals that no one else is interested in.
- Before you buy on eBay, craigslist, or other online sellers, follow the auctions and prices of several models you might be interested in. Which instruments consistently create bidding wars? After three weeks or so, you'll know which models are hot and which ones no one will touch with a 10-foot pole.

- Reviewing past sales also shows you which models (usually at bargain prices) show up again and again and are probably cheap imports that look shiny but will be corroded and falling apart in a year.
- On eBay, always search for your instrument on completed auctions that resulted in a sale. Do sales of your instrument often end with a "red" (no purchasers) sales price? Check the sales prices of completed auctions. You might be amazed at the deals people have gotten, and you can, too, if you're patient.
- Don't be shy about contacting a potential seller with additional questions. The answers you receive make you a more informed buyer and give you extra clues about the seller's sincerity.
- When you send messages to eBay sellers, communicate only through your eBay identity and not through your personal e-mail address. Some dishonest sellers use their sites as a front to mine for e-mails and other personal information.
- When sending a message, always check the "hide my address from seller" box. Be cautious about clicking on links on the seller's website, because some links take you away from eBay to a mystery site you know nothing about. You could end up paving the way for spyware and even viruses to download onto your computer. And just think, if you're forced to wipe out your computer's hard drive and reload your entire system, you'll have no time to practice!

RENT OR BUY?

If this is your first time trying an instrument, or you're unsure whether you'll be committed for the long term, rent. A woman once brought her very young daughter to a flute lesson, and by the end of the lesson the daughter had decided she wanted to play the saxophone instead. Good thing she hadn't bought a flute! A trial period of about one year is a good test to see whether a child will stick with it.

Make sure you're given an instrument of good quality and in good working order. If a friend or relative offers to lend you an instrument or give it to you, thank them profusely, and then take it to a professional to be sure it's in good enough shape to play. Even if an instrument is free, it may not be worth it when the sound is bad because it's damaged or ancient or just wasn't a good instrument to begin with.

If your budget is small, many stores have special financing or a "rent to own" plan where they apply all or part of the monthly rental fee toward the purchase price. After a year or so it may make sense to purchase the trombone you've played or else look for a better instrument. Some music stores that push their "rent to own" program are not offering you a good deal, though. They apply only a small portion of the monthly fee to the purchase price, and others make sure you'll end up paying far more than the instrument is worth.

Ask the store if they can give you a discount, if they have a certain model on sale, or if they will soon be having a sale. Most instrument prices are fairly standard, but it doesn't hurt to ask.

It's a plus to be able to order an instrument entirely to your own specifications. But as with everything, the more perks, the higher the price. Some instruments come with additional accessories or parts you can replace. For example, the mouthpieces for brass and woodwind instruments included by the manufacturer usually won't give you the best sound and playing comfort. A full service store will have a wide selection and allow you to audition mouthpieces.

CHOOSING AN INSTRUMENT

If you're a beginner, you probably have no idea what you need from an instrument, and spending thousands of dollars on your first instrument is a bad idea. When you don't know how to play well, the nuances, quality, and potential of a premium instrument will be lost to you. And what if you decide to give up playing clarinet for hockey? In most cases, a good-quality student model will meet your needs. At this stage of playing, you need to focus on learning technique, not playing an advanced instrument. But once you know you're maintaining your interest and beginning to advance, a higher-quality instrument will make more sense. If the instrument is bad, you'll sound bad and want to quit.

IS IT TIME TO BUY?

Once you've played for a while and fallen in love with playing an instrument, it may be time to buy your own. I would advise renting for the first year, then assessing your commitment. Owning your own instrument is not only a valuable investment in your ongoing musical training. It can also be a good financial investment.

Let's say you buy a beginner flute for about $600. If you play it for three years, that adds up to $200 a year. But after those three years, you can sell your old instrument for $300, which in effect makes the cost $100 per year. If after buying an intermediate or advanced flute, you decide to keep your old flute to take to school through high school, the yearly amortized cost would be only $50 per year. Now that sounds like a pretty good deal! Owning your own instrument can also be a real motivator to practice and continue playing for a lifetime.

Brand names

The designer T-shirt may not always be worth the extra money, but a brand-name instrument usually is. When you choose an instrument, you're choosing the reputation of the company, too. If the instrument is new, you are also choosing their customer service and guarantee. A brand-name instrument will also be easier to resell.

Should I sell my old instrument?

If you're buying an instrument to replace one, you may get a better deal selling your current one outright rather than trading it in. If you can afford to keep it, it may come in handy as a backup when your new one needs fixing or to play in marching band or around the campfire.

Take a knowledgeable person with you.

Used instruments may be appealing to your wallet, but with an inexperienced eye, how do you know if you're getting one that's been trashed? If you're a new player, it may be hard to tell if an instrument has a good sound or timbre. Ask a more experienced player to come with you to test instruments, or ask if you can take a couple instruments for a few days on loan. Play as many brands and models as possible to find the ones you're most comfortable with. Don't worry about price at this stage; you want to get a feel for the range of what's available. Later you can narrow your choices to models that strictly fit your criteria.

If you can barely play, ask someone to play the instrument for you to make sure it's in good condition. You may be able to take home the instrument for approval by your teacher or someone who plays. But remember, the person playing it can be a huge variable and with different needs than yours, so their approval doesn't guarantee you'll sound the same.

Carolyn Nussbaum, who owns one of the biggest flute stores in the United States, advises: "Many times a payment plan is better than a rental, as at the end of the payments you own the instrument. If the student only wants to try an instrument out for a few months, then a rental is good, but if they are going to stick with it for more than three to four months, then a payment plan is a much better way to go. Also, the beginner instrument becomes the marching instrument, the one you take on camping trips, or the second instrument to use when the good one is in the shop. Used instruments that are cheap are usually a money pit. I would suggest if someone is looking at a used flute, they should take it to their mechanic/instrument repair shop, not only the flute teacher, to determine the condition before purchasing—just as you would with a car. A private teacher can determine whether the flute sounds good, but they usually cannot really tell how much work the pads need or how worn the mechanism is or if there has been any damage or poor repairs. You can find good beginner instruments for a reasonable price. Instruments that are available only off the web are usually disposable, and most repair people will not touch them. A good instrument from the start is the best investment because resell value is usually pretty good. The student has a better chance of really loving music from the start and not struggling just to get the sound out of a poor instrument."

Questions to Ask When Buying New

Many people go to the store with a dollar amount in mind and look for an instrument in that price range, but there are more things to consider:

Knowledge

Bottom line: do the salespeople know what they're talking about? Are you buying a cello from a 17-year-old kid who plays drums? Be sure you're getting the right advice, especially before you purchase. A knowledgeable salesperson will help make the perfect match between you and the instrument.

Repair policy
- Who pays for repairs when the instrument is a rental?
- Are repairs done in the store or at another location?
- How long do repairs usually take?
- Do they provide a loaner when your instrument is in the shop?
- Is there a warranty for a certain number of months after purchase?
- If the instrument is purchased, then found to have problems, will they make the proper repairs, give a refund, or tell you that you're out of luck?

Inventory
- Is there a selection of instruments in stock in every price range?
- Are there quality instruments to rent?
- Can you try out brand-new instruments?

Accessories

Does the store provide everything that goes with the instrument? Do they have guitar, violin, viola, and cello strings? A selection of tuners and metronomes? Beginning books? Cleaning supplies?

Renting and trade
- Does the store have a "rent to own" policy?
- Is it cost-effective?
- Do they have a trade-in policy?

Relationships

Price may not be the most important factor in deciding where to buy your instrument. I have worked with a few stores for years; I trust them to give my students the instrument that fits their situation and to give them a fair price. They may cost a few dollars more than some catalog or eBay deal, but I know they will stand behind their products and do everything to make their customers happy. Priceless!

Questions to ask the owner:
- When did you purchase it?
- Did you purchase it new?
- Why are you selling it?
- Has the instrument ever been repaired? If so, what was done?

If the seller brings out the instrument with a bundle of instrument cleaning and care supplies, take this as a good sign.

Invest in Insurance

Insure your instrument just in case something happens to it while being transported. Have it appraised if it's not new. Your parents can add it to their homeowners' insurance policy, but they may need a rider for extra coverage. If you're renting, ask if the rental fee includes replacement insurance. Heaven forbid that the school bus runs over your trombone!

RESOURCES AND REFERENCES

For reviews by other players for all sorts of instruments, see www.musicians friend.com. For articles, tips, and resources for buying instruments, see www .inexpensivemusicalinstruments.com.

Have fun finding your musical match. Keep your options and your mind open every step of the way. Remember when you're shopping that you're not only buying an instrument, you're also opening the door for many years of learning and fun. What a payoff!

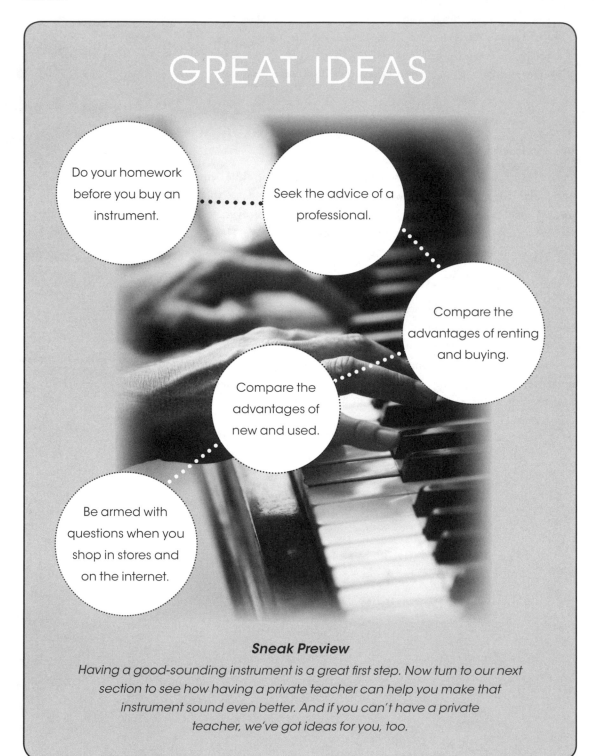

GREAT IDEAS

Do your homework before you buy an instrument.

Seek the advice of a professional.

Compare the advantages of renting and buying.

Compare the advantages of new and used.

Be armed with questions when you shop in stores and on the internet.

Sneak Preview

Having a good-sounding instrument is a great first step. Now turn to our next section to see how having a private teacher can help you make that instrument sound even better. And if you can't have a private teacher, we've got ideas for you, too.

PART TWO

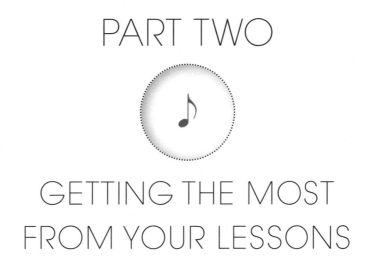

GETTING THE MOST
FROM YOUR LESSONS

SIX

Are Private Lessons for You?

Tom and his friend John got their new trombones the same week. Neither one had played an instrument before, and both were excited to start. Tom's parents found him a good teacher who demonstrated how to put the trombone together, showed Tom the correct fingerings, and coached him on how to get a good sound. Tom's teacher had a step-by-step plan for teaching the basics. Tom learned music theory, played scales and tone exercises, used étude books, and played some fun solos and duets. Tom's teacher was very demanding, but Tom liked learning and wanted to please his teacher. And besides, they told jokes and laughed at every lesson. Playing the trombone was fun.

Meanwhile, John struggled to learn the trombone on his own. He read the book that came with the instrument, but it was hard to figure out. The sounds that came out of his trombone sounded more like a sick cow than music, so it wasn't much fun practicing. The worse he sounded, the less he wanted to practice. Besides, what the heck was he supposed to practice? Then John signed up for school band. It was fun being in band with his friends, and he liked the teacher, but the music was hard. Instead of counting on his own, John just imitated the other kids and pretended to play the parts he couldn't get. His teacher was a clarinetist, so he didn't have many pointers for the trombonists, and he had his hands full with all the other kids. John sat next to last chair in band all year (you should have heard the kid who was last chair!), then quit playing trombone. Meanwhile, by the end of the year, his buddy Tom had worked his way up to first chair.

Tom and John started out with the same excitement and probably the same ability, but having a teacher made all the difference. You can struggle with teach-yourself-to-play books or just join your school band or orchestra, but a private music teacher can help you learn faster and more effectively. You may worry about the cost of lessons or how much time it will take to go to lessons and practice, but I promise you that the time and money you spend taking music lessons will be one of the best investments you (and your parents) will ever make. It may be a big sacrifice, but learning to play with a living, breathing

🔊

teacher can be the difference between developing a lifelong passion and giving up in frustration.

🔊
"That one-on-one connection helps because the teacher can answer any of your questions, and you don't have to feel embarrassed asking it in front of your friends. You get better faster with private lessons because you have a sense of security." (Andy, age 14)

WHY CAN'T I JUST LEARN BY MYSELF WITH A BOOK?

Books may tell you how to finger the notes and count, but they can't catch you when you make a mistake, coach you to get a good tone, or teach you to play musically. They can't check your posture and hand position or tell if you play out of tune. A book may help you with some basics, but a private teacher acts as a personal trainer who can collaborate with you to solve your problems and work with your own learning style. A book never tells you to go home and practice more, helps you with stage fright, or holds a recital. Interactive DVDs and CDs are better than books because they give you a sound to imitate, but they still can never replace a real teacher.

🔊
Thirteen-year-old James has taken piano lessons for seven years, and he plays both piano and percussion in band. He also loves soccer and other sports. His favorite music? Classical and rap. "Lessons are better because if you hit a spot in the books you're reading from and don't understand it, you won't be able to figure it out. A teacher helps you figure out where to put your hands for certain notes and how to read rhythms. My teacher helps me choose music. She's already gone through the books, so she knows what I would like."

🔊
Fifteen-year-old flutist, Kristin, who now plays in a youth orchestra, remembers her rocky beginning: "I started taking lessons in a group at school. The first few weeks of playing were hard because I didn't understand how my instrument worked and which keys to press. It's boring when you don't get it, and I didn't care about playing. I quit band in less than a year. I thought I could just read the book by myself and that lessons were a waste of time. But when you try to do it just with a book, you can't tell what you're doing wrong, and then you keep playing it wrong. I learned so much more when I started private lessons."

ISN'T PLAYING IN MY SCHOOL BAND OR ORCHESTRA ENOUGH?

Playing in school band or orchestra is a great way to meet friends, practice teamwork, learn new music, support your school, and sometimes take exciting trips. But if you look around, you'll notice that the kids who play best are usually the ones who take private lessons.

Being in your school music program can be great fun, but it's hard to get the personal attention you need in a traditional band setting. Your band or orchestra conductor usually has 100 kids to teach at one time and might never hear you play individually. Conductors have to teach all the instruments. If your teacher is a trumpet player, he or she may know everything about the trumpet but little beyond the basics to help you with your oboe. And besides, who wants to just play band music? Only a private teacher who is an expert on your instrument can give you the best help you need.

> *Eleven-year-old Rana started flute in fourth-grade band. "For the first year I took the school band program. We only played out of a beginning book, and by the end of the year I could play a one-octave B♭ scale. I could do the fingerings, but I didn't know the note names. None of the flutes in fifth-grade band took lessons, and I was the only flute who didn't quit. Once I started taking private lessons in sixth grade, I could easily play all the band music without practicing. I was ahead of the others and spent a lot of time waiting for them to catch up. I read books a lot in sixth-grade band. Now that I'm in advanced band, the music is still easy but more fun, and I like playing in a big group."*

This is what some parents say about starting private lessons and how you can change their minds:

"You have to play in band a year or two first. Then if you have talent, I might be willing to pay for private lessons."
Should you try to learn math on your own for a couple of years before you get a teacher? Should you drive a car for a couple of months before you have someone show you how? I hope not!

"You take gym class at school and don't need private tennis lessons. Why would you need private music lessons if you have music class at school?"
If tennis was your passion, and you wanted to get really good, you would want to take private lessons. Being only in band limits you to the kind of music you can play and how good you'll get.

"You don't practice enough to justify paying for private lessons."
No one would expect you to study before taking a class. How can they expect you to practice when you've never been taught how to practice? Or how much to practice? Or what to practice?

"I don't want to pay for private lessons. You're never going to be a professional musician, and lessons would be a waste of money."
Private lessons help anyone who wants to learn an instrument the right way, for those who want to be music majors, and for those who just want to play for fun. Do you only take tennis lessons or join the football team because you're going to be a professional athlete? Without private lessons, you'll never know the possibilities of your instrument, how good you can be, or how much fun you can have.

"I played the clarinet in high school. I can teach you how to play the sax."
Your parents can be invaluable coaches when you are beginning to learn. They can help you learn to read music and count and can help you organize your practice. But you need an expert on your instrument to take you beyond the basics.

As a teen, as much as you might love your parents, it's a lot easier taking directions from someone else. Working with a parent may work well for a few very patient parents and children, but it most often degenerates into World War III.

"You can learn to play the guitar on your own. All great guitar players are self-taught."
Some rock and jazz guitar players have never had private lessons, but they have studied the techniques of the great players who came before them. They joined bands and asked for pointers. They had to become their own teachers. Sure, you can try to pick it up on your own, but why not start out with lessons as a beginner to get over the initial hurdles, and then continue to develop your own style?

🔊

> *"I take private lessons because then you can really focus. When you look around the band, you see that the people who take private lessons are more dedicated." (Lauren, age 16)*

WHAT HAPPENS WHEN YOU TAKE PRIVATE LESSONS

You'll learn to play correctly from the beginning.
It's hard to unlearn bad habits.

You'll leave the tough beginning stages faster.
Why start from scratch when your teacher already knows the shortcuts? If you have a hard beginning and no teacher, you may be tempted to quit—or everyone who hears you may beg you to quit!

You'll learn tricks to make playing easier and more fun.
Private teachers can teach you hundreds of tone tricks, easier fingerings, and how to play with the right touch. This list goes on and on and could never be written in a book.

You'll gain a new adult friend.
One of the best things about having a private teacher is the personal relationship the two of you develop. Private music teachers are different than your teachers at school. They share their passion with you and really get to know you and will live through your ups and downs for years as you take lessons. It's great to have a friend outside of your family.

You'll meet kids your age who play instruments.
Sometimes it may seem as if you're the only one doing this "weird thing called

music." Private lessons will introduce you to other students who have the same interest and commitment as you.

You'll be motivated by your teacher.
It's hard to stay on track when you're learning by yourself. Your teacher will help you know what to practice and how to practice. A teacher will also make sure you do practice.

You'll enjoy more musical opportunities.
A well-connected teacher knows about opportunities like concerts, contests, ensembles, and performances.

> *Dan, a school district webmaster, had a rocky start becoming a musician. He was his own teacher for 30 years! "My early musical experience was limited to the clarinet in grade school band. I rarely practiced at home, and with 50–60 students to deal with, the teacher couldn't give me the guidance to get any better. Eventually I dropped out of band.*
>
> *"I taught myself to play the flute as a young adult in the navy. After a few weeks, I had control of the first two octaves. Playing by ear and 'jamming' with other sailors and friends brought me some satisfaction, but the flute was really just a diversion, nothing serious.*
>
> *"Over time, I became agile enough to play almost any tune I heard. I even began playing in church on Sundays, but I never soloed, and I still could only play two octaves.*
>
> *"In my professional life, I had taken countless hardware and software classes. It finally dawned on me, after many years, that I could afford private lessons for my own enjoyment. Off I went to the local community college to finally learn about my instrument.*
>
> *"My teacher, a professional flutist, was very patient and helped to identify many bad habits that were actually hindering me. My tone improved almost immediately. Playing became less 'strenuous' as I learned better posture and breathing, the proper way to hold the instrument, etc. I now play in a flute choir and participate in online music collaborations. Learning from a professional has opened the door to gaining more enjoyment from my horn than I had imagined possible. I only wish I had taken lessons earlier."*

WHAT IF YOU WANT TO TAKE LESSONS BUT CAN'T AFFORD THEM?

Even if money is tight in your family, you have lots of options.
- Try the barter system. I've traded housekeeping, sewing, cooking, gardening, babysitting, and computer and office work for lessons.
- Contact the local chapter of the Music Teachers National Association about their Music Link scholarship programs. There are MTNA chapters in most communities in every state.

- Contact your local Rotary chapter about the Music for Life program.
- Ask a private teacher if you might have a partial scholarship. If you show commitment and work hard, the teacher may be encouraged to help.
- Ask a teacher if you can have lessons every other week.
- Find a beginning teacher who may be good but who has lower fees. New teachers need students as much as you need a teacher.
- If you're a beginner, ask a local teacher to recommend an advanced high school student to teach you.
- Find a teacher who teaches group lessons, or ask if you and a friend could take lessons together.
- Contact a local community college for lessons in their not-for-credit program.
- Take half-hour instead of hour lessons.
- See if you can get a discount for coming at a hard-to-schedule time slot.

"I didn't want to take private lessons at first, but my parents signed me up anyway. It was the best decision they ever made for me." (Stacy, age 14)

"I went from practicing 20 minutes a day to 45 minutes a day when I got a private teacher. Private teachers don't want you to be good; they want you to be great. I practice more now because I want to get better but also because I want to impress my private teacher. Private lessons also teach you about things like music theory and more complicated music. I also like the studio activities because it gives me a community of students, a family away from home." (Rana, age 11)

WHAT SHOULD I DO IF I CAN'T TAKE LESSONS?

Not everyone lives close to a teacher, has the time to take lessons, or has the money to afford them. If you're not able to or it's too difficult to take lessons, you'll need to be more self-motivated. Keep yourself open to new opportunities and reevaluate your situation a year from now.

Here are some helpful compromises that can still jump start your playing:
- An occasional lesson from a private teacher is better than none at all. Can you afford a lesson every other week or once a month?
- Ask an older high school student or a friend who plays your instrument for help.
- Ask your school music teacher for ideas and music.
- Go to concerts, listen to CDs, and turn on the radio. Try to imitate these famous players.
- Have fun with play-along CDs, DVDs, and computer programs.
- Check out free advice online.

- Enter a solo contest to get feedback on your playing. Stay and listen to the other students, too.
- Join your school music groups, play with friends, and start a band.
- READ THIS BOOK!

WHAT IF I DON'T *WANT* TO TAKE LESSONS?

Private music lessons aren't for everyone. Millions of student musicians in the world don't take private lessons and still love playing and singing. Music can be fun at all technique levels and at all commitment levels. Just because you can't or don't want to take private lessons doesn't mean that music isn't important to you or that you won't have fun experiences. The most important thing is to keep listening and keep playing and have music in your life.

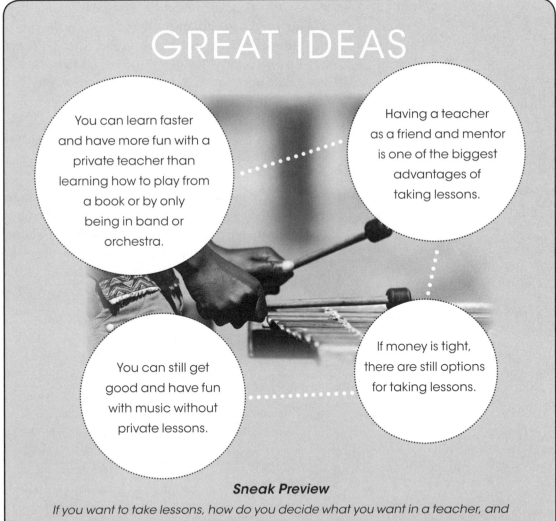

GREAT IDEAS

You can learn faster and have more fun with a private teacher than learning how to play from a book or by only being in band or orchestra.

Having a teacher as a friend and mentor is one of the biggest advantages of taking lessons.

You can still get good and have fun with music without private lessons.

If money is tight, there are still options for taking lessons.

Sneak Preview

If you want to take lessons, how do you decide what you want in a teacher, and how can you find the perfect teacher? Our next chapter gives you a step-by-step guide and everything except your new teacher's name!

SEVEN

Finding the Perfect Teacher

I have never heard one adult say, "I'm sure glad I quit music lessons. I don't really want to know how to play an instrument." So why did they quit? Many people stopped because they felt isolated, they didn't get to play the kind of music they wanted, or they didn't have time to practice. But most people quit because they didn't learn very much or they didn't like their teacher.

My flute students might not tease me so much about my piano playing if I'd had a motivating piano teacher when I was young. My teacher didn't care if I practiced, so I didn't care either. She never taught me to read music, count, or think for myself, so I was a beginner for a long time. She was a terrible teacher, and I was a terrible student. I wish I could turn back the clock and take piano lessons from someone who inspired me and encouraged me.

Of all the tips and tricks in this book, here is one of the most important: find a teacher who will set high standards, who will give you a positive push, who likes you as a person, and who will make learning fun. A teacher who believes in you and is willing to work hard to help you can make all the difference between becoming discouraged or having a blast.

Anna, age 16, was in for a bit of a shock when she first started taking lessons. "My first experience with a 'real' flute teacher at age 15 was very exciting—until my third or fourth lesson. Unlike my other teachers who would just go along with whatever I played unless I made a big mistake like counting or wrong notes, my new teacher was not afraid to point out all my mistakes, and I mean all. From too-short eighth-notes to tone and phrasing, she would write down everything so I wouldn't make the same mistake twice. She really cared about me and my playing. One week I slacked off, and I was very sorry for the price I had to pay. My teacher was quite impatient, and I could hear the stiffness in her voice. Of course I couldn't blame her, considering she is used to hearing the best out of her students. I'm glad to have a teacher with good students, even though I'm not a very good musician yet. With her help I know I will sound better, play better, and perform better."

Of course, you may be close to perfect yourself, but there are no perfect teachers, just as there are no perfect students, friends, teachers, or kids. How do you find the teacher who will be a good match for you?

If this is your first time taking lessons, you may not know what you are looking for in a teacher. Take a minute to think about what may be important to you.

What do you want to do?
- Learn to play the right way from the start?
- Play a beautiful piece you heard?
- Have more music in your life?
- Keep up with your friends who play?
- Earn first chair in band or orchestra?
- Learn to play an instrument as a hobby?
- Confidently play a solo in a concert?
- Prepare to take music classes in college?
- Be a professional musician?

Are you taking lessons because your parents are making you?
Even if this was all your parents' idea, give it a try. You'll never know how much you can learn and how talented you really are without a teacher. This "one time" your parents may be right.

"A good teacher can inspire students to love to play music and to want to make it sound good. They make it fun and enjoyable while still achieving a high level of performance. A bad one always points out faults or lets large mistakes go by and never works to fix them." (Lauren, age 16)

What are you looking for?
- A teacher who specializes in beginners? Or someone who can teach all levels?
- Music theory and history to be included as part of learning your instrument?
- Different styles of music or improvisation?

"My guitar teacher, instead of talking like grownups do, puts things into kids words so I can understand it better. He listens to the same music I listen to and points things out in a song I know, like, 'Remember that part in the song where he plays like this?' I got to pick the music I play, like Led Zeppelin, my favorite band." (Andy, age 15)

52

Part Two

WHAT TYPE OF TEACHER WILL BLEND
WITH YOUR PERSONALITY STYLE?

We all have different personalities and temperaments. The teacher your friend thinks is hilarious you think is lame. Your sweet, soft-spoken teacher may totally bore your friend. Find the teacher who keeps you interested and learning.

What kind of teacher would that be?
Someone who:
- Forms a close relationship with students?
- Makes learning fun?
- Is warm and friendly, is "all-business," or a little of both?
- Tells you where to improve and pushes you to get there?

🔊 *"I play two instruments and have had four teachers. All of them were different. The first one always wanted me to improve and encouraged me. The next one was always laidback, and she let me play whatever I wanted to play and helped me when I got stuck. The third teacher didn't care at all, and the teacher I'm with now is very hands-on. She asks me to play my songs to the fullest and as perfectly as possible. I like this teacher the best because she helps me play better." (James, age 13)*

🔊 *Sixteen-year-old Lauren is well on her way to becoming a professional musician. "I found a teacher who had many good students, so I decided to take lessons from her. My teacher pushes me to be the best, but at the same time she is fun to be around and play music with."*

What are your restrictions in cost and convenience?
- Are the times you can take lessons limited?
- Do you need a teacher who can teach at your school or come to your house?
- Are you willing to travel far for the perfect match, or do you need a teacher in the neighborhood?
- What can your budget support?

Do you want a teacher who offers extra enrichment beyond the lesson room?
Many teachers see you only once a week in their studio and for your recital at the end of the year. Other teachers have frequent recitals, master classes, ensemble opportunities, contests, and parties. Teachers who offer extra enrichment make learning more fun and give you a chance to make lifelong friends. From a student's perspective, this may be one of the most important things to consider—your social life. Students in my studio feel they're part of our flute family. They play together in ensembles, create skits for recitals, perform for each other in contests, concerts, and master classes, and have fun at our many parties. Through the years they become close friends.

- Perform in many student recitals?
- Get to know other students who play your instrument?
- Have fun playing in ensembles with other students from the same studio?
- Learn in ensemble classes? Group lessons? Studio parties?
- Feel you belong to a special club?

SHOULD YOU TAKE PRIVATE OR GROUP LESSONS?

The advantages of group lessons

Many teachers, especially those who teach piano, offer group lessons or a combination of group and private lessons. The cost per student per lesson is much lower in a group, although scheduling can be a challenge. You'll have a chance to meet other kids who play at your level, have friendly competition, play games, do drills, and perform for each other.

The advantages of private instruction

In private lessons, you don't have to spend any down time in the lesson waiting for a classmate to understand or play something until they get it just right. If you're struggling with a concept, your teacher can give you all the attention you need, and you won't feel embarrassed in front of others. When lessons are just with the two of you, you and your teacher can get to know each other better.

Combination lessons

Private lessons and group lessons make a great combination. Many teachers who teach group lessons also offer private lessons. Others who teach private lessons offer master classes, group classes once a month, or frequent performance classes.

WHERE SHOULD YOU TAKE LESSONS?

Private homes

Most private teachers teach in a home studio or in their living room where they have everything they need. It's comfortable learning in a home, and students see the teacher as a personal friend, not just another teacher. Sometimes I wonder if my students only come to pet my loving black Labrador, Angie, and to dip into my stash of candy!

The downside of learning in the teacher's home would be if the teacher lives far away or if the setting is not organized or professional. (It's hard to concentrate with MTV blaring in the next room and the teacher's screaming children streaking through the studio.)

Music stores

The teacher has access to instruments and music at the store, but usually teaches in a cramped space. Many great teachers teach at music stores, but unless the store screens the teachers and is involved in professional development, these lessons may be taught by someone who teaches many instruments but can't take students to an advanced level in all of them.

Group lessons at school

Group instruction at school usually begins in fourth or fifth grade and teaches kids the basics. Many kids would not even think about playing an instrument if beginning instrument class weren't offered at school. Lessons at school are free and convenient, and learning in a group may be fun, but because there is so little time and so many kids, progress is usually slow. This means that students may develop bad habits that the teacher doesn't have enough time to correct (or even to observe). It's fun to learn with other kids at school, but the kids who are most successful in this setting are those who are also taking private lessons. Many students who don't take private lessons become discouraged with their slow progress and quit the classes.

Private lessons at school

Many band and orchestra teachers excuse students from class to take private lessons. The lesson fees are usually fairly reasonable, and the commute is great. If you have after-school sports every night or other activities, lessons during school can be a good solution. While lessons at school are convenient, they're not ideal. Most lessons are short and taught in noisy, ugly, often tiny practice rooms and may be cancelled due to school events, vacations, and during the summer. Your parents may never meet the teacher, and you may never have the chance to form that special relationship with your teacher. But if you can commit to staying focused under these conditions, lessons at school can be a big help.

Community music schools

These local schools offer young students and adults a group of teachers who teach many instruments, all in the same place. Like medical buildings, these schools run like businesses with a central office. Some teachers are there because they don't want to teach at home. Others came there for the steady flow of new students. Students who study at these schools enjoy bigger facilities for concerts, more opportunities to play with other students, and a variety of classes.

WHAT QUALITIES SHOULD EVERY GOOD TEACHER HAVE?

You can put up with a lot of things in a teacher. Who cares if he wears ugly ties or if her music studio is a mess? But don't sign up for lessons until you've found a teacher who will:

- Know the standard music for your instrument and inspiring pieces.
- Be interested in you as a person, not just as a student.
- Boost your confidence and believe in your ability to play well.
- Be excited about teaching you.
- Be patient and take time to help you improve—even
  after reminding you of that F♯ 12 times. (OK, I admit
  after 12 reminders, I'm not so patient!)
- Use creative ways to help you understand techniques
  and keep lessons interesting.
- Motivate you with praise.
- Broaden your horizons by connecting you to the larger musical world.
- Be prepared for each lesson and have a long-range plan.
- Make each lesson fun.

Look for a teacher who has a strong commitment to students and an overwhelming enthusiasm for teaching. If your teacher is excited about your lessons, you will be, too.

CHOOSE A TEACHER WHO HELPS YOU FULFILL YOUR POTENTIAL

Kasumi's parents chose me as her teacher because other parents told them I got good results by setting high standards. Fifth-grader Kasumi knew she wanted a teacher, but she had heard that the one named Bonnie was a hard teacher who made her students practice a lot. Luckily, Kasumi's parents didn't tell her the name of her new flute teacher until she was getting out of the car. By then it was too late to turn back! Kasumi and I enjoyed eight years of wonderful lessons together, and she is at a top conservatory on her way to becoming a professional musician, all because her parents gave the "mean" teacher a chance. Having high standards implies that the teacher cares, not that the teacher is being mean.

YOU ARE MORE IMPORTANT THAN THE MUSIC

Seventeen-year-old Sandy studied voice for two years with a respected teacher and made great progress. But that progress came at a price. Whenever Sandy made a mistake, his teacher came unglued. "How could you be so stupid? Why don't you ever practice? Can't you hear?" Sandy left each lesson with a headache. But Sandy and his parents put up with the verbal abuse. Sandy's mom remembers, "We thought good teachers had to be harsh to get results."

Then Sandy's younger brother, Evan, started cello lessons. Evan also made remarkable progress, but Evan looked forward to every lesson. His teacher seemed delighted each time Evan walked through the door. Evan's teacher had the same high standards as Sandy's teacher, but he praised Evan, asked about his life, and joked around at each lesson. Evan became a good musician as well as a happy one.

Learning is not just about the end result but about the journey along the way. Who cares if you're good when you're miserable? You are more important than the music, and you deserve a teacher who cares about you as a person, not just as a musician. Years after quitting lessons you may forget how to play the concerto, but you will never forget how your teacher made you feel.

WHAT'S THE FIRST THING I SHOULD DO TO FIND A TEACHER?

Look around. Teachers who advertise for students may be beginning teachers or those with a large class turnover rate. But they may also be an experienced teacher who just relocated, had many seniors graduate, or wants to build her studio. If you consider taking lessons from someone at a music store, make sure the teacher specializes in your instrument. Student teachers at universities are often brimming with new ideas and enthusiasm, but most have little experience and may move on, leaving you to start your search again.

As with everything, referrals are your best bet. With whom do the best students study? Talk to band and orchestra directors. Attend concerts or contests. Contact the local Music Teachers National Association (MTNA) or professional society for your instrument. Ask teachers of other instruments; they know who is doing a good job. Talk to students about their lessons. Do they like their teacher and lessons? Are they learning a lot? Who has a good reputation? You may hear the same teacher's name mentioned again and again. That's the teacher you should call.

A WORD OF CAUTION

The teenager who baby-sits your neighbor's children, the kindly lady who lives on your block, or the teacher whose lessons cost half that of others may be wonderful teachers, but please don't base your entire decision on cost or convenience. Search for the best teacher you can afford, not the cheapest teacher. You get what you pay for! One month learning from a good teacher is worth a whole year of learning in your school band or orchestra. A good teacher is a wise investment whether you become a professional musician or just play for fun.

"I've moved four times all across the United States, and I've experienced the styles of four teachers. There's a big difference between a good teacher and a not-so-good teacher. When you first start to take lessons, it's okay to get a really nice teacher, but as you become more serious in your playing, you don't want someone who tells you that everything you play is good. You need a teacher who tells you where you need to improve. The teacher should teach you about music theory and musicality, not just playing the right notes. Choosing a great teacher doesn't just change your playing; it may also change the way you look at music for the rest of your life." (Irene, age 14)

You have a couple of names of teachers, but how do you choose? The best way is to go to a recital. Are the students well prepared? Are there beginners and advanced students? Is the atmosphere fun and accepting? Do the students and parents have an easy rapport with the teacher? Does this look like a cool thing to do?

If you're just a beginner and the students you hear are all amazing musicians, don't be overwhelmed. Those students started out as beginners just like you, and the teacher coached them into being superstars. You can be a superstar, too!

THE PHONE CALL

If you can't attend a recital, you can learn a lot by talking to the prospective teacher on the phone. It's best if your parent, instead of you, calls the teacher. First ask if the teacher has any openings. If the teacher's class is already full, ask to meet anyway for an interview. The teacher may be so intrigued with you that she may "miraculously" find a spot in her schedule. If not, after having met you, the teacher may be able to refer you elsewhere. Once you've met the "perfect" teacher, you will have a better idea of what you're looking for in another teacher, or you may decide to be put on a waiting list.

During the phone interview or first lesson, you or your parents may want to ask about the teacher's program: are music history, theory, and technology included? Are there performances? Does the teacher have beginners as well as advanced students? Does she seem to have a plan?

Ask about studio policies. Are parents welcomed, required, or forbidden to attend lessons? How much practice time is required? What is the fee? How are payments made?

What is the cancellation policy? Is there a policy for makeup lessons? What happens in the summer?

TAKE A TEST DRIVE

If you like what you hear, arrange a trial lesson. This is a chance for your parent, you, and the teacher to have a "blind date" with no commitment.

Is the studio a fun place to be? Do you feel at ease with the teacher? Does the teacher talk to you or just to your parent? Is the music studio organized and interesting? Does the teacher have good ideas? Does the teacher offer suggestions without putdowns, or is he or she a grouch or a perfectionist? Does the teacher seem excited to meet you and happy to work with you? Do you laugh together?

If you love the trial lesson and want to start lessons right away, go ahead and tell the teacher, but don't feel rushed. Choosing a teacher is a big decision, and you might want to try another teacher first or talk it over with your parents. When you find the right teacher, you'll set the stage for many hours (days/years/a lifetime) of happy music making.

GREAT IDEAS

Answer these questions before you look for a teacher:

What do I want included in the lessons?

What are my goals for taking lessons?

Where do I want to take lessons?

Find a teacher who:
1. Sets high standards.

2. Motivates you to practice.

Do I want private or group lessons?

4. Is interested in you as a person.

3. Makes lessons fun.

5. Loves to teach.

Sneak Preview

You and your teacher are a team. Now that you've found the perfect teacher, what do you have to do to make it the "dream team"? Here's a hint: it takes more than just showing up for lessons. To learn how you can be the perfect student, see chapter 8.

EIGHT

How to Be a Great Student

You have talent, supportive parents, a good instrument, and a motivating teacher. Everything should be perfect, right? Now the rest is up to you. What does it take to be a great student?

- Come to every lesson. Don't cancel unless you're headed to the hospital, your grandmother has died, or your lesson is scheduled for midnight on New Year's Eve. Consistent lessons are the only way to improve. Your teacher has reserved your time for you; this is not a drive-in restaurant. If you must cancel, call immediately and try to arrange a makeup lesson.
- Feel free to call your teacher if you have a question, but don't expect that she will be on call 24/7. Give her a break on Saturday nights.
- Involve your parents. Behind almost every good student is a supportive parent.
- Pay promptly. Teachers may have to beg you to practice, but they shouldn't have to beg you for money.
- Arrive on time. Why cheat yourself out of part of a lesson you have paid for? If you must be late, call the teacher so she doesn't worry.
- Bring all your music and manuscript books. It's hard for the teacher to scramble to get your books or remember your lesson assignment without your assignment book. Just because you didn't practice your étude is no reason to "forget" it at home.
- Walk in with a smile. Greet your teacher. Ask how she is. Remember, she's a person, too.
- Quit whining. Of course you go to the hardest school, you have the hardest teachers, and you just took the hardest test. Don't spend 15 minutes of every lesson complaining. Put your teacher in the psychiatrist role only for really important problems.
- Be prepared. Your lesson is only one hour a week. There is only so much the teacher can do. The real learning happens in the other six days during practice.
- Focus not only on the results but also on the effort. You can't win every time, but you can always improve.

- Complete your assignments on time. Order the
music, arrange the rehearsal, call the accompanist, buy the CD, and send in the contest form.
- If you haven't practiced, be honest. Don't waste your teacher's time and temper on faking it. If you haven't had
much time, come with only a couple of things practiced well, instead of everything practiced poorly.
- Don't try to talk your way through the lesson to avoid having to play the pieces you have not prepared. Spend
your lesson talking about Bach, not baseball.
- Don't pick and choose what you want to practice from the
weekly assignment. Of course the scales aren't your favorite part, but you must practice what your teacher has assigned. Remember, it is important to work on the basics
and not just prepare for the contest. Dessert comes last.
- Be open. Be willing to change. Even if you think your way
is better or it's too hard to do something different, give
it a try. Some things just take time. Don't be defensive. You pay your teacher to give you help. Use it.
- Be curious and develop your own opinions and style.
- Keep focused. Don't look at the clock and sigh.
Don't say, "Do I have to play that again?"
- Communicate. If you feel frustrated or confused, let the teacher
know. You can avoid tears over some misunderstanding at the les-
son if your teacher knows your feelings. Ask for help or a break.
- If you feel your teacher is too demanding or doesn't give you enough
to work on, tell him. Work together to set goals and standards.
- Be persistent. Rome wasn't built in a day, and neither is a good musician.
- Before you decide to quit lessons, discuss your problems with the
teacher. Give her a chance to accommodate your needs.
- Always rehearse music with your teacher that
you will be performing in public.
- Treat your teacher with respect. Reserve your slang for school.
Be courteous. Let your teacher know she is appreciated.
- Be grateful. Most teachers really care, and teaching is more than just
a job to them. If your teacher does something "beyond the call of
duty," such as extra lessons, consulting on the phone, writing a
recommendation letter, hosting a special recital, forming chamber groups, or attending performances, show your gratitude.
- Be thoughtful. You would be surprised how far a flower, a card,
or a treat will go—especially if you haven't practiced!
- Enjoy this special hour. When you learn something exciting, express your delight. Take pleasure in your lessons and your relationship with your teacher.

- When you leave, always smile and say, "Thank you for the lesson."
- Remember the goal is not just to become a better instrumental-
  ist but to become a better person through your music.
- Practice being a good student. Who knows?
  You may be the teacher some day.

Following is something my student Alisa, age 17 and a fabulous student, wrote when she was 12, as a joke. I hope you don't agree except for number 6!

How to Be an A+ Student

1. If you didn't practice, buy a present for your teacher
   and give it to her *before* your lesson.
2. Comment on what she is wearing and tell her
   that it is nice, even if it is tacky.
3. Laugh every time your teacher makes a joke, even if it is dorky.
4. Tell your teacher how much you love your instrument
   and your lessons to butter her up.
5. If you're bored while your teacher is talking, look
   straight at her and pretend you are listening.
6. PRACTICE!

GREAT IDEAS

Treat your teacher with respect and do your best at the lessons, and you, too, can be a great student.

Sneak Preview

But what if you are the "perfect student" and the lessons aren't going well? Could it be time to change teachers? Read why and how to change teachers in our next chapter.

NINE

Is It Time to Change Teachers?

"My teacher doesn't teach me anything! I'll never improve if I stay with him."

"My teacher thinks that music should be the only thing in my life. She wants me to practice all the time and play in too many recitals. She's so impatient, and nothing I do is ever good enough."

"My teacher is nice, but she's also boring. Every lesson is the same. I want lessons that are fun."

No teacher is the perfect match for everyone. The nicest teacher may not teach well. The hardest teacher may not be on your wavelength or may be too impatient. The teacher who teaches only facts and technique may not inspire you to play musically or to practice. Your lessons may be all work and no fun. You may have outgrown the teacher who was perfect when you were a beginner. Perhaps your teacher is too strict and demanding now that you're busy with other activities. And if you chose a teacher only because he or she was convenient or a bargain, you're probably seeing how well that's working out.

In this chapter we'll talk about how to decide if it's time to change teachers, what to do before you make that final decision, how to break it to your present teacher, and how to move on with no hard feelings. A great teacher can make all the difference in your performance and love of music, so I urge you and your parents to think about what you need and go after it.

Yijia, age 16, finally had the nerve to change teachers. "'Please don't let him be there so I can turn around and go back home,' I thought as I trudged toward the parking lot of the music store. I hated my music lessons with a passion. Anything sounded better than having to spend 45 minutes in a stuffy room with a guy who hardly said more than 10 sentences to me.

"My lessons were very routine. I walked in and mumbled, 'Hi,' and my teacher acknowledged my presence with a similar greeting. Then we used half the time to sight-read whatever random duet he happened to carry with him that day. This was the worst part. I hated sight-reading because my rhythm was so bad. He often got impatient, and I was frustrated. Next he would play

some music, and I had to mimic him. He never taught me how to play musically or with feeling. At the end of each lesson, he always told me how much I had improved.

"Over time he came in later and later to my lessons, often sweaty and apologetic. Sometimes he called a half hour before to cancel or never showed up at all. If I had a scheduling conflict, he would have this extremely pained look on his face. After spending a long time debating the situation, we often ended up just skipping the lesson. Then he started ending the lessons earlier. He also glanced at his watch not so discreetly every two minutes. I can't blame him because I started to do the same thing.

"All the negatives could have been overlooked if I'd been improving, but everyone was playing better than I was, and yet I worked just as hard. I wanted to quit altogether. What was the point if I dreaded the lessons and disliked my teacher?

"I really regret not changing teachers sooner. Sometimes I wonder what he really thought of me as a student. Did he despise the lessons as much as I did?"

Perhaps your situation isn't as bad as Yijia's, but you may have some serious concerns about your present teacher. Here are some issues students sometimes face, as they consider whether or not their current teacher is a good fit.

I don't want to hurt my teacher's feelings.

Even if you're not happy with your lessons, you may really like your teacher and have put off making a change. No one said it would be easy, but changing teachers may affect whether you continue playing or not.

Should I change teachers just to get another viewpoint?

Jumping from teacher to teacher to get different viewpoints is not wise. Instead, attend master classes, contests, and summer camps to receive input from many outside sources. Find a teacher who can guide you to the next level and who can be a friend and an advocate. Changing teachers is not like switching brands of laundry detergent or going to a different hairdresser. Give a lot of thought to this important decision, as it affects you and your teacher.

HOW TO DECIDE WHETHER A CHANGE IS NEEDED

Step 1: Think about how well your lessons are going.
Do you:
- Enjoy your lessons?
- Feel stressed because your teacher asks you to do too much?
- Feel bored?
- Learn quickly for your own talent and experience level?
- Believe in your teacher's abilities and knowledge?

- Learn the fundamentals of music rather than
    just playing through pieces?
- Admire and respect your teacher?
- Like your teacher only because she's nice or easy?
- Like your teacher only because he's close or inexpensive?
- Leave each lesson having learned something?
- Look forward to your lessons?

Does your teacher:
- Challenge and reward you?
- Give you chances to perform?
- Prepare you well for performances?
- Care about your feelings and help you when you're frustrated?
- Act impatient or irritable most of the time?
- Admire and respect you?
- Care about you as a person?
- Make teaching a priority? Does he skip lessons
    or seem tired and distracted?
- Give the same amount of energy and commitment he expects from you?
- Have a "plan"? Is the curriculum taught in a haphazard manner?
- Individualize the lesson, or teach "by the book"?

Keleah, age 15, has wanted harp lessons since she heard her teacher talk about the harp in Bible school. "When I was 10, I saw a harp for the first time at a Mexican restaurant. The harpist let me pluck the strings while she talked to my parents. She was only 15, and she gave harp lessons, so she became my teacher. She showed me where the notes were, and I copied her. But it turned out she was teaching me wrong because when she later changed teachers herself, she began teaching me in a different way, and it confused me. After almost two years I still didn't know how to read music or play with a consistent style. So we looked for a new teacher.

We found a teacher with a good reputation. I had to start all over. My new teacher is patient, and she knows what she's doing. She pushes me to improve, which makes me work harder and learn faster. My first young teacher was very nice, but now I'm going to become a good harpist because I finally found a good teacher."

Keleah's problem was that she was working with an inexperienced teacher. But sometimes it's not all the teacher's fault.

Step 2: Examine your own behavior to make sure you aren't part of the problem.
    "My teacher doesn't care if I practice," Heidi told me. "I want to study with you so you will push me to improve." Heidi thought I would inspire her to take her lessons seriously. I soon learned that Heidi was all talk. She said she wanted

to practice and improve, but she wouldn't work. Studying with a good teacher can't help unless you *want* to learn. Don't use your teacher as an excuse for your own laziness, and don't expect a new teacher to change old attitudes.

Do you:

- Really want to learn?
- Follow your teacher's instructions?
- Practice daily with concentration?
- Come to every lesson?
- Treat your teacher with respect?
- Listen and incorporate your teacher's suggestions?
- Take responsibility for your problems?

Step 3: Talk to your present teacher honestly.

My adult student Jeanette was always prepared and eager to learn. I heaped on the assignments, and she came prepared to every lesson. I thought everything was going fine until one day she told me she couldn't take the pressure anymore. I was shocked. If she had told me how she felt, I could have easily given her less, but her anxiety built up to the point of no return.

Don't blindside your teacher by saying you want to quit without first being upfront about the problem. You can't change a teacher's personality, but there are things you can change. It's only fair to tell your teacher about the problem before you quit. Enlist your parents' help if it's too uncomfortable for you to be honest with your teacher. If you're afraid at lessons, let the teacher know. She probably has no idea how her tone of voice or teasing affects you. Let your teacher know if the workload is too light or too heavy. If you think you're not prepared well for performance, talk about it. If you and the teacher have different goals—for example, he wants you to be a music major and you want music to be a hobby, then your teacher needs to know.

Perhaps you expect too much of your teacher. No teacher can guarantee you win every contest or make every minute of every lesson fun, or be on call 24/7. But if things aren't going well, it's only fair to give your teacher a chance to change or at least tell the other side of the story. If there's no chance of compromise, then it's time to leave.

HOW TO BREAK IT TO THE "OLD" TEACHER

What's the best way to tell your current teacher you're leaving? That's a tough one. I've had students call me, e-mail me, tell me at the beginning or end of a lesson that this is their last time, give me two weeks' notice, leave a note for me to find after they left, and just not show up again after a vacation. Sometimes I've been shocked, other times puzzled, and many times relieved.

Of course, it's difficult for everyone, but you can ease the transition. Be kind when you tell your teacher you're going to quit. Give the teacher a "compliment sandwich." First say what you've learned, then explain that you've decided to change, and end with how much you've enjoyed and appreciated the lessons. Give your teacher a chance to respond, but be firm once you've made the decision. Thank your teacher for your time together and speak with gratitude and respect. Don't place blame or make comparisons with other teachers. You want to remain friends so that you don't have to hide behind the toilet paper display when you see your former teacher in the grocery store.

It's important for both parties to say good-bye in person. There may be tears at the last meeting, but that means you care about each other. It's thoughtful to give the teacher a present, a lovely note showing your appreciation and affection, and a final warm hug.

FINDING A NEW TEACHER

Once the decision to leave is made, start calling other teachers. Use our suggestions in chapter 7, "Finding the Perfect Teacher." When you talk to prospective teachers, tell them what you're looking for in lessons and not why you were unhappy with the former teacher. It's diplomatic to keep the former teacher's name private. Out of respect for the first teacher, don't start lessons with the new teacher until you've made a clean break. Having the right teacher can make all the difference, so follow your heart and find a teacher who is right for you.

- Changing teachers is a big decision.
- Decide what you need from lessons.
- Ask yourself if you are part of the problem.
- Talk with the teacher about solutions before you quit.
- Be kind when you tell the teacher you are leaving.
- Don't complain about the first teacher to the new one.

Sneak Preview

Singers, if it seems as if this book has been only about instrumentalists, the next chapter is for you. Find out how to learn a song faster, sing it better, and keep your voice healthy.

TEN

Singers

You Are the Instrument

Singers have the best instrument of all. It's free. It's portable. It's beautiful and versatile. The human voice may be the most convenient instrument, but it's also the most mysterious. You can check your finger, bow, or embouchure position when you play other instruments, but the singer's instrument is inside the body. You can only hear the results.

We're all born with the capacity to sing. So why take lessons? A teacher acts as a vocal X-ray machine to help you connect the sounds you make with the mysterious moving parts that form them. Have you ever heard a recording of yourself and wondered who that was? A good teacher serves as your "outside ears" to give feedback.

Singing is intensely personal. Some say singing is the sound of the soul. The quality of your voice mirrors your physical state. It changes with age, illness, injury, and experience. It also changes with emotion—think how hard it is to talk or sing when you are upset. No other instrument changes as much through its life as the voice, and a private teacher can help you keep on track. Even top professionals continue to go to teachers throughout their career to help them navigate through the life of their instrument and keep all their vocal muscles in top form.

WHY SHOULD I TAKE VOICE LESSONS?

Untrained singers who think they don't need lessons usually fall into two groups. The first group has family and friends who are too polite to tell them they can barely carry a tune. (They probably don't tell them when they need to use deodorant, either!) People in the second group don't sound as if they are in a medieval torture device, but their delivery is plain and full of rough edges. They can sing, but they haven't learned how to be musical—how to phrase and interpret the music, how and when to breathe, and how to produce the most beautiful tone. On their own, singers in both groups can struggle for years, singing with unhealthy habits and even damaging their voice.

While there are some "natural singers," almost every professional (and all professional classical singers) have had lessons. Sure, you may be able to sing along with your favorites on TV or be the best in your church choir or on karaoke night, but you'll never know how good you can truly be if you don't have voice lessons. Even professional sports stars work with their coach every day to make sure they don't slip into bad habits. If you think you don't need lessons, your first lesson will probably change your mind!

VOICE TRAINING IS THE PATHWAY
TO ACHIEVING YOUR POTENTIAL

Untrained singers may be able to sing easy popular songs pretty well, but they fall apart when singing more complex music. They don't know how to breathe correctly, so they can't project sound, sustain high notes, or sing difficult runs. They rely on force instead of technique to sing louder. And let's not even talk about their pitch. Untrained singers have a hard time reading new music and take longer to learn their parts. Voice lessons can change all that.

An experienced voice teacher can help you in many ways. Even if you have a naturally good voice, lessons will help you explore your true potential and prevent damage to your vocal cords.

Develop your voice.
- Expand your range, power, and stamina.
- Practice breath support and control vibrato.
- Prevent vocal damage.
- Add beauty and richness to your tone.
- Smoothly bridge the chest and head registers.

Use your body efficiently.
- Expand your lung capacity.
- Control your air supply for better tone and longer phrases.
- Use correct posture and alignment.

Become a true performer.
- Interpret music and lyrics in a variety of styles.
- Sing with appropriate emotion.
- Conquer stage fright and connect with your audience.
- Improve self-confidence.
- Learn about performance opportunities.

WHAT SHOULD I SEEK IN A VOICE TEACHER?

Just because someone has sung in a rock band, at a piano bar, in a church choir, or on *American Idol* doesn't mean they can teach. Look for a teacher who knows how the voice works, not just someone who can sing. A skilled teacher will help you use better technique (such as good breath control and support), regardless of the quality of your voice, your age, your experience, or the style you sing. A teacher with a music degree and a background in the fundamentals of music can help you with ear training, sight-singing, and musicality, not just the quality of your voice or the ability to stylize songs.

WHY STUDY CLASSICAL VOICE?

Singers in rock bands, musical theater companies, and jazz bands all produce sound the same way. You don't need a teacher who performs your style of music. Classical teachers can help pop singers improve their breathing, tone production, expression, and even their acting skills. Classical singers can learn about freedom of expression, song styling, and stage presence from pop singers, although they still need coaching from a classical teacher on style and repertoire.

Find a teacher you like who encourages you, welcomes your questions, and challenges you. The National Association of Teachers of Singing (NATS) has chapters all over the country and can be a great resource for someone seeking a skilled vocal teacher.

CAN'T I LEARN TO SING WITH AN ONLINE COURSE OR DVD?

CDs and DVDs are great learning tools—if they come with a real live teacher to tell you if you're interpreting them correctly. Online courses and DVDs are cheaper than private lessons, easier to schedule, and you don't have to get off of the couch. These courses may be more convenient but nothing beats the results you'll get from a real teacher. Use "electronic lessons" when you can't take private lessons or want to supplement private lessons, but let the buyer beware.

Plug "singing lessons" into any internet search engine, and you will be overwhelmed with links to "learn-to-sing" programs.

Here's a sample of the advertising:
Skip all those vocal exercises. Our new technique allows
    you to warm up in just five minutes!
Classical teachers can only teach classical music. They try to turn
    everyone into an opera singer. Learn pop music with us!
Develop perfect pitch after listening to our five DVDs!
Learn to sing while driving!
Add one octave to your range—guaranteed!
Never have to sing in falsetto again!
Sing as high as you want!
Sing in virtually any style!
Learn to sing like a pro in only three months!
Sing like a star in 10 easy lessons!

Do these claims sound too good to be true? They probably are. Learning to be an accomplished singer takes time and practice. Books and DVDs may have tips and tricks, but nothing replaces a teacher who will tailor lessons to you, your voice, and your learning style, and who can give you immediate feedback.

HOW OLD DO I HAVE TO BE TO START VOICE LESSONS?

The ideal start time varies. Some teachers will accept students around age 12 when their voices begin to mature, while other teachers only accept students who are well into their teens. If you're physically coordinated, your voice is mature, you're able to pay attention and understand new concepts, and you're committed to practice, then you're ready to begin.

HOW CAN I START LEARNING BEFORE I TAKE LESSONS?

In the beginning stages, ear training is even more important than voice training. If your brain doesn't know what to sing, your voice sure won't! Young students who aren't quite ready for private voice lessons will have lots of fun in group music classes. Singing, rhythm, and movement games will help develop listening skills and a better understanding of music. Singing in choral groups is a great way to find your voice and learn basic techniques. Look for children's choirs in your community, at your school, and at your place of worship.

Learning another instrument, especially the piano, helps you learn to read music, understand music theory, and teach yourself parts. Playing a string instrument can better help you understand intervals (so valuable in sight-singing) and help you analyze pitch and tone.

Young singers usually have less knowledge of music concepts than instrumentalists their age, unless they've had previous musical training. The 15-year-old violinist can play Mendelssohn's violin concerto, while the 15-year-old singer without previous training is still trying to learn how to read music. Learning the building blocks of music before you start lessons can help you catch up.

WHAT IF I ALREADY SING LIKE AN ADULT?

You may only be 10 and be able to sing "Tomorrow" from the Broadway hit *Annie*, but a good voice at an early age doesn't necessarily mean a singing career ahead. In fact, if a young singer is pushed too much, that potential voice can be ruined. A child who can sing with an operatic sound, with lots of power and vibrato, rarely maintains it. Just as kids who learn to read at age 3 often level out to become average readers by second or third grade, "natural" singers often run into problems later on when they discover they really didn't know how to make their voice *work*.

Children's voices must receive the same care as the rest of their bodies. Doctors are seeing more sports injuries because parents and coaches push kids to train too hard and too long when their bones and muscles are still growing. Young voice students have the same problems. Children and teenagers still have very flexible larynxes (voice boxes) that are more susceptible to damage. When pushed to sing out of their range, or pushed to sing too loudly or too long, they can develop bad vocal habits and risk injuring their voices.

It's never too late to start an instrument or take voice lessons. If learning to be a better singer has always been your dream, go for it!

HOW CAN I GET THE MOST OUT OF MY VOICE LESSONS?

Have you heard the old joke: "How many psychiatrists does it take to change a light bulb? Only one, but the light has to really, really want to change." You'll get out of voice training only what you're willing to put in. Even the best teacher can't work miracles on students who are unwilling to try new things and practice. Training your voice is a gradual process. It takes time to strengthen your muscles and train them to respond in new ways. For singing techniques to become second nature, you need daily practice, dedication, and the coaching of a trusted teacher.

Suggestions for voice students:
- If you can't afford private lessons, look for group lessons.
- Remember that the first lesson is the hardest.
- Take enough lessons to make a difference. Your voice won't change overnight.
- Be willing to try new methods even if they feel odd or embarrassing.
- Tell your teacher if a technique is uncomfortable or if it hurts.
- Ask your teacher questions about how the voice works or if you don't understand exactly what your teacher is asking you to do.
- Understand that training your voice is more important than just learning new repertoire.
- Tape your lessons.
- Don't skip lessons, even on days you feel unprepared.
- Begin with short sessions and gradually build up time.
- Make good singing a habit even when you're in the shower or the car.
- Keep trying. One day everything will make perfect sense.

THE INTELLIGENT VOICE

It's not enough to be a dramatic singer; you must first be a musician. People get hijacked by what they think is emotion. Just because a singer is "really into it," the audience may think, "Wow, what a great singer!" But being a singer is more than having a beautiful or loud voice or wearing your emotions on your sleeve. A singer must have the same musical values as any other musician, including rhythm, pitch, and musical line. Singers who have the total package—a solid background in music theory, ear training, sight-singing, and musicality—will have a better chance of success.

My longtime friend and fellow singer, Nancy Zylstra, contributed much of the material in this chapter. Nancy is a skilled and insightful voice teacher, historical performance coach, and singing voice specialist who has some training in working as part of a team with ENTs (ear, nose, and throat doctors) and speech-language pathologists. Nancy is a renowned expert who has made recordings with top international conductors and orchestras, and she teaches each summer at a top conservatory, Oberlin College. I am grateful for her input in this chapter.

Nancy suggests you first learn to sing in your own language. Understanding lyrics will help you improve your diction. If you sing *pot* instead of *pat,* the audience will be bewildered or amused.

Nancy recommends this four-step recipe for learning a new song:

Step 1: Learn the poem or prose. Write it out in poetic form. Without this step you will be tied to the musical notation, which is for the convenience of music, not the text. Read the poem silently. Read it aloud. Recite the poem to others with meaning and good enunciation.

Step 2: Read the text in the composer's rhythm.

Step 3: Learn the music and sing it on "la," or any vowel that is easy for you. Pay attention to tone, pitch, and phrasing.

Step 4: Put it all together.

PROTECT YOUR VOICE

Your vocal cords, also called vocal folds, are muscles, and they need gradual conditioning like other muscles you depend on. They can lose elasticity due to age, misuse, or lack of use. Forcing them to work too hard can lead not only to hoarseness but even to permanent damage. Pushing your voice for a long time out of your range, singing too long, singing too loudly, or screaming (you call that singing?) can lead to hoarseness, broken blood vessels, cysts, or nodules on the vocal cords. Yuck!

Use your voice correctly.
- Support your speaking voice with proper breathing and posture.
- Always warm up before you start.
- If you sing in a group, don't compete to see who is the loudest.
- Don't push to get the high notes; it makes the tone strident and flat.
- Don't strain your voice by yelling, coughing, and singing too loudly or too long.

Watch what you eat and drink.
- Drink lots of water. Limit caffeine intake, as it's a diuretic.
- Watch what you eat just before a performance. Some singers find that certain foods produce phlegm or cause reflux. Avoiding dairy or drinking honey and lemon may help some singers but may make others feel awful. The most important thing is to be observant and notice possible causes and effects.

- Don't scream at the big game.
- Don't sing when you have a sore throat.
- Don't confuse screaming with singing, even if you're in a metal band. (Scream now, lose your career in five years: your choice.)
- Never try a new therapy on the day of a performance. Ask a medical professional for a second opinion of your friend's "miracle" cure.
- Don't smoke! Listen to 20-year smokers speak, and you won't want another cigarette—unless you're a soprano wishing to sing tenor.
- Never take someone else's prescription medications.
- Pamper yourself.
- Eat well, exercise, and get enough sleep.
- Introduce yourself to an ENT who specializes in voice *before* you have a vocal emergency.
- Take care of your voice all day. It's an irreplaceable instrument.

HELP! MY VOICE HURTS

If you've seriously strained your voice, consult your teacher and another voice professional (another reason not to rely on DVDs and online classes). When you stress your vocal folds, they can swell and rub each other, creating tiny calluses called voice nodules. Nodules limit voice vibrations and your ability to produce a full sound. Even mental stress can cause nodules.

Early in his career, operatic tenor Luciano Pavarotti developed a vocal cord nodule. He decided to give up his (at the time) mediocre career. Once he chose to stop singing, he freed himself of the stress and tension that had restricted his voice. When he no longer "had to" sing, the emotional expression and natural beauty of his voice shone through.

Pavarotti returned with a better sound, and eventually the nodule disappeared. He recalled in his autobiography: "Everything I had learned came together with my natural voice to make the sound I had been struggling so hard to achieve." Other singers who have suffered from nodules include Julie Andrews, Mariah Carey, Elton John, Whitney Houston, and Joss Stone.

To speed your recovery:
- Try to reduce the amount of singing and talking you do for a couple of days.
- Don't whisper; it's even harder on your voice than speaking normally.
- Remember proper breathing and support for talking.
- Speak in your natural range; don't let your voice drop.
- Don't clear your throat. That causes your vocal cords to rub together with hurricane force.
- Try to be gentle with coughing.

- Keep your body well hydrated. It won't necessarily
clear phlegm, but staying systemically hydrated will
help keep phlegm from being too viscous.
- If the problem is serious or long lasting, see your
regular doctor or an ENT.

WHAT ELSE CAN I DO TO ACHIEVE MY SINGING DREAMS?

Connect with your audience.

To sing professionally, you must enjoy singing and performing. Emotion keeps your audience engaged. Be confident and assertive, onstage and off. You'll have an edge over the competition when you learn to accept criticism graciously and keep going even after rejections.

Give audiences the complete package.

Strive to be the best overall musician you can possibly be. Learn microphone styles and technique, even if you are an acoustic (unamplified) classical or operatic singer. Attend concerts and listen to recordings of great singers. Offer the total package: your body, your dress, your mannerisms, and your professionalism.

Keep learning.

Study singing anatomy and physiology. Use voice exercises to build your strength and muscle memory. Study a foreign language or two. Learn your intervals and practice sight-singing. Participate in master classes and contests. Use mirror therapy to prevent bad habits, distracting facial expressions, and poor body language. You might also videotape yourself while performing.

Become a versatile musician.

If you sing popular music, learn the classical style. If you sing only classical, learn a few pop songs. Study different styles in your genre. If you're a classical singer, include Baroque, lieder, oratorio, opera, and choir selections. If you're a pop singer, include jazz, Broadway, country, gospel, and blues. Learn to accompany yourself on the piano.

Gain as much singing experience as possible.

It's hard to make it professionally as a singer. Until you hit the big time, keep your steady day job and sing at night. Stay flexible. You may hope to sing on the stage of the Metropolitan Opera House, but don't let that stop you from singing in your church choir or community choir, where you may get solos that advance your experience and also bring your talent to the attention of others.

To introduce yourself to the life of a professional entertainer, perform at local charity events and offer your services free. Perform in community musicals, coffeehouses, parties, clubs, and retirement communities. Sing at weddings, anniversaries, and gospel events.

Once you choose your area of expertise, learn as much about it as possible. What sells? Who offers what kind of repertoire? Who is your competition? Market your talents with business cards and brochures. Make a demo. Network. Later, consider getting an agent, but never one who demands that you pay money upfront. Treat your music like a business.

Connect with the professional singing community.

Play well with others. No divas allowed! Join the National Academy of Recording Arts and Sciences to gain access to the resources you will need to advance in your career. Join the National Association of Teachers of Singing at NATS.org and attend their meetings and conventions. Read biographies of successful singers, books on singing, and publications for singers like *Classical Singer,* the NATS *Journal of Voice, Opera News,* and articles on the internet. Check out www.harmony-central.com and www.dictiondomain.com.

ENJOY BEING A SINGER

Singing brings such deep joy. Mastering your singing voice will open you to a world of self-discovery and exciting possibilities. Take chances. You'll never win if you don't try.

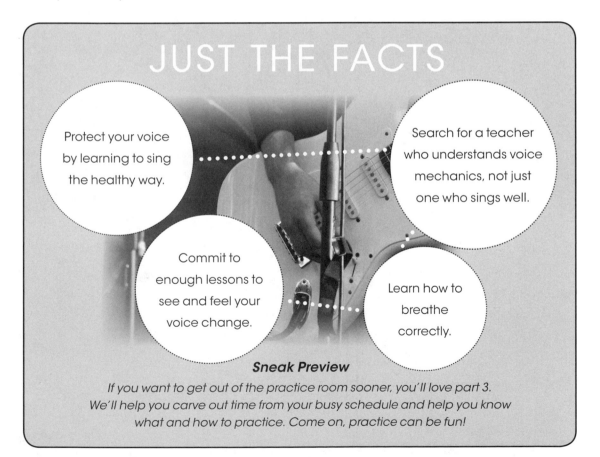

JUST THE FACTS

Protect your voice by learning to sing the healthy way.

Search for a teacher who understands voice mechanics, not just one who sings well.

Commit to enough lessons to see and feel your voice change.

Learn how to breathe correctly.

Sneak Preview

If you want to get out of the practice room sooner, you'll love part 3. We'll help you carve out time from your busy schedule and help you know what and how to practice. Come on, practice can be fun!

PART THREE

USING PRACTICE TIPS
FOR FASTER RESULTS

ELEVEN

The Attitude of Success

> Whether you think you can or think you can't, you're right.
> —Henry Ford

PICTURE YOUR WAY INTO SUCCESS

Seventh-graders Kevin and Nathan had both taken cello lessons for about six months. They liked their lessons and were happy with the progress they made in the beginning books. Then they played in their first recital. After they performed "The Happy Farmer" and "Spring Song," the older kids played the Bach suites and the Dvorak and Elgar concertos. Wow, were those kids ever good!

Kevin went home, listlessly tried a new piece, and then gave up in frustration. "I'll never be as good as those kids. Why should I even try?" At his next lesson he told his teacher he wanted to quit.

Nathan, on the other hand, was inspired by the older players. "I want to sound just like them in a couple of years." He tried imitating them and couldn't wait for his next lesson.

Have you ever heard an advanced student musician play at school or in your teacher's studio? Or heard an amazing professional play live at a concert or on a recording? As hard as it is to believe, those musicians once sounded just like you. They painstakingly learned scales and worked on their terrible tone just as you are. But they made it, and so can you. Picture yourself playing like one of the great musicians, and you'll have a better chance of becoming one. But picture yourself always sitting in last chair, and that may be all that you achieve. We move toward what we imagine. So plan big and aim high!

BELIEVE IN YOURSELF

In chapter 3, you read about the reasons so many music students give up in their first few months of playing. Learning to play an instrument takes perseverance, but many stop believing in themselves when they hit a rough patch. They can't see that where they are now will gradually transform into where they want to be. They don't think they have what it takes.

Abraham Lincoln said, "People are just about as happy as they make up their minds to be." People are as successful as they want to be, too. From the moment you pick up your instrument, tell yourself, "I can do this."

Success for some might mean playing your favorite song or being able to join a group. For others it might mean becoming a prize-winner or a professional. Or it might just mean being able to play well enough without your family and the neighbors running for cover. Your goals over the years may change, but your attitude should always be, "I can." It doesn't matter how you sound now, or if you had a slow start. It doesn't matter if the other kids you know are better than you, if you don't have private lessons, or even if you're the first one in your family to show an interest in music. As long as you want something badly enough and put in the work, you can do almost anything. Really.

BUILD CONFIDENCE WITH POSITIVE SELF-TALK

Parker paced the school hallway waiting for his turn to play at the contest. As he walked, he scolded himself. "I was so stupid to enter this contest. The girl in there playing now is much better than I am. I know I'm going to mess up. Oh, yeah, the judges will all be laughing when they hear me. Why did I think I could play? I'll never be any good. Yikes, I'm starting to feel sick!"

Success Begins in Our Minds

We talk to ourselves all the time. Whether you realize it or not, what you say to yourself affects what you do. Just as your self-esteem can be ruined by negative remarks from parents or teachers, your own negative self-talk drags you down, too. If you tell yourself you're a failure, you'll feel like a failure, act like a failure, and maybe even be a failure. People who say, "I can't," give themselves almost no chance of success. When they say, "I can't," they're really saying, "I won't," as in "I won't put in the time or effort or discipline myself."

When you talk positively to yourself, you become your own cheerleader. Imagine you're talking to your best friend. Would you tell your friend she's ugly and stupid? Can you imagine saying, "You don't have any talent. You'll never play well"? I sure hope not. So why say mean things to yourself? Respect yourself and say things that boost your confidence. What you say to yourself matters. It affects how you feel about yourself and how you perform.

TAKE RESPONSIBILITY FOR YOUR RESULTS

Jen made a face and put her hands on her hips. "Sam won the competition, and I didn't even place? It's not fair. He played last in the day, and I played in the middle, so the judge couldn't even remember me. I'd play better with a nicer cello. My mom forgot to pack my rosin. Sam's teacher is better and shows him more practice tricks. I didn't have time to practice because my parents made me visit my grandma. And I had to clean my room. My teacher gave me a piece that was way too hard. My dad came to listen and made me nervous. It's not my fault!"

Do some people, like Sam, have all the luck? Or do some people, like Jen, have all the excuses? Instead of whining that it's not fair, do something about it. Could you have memorized the piece a month earlier? Would performing more often tame your stage fright? Was the program you chose overly ambitious? Would you have been more successful if you had used your sheet music rather than your memory? Was there a problem with technique that you didn't address? Should you have practiced more?

A teacher at a private school told me that when students complain to him, saying, "I deserve a better grade than you gave me," he answers, "I didn't give you that grade. You earned that grade." And when they skip class or don't turn in homework, he warns them, "We are not going to kick you out. But you have just taken the first steps toward leaving this school." The student, not the teacher, is in charge of the outcome.

Of course, not everyone wins every contest, aces every audition, or plays beautifully every time. But as with most things in life, understand that what happens today is the result of what you did yesterday. If you want the results to be different, then your goals, thoughts, and actions must be different. The choice is yours. You can drop out, give up, slide by, and slack off, or you can believe in yourself and do something about it. Sure, it may mean uncomfortable changes, risk, and hard work. But you're worth it!

GREAT IDEAS

Picture yourself playing like a professional.

Believe you can do it.

Quit complaining.

Choose to be a winner.

Treat yourself like your best friend with positive self-talk.

Sneak Preview

You can practice nine hours a day and get nowhere unless you have the end in sight. Our next chapter will tell you how to know what you want and get it by using goals.

TWELVE

Get in Gear with Goals

There are no limits. There are only plateaus, and you
must not stay there. You must go beyond them.
—Bruce Lee, American actor and martial artist

GOALS GIVE YOU A PLAN

Why do some teens accomplish more than others do? Because they're smarter
or more talented? Are they more disciplined? Are their parents making them
do it? Successful teens achieve more using the power of goal setting. Have you
heard the saying, "No one plans to fail but many fail to plan"? Setting goals is
like creating an outline before you write your term paper or studying the map
before you hop into the car.

Elite athletes, musicians, and achievers in all fields set goals to achieve
their dreams, and you can, too. What holds others back? No plan and no focus.
Some teens' idea of a long-term goal is what they're going to do on the weekend. Goals like that only get you through the weekend, not through life.

You know you have all the talent you need to be a musician. Where do you
want to go with your music? What do you want to become? Are you coasting,
or are you visualizing something bigger and better? By the end of this chapter,
you'll be armed with a systematic plan for achieving your dreams in music and
in other parts of your life, too.

GOALS FOCUS YOUR EFFORTS

The harder you work, the more you'll accomplish. But hard work isn't enough.
You need to focus your time and energy on activities that move you toward the
end result. Many adults have not learned how to set goals and prioritize. Take
Tom, a computer programmer, for example. He puts in 12-hour workdays and
works hard, but not on the right things. It takes him an hour every morning
just to decide which project he will work on. Once he gets started, he forgets
to do the rest of his work and misses important deadlines. He daydreams and
wastes time looking up things on the internet, then complains that his work
is never done. It takes him 12 hours to do what other employees do in 6! Every
night when Tom's coworkers leave and he is still shuffling papers on his desk,
they think, "There's Tom, working *long and long* instead of *long and hard*."
Goals help you get the right things done.

Goals come in all shapes and sizes, from what you want to accomplish in a week to what you want to accomplish in a lifetime. Performance goals measure improvements. A college basketball player's *performance* goal might be to score 40 more points this year than he did last year. *Outcome* goals measure results, like getting an A in biology or winning a competition.

Outcome goals can be dangerous. Working to get an A in algebra is a good motivator. Don't you always study more before the big test? But what if *only one person* in your class can get an A? Winning in music often means that someone else has to lose. Even if you're the best cellist in town, you might fail to become the principal cellist in the big youth orchestra because an even better cellist moves into the neighborhood. Or you might play a piece in a contest that the judge really hates. We can control our own behavior, but not judges or competing musicians.

ACTION STEPS

Step One: Dream a Little Dream

What are your musical dreams? What are you willing to work a little harder to accomplish? Do you want to play solos? Perform in a garage band? Be admired by your friends? Get into a top performing group? Sing on *American Idol*? What do you really want?

My middle school student Janna brought in a poster of what she wanted to accomplish someday. Her goals started small with "Get through the *Tune a Day* book" and ended with her ultimate dream: "To play as a professional. Bonnie's old; I'm young. And I'm getting all the gigs!" I loved Janna's goals. Even the last one, although I hope it doesn't happen for a long time.

Sixteen-year-old Lauren started taking lessons in fifth grade with her long-term vision firmly in mind: "I decided right away I wanted to be good. In fifth grade I told my teacher that my dream was to go to Juilliard and become a professional flutist." Goals give you the means to turn your dreams into reality, and Lauren is on her way.

Step Two: Set Long-Term and Short-Term Goals

To show you how goals guide your efforts, let's follow the true story of my student Alisa. She started taking flute lessons in fifth grade. "I was excited to take lessons, but it wasn't my own choice. My parents were the ones who pushed me." When she was 14, she set her sights on earning a spot in the Seattle Youth Junior Symphony. "I had performed in the two lower youth groups," she recalls. "But I had always dreamed of being a member of the Junior Symphony."

Alisa's long-term goal was to win a coveted seat in that fall's Junior Symphony audition. "Only a few spots are available every year," says Alisa. "Other flutists wanted one as much as I did." She knew the danger of setting an all-or-nothing goal. "Even if I practiced as hard as I could, someone else could be

Get in Gear with Goals

practicing even harder." Depending on who else was trying out, her best playing might only earn her disappointment.

Step Three: Write down Your Goals

Experts call unwritten goals "nothing more than wishes." If you only think,
"I want to play better," how can you challenge yourself and measure your improvements? People who set specific, challenging goals and write them down
achieve more than people who just dream.

Once you've chosen your goal, you need to write the steps to accomplish it.
How? You create a to-do list of sorts. Did I hear a groan? I know, making lists is
like flossing your teeth. We know we should, but who enjoys doing it? Charging ahead seems faster than taking time to think and plan. But aren't you busy
enough? You can't buy more time at the dollar store. So why not plan how to
use what you have? Lists focus your time and effort on the important tasks.
They keep you organized and free memory space you would have used trying
to remember what's next. Once you've made your list, keep it handy on your
music stand or on the piano.

Alisa says, "Writing my goals helps me focus and clearly envision what I
want. In elementary and middle school, I wrote in journals and diaries. Starting in high school, I wrote my lists on my computer. Now I keep them on my
phone. I always write my daily schedule and a list of what I want to accomplish
each month. It helps me keep track of what I need to do and how I'm doing. I
look at them often and like to cross things off my list."

For a fascinating look at the power of writing and visualizing your goals,
read *Write It Down, Make It Happen,* by Henriette Anne Klauser. You'll learn
how to use visualization and other powerful tools to make your dreams a reality. For now, we'll focus on the nuts and bolts of making a plan.

Step Four: Believe You Will Achieve

To better her odds of winning the youth symphony audition, Alisa needed to
play a challenging piece. She chose the technically difficult *Carmen Fantasie*
by Bizet/Borne, the perfect piece to show off her skills. "*Carmen* was a stretch,
but I loved it," Alisa recalls. She imagined her goal as if she had already accomplished it. "I *knew* if I worked hard enough I could do it. I like to imagine
myself achieving my goal. Sometimes I feel unmotivated. But when I imagine
what could happen if I work hard, it helps me try harder."

Step Five: Break That Challenge into Manageable Chunks

"Success is the sum of small efforts, repeated day in and day out," wrote motivational speaker Robert Collier. Once you've set your long-term goal, your
next step is to break it into small steps. For example, if you want to clean your
room by next weekend, break that big job into chunks you can accomplish in

15 minutes or less. If the piles of clothes on your bed look like the Rocky Mountains, break your cleaning job into more manageable steps like these:

1. Locate my bed

2. Put the clean clothes on the bed in my closet and drawers.

3. Put the dirty clothes into the laundry basket.

4. Make my bed.

5. Find the things under my bed that smell and get rid of them!

TECHNICAL, MUSICAL, AND PERFORMANCE GOALS

Alisa divided her attention into three categories of improvement: technical (playing the instrument); musical (phrase, dynamics, expression); and performance (stage presence, confidence, satisfaction).

1. *Technical Goals*

A technical obstacle Alisa faced was playing what felt like hundreds of notes in one breath. "I struggled when I played long tone breath-building exercises," she remembers. "If I wanted to play long phrases, I had to be able to hold notes a lot longer than 25 seconds." She faithfully practiced her long tones, but progress was slow. Then one day she asked me, "How long can *you* hold a note?" I told her my best was about 45 seconds. Suddenly her eyes lit up. "*I'm* going to beat you!" she said, grinning. Keeping her goal in mind, Alisa began playing hundreds of long tones at home. Every time she came to a lesson, she added one or two more seconds to her record. As she left, she always remarked, "I *am* going to beat you!" In six months she did, indeed, beat my record. (I guess I need to practice more.)

Alisa was equally dedicated to meeting her other technical challenges. She set goals for double tonguing, playing strong low notes and even sixteenths, smoothing big skips, and bringing out the melody between fast notes. "The more I worked on my technique for the piece, the more my overall playing improved," she says, "and the more committed I became to playing a winning audition."

2. *Musical Goals*

We all know music is more than notes and rhythm. Alisa needed to play each page of *Carmen* with beautiful tone and exciting musicality. To prepare for her musicality goal, Alisa first circled the dynamics and marked the breaths. Next she listened to professional recordings of *Carmen* and watched the opera *Carmen*. She rehearsed several times with her piano accompanist, who helped her really understand the music. "I lived and breathed *Carmen*," she says. "And finally I was ready to put my own stamp on the music."

3. *Performance (Audition) Goals*

A sign in my teaching studio reads, "But I could play it at home!" Every musician relates to that message. Alisa wanted to play her best *Carmen* not only at home and in my studio but also at her audition. She needed to know *Carmen* so well that not even stage fright could rob her of her technique, musicality, and confidence. "I wanted to enjoy pleasing the audience," she says. "The final performance goals I wrote in my book were to walk into the audition with confidence and a smile and announce my piece without stumbling. Next I wanted to play my piece as musically and technically correct as I could and then finally to bow and smile, *not faint,* and leave knowing I had a good time."

Alisa is shy by nature, and to play her best, she had to come out of her shell. "I knew playing in front of a group of strangers would be a challenge for me," she says. "I started with a small audience and worked my way up to bigger audiences." Did she ever start out small! Her first audience was the chair in her bedroom, followed by her stuffed animals, her little brother and sister, and then her parents. Next, she branched out to neighbors, friends, and students who had lessons before and after hers. "I played for just about anyone I could drag in off the street," Alisa says, laughing. She gave a final student recital, and by the time of the *real* audition, she was ready.

Step Six: Take a Reality Check

Avoid these goal-setting mistakes:
- *Trying to do too many things.* You can accomplish only so much or make so many changes in a short time. Choose one or two goals and commit to achieving them.
- *Not being specific about what you want.* Saying, "I'm going to try my hardest to play this piece fast" is not as helpful as saying, "I will play this piece 10 metronome notches faster than I am today, with no mistakes."
- *Setting unrealistic standards.* Is your goal set too low? Or is it set so high that you'll probably end up being disappointed? It's not a real goal unless it is demanding yet reachable.
- *Setting negative goals.* Did you write what you want to accomplish in the positive? Remember, the brain doesn't handle the word *not* well. (For example, "Do *not* think of an ice cream sundae." Wow, that ice cream sundae sure looks good!)
- *Following other people's dreams.* Is this what you want, or is this what only your teacher or parents want? If your mom wants you to win a conservatory scholarship and you want to achieve your ambition of being a rock star or professional tennis player, it's time to discuss your long-term dreams with her.

- *Choosing conflicting objectives.* Keep in mind that every time you say yes to one thing, you're probably saying no to something else. You may not be able to win first chair *and* be on the all-star baseball team. It's a trade-off. Don't sabotage one goal for another.

Step Seven: Map out a Schedule

The first step in Alisa's plan was to set a schedule for learning the piece. Playing *Carmen* was a big stretch for her, so she made a promise to practice one to two hours every day. Although the Junior Symphony auditions were in September, she wanted to have her audition piece ready in early August to give herself some breathing room. She needed to play only a few pages for her audition, but her goal was to know the whole piece by that time. Although she began planning in March, to accomplish everything she had to get started immediately.

Step Eight: Set Priorities and Deadlines

> A goal is a dream with a deadline.
> —Napoleon Hill

Alisa's timetable included a schedule for learning the notes, gradually meeting the fast metronome markings, and memorizing sections of the piece. Alisa decided to tackle *Carmen* one page at a time, breaking down the long piece into short sections. Next, she set deadlines for each small goal she had to accomplish.

With her to-do list in writing, Alisa scheduled deadlines for learning parts of her piece:

Week 1: Learn all the notes. Play the runs tongued and leave out the grace notes.

Week 2: Add the right slurs. Play faster without mistakes.

Week 3: Play slowly but with the metronome, and add the ornaments.

Week 4: Memorize the first page

Step Nine: Anticipate Obstacles and Challenges

A sign on the door at a Weight Watchers meeting said, "Don't confuse what you really want with what you really want *now*." That gooey piece of chocolate cake sure looks good now, but it won't help the long-term goal of losing weight. What interferes with your goals? Your friends want you to go hang out, and you want to play electronic games, go to the mall, spend hours texting, or even sleep half the day. But doing those things now can sabotage your long-term plans. Rethink your goals if necessary.

My friend Mary Pat's capable 16-year-old grandson wasn't earning his usual good grades, much to his parents' dismay. He wanted to switch his look, and one day he asked his mom for permission to dye his brown hair. "Hmm," she said, thinking about it. "What color?" He responded, "Jet blue!" Sensing an opportunity, his mom replied with only a number: "3.8." Can you guess what it stood for? His Mom's shorthand meant, "If you want blue hair, you have to earn a 3.8 grade point average. Otherwise, I'll say no to this funky new accessory."

Months later, Mary Pat saw her grandson's new look. His hair was no longer brown, but it wasn't blue, either. "Hey," she said, "what's with the hair?" Greg answered, "3.5." Can you guess? Greg and his mom realized that a 3.8 GPA was too big of a stretch, so they adjusted his goal. They compromised on a realistic 3.5 for his bright blond hair, and both were happy. If your dream to be the next superstar isn't attainable, readjust your goals to something you know you can do. But what if even that smaller goal doesn't work out?

Step 10: Enjoy the Journey

I lost two students who took their goals way too seriously. Emma wanted to compete in the state contest. Once she achieved that goal, she quit taking lessons. Robert was so intent on earning first chair that when he didn't, he wanted to quit playing altogether. Goals are not ends in themselves. There's more to the journey than arriving at your destination. Don't wait until you win the contest to be happy. Appreciate the fun in learning and be happy for your baby steps along the way.

As I write this, it's hard to believe it's been four years since Alisa auditioned for junior symphony. Here's what happened: Alisa achieved every one of her performance goals. She played *Carmen* well and didn't make a single mistake on her sight-reading test. As for her outcome goal? Even though she played well, Alisa did not get into Junior Symphony. Instead, she earned a spot in Classical Youth Symphony. How did Alisa take it? She was disappointed, but then she reminded herself that Seattle Classical and Junior Symphonies are on the same level; they just perform different repertoire. And she was proud of herself for how much she improved.

Alisa's story is the perfect example of why it's a good idea to set both performance and outcome goals. Even though she didn't earn a seat, Alisa played in Classical Symphony for one year, auditioned again, and then played in the Seattle Youth Symphony, the top group, the next year. Though it didn't happen in a straight line, Alisa achieved her goal!

GREAT IDEAS

Energize your playing with specific playing goals.

Read them every day and imagine achieving them.

Address obstacles.

When you've reached your goal, celebrate.

Focus your efforts and reward yourself along the way.

Don't stop there! Energize your playing with new goals . . . and BEYOND!

Sneak Preview

In the next chapter, you'll learn about a key element to your success: making practice a priority.

THIRTEEN

How to Fit Practice into Your Already Busy Life

Thirteen-year-old Matt loved playing sports and music. He played a little trumpet on his own and was excited to start taking private trumpet lessons now that he was in eighth grade. He pictured himself in the top jazz band within a year and playing some really flashy stuff. But he didn't make practice a priority. That fall he played soccer and basketball, and in the spring he played baseball. He often cancelled lessons. When he came home from playing sports, he was just too tired to practice.

Matt's parents never made practice a priority, either. They thought that after his games, swim lessons, youth group meetings, and church, he needed "down time," not practicing on the weekends. Then there were the days when he felt sick or too tired to have a lesson or his parents were out of town or too busy to bring him.

School holidays and vacations also got in his way. On weeks with a school holiday or weeklong break, he rarely practiced and he missed lessons to do things with his friends. That summer Matt put his lessons on hold and took the whole summer off for family trips and to hang out with his friends. Besides, who wants to stay inside to practice? The year of private lessons Matt had counted on to prepare him had shrunk to only four months of lessons spread over a year.

As a result, each of Matt's lessons turned into a refresher course. His teacher spent so much time reviewing old material that he had little time to teach Matt new techniques. Without consistent lessons and practice, he had barely improved his skills and was still light years away from soloing in the jazz band.

Frustrated by his lack of progress and convinced he wasn't musical, Matt gave up playing. He never made his music a priority, so he never made his dream come true.

Taking lessons will help you improve, but only if you go to them! If you cancel lessons for tests, the track meet, a party, or because you didn't practice, your progress will drag to a halt.

Going to lessons regularly is a good start to building your skills, but remember, you make your biggest improvements on the six days *between* lessons when your teacher is nowhere in sight. Until the magical "Music Mastery Pill" is invented (followed quickly, I hope, by the "Wonderful Weight Loss Pill"), the only way to improve is with consistent, effective practice. Just think about this: one month of lessons plus a half hour per day of practice equals the improvement you'll get from one year's worth of band class with no practice. One hour of daily practice will get you two years ahead.

GET A GOOD START RIGHT FROM THE BEGINNING

If you've never taken lessons or had to practice, you may need a few weeks to fit it into your schedule and remember to practice. To make practice part of your life, keep your instrument available in a place where you'll see it while you're at home. Every time you pass your instrument in the living room or kitchen, pick it up and play it for a few minutes. If you practice 10 times a day for a few minutes each time, those few minutes of playing here and there will really add up. After your first good solid week of practice, you'll be surprised at how much you've improved in just one week.

> *Thirteen-year-old James, who plays three instruments, advises beginners: "For the first month or so, try playing a little bit every day, maybe a half hour every day. Then you get more practice in than just one practice a week and you get better faster and you don't get stuck on one part for a long time. To get in the practice habit, always set aside one part of the day for practicing, or ask your mom to tell you when it's time to practice." (Author's note: it's always the mom who has to remind kids to practice!)*

HOW MUCH SHOULD I PRACTICE?

Once you've gotten used to playing, it's time to turn it up a notch. You, your teacher, and your parents can decide when and how often you should practice. I personally don't care how much my students practice as long as their assignments are done well. I rarely ask students to make a practice chart, but beginners in my studio usually average 20 minutes of practicing per day; after six months that time increases to 30 minutes per day. By the first year mark, students ages 12 and older are practicing an hour per day.

A rule of thumb for many teachers is to assign a minute of daily practice for each minute of the lesson. That means students with 45-minute lessons would practice 45 minutes per day. No matter how much practice your teacher assigns you, the more you practice, the faster you'll get better. It's up to you.

Can I ever practice too much?

Most students are never in danger of practicing too much. But practice sessions that are too long can mean diminishing returns. Shorter, more frequent practice sessions help you maintain your focus. Practicing so many hours a day that you don't have time to relax or see your friends makes both you and your music dull! Practicing too much can also hurt your body and can cause severe injuries, such as carpal tunnel syndrome and back problems. Music is a wonderful thing, but it can't be your only thing.

TIME MANAGEMENT

Do it today! Don't put off until tomorrow what you can do today (for tomorrow, you may break your arm).

Everyone can think of excuses to put off doing things that take more effort. Does this sound like you at your lesson? "I had so much homework that I couldn't practice. I would have practiced more, but we had company. I was up until midnight every night doing a big project I was assigned a month ago. I was going to catch up last weekend by practicing three times a day, but then we went away on a trip. I know the competition is next weekend, but I promise I'll have my pieces memorized by then. Really!"

Projects, homework, tests, sports, and practicing always compete for your time. If you consistently arrive unprepared for lessons or cancel them to finish homework or a last-minute paper, test, or project, you need to work on managing your time. But here's the secret: did you know that managing time is really managing you?

"But I'm so busy," you protest. Maybe not, says H. Jackson Brown. "Don't say you don't have enough time. You have exactly the same number of hours per day as Helen Keller, Louis Pasteur, Michelangelo, Mother Teresa, Leonardo da Vinci, Thomas Jefferson, and Albert Einstein."

Have you ever noticed how you actually spend your time? According to Neilson Media Research, in the average home, a television set is turned on for more than 8 hours a day. The average American watches more than 1,600 hours a year. Plus we spend time talking on the phone, surfing the internet, texting, and playing electronic games. How much more could you do in 4 hours a day?

Prioritize your life.

Try this: list your activities and the amount of time spent on them each week. Assign a priority number to each one. Ask yourself, "Am I spending my time on the most important items?" How much time do you spend on "optional" activities like chatting with friends and watching TV? Where can you carve out time for practice? Still don't think you have time to practice? If someone offered to pay you $10 for every minute of practice, do you think you might find an extra hour to collect $600 every day? If you really want to do something, you'll find the time. And no, I'm not suggesting your parents pay you $600 a day!

🔊

Eighteen-year-old Leslie wants to be a professional musician like her dad. "My family life is hectic. I take clarinet, piano, and flute lessons and have tons of homework. When I get discouraged or overwhelmed, I take a deep breath and try to remove myself from the situation. I think about what actions I need to take to get it done. Instead of freaking out over having to prepare seven pieces by next week, I make a list of everything I want to accomplish during my practice sessions. My list might be fixing the intonation on the Mozart concerto or learning the notes in a difficult passage or memorizing the first page. Having a list keeps me organized, and I don't have to decide what to do next. Being organized helps me not become flustered, and instead of thinking of the million things I need to do, I can just focus on what I'm working on at the moment."

TIPS AND TRICKS TO KEEP YOUR PRACTICING ON TRACK

Practice consistently.
- Practice only on days you brush your teeth or on days that end with the letter *Y*.
- Get a day planner and mark out the things you have to do and also when you can have free time.
- Schedule daily practice as you would a dentist appointment. If you skip the appointment, you must make it up on another day.
- Keep your instrument out. The hardest part about practicing is remembering to do it and then getting started.
- Never let more than one day go by without practice, or you'll get out of the habit.
- Play at the same time every day.

Work with your parents and teacher.
- Ask your teacher to show you how to practice. Try a new piece at the lesson, and work on a strategy together.
- Ask your parents to remind you or to help you practice.
- Make a practice agreement with your teacher or parent.
- Give yourself a treat (or persuade your parents to reward you) after a week of good practice.
- Enlist your parents' help to check on your progress during the week and help you stay on target.

Other ideas to help keep on track:
- Play 20 minutes after an hour of study.
- Practice before school.
- Go to the band room during lunch to practice.
- Practice right after school, before you start homework.
- Play two sessions on Saturday to catch up.
- Practice more in the summer when you have more free time.
- Practice a new concept when you come home after your lesson.
- Set daily goals, such as learning just two lines of a song or working on two pieces one day and the other two pieces the next.
- Chart long-term practice goals on a calendar.

- Don't schedule lessons for every other week; you'll end up
  only practicing the few days right before the lesson.
- Create a practice chart to keep on track. The chart need only include the total amount of time spent each day, a tally of minutes
  spent per assignment, or a list of what is to be accomplished.

Fifteen-year-old Kristin has to use good time management to fit everything into her busy life. "Every week I have eight hours of tutoring on math, English, and writing. I take tennis lessons twice a week, play on the tennis team, go to church, and study and practice my instrument every day. Music made me more responsible because I have more things to do than kids who don't play music, and I manage my time better."

What to do if you're bored with practice:
- Ask your teacher to let you help pick out some of your
  pieces so you'll be playing music you like.
- Don't play the same pieces in the same order every day.
- Play at different times of the day.
- Concentrate on only one piece a day so that each
  day's practice will be different.
- Try playing in different rooms in your house.
- Practice with a friend. You can play for each other and give
  suggestions or play your ensemble music together
- Make everything you play sound like beautiful music,
  even it's just scales or a dumb étude.
- If you're stuck on the same piece for a long time, perhaps
  it's too hard and you need to change pieces.
- Make up stories to go along with your piece.
- Pretend you are playing for an audience.
- Take a day off if practicing prevents you from doing some-
  thing you really like, such as going skiing or to a
  party or even if you need a break to rejuvenate.

DEVELOPING NEW HABITS WON'T HAPPEN OVERNIGHT

Right now it may be hard to imagine being able to play the "flashy" pieces when all you can play now are the "stupid" or "easy" pieces. If you keep practicing, in time it *will* happen. Having patience and learning to consistently chip away at a task is one of the best ways to succeed in any task. The first time you played World of Warcraft, you probably weren't very good. But the more you understood the rules and strategies, the more fun it became. The same thing happens in music. Remember, anything worth doing is worth doing well, and that will take time.

Jean's mother ruled her daughter's practice sessions with an iron fist. She cut Jean no slack. Her rule for Jean was an hour of practice, seven days a week. If Jean missed a day, her mother made her practice for two hours the next day. If she missed three days, her mother called me and canceled her lesson. Her mother assumed that with only four hours of practice, Jean's lesson would be a waste of time. Jean resented her strict practice demands and begrudgingly put in her time, but her playing skills remained poor. I finally persuaded her mother to abolish the practice chart. The change in Jean was miraculous. She arrived at her lessons happier and well prepared. Now she focused on what she needed to improve, not on how many minutes had ticked by.

When the only thing that matters is time spent, practice becomes a game of "beat the clock." Have you ever been the kid who practiced piano with one hand and texted friends with the other to get through the jail sentence of practice? Quality of practice is much more important. Hours of practice done incorrectly or without focus on where to improve can be useless. Instead of planning practice according to the clock, make a daily practice plan that lists the time of day you'll practice and what you want to accomplish. Throw the clock out the window and focus on improvement instead of time.

SET GOALS FOR MORE TARGETED PRACTICE SESSIONS

You learned how to set goals in our last chapter. Now let's talk about setting specific practice goals like beating your last long tone.

Practice goals help you:
- Organize your practice sessions.
- Focus on fixing the hard parts instead of giving everything equal time.
- Practice with a plan and feel good when you've accomplished it.
- Achieve more in less time.
- Leave the practice room earlier because when you meet your goal, you stop!

Set specific practice time and improvement goals.
List daily practice goals with your teacher or parent and make a pact that your practice is over when you've met your goals. My sons like this kind of practice because it buys them free time. Using this system, my boys tell me at the beginning of their practice what they want to accomplish and then call me in to "test" them when they think they're ready. Many times their "early release" program is wishful thinking on their part, but they learn that a standard must be met to achieve the goal. This way they battle against their own mistakes, not the clock or me.

If you're a more advanced student, you should make your own daily goals, be responsible for attaining them, and be honest in your assessment. It doesn't matter how much time you spent to get the piece good, only that it *is* good.

If your parents say you're not practicing enough, suggest they ask your teacher how your lessons are going. If your teacher is happy with your results, you're doing great!

Practice Session Goals

Each week, talk with your teacher about what you should focus on during practice sessions the next week.

Sample goals:
- Play from an assigned list of music and cross
  off the pieces you've finished.
- Mark wrong notes and dynamics.
- Mark breaths and only breathe where you've marked them.
- Mark phrases and make a musical arc with each.
- Mark all fingerings or bowings and stick to them.
- Circle key signatures and accidentals.
- Play the first two lines of the étude with no mistakes.
- Play all the notes correctly in several runs
  using smooth, easy connections.
- Increase the tempo to a determined mark.
- Play a section with a tuner until the intonation is correct.
- Play a difficult measure five times right for every time wrong.
- Improve the tone on the double tonguing or double stop section.

LISTEN TO YOURSELF

How many times have you listened to a lecture from your parents and not heard a word? How many times have you practiced and not really listened but just gone through the motions? Wake up! When I hear students play without opening up their ears, I threaten to come home with them so that I can help them monitor their practice. I also threaten to send them home with a life-size cardboard cutout of me pointing my finger and mouthing the word *Listen*. Except in the highly unlikely case that you want your teacher with you during every practice session, it's up to you to analyze every note and fix the problems on your own. If you hit a really tough spot and your best practice techniques haven't worked, take a break and try another day.

GREAT IDEAS

Everyone has to practice. There's no getting around it.
The sooner you get into a routine and approach it with a good attitude,
the sooner you'll be reaping the rewards of playing your instrument.

Use daily practice goals and not the clock.

Make a habit of practicing almost every day.

You can find the time if you really want to.

Sneak Preview

Okay, you promise to practice, but where do you start? Is it good enough to just play each piece straight through over and over? In our next chapter you'll learn how to plan your practice sessions and target your trouble spots so you can get out of the practice room sooner.

How to Fit Practice into Your Already Busy Life

FOURTEEN

Quit Wasting Your Practice Time

Thursday's lesson wasn't that great, and Jim's teacher reminded him that he needed to practice on a daily basis. Jim vowed to *really* practice more for the next lesson. But on Friday the next lesson seemed so far away and, hey, he needed a break. The weekend was crammed full of sports activities. He had to work on the science project, his parents wanted him to help clean the house, and he wanted to catch up on those computer games he had missed during the week.

Practice? He thought about it once, but couldn't find his manuscript book, and then it slipped his mind. Monday afternoon rolled around. "I've got to do homework and, oh yeah, I've got to practice!" But first Jim had a snack and a little TV after school. Then soccer practice. Then dinner. Then homework. Then a friend called. *Then* practice. "I'm so tired, I think I'll just play the parts of the song we worked on last week and leave learning the new section until tomorrow. Yeah. This part sounds really cool when I play it fast. There were some weird notes somewhere on measures 20 to 26. I'll circle those measures . . . when I can find a pencil. I'll play the whole thing now again, but faster this time so I can get done sooner. I guess I better try that stupid étude. How does this thing go anyway? I don't get measure five; I'll just wait to ask my teacher at my lesson."

Tuesday is no better. "Where's my manuscript book? I guess I better learn those scales she told me to practice. Ugh. I'll play through the first three scales two times each and just tell her I didn't have time for the rest. How does she expect me to remember all those key signatures anyway? I'll try the étude again but skip those hard measures. Hmm . . . I wonder what's for dinner. I've got to ask Mom if Tom can come over on Friday. I wonder why the sky is blue. Where was I?"

Wednesday. "Oh, my gosh. My lesson is tomorrow. I can do the theory homework in the car on the way to the lesson. I'll practice for a whole hour today and play through everything. If I have another bad lesson, she's going to kill me."

Jim was doing everything right—if his goal was never to improve. Even though he was busy, he needed a plan.

You can get more done in less time if you practice right. Try these hints to make practice more efficient and effective, then watch yourself zoom ahead.

PRACTICE RIGHT

Practice Hint 1: Develop a Practice Routine

"Where do I start?"
Having a routine makes it easier to get started and to cover everything in a practice session. A good routine might include a stretching exercise for your body and a warm-up exercise on the instrument to help your muscles and your mind get ready to play. Next are scales to concentrate on all aspects of playing such as tone, vibrato, bowing, breathing, and position. Next comes the assignment: études, work on pieces already in progress, learn a new piece or a new section, and finally, playing something for review or just for fun.

Practice Hint 2: Make a Timetable

"So much to do, so little time. How can I get it all done by the deadline?"
Do you feel overwhelmed? Do you not know where to start? Are you allergic to scales and études, but love duets and solos? Does it seem as if the week has only three days? As we mentioned in the last chapter, if you have a problem using your practice time wisely or are running out of time, ask your teacher to assign a daily practice chart with definable goals. You'll get much more done if you know what you are trying to accomplish.

A daily practice chart might look like this:

Monday: Mark the beats in the tricky measures of the sonata, practice each measure five times on the first half of page 11 in "The Big Fat Étude Book," and practice the D and G major scales.

Tuesday: Practice the E♭ and B♭ scales, gradually bump up the metronome marking on the first half of page 11, and play the tricky measures in the sonata with the metronome.

Wednesday: Review the D, E♭, G, and B♭ scales and add the arpeggios, complete the theory homework, start on the second half of page 11, start on the last page of the sonata and work backwards one measure at a time, and circle every mistake.

A daily practice chart takes the guesswork out of what to practice and where to start. It helps you see one step at a time, keep track of your assignments, and prepare for the entire lesson seven days later. At first you should ask your teacher to write out daily assignments, but soon you'll be able to plan it yourself. You can write in the time spent on each assignment or just check it off.

PLAN CONSISTENT PRACTICE

"My lesson isn't for six more days; I'll practice later."
Cramming doesn't work. Your brain needs time to digest what you've put into it, and your fingers need time to develop muscle memory. Try to pick up the instrument every day, even if you plan only five minutes of practice (which will probably end up as much more once you get going). Practicing every day gets you into the habit, and you'll practice more hours during the week than if it's done all in a couple days. Daily practice strengthens your body and reduces tension. If you skip days and cram right before your lesson, you're going to hate practicing, and you'll dread your lesson.

KEEP TRACK OF LONG-TERM PROJECTS

"The contest is in three weeks? Help!"
Create a plan to be prepared by a deadline, and get started now! Like building contractors who use flow charts, use a calendar for a countdown of days left before the performance. A good trick is to make an artificial deadline; if the concert is in five weeks, pretend it's in three. Make weekly practice goals to mete out equally what needs to be accomplished so you don't have to stress at the end.

Practice Hint 3: Check Out a New Piece First before You Start to Learn It

"Can't I just play it through a couple of times first and worry about all that stuff later?"
If you stand at the top of the cliff and take the long dive into the river below without looking first, you could break your neck! Learning a new piece of music may not be quite so dangerous, but diving headlong into a new piece without looking first can be just as foolhardy. Discover as much about the piece as you can before you start so you don't waste your time on meaningless repetitions and learning mistakes. Amy Porter, flute professor from the University of Michigan, advises, "Take your music to bed with you and read it like a book. Pay attention to *everything* that's written."

As with sight-reading, analyze the form, key, meter, motives, and notes. Check out the rhythm, tempo, meter, and pulse and clap the interesting measures. Work out the difficult passages by naming the notes in tempo and rhythm out loud (say the sharps and flats). Pay attention to the key, accidentals, the form, patterns, and written instructions.

Practice without the instrument before actually playing the piece. You'll be surprised at how much more closely you watch the score and how quickly you can learn something when you don't have to unlearn all the mistakes.

"What do you mean, I have to 'feel the music'? This is just practice!"
Music isn't math or typing. Anyone can play the notes and rhythm, but there's so much more. Don't get so hung up on playing every measure technically right that you forget about the beauty and emotion of the piece as a whole.

Practice Hint 5: Try to Enjoy Practicing

"This is supposed to be fun?"
Practicing your instrument shouldn't feel like completing a jail sentence in solitary confinement. Think of it as *playing* your instrument instead of *practicing*. In addition to learning the music and becoming a better musician, think of the other benefits of practicing. Learning a new piece can be as stimulating as doing a crossword puzzle. It can be a break from homework and a chance to do something personally satisfying that's also good for you. It can make both you *and* your parents happy. Practicing may not feel like going to a party or riding a roller coaster, but it can be exciting and rewarding to learn new music. Remember that music is fun!

Practice Hint 6: Appreciate Your Progress

"Will I ever get good? Why is this taking so darn long?"
Learn to be patient with yourself. Rome wasn't built in a day, and neither is the technique of a good musician (except in the case of Mozart). We've all felt like throwing our instruments out the window now and again, but when we're impatient with ourselves, all of our energy goes into *frustration* instead of *learning*. Don't waste time beating yourself up or banging your head on the piano; just concentrate on the job at hand.

Realize that everything is a process. Sometimes learning a new way to do something, like double tonguing or a new bowing, initially seems harder than the old way, but trust the teacher's path and goals. When I was young, I decided that I could count on my fingers instead of learning the addition and subtraction tables because it was easier. Well, that only works up to the number 20 if you use your toes! I guess my first-grade teacher really did have a better way. Learning an instrument *is* a lot like learning math: every grade has different material to learn and builds upon itself. You expect that it will take 12 years to learn math, and you should expect that same step-by-step progress in learning music. There will always be the next level to attain, no matter how good you are. That's what music and learning are all about.

"But it's such a waste of time to play the same piece over and over."
Practicing one piece makes all your technique better, so the work you do on learning a beginning piece today will pay off by giving you the technique to play a harder piece next month. Short-term successes have a long-term effect.

"Why keep playing it when I already know it?"
Your brain and your hands need repetition. You need to practice enough to make improvement but also to make a lasting memory in your brain. Just because you can play it or understand it does not mean you will remember it. Practicing the same way (with the same fingering and hand position) over and over will produce kinesthetic memory and allow your body to automatically play.

"But it's such a lot of work now."
To keep motivated during the "long haul," set small attainable goals and give yourself a reward: "When I get these eight measures right, I'll take a break; when I finish my étude, I get to play the duet; when I can get the tempo up to 120, I will go to another section; when I can make every breath on this page, I'll eat a cookie." Congratulate yourself for larger projects like finishing the étude book, playing in the recital, or just making it through another year of lessons. Like losing weight, think about the next five pounds, not the next fifty, and give yourself success along the way.

"But I practice, and Nathan's still better than I am."
Just as in any endeavor, science or soccer, people progress at different rates. You aren't going to quit the soccer team if you aren't the best player, nor will you drop out of the science class if the student across the aisle scores better on the first test. Try to accept your skill level. I've had students who started out great the first six months and then stagnated in their development, and I've had others who seemed "hopeless" but turned out to be superstars.

Practice Hint 7: Practice with Focus and Concentration

"What was I supposed to be thinking about in this piece?"
"I can't remember because I have so many ideas in my mind at once. What are the sharps in B major? How do bees fly? How many beats in a dotted quarter-note? How many quarters will it take to buy that baseball mitt? How many counts does this rest have? I deserve a rest from all this thinking."

🔊 *Ten-year-old Luke is working on staying focused. "It's hard to concentrate while I practice. If I see a bug on the floor, all I can think about is the bug. I'll play and hear something funny but barely notice. I think, 'Hmmm, that sounded interesting. I better go on.' The only time I really concentrate is when I'm trying to prove to my mom that I don't have to practice slowly. I really narrow my focus so I can show her I can play fast and still get it right. (Note from Luke's mom: that never works.)*

"When I have a problem in the music and my mom's not in the room, I skip it. If she's in the room, I do what she says. If she's not in the room but promises me a treat after the practice—and if I'm in a good mood—I'll practice it three times. But a lot of the times if she promises a reward, all I can think about is the ice cream cone or going somewhere for the reward. If I could change my ways, I would pay more attention and go back and mark and fix my mistakes, play it with different rhythms, play out the sixteenth-notes, and play it slower." Luke is really trying and may be able to stay more on track when he's a teenager.

SAVE TIME BY PAYING ATTENTION

There is no substitute for time and repetition, but you can cut down on both with concentration. (No, practicing in front of the TV during commercials won't cut it.) We've all read a page in a textbook five times and not remembered a thing because we were dreaming about something else. Keep your mind on the task at hand and make every minute count. I call this type of practice "microwave practice" because it's concentrated and goes three times as fast. If you concentrate hard, you'll get more done and get done quicker! And isn't that what we all want?

Sayoko, who first started playing flute as an adult, observes, "Learning to play an instrument is like learning to drive a car. There are so many things to think about at the same time. How am I going to shift gears? How can I look in the front mirror and the side mirror? Which lever is the turn signal, and which one is for the windshield wipers? How am I supposed to think about the notes, rhythm, dynamics, pitch, and vibrato all at the same time? I have to keep my mind focused so that I don't drive off a cliff."

My son Kyle would always amaze his family and teachers at contests and recitals. When the stakes were high, he would really concentrate and play so much better than at any lessons or practice. One year I "bribed" him. "If you get into Junior Symphony, I'll buy you a video game." That's all it took. Everything his teacher had been coaching him on miraculously came together. All it took was extreme concentration.

You should work on your concentration by practicing in a room with few distractions and then practicing where there are many distractions so that you can learn to ignore them. If you can practice while your brother is playing video games, your sister is talking on the phone, and your parents are making dinner, playing a concert will be easy.

TIMING IS EVERYTHING

"I can't concentrate that long."

Practice at the right time. Focus on your practice or wait until you're ready to concentrate. Don't practice if you're upset or worried, overly tired, or hungry. (You're not *always* worried, tired, or hungry!) Break up your practice sessions. Even a short break can help clear out the cobwebs. Walk around the house, step outside, pet the dog, feed the cat, get a drink, do some stretches, or play another song for a few minutes before returning to the task at hand.

DON'T MAKE THE MISTAKE THE FIRST TIME

"I keep making different mistakes!"

A mistake isn't just an accident. It's a possibility you have given your brain. If you're learning the driving route to a new place and go a different way every time, your brain will understand each way as being a correct choice and will be paralyzed with indecision under pressure. "Do I turn left or right at the light? Do I go past the school or turn before I come to it?" Making mistakes in music leaves your brain similarly befuddled. "Which fingering should I use? Do I shift into fifth position here or stay in third? Where should I pedal? Where should I breathe? Should I be playing at the bow tip or the frog? Was that an F♯ or F♮?" It's very hard to unlearn mistakes and bad habits, so try not to make them the first time.

Let the metronome and the tuner be your at-home teachers. Always keep them by your stand and rely on them for accuracy.

Practice Hint 8: Specifically Mark All Mistakes

"How can I remember not to play that wrong note again?"

Do everything possible so that mistakes are not repeated. Remember, practice doesn't *make perfect,* practice *makes permanent.* When you make a mistake, mark it! Never practice without a pencil. (Marking with a pen shows over-inflated self-confidence!) So many students say, "I always make that mistake!" Well, if it was marked, I bet you wouldn't! However, marking mistakes is not license to write in every accidental, key signature, enharmonic or high note name.

To mark mistakes:
- Don't just circle the mistake, but specifically mark what you did wrong. Write in the number of beats, add a sharp or flat before the note, circle the connection, put an arrow up or down for pitch, etc.
- The first time a mistake is made, circle it. The second time, circle it in red, the third time draw a pair of glasses before the mistake, the fourth time draw a skull and crossbones, the fifth time go to jail!

- Try using different colors for each dynamic (yellow is *piano,* blue is *mezzo forte,* and red is *double forte*) or different colors or shapes for changing tempi like *rallentando, stringendo,* and *allargando.* Anything to easily draw attention to the markings.
- Don't circle everything. If you mark every D♯ in E major, you'll never learn the key signature. Use your brain!
- At the next practice session, first review the marked measures. Practice them before putting them into context.
- If you don't want to mark up the music, use sticky notes for trouble spots. When the spot is conquered, the sticky note can be ceremoniously crumpled.
- When it is close to performance time, make several copies of the music. Have your teacher mark in only that week's mistakes.

Speaking of marking mistakes: A friend of mine played violin in a community orchestra and shared a stand with a 14-year-old boy. The music had been used before and contained several markings from the previous performer. Eyeglasses were marked everywhere denoting places to really watch out for. The boy turned to my friend and innocently asked, "What are all those bras in the music for?"

Practice Hint 9: Practice the Notes *before* the Mistake

"I stopped and fixed the wrong note. Why do I still miss it when I start from the beginning?"
You played the E♮ in the long run wrong. You noticed it, circled it, and then played the E♮. You fixed the problem. Wrong. The problem is not the E♮ but the notes leading up to it. Even if you mentally remember that the note is E♮, your fingers won't remember. You must practice all the notes in the run before the missed notes to cement the run in your mind and in your fingers. Play the few notes before the E. Now go back farther and practice the two lines before the run and the two lines after. By George, you've got it!

Practice Hint 10: Don't Practice Everything Every Day

"How am I ever going to get through all these pieces in one practice session?"
Warm-ups, scales, and exercises for basic technique like bowing, shifting positions, tone, and breathing should be practiced daily, but you can be "spread too thin" by trying to work through every piece every day in a limited amount of time. Choose three pieces out of five, or two sections from each piece on which to concentrate. Rotate pieces and start at different sections.

What do you do when company's coming for dinner and there's no time to clean the whole house? Just clean the living room, kitchen, and bathroom and don't allow the company into the rest of the house. Similar choices must be made when practice time is short. Come to the lesson with only two out of five assignments prepared well rather than having played through everything with little accomplished.

Practice Hint 11: Don't Skip the Hard Parts

"Why can't I just practice the parts I know and wait for my teacher to help me on the hard parts?"
Stopping at every roadblock is easy and makes you feel good because everything sounds good and practice is no trouble at all. But nothing new gets learned. *Don't wait for your teacher; be your own teacher.*

Practice Hint 12: Don't Always Play Straight through the Piece

"What do you mean I didn't practice? I played it three times from the beginning to the end without stopping!"
There's a big difference between playing and practicing. Playing without stopping is play; practicing is problem solving. It's fun to hear the whole song, but this is practice, not a performance.

Practice the same way you would memorize a poem, stanza by stanza. Pick a section to work on, and be sure it's better before you leave it. When you make a mistake, don't start back at the beginning of the piece or even at the beginning of the section. Correct the measure of the mistake and only then go back

For long-term projects, start with the hard section first; it will take the most time to conquer. Don't always start at the beginning of the piece at each practice session. Play only a few sections, work backwards from the end, or play the hard parts first. Allow yourself a run-through as a reward.

Practice Hint 13: Take Small Bites

"How am I ever supposed to learn the really hard parts?"
Divide the hard sections into tiny parts and take small bites. (We all need to learn this lesson with *food,* too!) Work to focus your eyes on signposts of only one note, measure, or beat at a time. Looking at the whole run makes us feel like we are taking off on a roller coaster. Play a difficult run or measure one beat at a time with a break afterward. Play first with each note articulated, then faster, then with the correct articulation, then as fast as possible. Now go on to the next beat or measure. This is a practice trick called chunking. It allows the brain to concentrate on only one small piece of information first. When practicing in small chunks, be sure to put them all together afterward to get the transitions from section to section, and to understand the structure and emotions of the piece.

Chunking is a good technique for mastering long runs with many notes as well. Subdivide into groups of no more than five notes at a time, and then chunk them. Subdivide a seven-note run into 3+4 or 4+3. A nine-note run becomes 3+3+3. Thirteen notes might be 3+3+4. (Another little trick: for five-note runs, think Hip-po-pot-a-mus or, for the high-browed, I-gor-Stra-vin-sky.) Even when the piece is learned, continue to subdivide in your head for a clean performance.

> *Fifteen-year-old Zoë learned the value of chunking. "There is one passage in the piece Poem, by Charles Griffes, that I absolutely could not play. It was a really hard run, and I was so frustrated that I couldn't get it that I broke into tears at one of my lessons. My teacher told me to keep on practicing it in different articulations and rhythms, chunking it and playing very slowly. By the end of that year at the Horsfall Flute Competition, I stood up and played that run with ease and confidence. I finally had it, and I was one of the winners."*

Practice Hint 14: Chew Slowly

"Why do I have to practice slowly? This is a presto!"
Don't race through practice; it's not a contest. Practice slow, slower, then slower yet. Some younger students, especially boys, have a really hard time with this. They like to prove that they don't need to work slowly, and they can get good fast, without gradually working up the tempo. (They don't like to ask for directions, either.) Success comes much faster when we play slowly 10 times correctly rather than 50 times fast. Trust me! (And please convince my sons, who want to turn everything into the *Minute Waltz*.)

If you play too fast, either you can't hear your mistakes or you are so focused on the speed that you want nothing to interrupt it and you ignore the mistakes. You can fool all the people some of the time, and some of the people all the time, but you cannot fool all the people all the time!

Practice Hint 15: Gradually Build up Speed

"It says presto. How can I ever get it that fast?"
It's a long way from *andante* to *presto,* but these pointers can speed the way. First, make sure the piece is airtight at a slow tempo before edging it faster.

Analyze technical problems that may be holding back the speed and devise ways to conquer them. If big octave leaps, flying fingers, major shifts, double tonguing, or crossing over hands on the piano is the problem, take a time out. Use other études and exercises to fix your technique, then revisit the piece.

After inching up the metronome, give the piece an overnight rest to sink in, and return to a lower metronome marking.

Sometimes try the tempo at a breakneck speed, just to see if it's possible, but concentrate on relaxed hand and fingers (and neck, back, and shoulders). Tension slows down movement, so practice playing only as fast as you can without a clenched fist and a furrowed brow. Playing too fast is a good diagnostic tool, as unreliable parts will fall out under pressure. Take the piece down a few notches from its all-time high for the actual performance, and the original tempo marking will be easy.

Practice Hint 16: Practice Enough Perfect Repetitions to Ensure Success

"I played it right two times. Isn't that enough?"
I remember playing a piece "perfectly" at home and then falling apart at my lesson. How could this happen? After 20 tries, I had finally gotten the hard parts right and considered them fixed. But the little bit of nervousness I had at the lesson made the mistakes come back.

Repetition is insurance, but playing something wrong 10 times and right once is not good odds. Don't count the phrase as learned until it can be played 10 times right and not once wrong. Practicing is only really over when there is no chance of a mistake.

Practice Hint 17: Try Different Practice Methods

"I played that same measure over and over, and it's still wrong.
What else can I do?"
When concentrating on a problem spot, try to approach it from different angles. Attacking the problem often helps to solve it, and this keeps you engaged and willing to practice longer. Try variations, such as playing single notes on stringed instruments as chords to check intonation, playing chords on the piano as single notes, playing without any ornamentation, playing solo instrument notes on the piano (this especially helps when learning scales), or writing out hard rhythms in half-time (sixteenths become eighths) to count them more easily. You'll find lots of ways to conquer those tricky parts in our next chapter.

Practice Hint 18: Listen to Yourself and to Others

"Are you sure it was out of tune? It sounded good to me."
It's easier to hear when someone else is out of tune or has a scratchy sound than to hear it in yourself. The answer? Record yourself. Review the recording with a teacher or parent, while watching the music and marking mistakes and places for improvement. Always include in the review the wonderful things about the performance, too.

"How am I ever going to sound as good as the CD?"
When you learn a language, you learn by mimicking. Learning music is the same. Ask the teacher to demonstrate. Go to concerts. Listen to CDs, play along with them, or buy Music Minus One play-along CDs. Listening to professionals gives you valuable insight. You will understand how to play better by surrounding yourself with good playing.

PRACTICE METHODS
FOR DIFFICULT PASSAGES

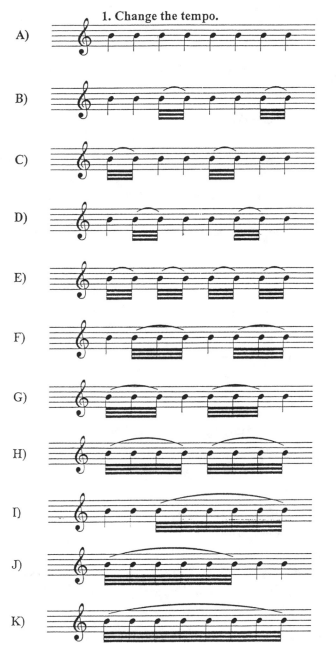

FOR EACH:

1. Change the tempo.
Alternate playing notes fast and slow. Quarter notes can be played out of tempo, but slurred notes should be played as fast as possible.

2. Use dotted rhythms.

3. Build the passage from both ends. Play the first two notes as fast as possible, then the first three notes as fast as possible, then the first four notes as fast as possible, etc. Then play the last two notes as fast as possible, then the last three, etc.

4. Play one time very very slowly with perfect connections, tone, and pitch. Then play three times very slowly, once more a little faster, once again too fast, then

LEAVE IT!

Quit Wasting Your Practice Time

Practice Hint 19: Never Put Mistakes to Bed

Short-term memory lasts about an hour, but long-term memory kicks in at about 24 hours and becomes permanent. Always leave the piece with all the right notes. Make sure the last run-through is good so that your brain will store the right information and not the mistakes.

Practice Hint 20: Just Do It!

Now that you have learned the 20 basic practice hints, try these ideas for even more successful practice.

If something is hard, make it harder in practice.
- To master a difficult high note in a phrase, replace it with a harder note and then come back to play the original more easily. For example, if the last note is a high E, play a high B instead. Now come back to the original. Instead of reaching up and straining to get the high E, it will seem easy compared with the harder B.
- If it is hard to *diminuendo* to a *mezzo forte,* practice the *diminuendo* to *pianissimo.*
- Play the piece faster than necessary and then relax at the required tempo.
- If it is hard to play many notes in a bow or a breath, add to that number.

Work from a point of strength.
- When learning new notes or working on tone, play a note that is easy and gradually stretch outwards.
- Practice first without ornaments to get the rhythm stable, then put them in.
- Of course, play slowly and then build up.

Change the articulation.
- Trade slurs for separate notes.
- Slur in twos, threes, and fours.
- Play everything tongued or on separate bows, then play with everything slurred. (This will really help get the rhythm steady and the notes even.)
- If the pattern is four notes slurred, play the first note separate and slur the next four notes. (This helps with a feeling of forward motion.)

Change the rhythm.
- Play sixteenth-notes in dotted eighths and sixteenths, sixteenths and dotted eighths, triplets, and whatever else you can think of. (This method of practicing puts the focus on different notes and different connections.)

- Put fermatas over difficult notes or notes that are missed in a run.
- Practice by putting one big pulse on every note of a run. Do it slowly, then speed up. Gradually transition to accents on every beat, then on beats one and three, then just on one beat in each measure.

More Practice Tricks

- Practice from the score. Learn entrances, harmonic structure, and when there is freedom to, use rubato.
- Practice with just fingers, not blowing or bowing.
- For a *gruppetto* (three repeating notes slurred, followed by a staccato note), circle the melody note to let your eyes focus on it and to set it apart musically from the repeating pattern.
- Just because you fingered the note doesn't mean it sounded. Count on your ears and not just your fingers for accuracy control.

GREAT IDEAS

Practicing smarter means getting better faster. These hints will save you loads of time and tons of frustration. So promise me you won't just keep playing through the piece from beginning to end as fast as possible and piling up the mistakes. Transform your practice and your playing with deliberate practice.

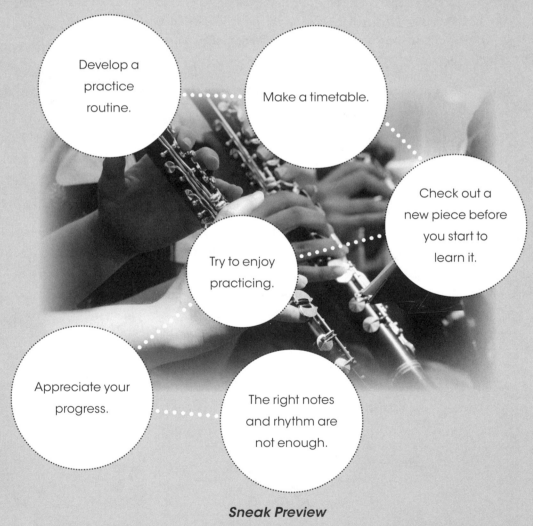

Develop a practice routine.

Make a timetable.

Check out a new piece before you start to learn it.

Try to enjoy practicing.

Appreciate your progress.

The right notes and rhythm are not enough.

Sneak Preview

Now that you've learned the ways to structure your practice, turn the page for ways to attack the problems from different angles and to prevent boredom in your daily routine. You'll never say, "I don't know how to practice this spot" again.

Practice with focus and concentration.

Specifically mark all mistakes.

Practice the notes *before* the mistake.

Don't practice everything every day.

Don't skip the hard parts.

Don't always play straight through the piece.

Take small bites.

Chew slowly.

Gradually build up speed.

Try different practice methods.

Listen to yourself and to others.

Never put mistakes to bed.

Practice enough perfect repetitions to ensure success.

Just do it!

FIFTEEN

Shake Up Your Practice Routine

Practice! Practice! That's all you hear from your teacher and your parents. It can become very tiring and boring to practice the same way day in and day out, year in and year out. *Yawn.*

I've come up with a huge list of ways to practice that can help you attack the problem from different angles and keep you from going out of your mind. Different technical problems need different solutions. These ways to tackle the problem will get it fixed faster than just playing through the piece again and again. Having different ways to practice will also keep you interested longer and willing to put in more time at your instrument. Keep this list propped up beside your music. Try keeping a practice diary to see if you can use them all.

If you're an experienced player, you can skip ahead to our list of 75 practice strategies. But if you're a beginner, this next section is for you.

TO THE BEGINNER

As a beginner, it's hard to know how to practice. Here's a tried and true way to learn your pieces right from the start. This method gives you one thing to worry about at a time, then builds up your skill. Don't go on to the next step until the one you are on is perfect. Absolutely perfect. "But this is boring and doesn't sound like music," you think. "I want to just play through the piece fast; it's more fun." Let me assure you, practicing deliberately may be boring at first, but if you take each piece through these stages, you will learn them right the first time and get better faster! And that's when the fun starts.

Beginners' Steps to Perfection

1. Say the note names out loud (G, G, G, D).
2. Say the rhythm. For quarter-notes say *ta;* for two eighth-notes say *tee-tee.* Or say words like *pie* for a quarter-note, *apple* for two eighth-notes, and *huckleberry* for four sixteenth-notes, or just *la la la.* Be sure to say *shh* every time there is a rest. (For more rhythm words to help you count, check out *String Rhythms* by Sally O'Reilly, Kjos Music.)

3. Say the note names in rhythm (G, G, GG, D).
4. Finger the notes on your instrument and
    say the note names in rhythm.
5. Pianists play one hand at a time.
6. Play without mistakes very, very, very, very slowly.
7. Add articulation (tonguing and slurring and phrasing or pedal).
8. Play with the metronome very slowly.
9. Gradually work up to tempo.
10. Impress your teacher.

75 WAYS TO PRACTICE DIFFERENTLY EVERY DAY

Play Slowly

If you think playing slowly is boring, just think how boring it is to play badly!
1. Play very, very slowly. (My husband paints very slowly, whereas I
    paint very fast. Guess who takes twice as long to clean up mistakes.)
2. Even slower. (Trust me! I know it's not fun, but I *promise*
    that slow practice adds up to fast learning. No, really.
    Stop fighting with your parents and play slowly.)
3. One measure at a time. Play the first measure, then the second mea-
    sure, and then play the first two measures. Continue on with the
    third measure and fourth measure, then the first four measures.
4. One phrase at a time. Concentrate on the phras-
    ing, not just the notes now.

Study

Your parents might not believe you're practicing if they don't hear music, but
using your head first can save lots of mistakes later.
5. Silent practice. Read chapter 28 for tips on how to sight-read.
6. Listen to a recording of your piece while looking at the score.
7. Write out measure-by-measure instructions as if you were writing
    a friend a letter about your piece. (Start *forte* on m.1, accent
    the G, watch pitch on the E, smooth connection to the B.)
8. Read the music like a book. Notice everything for your next
    practice. Make sure you know all the terms and tempo mark-
    ings. This is also the time to learn about the composer.
9. If you play a solo instrument, now study the piano
    part, too, and see how the two parts fit together.

Focus

You can play for 10 hours in a row, but if your mind is outside playing baseball, nothing will be accomplished. Concentrate on one thing at a time.

10. Pitch
11. Dynamics.
12. Tone.
13. Rhythm.
14. Articulation (tonguing and slurring, bowing, and the attack and length of the notes).
15. Speed. Use the metronome to slowly build up speed and to keep a steady tempo.
16. Breathing. Are your breaths in the right places? Can you play every phrase without running out of breath? Are they noisy? Are you breathing correctly?
17. Bowing and attack. Is it a down bow or an up bow? Are you using the right kind of attack? Is it *spiccato*? Are you using the right part of the bow? Is your bow straight? Even if you are not a string player, are you using the right attack (amount of pressure) and playing the note the correct length?
18. Pedaling (for pianists). Is your technique good? Are you following the pedal markings?
19. Fingering. Are you using the correct fingering? String players: are you on the right string in the correct position?
20. Vibrato. Is the vibrato produced correctly? Do you sound like a nanny goat or a dead battery? Does it vary with the emotions of the piece?
21. Posture and position. Are your hands and your entire body in maximum performance position?
22. Intonation. Have you tuned correctly? Are you flat or sharp on particular notes or with particular dynamics?
23. Phrasing. This is music, remember. The notes are not enough. Does your music have forward motion? Tension and release? Emotion?

Write

Why make the same mistake again? Mark your music at home.

24. Mark the beats.
25. Mark the breaths.
26. Mark the fingerings.
27. Always mark your mistakes. If your music is clean after a week of practice, that means you either made no mistakes or you didn't care.
28. Color code the dynamics to make them stand out. How about purple for loud, pink for soft, and turquoise for a crescendo?

29. Write the hard part out in a manuscript book.
30. Write out the part you are trying to memorize.
31. Write a story for your piece.

Do Something Different

Think of ways to make the music easier and to keep your interest.

32. Put more beats in the measure to make it easier to count.
    If the piece is in 4/4 (four beats per measure and the
    quarter-note gets the beat), play it in 8/8 (eight beats
    per measure and the eighth-note gets the beat).
33. Work from the end. Play the last bar, last two bars,
    last three, or start with the last section or last page.
    This way the end won't always get cheated.
34. Practice in different rooms in the house. Get used to the dis-
    tractions and different acoustics. Can you sound as good
    in the living room as you did in the bathroom?
35. Concentrate on time and phrasing by playing tongued or sepa-
    rated bowed notes slurred. Play slurred notes tongued or bowed
    to focus on playing each note correctly and in strict rhythm.
    Slurring helps you concentrate on tone and phrasing, while bow-
    ing helps you concentrate on note and rhythm accuracy.

Play Musically

Remember, this is music, not math. Playing the right notes at the right time is
just the beginning.

36. Listen to recordings and take notes. Don't be a parrot or just a
    trained seal; be open to ideas from professional recordings.
37. Concentrate on the flow of the music. Does the first phrase connect
    with the second? Does the fourth phrase complete a section?
38. Practice the performance, not just the piece. Pretend you're
    onstage. You can even wear the outfit you will wear for
    the performance and practice announcing yourself.

Be Wild

Our job as musicians is to communicate. That may mean going over the top so
the audience gets it.

39. Use extreme dynamics. This is like extreme sports only
    with volume. Only *ppp* or *fff*. No *mezzo* allowed.
40. Be dramatic. Sometimes forget about playing every note right
    and concentrate on making every note dramatic. Pretend you're
    playing music for a movie. Be wild. Be crazy. Come on!

41. Try different moods for sections or for the entire piece. Use your imagination. The same notes can have different meaning played different ways. Don't always look for the "right" way; look for "your way."

Repeat

42. Chunk notes. Play two notes at a time very fast, then pause. Play three notes very quickly. It's fun to play straight through, but that is called playing, not practicing. You can play a piece over and over with the same mistakes. Practicing is concentrating. Now, chunk measures.

43. Practice scales with a clock and see if you can shave time off each perfect repetition.

44. Repeat a set number of times for a phrase, hard section, or piece. (Like a jail sentence—30 years, then you're out!)

45. Repeat a set number of times with no mistakes. Make a mistake, and you start counting over. This does wonders for your concentration.

46. Even harder, play a set number of times with no mistakes *in a row*.

47. Practice five minutes on each tricky section. (Come on, you can concentrate for five minutes!)

48. Practice a hard section for only five minutes at a time, but play it several times a day. Put no pressure on yourself, and it will gradually get there.

49. Play more times right than wrong. Every time you play the phrase wrong, it cancels out a perfect phrase.

50. After so many mistakes you must play for 10 more minutes.

51. Put some M&Ms on the stand. Every time you play the passage correctly, you get to eat one. Or every time you make a mistake, you have to give one to your mom. (Can you tell this was written by a mom who likes chocolate?)

52. Play the last two notes of a hard phrase really fast, then the last three notes, the last four notes, etc. Continue until you can play the whole phrase.

53. Now start from the beginning and play only the first two notes as quickly as possible, then the first three notes, etc. Continue until the whole phrase is fast and perfect.

Use a Different Road Map Every Day

54. Practice the hardest part first. (Don't avoid it. Get it over with! The rest of your practice will seem easy.)

55. Practice only the hard parts. (If you don't have much time, this will make the most of it.)

56. Don't play everything every day. Practice just one section from each piece.

57. Or play just one or two pieces instead of all of them every day.

58. Take a day off. Really. You will have renewed enthusiasm when you return.

Play with Help

(Notice that none of these ideas suggests just waiting for your teacher to tell you what to do!)

59. Use the metronome. The metronome can help you count, keep
   an even tempo, or build up speed one notch at a time.

60. Use the tuner. Check your pitch on those normally out-of-tune notes that you play.

61. Play with someone shadowing you on the piano.
   (This is especially helpful for pitch.)

62. Record yourself. (It's always easier to spot the mistakes in someone else. Listen to your recording and pretend you are a judge.)

63. Play along with Smart Music, Music Minus One, or a recording.

64. Play along with your parents. (Yes, they can help!)

Handle the Hard Parts

65. Make a daily list of problems and how you can solve them. (If
   there is a rhythm problem, the solution might be to mark
   the beats, use the metronome, count out loud, etc.)

66. Figure out the note you are missing in a run and put a fermata on it.

67. Write out the hard measures or play them on the piano.

68. At the end of the practice session, put a sticky note on the measures
   you need to work on. Keep the sticky note on the measure
   every day until you have conquered the section.

Try These Other Ideas

69. Memorize. Then you know it's solid.

70. Choose any section and just enjoy it.

71. For a feeling of forward motion, walk across the room as you play a
   phrase, reaching the end of the room at the climax of the phrase.

72. Play it through and enjoy it. Yeah, it sounds like music!

73. Ideas from your teacher:

_____

74. More ideas from your teacher:

_____

_____

75. Your own ideas:

_____

_____

_____

Whew! I guarantee those tricky parts won't stand a chance once you have used these different ways to practice. Soon you'll become an expert at attacking your problems. If you get stuck on a tricky spot and don't know how to approach it, ask your teacher to help you choose practice methods to solve the problem. Use these tricks and get out of the practice room sooner.

Sneak Preview

Knowing how to practice can get your work done sooner. But did you know that understanding music theory can help, too? Our next section is a step-by-step workbook for you to do alone or with your teacher. By the end of part 4 you'll know basic music theory and be able to use your knowledge to sight-read, play faster, memorize, and play more musically. And you thought scales were only invented to torture you!

PART FOUR

SOLVING THE MYSTERY OF
MUSIC THEORY

SIXTEEN

Note Names on the Piano, Sharps and Flats, and the Chromatic Scale

WHY THEORY?

Diminished chord? Melodic minor? Authentic cadence? Augmented fifth? Beethoven's Fifth? What? I was a reluctant student in my college music theory classes. I had never been taught music theory or even how to play a scale. I was completely bewildered. I sat in the back of the class hoping never to be called on.

Fast forward to today. I'm still not a music theory whiz. I don't compose my own music or transpose, but I use music theory in my teaching and in my playing. Why? Music theory helps you play more musically and sight-read faster.

Scales and chords are the backbone of music. Without knowing them, you have to read note by note. However, when you know your theory, you can understand why a note sounds wrong, how to spot patterns, why you play certain dynamics on some notes, why you breathe after the tonic, why you use terraced dynamics on sequences, and much, much more. It may seem as if music theory is just some kind of perverted math invented to torture you, but I guarantee, you will be a better musician if you know the basics. (Singers, this means you, too!) My old theory teachers will get a big laugh now that I'm writing a chapter on theory. (See, I paid attention from the back of the room.)

This chapter is written to take you through the basics of how music works. You can work through it alone or, better yet, with your teacher. Let's start from the very beginning—a very good place to start.

PLAY THE PIANO

It's so much easier to understand music theory if it is related to the piano; it's all in black and white! When I first started music theory classes, the only way I could find the answers was to pretend I had a keyboard on my desk. Playing the piano will also help you when you have to write music. You can use the piano to train your ears to hear more than one note at once and to recognize notes just by their sound. You don't play the piano? No problem! Here's your first easy lesson. Practice these exercises on a real piano or keyboard if you have one; if not, just use the diagrams.

Music uses the first seven letters in the alphabet: A, B, C, D, E, F, G. After G, start again at A.

NOTE NAMES ON THE PIANO

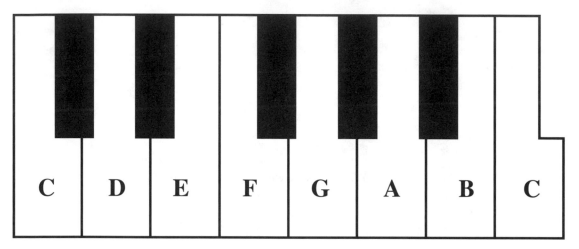

Step 1: To the left of the two black keys is C.
    To the left of the three black keys is F.

Step 2: Play all the Cs on the piano and all the Fs.

Step 3: Going to the right on the piano is higher and to the left is lower.
    If you know where C is, play up one white key higher
    to D. Play down one white key lower to B.
        Play all the Ds, then all the Bs. Repeat this process with F.
    One white key higher is G, one white key lower is E. Now that
    you know B, C, D and E, F, G, it is pretty easy to figure out A.

Step 4: Write in all the names of the white keys on the piano.

Step 5: Play any note on the piano and say its name. Keep prac-
    ticing until you recognize all the notes.

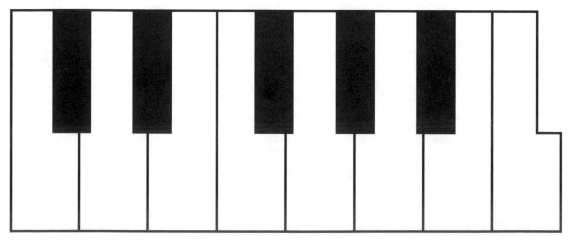

An interval is the distance between two notes. The smallest interval is a half step. If you play any note on the piano, then play the note right next to it, whether it is a black note or a white note, that will be a half step. Another name for a half step is a minor second. Play all the white and black keys on the piano. Each one of those notes is a half step away from the next.

SHARPS AND FLATS

Now let's name all those half step notes. To sharp a note means to raise it one half step. To flat a note means to lower it one half step. Remember, sharp = higher, moving to the right on the piano. Flat = lower, moving to the left. The white notes on the piano are called naturals, and the black notes are called sharps and flats.

Remember:

♯ = Sharp

♭ = Flat

♮ = Natural (cancels a sharp or flat)

Play the sharps:

Step 1: Play C on the white key. Now play the black key right above C. That is called C♯.

Step 2: Play D/D♯, skip E, play F/F♯, G/G♯, and A/A♯. The interval in each of those pairs of notes is a half step.

Play the flats:

Step 1: Play B on the piano. Now go down (to the left) to the black key right below B. That black key is called B♭. B♭ is one half step lower than B.

Step 2: Play B/B♭, A/A♭, G/G♭, skip F, play E/E♭, and D/D♭.

Step 3: What is a half step above C? _____ Above D? _____
F? _____ G? _____ A? _____
What is a half step below B? _____ Below A?
_____ G? _____ D? _____ E? _____

ENHARMONICS

Step 1: Let's play all the white keys and the black keys on the piano going higher (from the left to the right). Each note you play will be the interval of one half step above the last note.
You should play C, C♯, D, D♯, E (no black key),
F, F♯, G, G♯, A, A♯, B (no black key), and C.

Step 2: Now play all the black and white keys on the piano, but start from high to low, so you will be going to the left.

Step 3: Start on C. Since there is no black key below C, the next note a half step lower will be B. Play C, B, B♭, A, A♭, G, G♭, F (no

Note Names on the Piano, Sharps and Flats, and the Chromatic Scale

black key), E, E♭, D, D♭, and C. Each note you play will be the interval of one half step lower than the last note.

Step 4: Play C, one half step higher to C♯, then one half step higher to D. Now play D, one half step lower to D♭, then C. Did you notice that the black key in between C and D had two names? When you went higher, it was called C♯, and when you went lower, it was called D♭. The sharp of one note will be called the flat of the note above. Get it?

All the black keys have two names. C♯ = D♭, D♯ = E♭, F♯ = G♭, G♯ = A♭, A♯ = B♭. Instead of saying two names for the same note, musicians use the word *enharmonic*.

It's important for you to learn both names for each note, because composers use all of them. You may be used to playing B♭, but when you get into more complicated music, composers will use both B♭ and A♯. Be ready by learning two names (the enharmonics) for all the notes. And don't write in B♭ every time you see an A♯. You can remember both names.

Step 5: Play C, C♯, D, D♭. What is the enharmonic for the black key between C and D? If you said C♯ and D♭, you're right.

Now play D, D♯, E, E♭. What are two names for the black key between D and E? _____

Play F, F♯, G, G♭. Two names for the black key between F and G? _____

Play A, A♯, B, B♭. Two names for the black key between A and B? _____

Step 6: Now it's your turn. Write in the names of all the white notes and two names (enharmonics) for every black note:

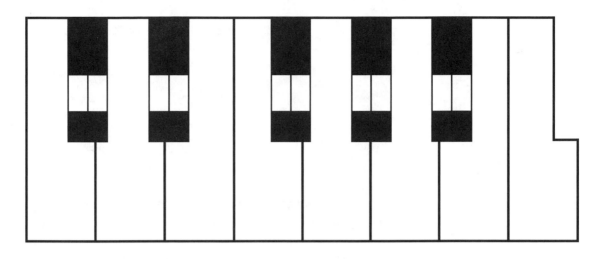

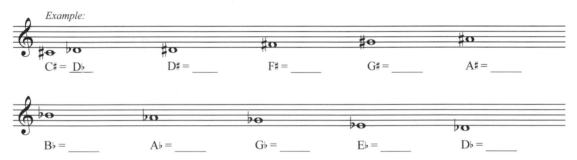

C♯ = _D♭_   D♯ = ____   F♯ = ____   G♯ = ____   A♯ = ____

B♭ = ____   A♭ = ____   G♭ = ____   E♭ = ____   D♭ = ____

You'll notice on the keyboard that there are no black keys above E or B. This is really important to remember. You already know that the note right next to another note is a half step away. On all the other notes, the sharps and flats have been a black key, but there is no black key between E/F and B/C. So a half step above E must be F, and a half step above B is C. Even though the pairs of E/F and B/C don't have black keys, they still have enharmonics; they're just not on the black keys. In other words, B♯ = C, E♯ = F, C♭ = B, F♭ = E.

To recap, a half step above E is F, so E♯ = F. A half step below F is E, so F♭ = E. The same is true for the B/C pair. A half step above B is C, so B♯ = C, and a half step below C is B, so C♭ = B. Got it?

Step 7: Write in the names of the enharmonics for the B/C and E/F pairs. Always use notes on the staff, not just letter names when you do this homework.

THE CHROMATIC SCALE

Remember that the smallest interval (distance between two notes) is the half step. When you play all the half steps in order going up and down on the piano, it's called the chromatic scale. We usually use sharps when we go higher and the enharmonic flats when we go lower.

The chromatic scale is a great way to learn your enharmonics and is a good warm-up. It is also required at many auditions. Composers use the chromatic scale when they want the piece to be exciting or for the soloist to show off. Practice the chromatic scale first on the piano and then on your instrument so that you can play it fast!

This is the chromatic scale. Notice that it goes up (to the right) in sharps and down (to the left) in flats.

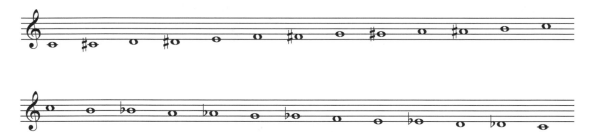

Step 1: Play the chromatic scale on the piano while saying the note names.

Step 2: Write the chromatic scale in sharps going up and in flats coming down:

Step 3: Practice saying the names of the chromatic scale while looking at the notes.

Step 4: If you're not a pianist, ask your teacher to show you the chromatic scale on your instrument and to quiz you on knowing both names for all the notes.

Step 5: Ask your teacher to play the chromatic scale on the piano while you play it on your instrument. The chromatic scale can start on any note, but in practice we'll start on C.

Step 6: Since the chromatic scale appears in music so often, it's important that you memorize it. Say the names of the notes as fast as you can.

Step 7: Say the note names in the chromatic scale one at a time out loud, and then play them on your instrument. Say, "C," then play C, say, "C♯," then play C♯. You've got the idea. When you come to E, go right to F, and when you come to B, go right to C. When you reach an octave (all the way to the next C) or as high as you can play on your instrument, play down the scale. This time say the enharmonic notes in flats, as we wrote in the above diagram.

Step 8: Now play the chromatic scale without looking at the notes and without saying them out loud. If you make this part of your practice routine, you'll be ready for some exciting music.

Guess what? You've just learned to recognize all the keys on the piano, and you can play the chromatic scale on the piano and on your instrument. That's huge! Good job!

Sneak Preview

Now let's find out why all major scales sound similar.

SEVENTEEN

Major Scales and Key Signatures

BUILDING MAJOR SCALES

Music is built on major and minor scales. This means that a composer chooses a pattern of eight notes, called a scale, and then composes the piece using the notes in that scale as the base of the piece. If you can recognize scales in your pieces and have practiced them on your instrument, you're already halfway to knowing the piece. The notes are like the letters in the alphabet, and the scales are like the words. As boring as learning scales may seem, when you sight-read a piece with a lot of sharps or flats and fast scales, you will be so thankful for all those hours in the practice room.

Let's start off with major scales. While the chromatic scale has a half step (minor second) between each note, major scales have both half and whole steps. The shorthand for major is a capital *M*, while minor is a lowercase *m*.

A whole step is two half steps. For example, C to C♯ is one half step, C♯ to D is another half step: two halves equal a whole, so C to D is a whole step. Another name for a whole step is a major second.

Step 1: Under each pair of notes, analyze the interval (distance between two notes). Is it a whole step or half step?

Step 2: As we said before, major scales have both half steps and whole steps. Now analyze the whole and half steps in a C major scale. Is it a whole or half step between C and D? Between D and E? E to F? F to G? G to A? A to B? B to C?

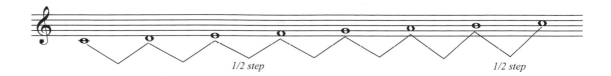

1/2 step   1/2 step

Did you remember the half steps between E/F and B/C?
Now analyze the whole and half steps in the G major scale.

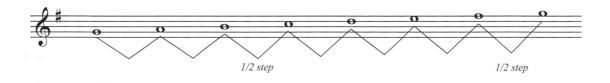

1/2 step   1/2 step

All major scales have every single letter name: ABCDEFG. All major scales
have the same intervals: a whole step between the first two notes, then another
whole step, a half, whole, whole, whole, half. To help you remember: that's two
wholes and a half, then three wholes and a half. We can write that in shorthand
like this:

1, 1, ½, 1, 1, 1, ½

Step 3: Memorize the intervals in a major scale.

All major scales sound alike because they use the same pattern.
Music is built from scales, so you can hear a wrong note because it
doesn't fit the patterns we are accustomed to. Music from other cultures can have ¼ steps and ⅛ steps, but those notes sound wrong to our
ears. Just imagine how complicated their music theory classes must be!

Step 4: Since every major scale is the same, you can start on any
note and figure out what the flats or sharps will be for that
scale. Let's build the major scale that starts on A.

Hint 1: First write out the letter names (A B C D E F G A). Now
figure out which sharps and flats you must have to make
the intervals whole, whole, half, whole, whole, whole, half.

Hint 2: Major scales will have all sharps or
all flats, never a mixture.

Hint 3: Remember those two tricky pairs of
half steps between E/F and B/C.

Hint 4: Once you have written out the major scale, play
it, and you'll be able to spot your mistakes.

Step 5: For more advanced work, build these pairs of scales:
F# and G♭ on the first staff, C# and D♭ on the second, and B and C♭ major on the third staff.

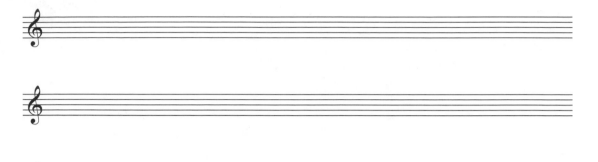

Step 6: Play each pair of scales. Notice that each pair sounds exactly the same, just written with different enharmonics.

KEY SIGNATURES

The sharps or flats in a scale are called the key signature. The key signature tells us which sharps or flats to play and which scale, or key, the composer used to build the piece. For example, when we figure out the whole and half steps in the D major scale, we get D E F# G A B C# D, so we say the key signature for D major is F# and C#. If the composer wants us to play in the key of D major, F# and C# are written at the beginning of the piece, instead of having to put a sharp in front of every F and C.

The sharps or flats at the beginning of a piece are always in the same order.

Sharps

If there is one sharp, it will always be F#. Two sharps are always F# and C#. The order of the sharps is F C G D A E B.

Step 1: Learn this mnemonic to remember the order of the sharps:
Fair Cinderella Goes Down And Eats Bugs or
Funny Cows Go Dancing At Every Bar
      F#   C#   G#   D#   A#   E#   B#
If you picture Cinderella or the cows, you'll remember.
Here is the order of the sharps as they appear in the key signature:

Step 2: Write the order of the sharps in the key signature. Make
sure to write them on the correct lines and spaces.

Now that you know what order the sharps are written in, how do
you know what the name of the scale is? For instance, if you saw F♯
and C♯ written at the beginning for the key signature, how would
you know that the piece is written using the scale of D major? Here's
the trick: *The name of the key is a half step above the last sharp.*

For example, if the key signature has F♯ and C♯ written in that order, the C♯ would be the last sharp. What's a half
step above C♯? Just think of the chromatic scale. D is the answer. So the key signature with F♯ and C♯ is D major.

Step 3: Write the key signature with one sharp and the name of the key.
I'll talk you through the first one. You know the first sharp is F♯
(remember Fair Cinderella). A half step above that F♯ (which is
the first and last) is G. So the key that has one sharp is G major.

Now it is your turn. I made it really easy for you by writing in the
names of the sharps in order. Your job is to write the name of the key
below the staff. It's a piece of cake since you know the chromatic scale.

Big hint: Remember those tricky half step pairs, E/F and B/C. E♯
is F, so ½ step above E♯ is F♯ and ½ step above B♯ is C♯. Once you've
written out each major scale, check down below to see how you did.

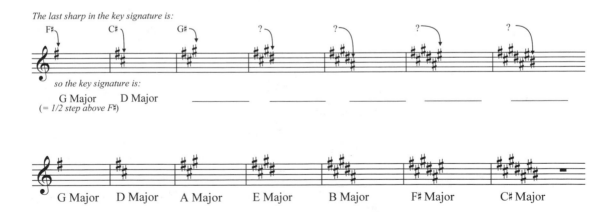

If you didn't get the last two key signatures, F♯ and C♯ major, this may be why:

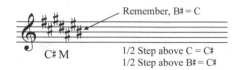

Remember, B♯ = C

C♯ M

1/2 Step above C = C♯
1/2 Step above B♯ = C♯

But what if you know the name of the scale, but don't know what sharps it has? Just work backwards. Let's figure out the sharps in E major. You could start with E and build the scale using the 1, 1, ½, 1, 1, 1, ½ pattern, but let's save some time here.

Remember: The name of the key is one half step ABOVE the last sharp. So if you know the name of the key, go down one half step from the name of the key to get the last sharp.

The key signature will include all the sharps up to the last one.

Key name	E major
Down ½ step	Key signature for E major is F♯ C♯ G♯ D♯
Last sharp	D♯

Step 4: If you know the scale is A major, how do you know what the sharps are?

First think, "What is the last sharp in A major?" (go down ½ step). The key signature is all the sharps through that last sharp.

Let's review:

The name of the key is ½ step above the last sharp.
The last sharp is ½ step below the name of the key.

Step 5: Write each key name and under it write the last sharp.

For example, write GM and under it write F♯.

Name of Key:	G	D	A	E	B	F♯	C♯
Last Sharp in the Key Signature:	F♯	___	___	___	___	___	___

Step 6: Now that you know the last sharp for every sharp key, write each key name and all the sharps in the key. Be sure to write the sharps on the correct line of the staff.

It should look like this, but be written on the staff.

GM	DM	AM	EM	BM	F♯M	C♯M
F♯	C♯ (F♯, C♯)	G♯ (F♯, C♯, G♯)	D♯ (F♯, C♯, G♯, D♯)	A♯ (F♯, C♯, G♯, D♯, A♯)	E♯ (F♯, C♯, G♯, D♯, A♯, E♯)	B♯ (F♯, C♯, G♯, D♯, A♯, E♯, B♯)

It's easier than you think if you just remember that Fair Cinderella Goes Down And Eats Bugs. Once you have the key signatures memorized, it will be so much easier to remember them when you're playing. If you don't know that E major has four sharps, it will always be hard to remember which notes are supposed to be sharped, especially for that tricky D♯. Memorizing all your scales and being able to play them on your instrument will help you learn so much faster and make fewer mistakes. I guarantee it.

Flats

Now let's learn the major scales that have flats.

The order of the flats is:

Bears Elephants And Dogs Go Crawling Forward or

BEAD Greatest Common Factor

B♭　　E♭　　A♭　　D♭　　G♭　　C♭　　F♭

These mnemonics aren't as funny, so maybe you can make up something better.

Step 1: Memorize the mnemonics for the flat keys.

Step 2: Write the flats on the staff. Remember to put them on the right lines and spaces.

Step 3: The name of the flat keys is the name of the second to the last flat. (You just have to memorize that F major has 1 flat.) B♭ major has B♭ and E♭; B♭ is the second to the last flat, and so B♭ is the name of the key.

Step 4: Everyone, and I mean *everyone*, mixes up the rules for naming the sharp and flat keys. Why don't you be the first exception?

Write out the rule for naming the flat keys:

_____

Write out the rule for naming the sharp keys:

_____

Major Scales and Key Signatures

Step 5: Write every flat key signature and label:

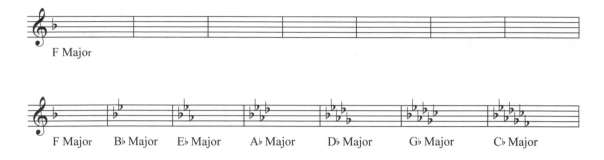

F Major   Bb Major   Eb Major   Ab Major   Db Major   Gb Major   Cb Major

Step 6: Now you know that the name of the flat key is the name of the second to the last flat. But if you know the name of the flat key, how do you know which flats it has? That's easy. *If you know the name of the flat key, add one more flat to get the key signature.*

For example, to name the flats in Ab major, start at the beginning with Bb, Eb, Ab, and just add one more flat, Db. There's your answer.

Step 7: Write each key name and add one more flat. Now write the whole key signature. (Start out with F major, with only Bb.) Notice that the name of the last flat will be the name of the next key. (Do your best to fit the key signatures on this staff.)

The last flat in the Key of F is Bb which is the name of the key with one more flat!

The Key of Ab has 4 flats The last flat is Db which is the name of the key with one more flat.

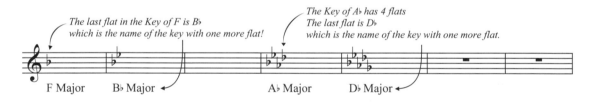

F Major   Bb Major   Ab Major   Db Major

Did you get it right?

FM has one flat.

Bb + one flat = Bb + Eb

Eb + one flat = Bb, Eb, + Ab

Ab + one flat = Bb, Eb, Ab, + Db

Db + one flat = Bb, Eb, Ab, Db, + Gb

Gb + one flat = Bb, Eb, Ab, Db, Gb, + Cb

Cb + one flat = Bb, Eb, Ab, Db, Gb, Cb, + Fb

You now know how to build scales and key signatures. You'll use this knowledge every single time you play your instrument or sing. Now let's learn how to see and hear the distance between any two notes.

EIGHTEEN

Intervals

Earlier we talked about the two smallest intervals: a half step, called a minor second, and a whole step, called a major second. You already know how to identify them by looking at the chromatic scale on the piano. But wouldn't it be great to know how they sound just by looking at them? If you know what each interval sounds like, you can pick up a piece of music and sing it without having heard it before. That's called sight-singing. If you become a music major, sight-singing will be a required class. But even if you're not going to major in music, being able to identify all the intervals helps you know if you played a mistake and will help you memorize faster. It will also enable you to pick up a piece of music and sing it without ever having heard it before. How cool is that?

ANALYZING INTERVALS BY SIGHT AND SOUND

To figure out any interval, start with any note on the piano. Call that first note #1. Count how many white keys/letter names there are between note #1 and the next note. For instance, if you want to know what the interval between C and E is, C is note #1, D is #2, and E is #3. So from C to E is a third. If you went from C to F (CDEF), that would be a fourth.

It's much easier to hear and see the intervals on the piano. If you don't have a piano, try playing them on your instrument to memorize the sound. This is another time when your teacher can come in handy by quizzing you.

Learn to recognize intervals with the help of your teacher:
- Your teacher plays intervals on the piano, and you name them by looking at the keyboard. (Your teacher plays D and F, and you say, "That's a third.")
- Your teacher asks you to recognize the intervals without looking at the keyboard. (Your teacher says, "What is the interval between D and F?" You gleefully answer, "That's a third!")
- Your teacher plays two notes on the keyboard, and you say what the interval is just by listening. (Your teacher plays D and then

F, or both notes at the same time. She is so proud of you when
you jump up and down and say, "I know! That's a third!")
- Your teacher plays one note on the piano and asks you to sing a certain
interval. (Your teacher plays D on the piano and says, "Sing a third
above this note." Your voice rings out loud and clear on an F.)
- Your teacher says, "You're so smart!" You just smile
and thank me for writing this theory section.

INTERVAL SYMBOLS

Let's get started with a review of the two intervals you already know, the major
and minor second (M2 and m2). Remember that the shorthand for major is M
and that the shorthand for minor is m. Two more kinds of intervals you will
learn are augmented, which is a plus sign (+), and diminished, which is a circle
(°).

Step 1: Write the shorthand symbols for major, minor,
augmented, and diminished:

MINOR AND MAJOR SECONDS

Minor second = 1/2 step to the next letter name.
A minor second sounds like the chromatic scale
and the shark theme from *Jaws.*

Step 2: Write m2 above these notes:

Major second = 1 whole step to the next letter name.
A major second sounds like the first two notes of a major or minor scale, or
the first two notes of "Silent Night," "Rudolph," and "Happy Birthday."

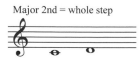

MINOR AND MAJOR THIRDS

The next interval you will learn is called a third. Chords are built on thirds, so please pay close attention. Count up three notes from note #1 and you get a third. Another way to think about a third is to start on note #1 and skip one letter name in the alphabet.

Step 1: Circle the thirds (skipping one letter name) in the alphabet:

A B C D E F G A B C D E A B C D E

Step 2: Now do the same thing, but write the thirds in notes on the staff:

There are two kinds of thirds. To build them, you must always first skip a letter name.

A minor third has three half steps. Let's say you want to find a minor third above D. Finding intervals is like a game that has two steps.

　　　　1. Start on D and skip one letter name. The answer is F.

　　　　2. Now count three half steps above D: one half
　　　　　　step above D is D♯, two half steps above D is E,
　　　　　　and 3 is F. So a minor third above D is F.

Let's try another one. If F is note #1, a third above it will be A, skipping the note G. Now count out three half steps above F: one half step is F♯, two half steps is G, and 3 half steps above F is G♯. But wait, the game has two steps. Step #1 is to skip one letter name above F. The third has to be some kind of A, so you must call that G♯ by its enharmonic spelling, A♭. A minor third above F is A♭. Hint: All of this will be easier if you look at a keyboard.

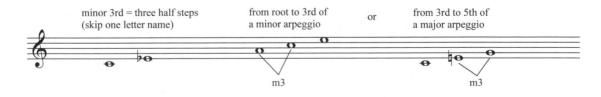

minor 3rd = three half steps (skip one letter name)　　　from root to 3rd of a minor arpeggio　　or　　from 3rd to 5th of a major arpeggio

Step 1: Write minor thirds above these notes. The answer to the first one is C.

A major third skips one letter name and has four half steps. The most famous major third is the opening of Beethoven's Fifth Symphony. A major third is the interval between the bottom note (the root) and the middle note (the third) of a major chord. A major third also sounds like the first two notes of "Swing Low, Sweet Chariot," "I Could Have Danced All Night," and "For He's a Jolly Good Fellow."

Major 3rd = four half-steps   From the root to the third
(Skip one letter name)   of a major arpeggio

Major 3rd

Step 2: Write major thirds above these notes.

Now that you understand how to build intervals, let's quickly go through the other intervals.

PERFECT AND AUGMENTED FOURTHS

Perfect Fourth

A perfect fourth skips two letter names and contains five half steps. A perfect fourth is one half step above a major third. So if you know that a major third above G is B, then a perfect fourth above G is C. A perfect fourth sounds like "O Christmas Tree" or "Here Comes the Bride."

Perfect fourths

Write a note a perfect fourth above the given note:

Augmented Fourth

An augmented fourth skips two letter names and contains six half
steps. An augmented fourth is one half step above a perfect fourth. Another name for the augmented fourth is a tri-
tone. In years gone by, it was also called the "devil's interval,"
and it was banned from music. An augmented fourth sounds
like the first two notes of "Maria" from *West Side Story.*

DIMINISHED, PERFECT, AND AUGMENTED FIFTHS

Diminished Fifth

A diminished fifth skips three letter names and contains six half steps.
A diminished fifth is the same as the augmented fourth, but
just spelled enharmonically, and it is much more common.

Augmented fourths/diminished fifths (tritones)

Write a note an augmented fourth above the given note:

Now write diminished fifths next to the augmented fourths you just
wrote. They sound the same but are spelled differently.

Perfect Fifth

A perfect fifth skips three letter names and contains seven half steps. Fifths
are the second most common interval after thirds. The interval between the bottom and top note of a major chord is a perfect fifth.
A perfect fifth sounds like the first two notes of "Twinkle, Twinkle Little
Star," "God Rest Ye Merry, Gentlemen," and "Star Wars."

Perfect fifths

Write a note a perfect fifth above the given note:

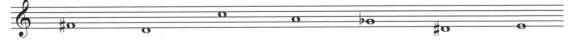

Augmented Fifth

An augmented fifth skips three letter names and contains eight half steps. An augmented fifth is one half step larger than a perfect fifth. Augmented fifths sound like the main theme of Scott Joplin's rag "The Entertainer," even though those notes are written as a minor sixth.

Augmented fifths

Write a note an augmented fifth above the given note:

MINOR AND MAJOR SIXTHS

Minor Sixth

A minor sixth skips four letter names and contains eight half steps. It is just a perfect fifth plus ½ step. A minor sixth also sounds like the third and fourth notes of "The Entertainer."

Minor sixths

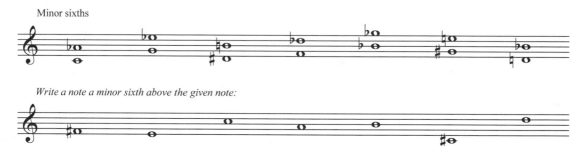

Write a note a minor sixth above the given note:

Major Sixth

A major sixth skips four letter names and contains nine half steps. A major sixth is a whole step above a perfect fifth. It may be my favorite interval because it sounds like "My *Bonnie* Lies over the Ocean," and the first two notes of the NBC TV three-note signature.

Major sixths

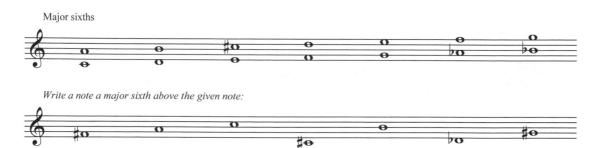

Write a note a major sixth above the given note:

Minor Seventh

A minor seventh skips five letter names and contains 10 half steps. A
minor seventh is an octave minus a whole step. It sounds like
the first two notes of "Somewhere" from *West Side Story.*

Minor sevenths

Write a note a minor seventh above the given note:

Major Seventh

A major seventh skips five letter names and contains 11 half steps. A
major seventh is an octave minus a half step. Think up one octave (the interval of 8 notes from one letter name to the same
letter name), then go down a half step for a major seventh.

Major sevenths

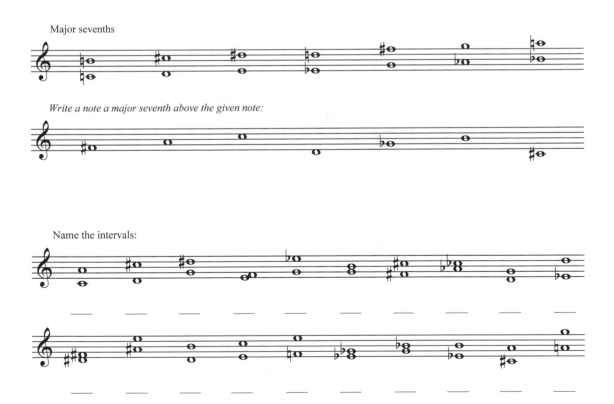

Write a note a major seventh above the given note:

Name the intervals:

Add a note which is the specified interval above the given note:

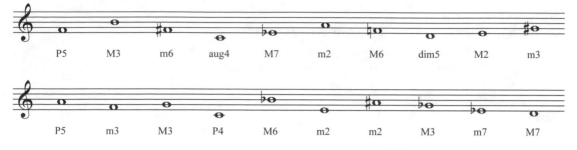

| P5 | M3 | m6 | aug4 | M7 | m2 | M6 | dim5 | M2 | m3 |

| P5 | m3 | M3 | P4 | M6 | m2 | m2 | M3 | m7 | M7 |

INTERVAL NAMES

It's easy to get the names of the intervals mixed up. Which intervals are minor? Major? Augmented? Diminished?

Let's review:

Minor: second, third, sixth, seventh

Major: second, third, sixth, seventh

Perfect: fourth, fifth

Augmented: second, third, fourth, fifth, sixth

Diminished: third, fourth, fifth, sixth, seventh

Here are the intervals from the smallest up to an octave.

Minor second = m2

Major second = M2

Augmented second = Aug2 (same as a minor third, but spelled differently)

Minor third = m3

Major third = M3 (same as a diminished fourth)

Perfect fourth = P4

Augmented fourth = Aug 4 (same as a diminished fifth)

Perfect fifth = P5

Augmented fifth = Aug 5 (same as a minor sixth)

Minor sixth = m6

Major sixth = M6

Augmented sixth = Aug6 (same as a minor seventh)

Minor seventh = m7

Major seventh = M7

Octave

Intervals larger than an octave are still named for the number of notes. For example, nine notes above note #1 is called a ninth.

Consonant intervals (those that sound beautiful to most ears):

m3, M3, P4, P5, m6, M6

Dissonant intervals (those that clash):

m2, M2, Aug4, Dim5, m7, M7

CHANGING INTERVALS

When the upper note of

a major interval is raised by a half step, it becomes augmented.

a major interval is lowered by a half step, it becomes minor.

a major interval is lowered by two half steps, it becomes diminished.

a minor interval is raised by a half step, it becomes major.

a minor interval is raised by two half steps, it becomes augmented.

a minor interval is lowered by a half step, it becomes diminished.

a perfect interval is raised by a half step, it becomes augmented.

a perfect interval is lowered by a half step, it becomes diminished.

Sneak Preview

Now you know everything you ever wanted to know about intervals.
Let's turn to chapter 19 to learn more about scales.

NINETEEN

Minor Scales

Just when you thought you knew everything about scales and key signatures, I have to break it to you that there's still more to learn. We've studied major scales, but there are also minor scales.

Step 1: Play this A minor scale on your instrument or on the piano:

Step 2: It sounds different than the major scale, doesn't it? Maybe a little sadder? The minor scale sounds different because it has a different series of whole and half steps. Remember the series of whole steps and half steps for major scales? That's right, it's 1, 1, ½, 1, 1, 1, ½. The minor scale has a different series of whole and half steps.

Step 3: Write in the whole and half steps in the A minor scale above:

_____

Did you get this answer?

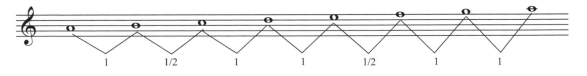

THE INTERVALS IN A MINOR SCALE

Every minor scale has the pattern of whole, half, whole, whole, half, whole, whole (1, ½, 1, 1, ½, 1, 1). You can start on any note, use every letter name, and figure out the sharps or flats in any minor key.

But wait! There's an easier way to figure out the key signature for minor scales.

Each minor scale has a relative major scale with the same key signature.
The relative MAJOR scale is a minor third (skip one letter name, three half steps)
ABOVE the minor scale.

Here is the formula:

Major scale

go down a minor third

= minor scale

For example, start with C major.

Count down a minor third. (To find a minor third, skip one letter name
and count down three half steps.)

So start on C, skip one letter name (C, skip B, end on A).

Now count three half steps below C. Start on C, count down one half step
to B, down two half steps to B♭, down three half steps to A. You have just
found the relative minor scale of C major: that's right, it's A minor.

So C major and A minor are related—they have the same key signature.

The C major scale is C to C with no sharps and flats. Its relative minor, a
minor, is A to A with no sharps or flats.

(They both happen to be my favorite key signatures for that very reason!)

Relative Scales With the Same Key Signature

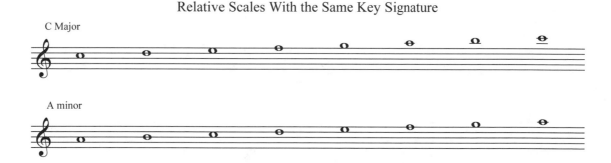

It's easy to forget that the major scale is ABOVE the minor scale, so think of
this: would you rather be in the major leagues or the minor leagues? The major
leagues, of course, because the major leagues are ABOVE the minor leagues.
The major is ABOVE the minor.

Major

minor

Step 1: Promise me you will always remember that *the major is a
minor third above the minor scale.* And please tell my students so that I never have to say this again. Thanks.

Step 2: Write the relative minor key BELOW each of these major keys.
(Just count down a minor third.) I'll even be nice and do the first
two for you. Each pair of scales has the same sharps or flats.

C major   G major   D major   A major   E major   B major   F♯ major   C♯ major
a minor   e minor
F major   B♭ major   E♭ major   A♭ major   D♭ major   G♭ major   C♭ major

I know you understand this, but just to drill a little more, let's go the opposite way. Say you know the minor, and you want to find the
major. What do you do? That's right. Go UP a minor third from
the minor scale to the relative major. You remembered that
the minor is below the major, right? Don't disappoint me!

Step 3: Write the relative major ABOVE each of these minor keys:

_____

a minor   e minor   b minor   f♯ minor   c♯ minor   g♯ minor   d♯ minor   a♯ minor

_____

d minor   g minor   c minor   f minor   b♭ minor   e♭ minor   a♭ minor

Step 4: Now you know that for every key signature there are
two key possibilities: the major and the minor.

You just learned the major and minor key possibilities for
each key signature. Now write the very same thing, but
write it on the staff with real flats and sharps.

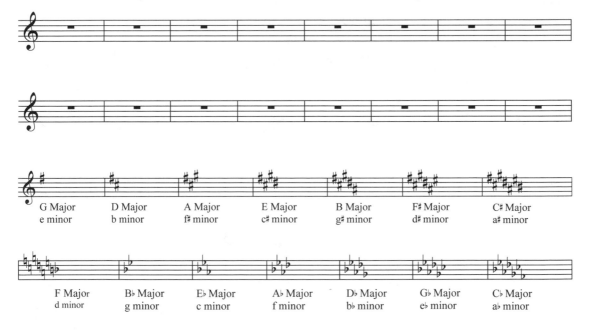

G Major	D Major	A Major	E Major	B Major	F♯ Major	C♯ Major
e minor	b minor	f♯ minor	c♯ minor	g♯ minor	d♯ minor	a♯ minor

F Major	B♭ Major	E♭ Major	A♭ Major	D♭ Major	G♭ Major	C♭ Major
d minor	g minor	c minor	f minor	b♭ minor	e♭ minor	a♭ minor

Now that you know the minor scales, there's just one more thing to tell you
about them. There are three forms of minor scales. Don't worry. You already
know the first form, which is called *the natural minor.* The natural minor is
exactly like the relative major.

This is the A natural minor scale, which is the same as the C major scale,
except that it starts on a different note (A).

The next form is the *harmonic minor*. The seventh note in the scale (the second to the last) is raised one half step in the harmonic minor. The harmonic minor has a "gypsy" or "foreign" flavor to it because, unlike any other scale, there are one and a half steps between the sixth and seventh scale degrees. There can also be both sharps and flats in the harmonic minor scale. Play this harmonic minor scale and picture a snake charmer.

Harmonic minor (raised seventh scale degree):

The last form is the *melodic minor*. The melodic minor has raised sixth and seventh scale degrees going up, and is just like the natural minor coming down.

Melodic minor (raised sixth and seventh scale degrees) ascending, like the natural minor descending:

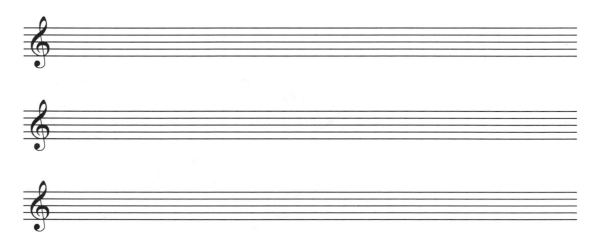

Now, write three forms of d, g, and e minor:

Step 1: You may find it tricky to remember the three
forms of the minor scale, so let's review:
1. The natural minor is like the relative major.
2. The harmonic minor has a raised seventh.
3. The melodic minor has a raised sixth and seventh ascending and is like the natural minor descending.

Do you have them memorized now?

Step 2: Label each form natural, harmonic, or melodic minor.
(Write the melodic minor ascending and descending.)

Step 3: Play different forms of each minor scale and learn to recognize them
by ear. Ask your teacher to quiz you on the forms of the minor scale.

How can you tell whether a piece is in a major or minor key?

1. Choose any piece you are working on. Play it. Which scale
do you hear? Does it sound "sad" or "happy"?
2. Analyze the notes in the beginning. A composer will try to es-
tablish a key by using the notes of the scale and the first, third,
and fifth notes of the scale to give you the feeling of the key.
3. Look at the accidentals. Are they forms of the harmonic or melodic minor scales?
4. Cheat and look at the last note of the piece. That
note will usually be the name of the key.

Step 4: Practice identifying major and minor keys by looking at a piece
and by playing it. Ask your teacher to play a few short excerpts
from songs and try to identify them as major and minor.

Sneak Preview

*Now that you're a major and minor scale expert,
let's move on to chords.*

TWENTY

Chords and Arpeggios

Now that you know the major and minor scales and intervals, you're more than halfway there. It's time to talk about chords and arpeggios.

A chord is a group of notes played all at once. An arpeggio, on the other hand, is a chord, any chord, with each note played one at a time in rapid succession.

Music is full of scales and chords. Remember when you were learning to read? You had to sound out every letter. "C-A-T. Cat." With a little practice, as soon as you saw those three letters, you remembered what they spelled, and you were on your way to becoming a good reader.

Learning chords is like learning words. When you first learn to read music, you read one note at a time. "C-E-G. That's the C major chord." With practice, whenever you see those three notes, no matter what order they are in, you will recognize them as the C major chord. When you can easily recognize chords, your fingers will kick into automatic pilot. Sight-reading, playing, and memorizing will become so much easier. It's really worth taking the time to memorize the chords/arpeggios. Trust me!

TONIC CHORDS

The name of the first note of every scale is the tonic. The tonic of the C scale is C, and the tonic of the G scale is G. Chords that are built on the first note of the scale are called tonic chords.

Step 1. Write out the G major scale.

Step 2. Number the notes of the scale 1–8.

Step 3. Circle the tonic chord: scale tones 1–3–5–8.

Step 4. Write out the tonic chord after the scale.

Step 5. Play the tonic chord.

Your work should look like this but in G major:

Step 6. Circle the tonic chords for all the major keys. Quit groaning.
I'll tell you the key signatures to make it go faster.

13

Step 7. Play the tonic chord.

Step 8. Now memorize the tonic chords. Yes, memorize all of them. And
keep them memorized now and forever. It may hurt
now, but you'll thank me for this some day. (In fact,
you'll thank me by the end of this chapter.)

INTERVALS IN TONIC CHORDS

In the previous section we wrote the notes one after the other in arpeggios, and
in this section we will write them on top of each other in chords.

Chords have three or more notes. The interval between every note in a
tonic chord is a major or a minor third. Because you skip a letter name when
writing thirds, chords will look like snowmen on the staff: line-line-line or
space-space-space.

Step 1: Write the F major and B♭ major chords on the
staff. See, they do look like snowmen.

The distance between the bottom note and the second note in a chord is a
third, and the interval between the bottom and top notes of a chord is a fifth.
When we talk about the notes in a chord, we call the bottom note the root, the
middle note the third, and the top note the fifth; it's pretty obvious how they
got those names. (If you can't remember what a third and a fifth are, you'd better go back and review the intervals chapter.) In this C major chord, the C is the
root, the E is the third, and the G is the fifth.

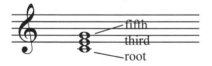

Step 2: What note is the root of the A major chord? _____

What is the third? _____

What is the fifth? _____

Step 3: Write the D major chord (the first, third, and fifth notes
of the D major scale) and analyze the intervals.

Is there a major third (4 half steps) or a minor third (3 half steps) between the root and the third? _____

Is there a major or minor third between the third and
the fifth? _____

Here are the intervals in the C major chord.

MAJOR CHORDS

If you analyzed your D major chord correctly, you should have gotten the same intervals. So here's the pattern for all major chords: every major chord has a major third on the bottom and a minor third on the top.

Major chord:

m3

M3

Step 4: Write these major chords: D♭ major, E major, B major (notice I gave you ones you might not have memorized).

Step 5: Write in the intervals between the notes.

MINOR CHORDS

Every minor chord has a minor third on the bottom and a major third on the top. The minor chord is the first, third, and fifth notes of the minor scale.

Minor chord:

M3

m3

It's easy to memorize major and minor chords because the name of the chord is the name of the first third: *major* chord starts with *major* third, *minor* chord starts with *minor* third. Now who can forget that?

Step 1: Write these minor chords: a minor, g minor, and d minor.

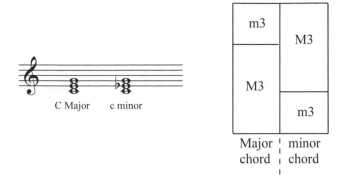

C Major   c minor

Step 2: Write these major and minor chords: E♭, E, F, and A♭. Notice that the root and the fifth of the major and minor chords stay the same, and only the third changes. If you have the major chords memorized, then you just lower the third to get the minor chord. Suddenly you have all the minor chords memorized, too! How easy is that?

DIMINISHED CHORDS

What? You had trouble with those chords? My joy in teaching is diminished!

Which brings us to the next kind of chord. To diminish means to make smaller.

A diminished chord has two minor thirds.

c dim   minor 3rds   d dim   minor 3rds

Diminished chord:

m3
m3

Step 1: Write these diminished chords; G, E, and D.

So you understood diminished chords? You just augmented my joy in teaching them. I know, bad way to introduce augmented chords. To augment means to make larger.

Step 1: What do you think the intervals are in an augmented chord? _____ and _____.

Augmented chords have two major thirds.

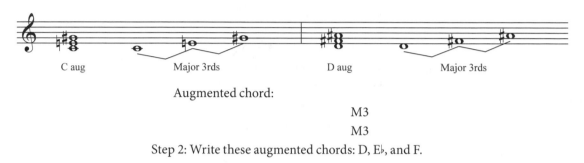

C aug   Major 3rds   D aug   Major 3rds

Augmented chord:

M3

M3

Step 2: Write these augmented chords: D, E♭, and F.

REVIEW

Step 1: The intervals in a major chord are _____ and _____.

Step 2: The intervals in a minor chord are _____ and _____.

Step 3: The intervals in a diminished chord are _____ and _____.

Step 4: The intervals in an augmented chord are _____ and _____.

Aren't you glad you memorized those major chords?

Remember, if you know the major chord and want to know the minor chord, just lower the third (the middle note) ½ step.

D major = D F♯ A   D minor = D F A. The third is lowered.

From the minor chord to the diminished chord, you lower the fifth (the top note). D min = D F A Ddim = D F A♭

From the major chord to the augmented chord, just raise the fifth.

Dmaj = D F♯ A   Daug = D F♯ A♯

Step 5: Write the C major, C minor, C diminished, C major again, and C augmented chords.

Step 6: From major chord to minor chord, lower the _____.

Step 7: From minor chord to diminished chord, lower the _____.

Step 8: From major chord to augmented chord, raise the _____.

Step 9: Now sit at the piano and play four forms of each chord and listen to their tone quality. (Major is happy, minor is sad, diminished is really sad, and I think augmented sounds like a train whistle. What do you think?)

Step 10: This is a good time for your teacher to play the chords for you and quiz you.

Step 11: Write four forms of each chord and label them (C, C♯, D♭, D, E♭, E, F, F♯, G♭, G, A♭, A, B♭, B, and C♭). I know it will take some time, but here's a little timesaver. Instead of writing out the words, use these signs:

major = M, minor = m, diminished = °, augmented = +

Remember, you don't have to figure out the intervals for each chord. Start with the major chord and just raise or lower the thirds and fifths. It's a cinch.

Write the chords as indicated, following the example of the first group:

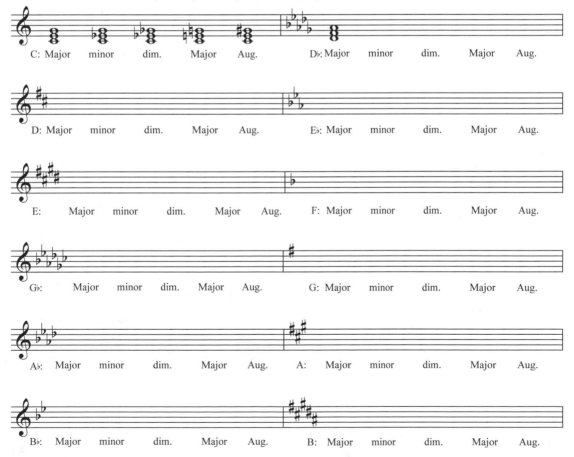

Chords and Arpeggios

Let's see what you learned. Analyze these chords:

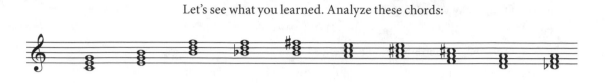

Sneak Preview

*Wow, that was a lot for one chapter. You only have one more
theory chapter to go. In the next chapter we will talk about
the "higher math" of chords. You can do it!*

TWENTY-ONE

Chord Inversions, Figured Bass, and Cadences

After writing all those chords in chapter 20, I bet you thought there couldn't possibly be more to learn. Sorry. If you play jazz or guitar, this is only the beginning. In this chapter, you'll learn about chords that have more than three notes, chords that have the notes in a different order, and a shorthand way of talking about chords.

DOUBLE SHARPS AND DOUBLE FLATS

Before we begin, let me show you some funny ways to spell certain notes. A double flat looks like this: ♭♭. A double flat before a note lowers the note one whole step regardless of the key signature. (B♭♭ is always A, even if there is a B♭ in the key signature.) A double sharp ✕ raises a note one whole step regardless of the key signature.

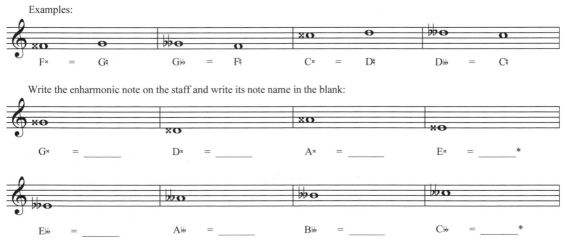

Examples:

F✕ = G♮   G♭♭ = F♮   C✕ = D♮   D♭♭ = C♮

Write the enharmonic note on the staff and write its note name in the blank:

G✕ = _____   D✕ = _____   A✕ = _____   E✕ = _____ *

E♭♭ = _____   A♭♭ = _____   B♭♭ = _____   C♭♭ = _____ *

* Yes, these are trick questions

Chords are named for the root (the bottom note). A C chord starts on C, and a D chord starts on D. But chords are not always in root position. Music would get boring if the notes of the chords were always in the same order. Sometimes the third is on the bottom, and sometimes the fifth is on the bottom. But no matter which note is the lowest in the chord, it's still essentially the same chord. Chord inversions are like having three sisters from the same family. You can list them from the oldest to the youngest, you can start with the middle sister, or you can start with the youngest. It's still the same three girls.

Step 1: Write the letter names of these chords with different notes on the bottom: C, D, E, F, G.

I'll do the first one for you:

C chord = C–E–G, or E–G–C, or G–C–E.

Now you write out the others:

D chord = _____

E chord = _____

F chord = _____

G chord = _____

Step 2: Circle the letters G B D in the alphabet: A B C D E F G A B C D E F G A

G is the bottom letter, (skip the A), next is B (skip the C), and the last note is D. Because there is one letter name between each of the letters when we start with G, we know the notes G–B–D create a G chord, no matter what order they appear in.

Step 3: What if the notes in the chord are B–D–G? Think of the alphabet again. How can you line up those three notes in the alphabet so there is one letter name between each note?

To name the chord, think: What note must go on the bottom so the others line up in thirds above it?

A B C D E F G A B C D E F G

That's right. Even in this mixed-up version, the G must go on the bottom so the other letters line up in thirds above it. Thus the notes B–D–G are still a G chord.

Step 4: Let's figure out what the bottom note must be in these chords in the following diagram. What note must go on the bottom so there is one letter name between each note? (The bottom note will be the name of the chord.) Use the alphabet to get started. A B C D E F G A B C D E F G.

Try to figure out the chord name first by looking only at the notes, then look at the answer. You can also write the notes on the staff and make them line up like snowmen: line-line-line or space-space-space.

You're on your own on the second line.

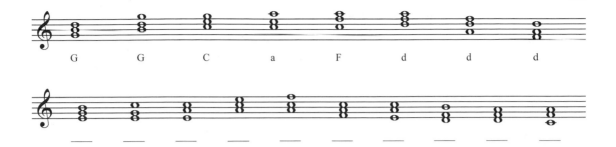

G   G   C   a   F   d   d   d

Step 5: Now that you know the root of these chords, let's analyze what
kind of chords (major, minor, diminished, or augmented)
they are by looking at the interval between each note.

A major chord has a major third on the bot-
tom and a minor third on the top.

A minor chord has a minor third on the bot-
tom and a major third on the top.

A diminished chord has a minor third on the bot-
tom and a minor third on the top.

An augmented chord has a major third on the bot-
tom and a major third on the top.

For example, if you have C–A–E, the A must go on the bottom to line up in
thirds. But what kind of thirds are they? A to C is a minor third, and
C to E is a major third. You remember that a minor third then a major
third is a minor chord. So you have just decoded the A minor chord.

To analyze a chord, ask:

• Which note goes on the bottom of the staff or first in the alphabet?
• Are the intervals between the notes major or minor thirds?
• Is it a major, minor, augmented, or diminished chord?

Step 6: Now go back to step 3 in the above diagram and
write M, m, +, or ° under each chord.

Naming Chord Inversions

Let's first review the names of each note of a chord: the bottom note of the
chord is called the root, the middle note is the third (it's a third above the root),
and the top note is the fifth (it's a fifth above the root.)

The bottom note of the chord is called the _____.

The middle note of the chord is called the _____.

The top note of the chord is called the _____.

You've seen that each chord can be written many different ways. When the
root of the chord appears on the bottom, the chord is said to be in root position.

When the first note of a chord is the middle note of a chord, it's in first inversion, and when the first note of the chord is the fifth, it's called second inversion. For example, a C chord starting on C is root position, a C chord starting on E is in first inversion, and a C chord starting on G is in second inversion.

Under each chord write root, first inversion, or second inversion:

FIGURED BASS

Every scale has seven chords that use the notes of the scale.

Step 1: Write the CM scale.

Step 2: Write the scale tone number above each note. (Above
   C write the number 1, above D write 2, etc.)

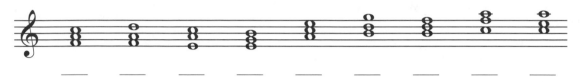

Step 3: You can find the seven chords in the scale by writing thirds
   above each note. Using only the notes in the scale of C major,
   write thirds above each note. (Remember, it is my favorite because it has no sharps or flats.) Above C write C E G, above
   D write D F A, etc. All notes will be in the key of C.

Step 4: Below each chord, write whether it is M (major),
   m (minor), + (augmented), or ° (diminished).

If you did it correctly, your chord analysis should
   be the same as in this example:

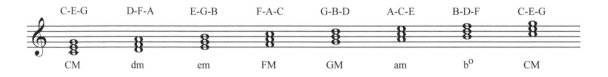

There's a shorthand way to talk about chords in the scale, called figured
   bass. It's been used for hundreds of years, and today *you* get to
   learn it. We use roman numerals to show what note of the scale the
   chord is built on *and* what kind of chord it is. I, II, III, IV, V, VI,
   VII, VIII. I just counted to eight. Each of those uppercase roman

numerals tells us the chord is major. CM: V tells us the chord built on the fifth note of the C scale is a major chord. If you want to show that the chord is minor, just use lowercase numerals: i, ii, iii, iv, v, vi, vii, viii. Augmented = +, diminished = °. Got it?

Here's how the chords in the G major scale would look:

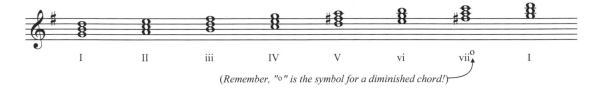

| I | II | iii | IV | V | vi | vii° | I |

(Remember, "°" is the symbol for a diminished chord!)

Step 5: Go back to your C major scale and write in the roman numerals under each chord.

Step 6: Now compare the chords in the C and G scales. Yes, you're right. They're the same!

Why should you care about figured bass? Keyboard players in the Baroque period were sometimes given only a bass line and figured bass (slightly more complicated than what appears here) upon which to create a keyboard part. Even today, figured bass is a fast, easy way to refer to chords. "Play a V chord there" or "End on the I chord" enables musicians to easily communicate. Knowing figured bass can also help you transpose (change keys), improvise, and compose.

CADENCES

There are three superstar chords: I, IV, and V. The I chord (i chord if it is minor) is the most important. Almost all pieces end, or cadence, with the I chord. The word *cadence* means "a feeling of rest." A piece in a major or minor key won't feel as if it cadences (ends) unless the last chord is the tonic major or minor (I or i) chord. Almost all pieces, and many phrases, end with the pattern of V chord, then a I or i chord. This pattern of V going to I at the end of a phrase or piece is called an authentic cadence. It sounds like "THE END." Ending with a IV chord going to a I chord is called a plagal cadence. You can hear plagal cadences at the end of hymns. They sound like "AMEN." When you hear a V–I or IV–I cadence at the end of the piece, you'll know it's time to wake up and start applauding.

And now it's time for you to wake up and applaud. Congratulations! You made it to the end of the music theory chapters. Of course, there's much, much more to learn, but let's leave that up to your teacher. If you go to college with the knowledge in these chapters, you'll have a great head start in your music theory classes and won't have to hide in the back of the room as I once did.

GREAT IDEAS

Music theory is more than an amusing puzzle to unravel. It's the math and the language of music. Just as learning grammar, verb forms, punctuation, and vocabulary enable you to become a better writer, learning music theory helps you to become a better musician. Incorporate your knowledge of music theory into your playing every day, and you'll become a sophisticated listener and more musical player.

Sneak Preview

To really understand classical music, you'll want to know the composers and how the world they lived in affected their music. In the next four chapters, you'll learn about the major periods of music in Western civilization and the key "players" in each.

PART FIVE

TUNE IN TO
CLASSICAL MUSIC

TWENTY-TWO

The Middle Ages and the Renaissance

Do you consider anything written before the 1990s to be "classical" music? Is it hard for you to imagine a world without rap music or hip-hop? If the answer is yes, it's time for you to take a trip back in time and make music history come alive! In this chapter and the next three, you'll learn about the major music events that helped shape the music you enjoy today.

We will be talking about music centered in Europe, but of course other musical traditions were growing around the world.

WHY SHOULD I LEARN ABOUT THE HISTORY OF MUSIC?

You'll see how the world the composers lived in affected their music.

Living conditions, architecture, religion, art, and wars have changed composers' views and the way they express themselves through their music. In fact, many pieces of music are religious or political statements in themselves. Beethoven originally dedicated his third symphony, the *Eroica,* to Napoleon, but tore up his title page in disgust when he learned that Napoleon had declared himself emperor of France. Shostakovich wrote his seventh symphony during the siege of Leningrad in World War II, with the sounds of battle in his ears and in his music. Classical music and musicians are part of history, just as political figures and the events they created are. To really study history, we must include not only politics but also art, music, and architecture. Political leaders and wars aren't the only important things that shape civilization.

You'll empathize with composers' struggles and triumphs.

Knowing that Mozart, desperately trying to find a job, had to travel through Europe in a cold carriage over pothole-filled dirt roads helps us understand the hopefulness and yet the sometimes underlying current of sadness in his music. When you know about Tchaikovsky's personal traumas and depression, you can better hear the emotions in his music. Knowing the emotions the composer intended makes it easier for us, as musicians, to understand the music.

You'll join composers' family trees while making your own musical "family" tree.

Bach came from a very long line of great musicians, spread over seven generations and three centuries. But when we play Bach, we too become part of his family tree. We carry on the "family tradition" as we keep the music of past centuries alive today. And you develop your own musical tree each time you add another composer to the music that you perform.

You'll learn how to imitate the styles of the times.

Do the trills start on the higher note? Was the piece really written for the harpsichord and not the piano? What kind of vibrato was common? Is it okay to stretch the phrases to make them more musical? How did the composer visualize the performance?

You'll discover more music to love.

To know it is to love it!

As you read each chapter of music history, please take time to listen to music of the great composers from those periods. Sampling each period's music will help you recognize some of the trends and composers. Remembering the composers and styles of each era without listening to music would be as tough as trying to remember artists and art styles by reading a textbook with no pictures. Don't be in a rush to finish. Enjoy discovering your own favorites.

You'll find suggested listening to get you started at the end of each musical period listed. In chapter 27, "Hey, Listen to This!" I've included my list of all-time favorite pieces. Web tip: of course, you can find much more about your favorites on the internet. So load that playlist and take a tour through history.

THE MAJOR MUSICAL PERIODS

Music changes with the times.

Have you ever watched a movie and guessed it was old just from the actors' hairstyles? Styles change. Tie-dyed shirts, jeans, beads, long hair, and lime green polyester suits—all high style in the 1970s! Nobody made us dress like that, but most people did. There are no laws or rules governing how a composer is supposed to write, but as in fashion, similarities in each period existed until one or more composers "broke out of the mold" and changed how music was written. Have you heard stories about the outraged TV viewers that "Elvis the Pelvis" shocked with his "indecent" hip moves? Talk about resisting a transition. TV producers "cropped" his future appearances so viewers saw him move only from the waist up. Or how about your parents' reaction when they first heard rap? You may not like your parents' music, and they probably rebelled against your grandparents' music.

Things weren't any different in the time of earlier composers. When Igor Stravinsky's ballet *The Rite of Spring* was first performed, it caused a riot. Transitions from one musical period to the next have always shocked audiences. Classical music of each period became an overreaction to what preceded it.

Historians divide the history of music in Western civilization into large spans of time called musical periods. Each period represents unique living conditions, types of instruments, performance possibilities, architecture, religion, art, and even wars. Musicians were influenced by the events of their day and by other composers, past and present. With careful listening, you can learn to identify what period a piece was written in and who the composer was just by listening.

THE MUSIC OF THE EARLY CATHOLIC CHURCH, 800–1100

Of course, people have been singing and making music on tree branches and gourds for eons, but we have no record of it. We know that music was of great importance to Greeks and Romans in the centuries BC, but we don't know how the music sounded. We get some idea from writing, art, and archaeology about the types of instruments they had, such as drums, harp, reed flutes, and bells. Every composer is limited by the types of instruments and types of performance available at the time and by what they have heard or played. Imagine what Jimi Hendrix or the Rolling Stones might have tried if they had lived in 960, when rhythm and sounds had such a limited palette compared with 1960! The pace of change in musical instruments and composition has been accelerating faster and faster in the past 50–75 years. What do you think will be the innovations in music in 2108? Which composers' or groups' music will still be played and loved as much as today?

Music of the Monks

The first written music was that of the Catholic monks. They lived in monasteries and had a very plain daily routine—and they had to wear those ugly brown robes! Their days were spent working, praying, and singing. The music the monks composed is called Gregorian chant, named after Pope Gregory I. Gregorian chant, or plainsong, is a simple melody sung in unison without any accompaniment. The melody follows normal vocal inflection in a sentence. If the voice would normally rise or fall for a particular word or syllable, the melody would imitate this pattern. Listening to Gregorian chant will take you back in time 1,000 years.

Harmony! What a great idea!

Imagine five eleventh-century monks huddled together in a vast cathedral chanting the daily prayers. Suddenly one monk has a brilliant idea: "Let's sing in harmony!" Well, kind of in harmony. He sings along an octave lower or higher. OK, it's a start. Sometime within the next century some other adventurous monks start to sing not only in parallel octaves but also in parallel fourths, fifths, or octaves and fifths at the same time. (That means they would sing the very same melody but four or five notes higher. What a concept!) As time went on, the monks got more adventurous, and two or more vocal lines became more independent and more beautiful. This weaving together of independent lines is called polyphony, which means "many sounds."

The first sheet music. Ever.

As music became increasingly "complicated," the old system of learning by imitation or rote was no longer efficient. Luckily, around the year 900, the monks began to figure out an effective way to write the music down, because it would be way too hard to learn by rote. (One of my favorite cartoons is of a monk coming into a room and seeing another monk sleeping over the manuscript he was copying and exclaiming, "Oh, no, the copier is down!")

The monks started out with a one-lined colored staff. Centuries later, the staff grew to five lines without any cool colors. In the fourteenth century, ways to show rhythm were developed. The notes were square because they were drawn with quills. When we look at these old manuscripts now, they look to us like electrocardiograms (computer printouts of heartbeats). But they were an amazing invention that allowed music to become more intricate and to be passed down from generation to generation.

THE MIDDLE AGES, 1100–1400

The first professional musicians

The monks of Europe soon lost out on their "exclusive rights" to write for the church as other musicians began writing intricate polyphonic music for the church service, called the Mass. Composers, though still mainly employed by the church, now began writing secular (nonreligious) music, too. These new compositions joined a growing repertoire of what we might call "folk music," written and passed down from musician to musician. Professional entertainers (men in tights) roamed Europe singing love songs and playing instruments. They also juggled, performed acrobatics, told stories, read poetry, and danced. Thus the hectic life of the professional musician began.

Great Composers of the Middle Ages

(In chronological order)
Anonymous (by far the most prolific composer!)
Hildegard von Bingen (a woman!) (1098–1178)
Guillaume de Machaut (1304–77)

Greatest Hits from the Middle Ages

Hildegard von Bingen: *Ordo Virtutum*
Guillaume de Machaut: *Messe de Notre Dame*

The Middle Ages was a time of wars and plagues. There was not much time or energy to spend composing. But things changed in the Renaissance, which means "rebirth." Looking back to ancient Greece and Rome for inspiration, Europeans experienced renewed interest in art and education. The Renaissance saw an explosion of painting, sculpture, architecture, travel, music, and invention. Once again music was a vital part of a well-rounded education. Even today, we use the term *Renaissance man* to describe a cultured person who has a broad education and is proficient in both the arts and the sciences.

New instruments are invented.

Composers matched the beauty of art by Michelangelo and Leonardo da Vinci with the beauty of more elaborate and energetic music. New musical styles included more appealing melodies and richer harmonies sung by multiple voices. Organs were already in use before the Renaissance, but now the harpsichord became popular. Small ensembles were composed of early forms of instruments we play today. Many of them had odd names like the shawm (oboe), fagot (bassoon), viol (violin), cittern (a cross between a lute and a guitar), and the sackbut (trombone). Try keeping a straight face when you tell friends about your fagot or sackbut!

Patrons provide paychecks.

Composers began to be recognized for their works, and music became a big part of daily life, even for poor common folk. Madrigals, songs written for three or more voices and often set to love poems, grew popular in the Renaissance.

Most Renaissance composers worked for the church, but as the patronage system grew, more were employed by wealthy music lovers. Royalty kept their own in-house orchestra and a composer who wrote music to celebrate every occasion. Although royalty gave composers the same status as maids, their support gave hungry musicians a steady job. Composers began to write more music outside the church that used instruments as well as voices.

Palestrina saves the day.

People across Europe were thrilled with the new music with its richer textures and melodies of the new polyphonic style. However, the Roman Catholic Church, still a major patron of the arts, was not the least bit thrilled. In the early 1500s, the church proclaimed polyphonic music too fancy and too complicated. It was deemed too distracting for worship services because sometimes the instruments and voices drowned out the words of prayers. Pope Marcellus II, who considered this style of music dangerous, recommended that sacred music return to the style of Gregorian chant. The church might have banned music from services altogether if composer Giovanni Pierluigi da Palestrina had not saved the day. The Mass he wrote (and cleverly named after the pope) in the new polyphonic style was so beautiful that the pope changed his mind. For centuries, the Roman Catholic Church continued to actively support the creation of new music and commissioned the best composers of the time to write new sacred works. It's hard to imagine how long unison sacred music would have lasted without Palestrina's talent.

The printing press brings power to the people.

The world of music changed dramatically with invention of the mechanical printing press by Johannes Gutenberg in 1436. Now music could easily be duplicated and mass-produced (so long, "sleepy monk" jokes). More music reached the hands and lives of ordinary people, and composers enjoyed widespread fame. Above all, the printing press ensured the survival of written music.

Great Composers of the Renaissance

Guillaume Dufay (1400–74)

Josquin Desprez (1440–97)

Thomas Tallis (1505–85)

Giovanni Pierluigi da Palestrina (1525–94)

William Byrd (1543–1623)

Giovanni Gabrieli (1553–1612)

John Dowland (1563–1626)

Greatest Hits from the Renaissance

Thomas Tallis: *Spem in alium*

Giovanni Pierluigi da Palestrina: *Missa Papae Marcelli*

John Dowland: songs for lute and voice

Giovanni Gabrieli: *Hodie Christus natus est*

Sneak Preview

Although the pope thought music was becoming too complicated in the Renaissance, he should have heard it in the Baroque period. Talk about fancy. Next, learn how music changed in the following 150 years.

TWENTY-THREE

The Baroque and Classical Periods

Have you ever heard someone use the expression "gilding the lily"? It means decorating an already perfect or beautiful thing. If so, they could have been talking about the Baroque era. Architects designed churches and palaces on a grand scale. Decorators adorned churches with ornate marble, gold, cherubs, domed ceilings with murals, and enough statues of angels and saints to make you think you had died and gone to heaven.

Baroque music matched these rich decorations with its own. Composers adorned their music with cascades of notes and elaborate ornaments (added trills and notes to make it sound fancier). If you ever have a chance to visit Europe, go! Standing in a cathedral under a cavernous dome will help you understand the beauty and power of the Baroque period.

Star performers

Although there were few public concerts, music gained an audience beyond churchgoers. Musicians became more skilled, and some even became famous. Composers wrote more elaborate music for these superstars. To hear a sample of a "show-off violin," listen to "Spring" from Vivaldi's *Four Seasons* concerto.

Improvements in organs made that instrument the crowning glory of the day, and almost every church and cathedral had a spectacular one. Instruments kept changing, and violins replaced the old, softer viols. Using a special wood, Stradivari crafted the highest-quality violins ever (now worth millions—and no, the violin in your attic is not a Strad.) The transverse or horizontal flute replaced recorders, and the hunting horn morphed into the French horn. In 1709 the first piano was made. It was truly remarkable because, unlike the harpsichord, whose strings are plucked when the keyboard is fingered, it could produce soft and loud sounds according to touch by striking the strings with padded hammers.

New groups and new forms of music

For the first time, musicians grouped instruments to form orchestras of strings, wind instruments, and kettledrums. More people owned instruments and invited friends to join them in playing chamber music. Remember, there were no televisions, radios, internet, recordings, or iPods. (How could you survive?) The only way to hear music was to perform it or hear it live.

Composers and performers during the Baroque period developed new forms of music.

- *Solo sonata:* For solo instrument, keyboard, and bass, in three or four movements of different speeds.
- *Trio sonata:* Like a solo sonata, but for two melody instruments and accompaniment.
- *Dance suites:* A group of dances loosely strung together.
- *Concerto:* A piece for soloist and orchestra usually in three movements.
- *Concerto grosso:* (No, not a *gross* concerto!) A "big" concerto for two or more soloists.
- *Opera:* A dramatic work where the actors sing rather than speak their lines.

Claudio Monteverdi, who was already famous for writing madrigals, became even more popular after writing his opera *Orfeo.* The operas that had been written earlier were just vehicles for singers to show off, and the words and plots were downright silly. In *Orfeo,* music was center stage, and Monteverdi's characters came to life through their arias. *Orfeo* paved the way for more dramatic, emotional operas, although some that are performed today still seem downright silly.

THE BAROQUE PERIOD, CA. 1600–1750

Johann Sebastian Bach and George Frideric Handel set the bar high for composers of the Baroque period. Even now when you go to music school, it's their music you study.

Bach's family produced several generations of musicians. Regarded as one of the great musical geniuses of all time, Bach was the grand master of polyphony (weaving several melodies together.) He wrote stunningly beautiful music for voice and instruments that ranged from sweet and simple to complicated and powerful. In Bach's time, composers created music for the needs of their employers. Like so many other composers, Bach held many jobs but struggled to earn a living. Plus, he had 20 children (and plenty of distractions while he composed). He was one busy guy!

People traveled far to hear his organ improvisations, sometimes trying to test him with melodies they thought were impossible to improvise on. But Bach was such a genius at composing on the spot and such a skilled organist (especially with his feet!) that he amazed everyone who heard him. Bach composed more than 1,000 works before he died in 1750, but he left his second wife poor. After his death, his reputation as a composer faded, and he was mainly remembered as an amazing organist, teacher, and father of musically talented sons. Not until many years later when Felix Mendelssohn revived and conducted the *St. Matthew Passion* did Bach's music reenter churches and concert halls.

Although Handel's father never wanted him to be a musician, George didn't listen. He became a very successful composer—one of those few who didn't have to wait until he died to become rich and famous. Handel's Italian operas were all the rage in London, but he is best remembered for the *Water Music* (composed for a trip down the river Thames by George I), the *Music for the Royal Fireworks* (which ended with a massive fire), and his beloved oratorio, *Messiah*. *Messiah* was written in just under three weeks (it's about two hours long) and contains the "Hallelujah Chorus," which is probably the most famous choral work of all time.

The greatness of music by Handel, Bach, Vivaldi, and other Baroque stars can be seen in the adaptations for many instruments even today. Andrés Segovia's transcriptions of Bach violin or cello sonatas for guitar and James Galway's transcriptions for flute retain their power even when they're played on different instruments. Not surprisingly, Bach's cello suites do not lose their sublime beauty even when played on an electric bass, if the soloist has skill and passion.

For many people, Baroque music at first may seem too complicated, but once you've had a chance to learn and perform one of these pieces, it opens the door to understanding and loving it. That door opened for me in high school when I was singing choruses from Handel's *Messiah,* and I hope you find a favorite Baroque piece of your own to sing or play.

PERFORMANCE STYLES

One of the innovations of the past 40 years is the interest in bringing back the performance style of the seventeenth and eighteenth centuries. Many artists have built entire careers playing on viols, real wood woodwinds, harpsichords, and valveless ("Bach") trumpets. Playing on "authentic" instruments with the style and techniques heard in the Renaissance and Baroque periods is now the preferred sound for many classical musicians.

At the same time, modern brass, woodwind, and piano makers have become so skilled that these new instruments produce a much richer sound and range than Bach or Handel ever imagined. Personally, I think Baroque composers would have loved to have our modern instruments—and they would have been thrilled to have indoor plumbing, too! It's valuable to learn about the performance practices of each period so we can make beautiful music no matter what era our instrument is from. Instruments are still evolving, and with advances in digital technology, who knows what music we will be playing and what instruments we will be playing 50 years from now?

Great Composers of the Baroque Period

Claudio Monteverdi (1567–1643)

Heinrich Schütz (1585–1672)

Jean Baptiste Lully (1632–87)

Arcangelo Corelli (1653–1713)

Johann Pachelbel (1653–1706)

Henry Purcell (1659–95)

François Couperin (1668–1733)

Tomaso Albinoni (1671–1750)

Antonio Vivaldi (1678–1741)

Georg Philipp Telemann (1681–1767)

Jean-Philippe Rameau (1683–1764)

Johann Sebastian Bach (1685–1750)

George Frideric Handel (1685–1759)

Domenico Scarlatti (1685–1767)

Greatest Hits of the Baroque Period

Claudio Monteverdi: *Vespro della Beata Vergine.* These vespers—prayers sung at sunset—are hauntingly beautiful.

Johann Pachelbel: His Canon in D Major is played at almost every wedding.

Arcangelo Corelli: You don't have to wait for the right season to listen to his *Christmas Concerto.*

Antonio Vivaldi: You probably already know the *Four Seasons* concerto. Don't miss his *Gloria* mass.

Tomaso Albinoni: The Adagio in G Minor is waves upon waves of beauty that can stop a war. It is the piece played by Vedran Smailovic 22 nights in a row in 1992 (wearing his full concert tuxedo with tails and white tie) in the bombed-out rubble of Sarajevo to protest the ongoing war and the 22 victims killed in a bread line. The beautiful Adagio and Smailovic's courage and elegance inspired the snipers to hold their fire every night!

Johann Sebastian Bach:

Famous tunes: "Jesu, Joy of Man's Desiring," "Sleepers Awake," Air on the G String, "Sheep May Safely Graze," and "Du bist bei mir." Also his Violin Concerto in E Major, Brandenburg Concertos, solo cello suites, flute sonatas, and orchestra suites.

Choral music: Magnificat; the Mass in B Minor; and the *St. Matthew Passion.*

George Frideric Handel: *Water Music* and *Music for the Royal Fireworks* are filled with hummable tunes. The *Messiah* is a Christmas tradition around the world.

THE CLASSICAL PERIOD, CA. 1750–1820

It can get a little tricky at times, but, yes, we call one of the periods in classical music the "Classical" period. In this period, music became available to an even broader class of citizens. People saw music as an "innocent luxury" and wanted new music.

The Classical period of architecture (including the style of our White House) imitated the ancient cultures and art of Greece and Rome. In music, classical composers went "back to the basics" and wrote their music to be clean, simple, and elegant. Gone was the "heavy, formal, fussy" polyphony of the Baroque. In contrast, the Classical style emphasized a single unadorned melody enhanced by blocks of harmony—more like singing and playing chords on the guitar.

Transitioning to the Classical Style

Bach's three famous sons, Wilhelm Friedemann, Carl Philipp Emanuel, and Johann Christian Bach, each had one foot in the Baroque style and one foot in the Classical style. Bach's boys thought their dad's music was old-fashioned, and after Bach's death in 1750, they paved the way for the new style. (Bach's daughters were home doing the dishes.)

Papa Haydn

Now composers wrote more music for instruments than for voices (they still do). In the Baroque period, the largest work was the orchestral suite, but in the Classical period, Franz Joseph Haydn began writing large-scale orchestral works in four movements, called symphonies. "Papa Haydn" is called the "Father of the Symphony." Although he didn't really invent the symphony, writing 104 of them should count for something. He also solidified the form of the string quartet, the most popular chamber music ensemble today. It has four movements written with contrasting speeds and emotion and is usually written for an ensemble of two violins, viola, and cello.

Although the orchestra that Haydn conducted was smaller than our modern symphony, it still needed a concert hall to be heard. People began to attend public concerts in concert halls instead of just in the king's palace or the nobleman's castle. Composers formerly employed by the church or noblemen now found themselves unemployed and hungry.

Haydn was one of the few lucky composers who enjoyed the luxury of being steadily employed by wealthy patrons. "My Prince was always satisfied with my works," he said. "I not only had the encouragement of constant approval but as conductor of an orchestra I could make experiments and be as bold as I pleased." Haydn had a long and successful career, and his music set the stage for the works of Mozart and Beethoven.

Little Boy Wonder

Later in the Classical period came child prodigy Wolfgang Amadeus Mozart. While most 4-year-olds were toddling around their houses playing with blocks and dolls, Mozart was busy composing and playing the violin. Mozart never had to go to school. Instead, he toured Europe with his talented sister, Nannerl, performing on harpsichord and violin for kings and noblemen. The boy astonished audiences, including royalty and successful composers. He even had a few lessons from Haydn, which brings me to this joke: Why couldn't Mozart find his teacher? Because he was Haydn!

Mozart struggled all his life to earn a living, but he never struggled to compose as Beethoven later did. Music came to him as if in a dream, and all he had to do was write it down. His elegant, emotional music became the crowning jewels of the Classical period. He wrote 41 symphonies, 40 concerti (plural of concerto), many chamber music pieces, and operas. The last piece he wrote (and never finished) was his dramatic *Requiem* (Mass for the dead), which he wrote as he was dying at the age of 35. We can only imagine the masterpieces that were left unwritten. Check out the movie *Amadeus* to get a feel for Mozart's life and music.

Great Composers of the Classical Period

> Christoph Willibald Gluck (1714–87)
>
> Franz Joseph Haydn (1732–1809)
>
> Luigi Boccherini (1743–1805)
>
> Wolfgang Amadeus Mozart (1756–91)

Greatest Hits of the Classical Period

> Franz Joseph Haydn: his cello concertos; Symphony no. 45 (*Farewell*), written to give his patron the hint that the orchestra wanted to go home; Symphony no. 94 (*Surprise*), written to wake up anyone sleeping in the audience; Symphony no. 103 (*Drum Roll*); and Symphony no. 104 (*London*).
>
> Wolfgang Amadeus Mozart: Symphony no. 39 in D Major, K. 504 (*Prague*); Symphony no. 40 in G Minor, K. 550; Symphony no. 41, K. 551 (*Jupiter*); *Eine kleine Nachtmusik* (*A Little Night Music*); divertimenti; and the *Requiem*.

Sneak Preview

Do you need a little more romance in your life? Read about the sometimes radical Romantic period in the next chapter.

TWENTY-FOUR

The Romantic Period

LUDWIG VAN BEETHOVEN

Although Beethoven lived in the Classical period (his dates are 1770–1827), he revolutionized music with a bang. The rules and controls of the Classical period gave way to a brand-new kind of music with more intensity, emotion, and freedom. Composers used more dynamics, chromatics, and modulation. Symphonies were longer and used bigger orchestras. Music became—you guessed it—more romantic.

A New Kind of Music

What led Beethoven to be such a rebel? When he was 31, Beethoven realized he was nearly deaf. At first he was despondent, but then his true character shone through. Instead of giving up on life, he devoted himself to creating a new kind of music. Until then, his music had been rooted in the Classical period, but everything changed with his third symphony, the *Eroica* (Heroic). This new kind of romantic music was like Beethoven himself. He was known for his convictions and emotional outbursts (he never did well with landladies or girlfriends), and his music had the same emotional character. The strong, driving rhythms like the "ta-ta-ta-daaa" of his fifth symphony, sudden dynamic changes, and intensely emotional passages depict sorrow changing to joy and hope. His perseverance shines through in his music.

When Beethoven premiered his famous ninth symphony to a packed audience, he had not appeared on stage in 12 years. He had to share it with the "official" conductor, who had instructed the singers and orchestra to ignore Beethoven. Now totally deaf, Beethoven stayed off to the side during the performance, turning pages of his score and beating time to an orchestra he could not hear.

The symphony ended, and the crowd broke into thunderous applause. Beethoven, still several measures behind, kept conducting. He had no idea of the ecstatic reception to his masterpiece because he couldn't hear the applause. A singer turned him to face his adoring yet sympathetic audience. They honored him with five standing ovations and, knowing he couldn't hear their cheers, raised their hands and threw hats and handkerchiefs into the air for him to see.

Composers do their own thing.

Beethoven had changed the rules, and because of this new freedom, composers were more creative and individual and much harder to "typecast." Their works are all so different, it is hard to place them in the same category. Some, like Beethoven and Mendelssohn, tried to imitate nature, while Paganini and Liszt wrote virtuosic music to further their dazzling solo performing careers. Other composers, such as Dvorak, Mussorgsky, and Rimsky-Korsakov, wrote nationalistic music as a tribute to their countries. Pianist Chopin wrote almost exclusively for his instrument, while Berlioz loved a huge orchestra and chorus. The operas of Verdi and Wagner are not at all similar. These composers can only be categorized together because they lived in the same era and they wrote wonderful music.

Program music

Music in the Romantic period began to tell a story. Program music (music that depicts a person, nature, mood, event, or literature) was used in the symphonic poem/tone poem (one movement composition using program music) and even in many quartets, concert overtures, and piano pieces. We can hear war, thunder, laughter, tears, sighs, birds, horses, and even the devil! These Romantic composers were pretty dramatic.

Listen to Beethoven's Symphony no. 6 (*Pastoral*) to hear his story about a day in the country. You'll hear the babbling brook, the nightingale, quail, and cuckoo, and country folk dancing. You'll almost feel the rain as it begins to drip, finally ending in a huge thunderstorm. Watch the movie *Fantasia* to see what Walt Disney did with this program music.

Nationalism

Composers from Russia, Germany, Spain, England, and Hungary showed their pride in their country by using folk songs and folklore to inspire their symphonies and other works. You can hear the music of nationalistic composers such as Antonin Dvorak, Bedrich Smetana, Gustav Holst, Edvard Grieg, Jan Sibelius, and Mikhail Glinka and immediately know where they were born. (Americans were too busy trying to form a nation and only later developed a national musical style.)

The main audience for music was now the middle class. No more kings and queens for patrons. Composers and instrumentalists had to fend for themselves. (Today we call this freelancing.) Going to concerts was the "in" thing to do, and many composers became famous.

The crowd goes wild.

Virtuoso performers were treated like rock stars. Niccolò Paganini was such a great violinist (sometimes playing concerts on only three strings) that he was rumored to be possessed by the devil. Women fainted, threw their jewelry onto the stage, and threw themselves at Franz Liszt when he played the piano. (Sometimes he fainted, too.)

Not content to write in the style of Beethoven or Brahms, some composers wanted to become even wilder. Richard Wagner, who was not afraid to walk over anyone, had such a distinct personality and musical vision that he became a superstar. Wagner changed traditional opera into music drama. In his operas, the music never stopped and was made up of themes that represented different people and things, called *leitmotifs*. Not content to stay in any key for long, Wagner's music modulates so quickly that sometimes you can't tell what key it's in. Audiences still throng to hear his very dramatic and very long four-opera cycle, *The Ring of the Nibelung*. He set the stage for composers of the contemporary period to abandon all rules about harmony and form.

Great Composers of the Romantic Period

> Ludwig van Beethoven (1770–1827)
> Niccolò Paganini (1782–1840)
> Gioacchino Rossini (1792–1868)
> Franz Schubert (1797–1828)
> Hector Berlioz (1803–69)
> Felix Mendelssohn (1809–47)
> Frederic Chopin (1810–49)
> Robert Schumann (1810–56)
> Franz Liszt (1811–86)
> Richard Wagner (1813–83)
> Giuseppe Verdi (1813–1901)
> Johann Strauss (1825–99)
> Alexander Borodin (1833–87)
> Johannes Brahms (1833–97)
> Camille Saint-Saëns (1835–1921)
> Georges Bizet (1838–75)
> Modest Mussorgsky (1839–81)
> Peter Tchaikovsky (1840–93)
> Antonin Dvorak (1841–1904)
> Edvard Grieg (1843–1907)
> Nikolai Rimsky-Korsakov (1844–1908)
> Gabriel Fauré (1845–1924)
> Edward Elgar (1857–1934)
> Gustav Mahler (1860–1911)
> Richard Strauss (1864–1949)
> Jean Sibelius (1865–1957)

Greatest Hits from the Romantic Period

This book would have to be a lot, lot longer if I were to list them all. Here are some of the blockbusters:

Ludwig van Beethoven: all the symphonies; Violin Concerto in D; *Leonore* Overture no. 3; Piano Concerti nos. 4 and 5; *Ode to Joy*; Piano Sonata no. 23 in F Minor (*Appassionata*); Piano Sonata no. 14 in C-sharp Minor (*Moonlight*); Piano Trio in B-flat (*Archduke*)

Niccolo Paganini: 24 Caprices

Gioacchino Rossini: *The Barber of Seville* (opera); *William Tell* Overture

Felix Mendelssohn: Octet, overture to *A Midsummer Night's Dream*; Violin Concerto in E Minor, op. 64; Symphony no. 4 (*Italian*)

Hector Berlioz: *Symphonie Fantastique*

Frederic Chopin: Piano Concerti in E Minor and F Minor

Robert Schumann: *Carnaval*, Symphonies nos. 2 and 3

Franz Liszt: Hungarian Rhapsodies

Alexander Borodin: *On the Steppes of Central Asia*

Georges Bizet: *Carmen, L'Arlésienne* Suites

Johannes Brahms: all the piano trios, quartets, and quintets; all four symphonies; violin concerto; and his *German Requiem*

Camille Saint-Saëns: *Carnival of the Animals;* Symphony no. 3 (*Organ*); Cello Concerto

Modest Mussorgsky: *A Night on Bare Mountain; Pictures at an Exhibition*

Nikolai Rimsky-Korsakov: *Scheherazade; Capriccio Espagnol*

Peter Tchaikovsky: Symphonies nos. 4–7; *The Nutcracker; Swan Lake; Romeo and Juliet;* Piano Concerto no. 1

Antonin Dvorak: Symphony no. 9 (*New World*); Cello Concerto; Slavonic Dances

Giuseppe Verdi: *Otello, Rigoletto; La Traviata; Falstaff; Requiem*

Richard Wagner: *The Ring of the Nibelung; The Flying Dutchman; Lohengrin; Tristan and Isolde*

Edvard Grieg: Piano Concerto in A Minor; *Peer Gynt* Suites

Nikolai Rimsky-Korsakov: *Scheherazade; Capriccio Espagnol*

Gabriel Fauré: Requiem Mass

Edward Elgar: Cello Concerto

Richard Strauss: *Also Sprach Zarathustra*

Sneak Preview

Wow! The Romantic period has such a wide variety and richness of music. Most teens like music from this period the best. Take your time and sample its music, learn about its composers, and discover your own lifetime favorites. But it doesn't stop here. Our next chapter will take you back to the future.

TWENTY-FIVE

The Contemporary Period

IMPRESSIONISTIC MUSIC

Claude Debussy: Rebel with a Cause

If you thought Romantic composers were individuals, wait until you hear what happened next. Frenchman Claude Debussy used whole tone scales (scales in which every interval is a whole step) to create impressionistic music. The Paris Conservatory called him on the carpet for not using the standard compositional forms, but he didn't care. He was tired of the same old rules for harmony and wanted music to be freer. In Debussy's music there are no distinct phrases, only themes that drift in and out and change, creating a dreamy mood. Debussy's music mimics the great Impressionistic painters of the day, such as Monet and Renoir. Look at some of their paintings to get a feel for what Debussy was trying to express. You might think of Debussy's music as written in chalk and slightly blurred—sort of like New Age music you would hear in a spa but lots, lots better. Debussy "broke the mold" and led the way for experiments with form and tonality.

The traditionalists

Other composers, though totally original in their own right, continued to use the traditional system of major and minor scales, but with new twists and turns of harmonies and rhythms. Those composers included Barber, Gershwin, Holst, Vaughan Williams, Rachmaninov, Bartok, Copland, and Britten. Others, including Prokofiev and Poulenc, wrote in a neoclassical style using the forms and style of the Classical period with a more modern harmony. Their music sometimes sounds like Bach or Mozart with wrong notes or surprises.

Igor Stravinsky Causes a Riot

Rabble-rouser Igor Stravinsky was the next composer to stun audiences. His ballets, *The Firebird* and *Petrushka,* caused a sensation, but the debut of his *Rite of Spring* in 1913 caused a riot. The clashing harmonies, short fragments instead of melodies, and jarring use of dissonance incited the frightened Parisian audience to walk out en masse. In the Disney movie *Fantasia,* the animation for the *Rite of Spring* depicts the beginnings of time and the violent extinction of the dinosaurs. This is really wild music!

What happened to the key signature?

Now composers didn't feel they had to have a key signature. At first composers such as Richard Strauss, Richard Wagner, and Gustav Mahler wandered at length through different keys. Later, others decided to break all the rules. Arnold Schoenberg and Alban Berg agreed that music needn't be in any key at all. *Atonality* meant that no notes were wrong—although sometimes it sounds as if no notes are right, either!

You call that music?

Schoenberg played intellectual games with music and made up rules called serialism. Following the rules of serialism meant you couldn't use a note again until you had used the other 11. Composers had to use the same notes in the same order over and over, upside down or backwards. Composing to Schoenberg must have been like playing chess. His compositional techniques, which seemed so odd to the audiences of his time, have become quite common to modern-day composers.

You call that an instrument?

Composers used instruments in different ways, too. String players began to play on the stick of the bow and past the bridge. "Prepared" pianos had small objects put inside them to make noises. Flutists slapped the keys, played two notes at once, and sang and played at the same time. Even computers and tapes became instruments. John Cage stretched the meaning of music by including the sounds of himself chopping vegetables and drinking juice, using four radios playing at the same time on different stations, and even "performing" four minutes and 33 seconds of silence. The possibilities are endless if not ridiculous.

Modern music leaves behind the idea that music must be pretty and have a form, a distinct melody, or repeated rhythmic patterns. Sometimes the music seems like a rebellious teenager who will go to any length just to be different, and other times it sounds fresh and creative. Who knows what will happen next? Let's keep our ears open and find out.

Great Composers of the Contemporary Period

> Claude Debussy (1862–1918)
>
> Richard Strauss (1864–1949)
>
> Sergei Rachmaninov (1873–1943)
>
> Gustav Holst (1874–1934)
>
> Charles Ives (1874–1954)

Arnold Schoenberg (1874–1951)

Maurice Ravel (1875–1937)

Ottorino Respighi (1879–1936)

Bela Bartok (1881–1945)

Zoltan Kodaly (1882–1967)

Igor Stravinsky (1882–1971)

Alban Berg (1885–1935)

Sergei Prokofiev (1891–1953)

Paul Hindemith (1895–1963)

George Gershwin (1898–1937)

Francis Poulenc (1899–1963)

Aaron Copland (1900–1990)

Joaquin Rodrigo (1902–99)

Dmitri Shostakovich (1906–75)

Samuel Barber (1910–81)

John Cage (1912–92)

Benjamin Britten (1913–76)

Leonard Bernstein (1918–90)

Greatest Hits of the Contemporary Period

Claude Debussy: *Clair de Lune; Prelude to an Afternoon of a Faune; La Mer* (The Sea)

Richard Strauss: *Also Sprach Zarathustra*

Sergei Rachmaninov: Piano Concerto no. 2; Symphonies nos. 1 and 2; *Rhapsody on a Theme of Paganini*

Igor Stravinsky: *The Rite of Spring; The Firebird*

Gustav Holst: *The Planets*

Maurice Ravel: *Bolero; Rhapsodie Espagnole*

Ottorino Respighi: *Pines of Rome; Fountains of Rome*

Sergei Prokofiev: *Peter and the Wolf; Romeo and Juliet*

George Gershwin: *Rhapsody in Blue; Porgy and Bess*

Aaron Copland: *Appalachian Spring; Rodeo; Billy the Kid; El Salon Mexico*

Joaquin Rodrigo: *Concierto de Aranjuez; Fantasía para un gentilhombre*

Dmitri Shostakovich: Symphony no. 10; String Quartet no. 8

Samuel Barber: *Adagio for Strings*

Benjamin Britten: *Young Person's Guide to the Orchestra*

Leonard Bernstein: *West Side Story*

Composers Making Their Mark in the World

John Adams (1947–)

Arvo Part (1935–)

Henryk Gorecki (1933–)

John Tavener (1944–)

Toru Takemitsu (1930–96)

Good job! You just took the jet set musical history tour around the world in 900 years. Having trouble keeping the order of the musical periods straight? Try this handy dandy mnemonic, or make up something just as silly on your own.

To remember the order of the musical periods:

Renaissance	Baroque	Classical	Romantic	Contemporary
Real	Blades	Can	Rip	Cloth
Rapunzel	Borrowed	Cherry	Red	Conditioner
Red	Bugs	Can	Rot	Cupcakes

GREAT IDEAS

If you study the history of the great composers and listen to their works, classical music will become something more to you than what you listen to in the elevator or in restaurants. Knowing about the composers will become more than just another history assignment as you associate them with your favorite pieces and imagine their lives.

Sneak Preview

To know them is to love them, and the more you know about classical composers and their music, the more classical music will become part of your life. Our next chapter gives you even more ideas for your listening journey.

TWENTY-SIX

Why Listen to Classical Music?

Why should you listen to classical music? Why not? You've been listening to it since you were a baby. Did your mom rock you to sleep humming Brahms's *Lullaby*? Did you laugh at Bugs Bunny tormenting Elmer Fudd to Rossini's music from the opera *The Barber of Seville*? Are you looking forward to walking down the aisle at graduation to Elgar's *Pomp and Circumstance*? You hear classical music in TV and radio ads, cartoons, video games, movies, restaurants, and elevators. If I played the top classical melodies, you'd probably recognize most of them. Classical music is everywhere.

WHY DON'T MORE PEOPLE LISTEN TO CLASSICAL MUSIC?

Many people have misconceptions about classical music that keep them from even trying it. They don't bother with classical because they assume it's not their "type." Why does classical music get such a bad spin? Mainly because our education system allows people to grow up with absolutely no exposure to classical music. You can't like what you don't know. But far too many people continue to believe stereotypes like these:

"It's not cool to listen to classical music."
Some people assume classical music lovers are all snobby or too rich to be normal people. Others look down on classical music fans as "nerds" or weird. They're wrong. All sorts of people love classical music. Don't think you should shun classical music so you can "fit into" some clique at school or because it's what your parents listen to.

"Classical music is for old people."
Who says classical music isn't for young people? If you enjoy pieces such as these, then you like classical music:

1. John Williams, *Harry Potter* soundtrack
2. Tchaikovsky, *The Nutcracker*
3. Hans Zimmer, *Pirates of the Caribbean* soundtrack
4. Saint-Saëns, *Carnival of the Animals*
5. John Williams, *Star Wars* soundtrack

In the United States, a growing number of symphonies dedicate programs and concerts to young people and those who don't usually attend the regular symphony season. The Seattle Symphony has had concerts of cartoon, movie, and video game music and even a concert with circus performers onstage. Crossover classical artists such as Wynton Marsalis, Yo-Yo Ma, and James Galway appeal to a wide audience, and the Young Eight are playing to sellout crowds with an eclectic mix of hits from Mendelssohn, 50 Cent, and Beyoncé.

Joshua Bell, a gifted violinist, charms audiences and has been called a "prince of music" and a "classics hunk." He has brought legions of young fans to classical music who never expected to like it (and who perhaps even had said they hated it). Check out his *Voice of the Violin* and *The Romantic Violin*. Classical isn't only for an aging, blue-haired audience of people with their hearing aids turned up. Anyone can join the classical club.

"Classical music is boring!"

Sixteen-year-old Simon has heard that one before. "Most kids think classical music is church music or anything played slow with lots of strings," he says. "They think it's boring and not stimulating." Zoe agrees. "Kids stereotype classical music and think it's all boring. They never take the time to sit down and listen. Lots of kids at school don't like classical music, so some kids are afraid to look uncool if they listen to it."

Your friends who appreciate classical will tell you it's anything *but* boring. Everyone seems perfectly okay when a spooky Bach organ fugue adds to the tension in a horror movie or Tchaikovsky's "Marche Slave" (part of his *1812 Overture*) is heard in an Indiana Jones movie. Do you think classical music will have you nodding off and drooling all over your iPod? Here's a high-energy classical piece that blows that stereotype right out of the water.

A blast from the past

I guarantee you won't nod off listening to Tchaikovsky's *1812 Overture*. It's the piece you've heard at Fourth of July celebrations played in sync with the fireworks display. You'll know the real excitement is at hand when you hear church bells ringing. Then: *Incoming!* Live cannon fire! Back then, cannon fire was not techno music; it was a slice of real life.

The *1812 Overture* really gets around. In the comic strip *Calvin and Hobbes,* Calvin asks his imaginary tiger friend, Hobbes, about the music heard with big booming sounds. "Those are cannons," Hobbes tells him. "And they perform this in crowded concert halls??" Calvin exclaims. "Gee, I thought classical music was boring!" The "wild and crazy" *1812 Overture* has been featured in everything from a 1960s puffed wheat commercial (the cereal is shot from cannons) to *Star Trek* (exploding spaceships) and Notre Dame home football games (starting fourth quarters with a bang).

"Classical music is too old-fashioned."
Many fans of popular music see classical music as stuffy and outdated. True, most classical music was written long before the invention of the computer and even the typewriter. But classical music isn't just a relic from the past. Composers are now writing some pretty wild stuff. And you might be surprised how many modern movie soundtracks include classical music or music written in the classical style. You can even find powerful symphonic music in games like *World of Warcraft* and *Wii Music*.

"Classical music is too confusing."
Classical often comes on a grand scale. Ninety or 100 instruments playing at once creates interesting harmonies and layers of sound. Add in 75 choral singers, and there is a lot going on. Most popular music lovers aren't used to following melodies that fade in and out, interweaving parts and changing time signatures. Not to mention that most people are used to listening to songs 3–5 minutes long. Just one movement of a symphony can last 20 minutes. Sure, classical music is more complicated and unpredictable. Would you trade that for simple and predictable?

IS ALL CLASSICAL MUSIC GREAT?

Do you like every rap song? Are you a fan of every rock group? No. Not all classical music is wonderful, either. Just like other kinds of music, classical music can be dull, ugly, meaningless, or just way too long. Sometimes I go to classical concerts and want to run to the nearest exit. But other times I sit entranced. By exploring recorded and live music, you're bound to find something you like.

We feel more comfortable with what we know.
When people say, "I don't know much about music, but I *know* what I like," what they're really saying is "I don't know much about music, but I *like* what I *know*." Whether it's food, clothing, or music, the unfamiliar is always a tough sell. It's no surprise kids who grow up eating tacos and enchiladas or kimchi and Korean barbeque like that food best as adults. We form our musical tastes the same way.

Musical habits can be hard to change.
Most people identify with music they loved as teens. "Ancient" Beatles songs are etched in *my* brain. People can even guess your age by knowing your favorite kind of music. A couple of San Diego radio DJs wowed their audiences by being able to guess any caller's age within two years. They only had to ask one question: "What is the name of the first album or CD you bought with your own money?" Their nearly spotless record came from knowing that most people make their first big music purchase when they are 14 to 16. That first purchase affects their musical taste for the rest of their lives.

Why Listen to Classical Music?

You will listen to music differently.

People who don't know much about classical music experience it only on an emotional level—how that music makes them feel. Once you understand how complex and clever classical music is, you'll enjoy it with both your heart *and* your brain. Listening to classical music develops your ability to listen more carefully to *any* kind of music.

You will understand the evolution of music.

Soon you'll recognize differences between musical periods and later even between composers. I used to play a car game with my sons. Whenever we heard classical music, we tried to guess the period of music and then the composer. Knowing the great classical works is part of a well-rounded education.

You will learn the basic rules of music.

I'll never forget the first time I saw my husband, Don, play rugby. What in the heck were those guys doing? What's a scrum? A line-out? A fly-half? I didn't know when to cheer or even when they scored. I didn't enjoy the game that much because I spent most of the time just being confused. Don started out at the same knowledge level with classical music. He was a reluctant listener, and I had to tell him whether I thought the performance was good or bad and even when to clap. As with almost anything, once you understand the basics, you'll enjoy it a lot more.

You will learn by (great) example.

If you wanted to speak French using a big vocabulary and a great accent, where could you learn most easily? In France, of course. In France you'll learn by leaps and bounds via "immersion" training. When you hear French pronounced correctly all day, it's easier to imitate and remember those new words. On the other hand, if you were stuck at home and only heard French at a one-hour lesson once a week, you'd still be struggling with your accent, with no fond memories of those éclairs. Learning music by immersion (listening all the time) will make you a better musician fast.

You will improve your sight-reading ability.

Listening to a variety of music even makes you a better sight-reader. Once you've heard common rhythms, note combinations, and phrases over and over, it will be easier for you to count and phrase on your own. When you've heard the major works for your instrument or ensemble, you can impress your friends, teacher, and directors with your uncanny ability to play it right the first time.

Classical sets the bar high.

Classical musicians are usually highly trained and give careful attention to each note and phrase. Even if you don't play classical music, why not learn to give that same care to your own music?

Singers, you benefit, too. In today's world of *American Idol* competitions, it seems everyone wants to be the singer to win next season's competition. The challenging vocal techniques of classical will get you there faster. Whether you sing show tunes, blues, country, gospel, or opera, there's no better way to strengthen your vocal "chops" and extend your range. And if you keep going through this book, you also will learn how to present yourself onstage like a professional and how to bypass stage fright.

Can a rocker learn from classical music?

Classical music gives you a great foundation for any kind of playing. Just ask my son Kyle. After seven years of cello lessons, he immediately could play rock guitar. The training he had received made his fingers fast and strong, taught him music theory, and made him a great listener and sight-reader.

BUT I (SNIFF) ONLY PLAY CLASSICAL MUSIC

And now for you "classical music snobs." Don't miss out on learning about other kinds of music. Listening to jazz, rock, gospel, blues, folk, metal, movie soundtracks, and more can loosen you up, connect you to more people, and be tons of fun. Get out of your shell and listen to all kinds of music. The more you listen to music, the more you'll enjoy it and the better musician you will be.

LEARNING TO LOVE CLASSICAL MUSIC

Who needs classical music? *Every* musician! If you didn't grow up around classical music, it may take a few tries for it to grow on you. That's how you learned to like new foods. As a baby, you didn't gobble up your first bite of pureed prunes. Like most babies, you scrunched your nose in disgust, locked down your lips, made a few gagging sounds for effect, and then launched your spoon into the next room. Babies who are picky eaters need to experience new foods many times before they learn to like them. Are you a "picky" listener? You, too, can listen to classical music without scrunching your nose, gagging, and then launching your radio across the room.

Try it, you'll like it!

When babies eat peas as their first bite of food, after ten days they almost all turn into pea-lovers. Not only do they not gag on peas. They *want* peas and even giggle at the sight of them. Not that I'm comparing classical music to peas, but you can warm up to classical music in the same way.

Most pop music has words, making it easy to understand the mood or the meaning. Classical music has profound emotions, too, but you can supply your own meaning. As you listen, think of how the music makes you feel. Let your mind wander to someone you love, someone who has died, or a favorite moment in your life, and let the music fill you with emotion.

Start with short listening sessions of 15 minutes or so, and stay with a piece until it becomes familiar to you. Sample different composers and think about why you like some pieces better than others. Before long, you may find yourself begging for Bach.

The more (music), the merrier

All music has its merits. Music isn't good or bad, right or wrong. Why waste time arguing about whose music is smarter, better, or cooler? Music isn't meant to divide people into camps according to their age, race, or preferences. Music can unify people with all different tastes. As music lovers, let's welcome our musical differences. It's all good. After all, it's all *music*.

GREAT IDEAS

The more you know about classical music, the more you'll love it.

The best way to learn to play classical music is to listen to classical music.

Listening to classical music will make you a better player, no matter what instrument or type of music you play.

Start by listening to movie and video game music and then progress to blockbuster hits.

Classical music isn't just for old people. It's not too complicated, and it's not boring. It just takes a little longer to understand.

Listening to a variety of music opens up new worlds to you and helps you become a better musician.

To know it is to love it.

Sneak Preview

How do you get started listening to classical music? What pieces are the most exciting? What pieces are the most famous? Turn to the next chapter, and you'll find lots of listening suggestions to get you started.

TWENTY-SEVEN

Hey, Listen to This!

INCORPORATE CLASSICAL MUSIC INTO YOUR LIFE

I want you to fall in love with the world's greatest music, just as generations of other young people have throughout history. It's great to know about the composers and to know how to play an instrument or sing. But that's just an introduction into a world that can enrich your life so much. In this chapter you'll learn about the world's most beloved classical music and get a list of my personal favorites, too.

Don't wait to attend the symphony to explore classical music. Play it while you do chores and homework, and let it lull you to sleep at night. Tune your radio to a classical station at home. Let it stream onto your computer and carry it with you on your iPod. Go to a concert instead of a movie. Weave classical music into your life.

CLASSICAL ON THE CHEAP

Not ready to spend your money on classical music? Visit your local library to check out classical works and read your newspaper's local events section to find free community or college concerts. Visit websites and Classical Live Online Radio to stream music live from more than 100 classical radio stations. Classical radio websites like King.org and Beethoven.com offer free music 24/7. You can also stream free excerpts of classical music at most online music stores and bookstores, like Amazon and Barnes and Noble. Visit the websites of symphonies and classical performers to hear clips of performances. Download classical music one song at a time. Free classical downloads websites like Classical Cat show you where. And don't forget YouTube! That site has tons of videos of some of the greatest performers of today and yesterday.

USE DIFFERENT MUSIC TO CREATE DIFFERENT MOODS

Think for a moment about your tastes in movies. Comedies are my favorite, but I also like animation, action, suspense, and drama. If the only movies you ever saw were "chick flicks," would you miss seeing chase scenes and thrillers? Classical is my favorite music, but I also listen to other kinds to fit my mood. I listen to rock music because it appeals to my "wild side." (Yes, I do have one!) To relax, I might pick cool jazz. I love getting together with friends to sing Renaissance madrigals or folk music. To stay energized for Saturday morning chores, I choose the Beatles, Rolling Stones, or even "Kashmir" by Led Zeppelin.

Choose classical music to fit your mood. These classical mood makers will help you relax or study: Debussy's dreamy *Prelude to the Afternoon of a Faun,* Beethoven's *"Moonlight"* Piano Sonata, Samuel Barber's *Adagio for Strings* (heard in *Platoon*), or the Bach Cello Suites. Want to raise your energy level? Listen to the *Four Seasons* by Vivaldi and Maurice Ravel's captivating *Bolero,* which helped an Olympic skating duo earn a perfect score.

SO MUCH MUSIC, SO LITTLE TIME

With so many composers and so much music, it's hard to know where to start listening. If you're new to classical music, follow our step-by-step plan to becoming acquainted with the world's most popular and loved pieces.

Start with Movie Scores

My son Scott has had years of lessons on the piano, violin, and viola. He's away at college studying to be a pilot, but still listens to classical music. "When I took piano lessons I liked the heavy stuff like Rachmaninov and *Pictures at an Exhibition,*" he says. "Now that I'm in college, I listen to classical music from movies I've seen. I think it's the best music written right now."

More people listen to more classical music in movies than anywhere else. Start with this amazing collection of music by composer John Williams.

Movie music by John Williams:
- *Close Encounters of the Third Kind*
- *Jaws* series
- *Indiana Jones* series
- *Jurassic Park* series
- *Harry Potter* series
- *E.T.*
- *Born on the 4th of July*
- *Catch Me If You Can*
- *Dracula*
- *Schindler's List*
- *Saving Private Ryan*
- *War of the Worlds*

Other great "classical" movie soundtracks:
- *The Lord of the Rings* trilogy
- *Star Wars* series

- *The Godfather* trilogy
- *Star Trek* TV series and films
- *Titanic* soundtrack (the biggest selling orchestral track in history)
- *Psycho* (with the scariest-ever shower scene)

After you've had your fill of classical movie and TV scores, continue your listening with the descriptive classical music that seems as if it were written for movies.

Dramatic Classical Music

- "Jupiter" from *The Planets* by Gustav Holst
- *Bolero* by Maurice Ravel
- "O Fortuna" from *Carmina Burana* by Carl Orff
- "Dies Irae" from *Requiem* by Giuseppe Verdi
- "Dies Irae" from *Requiem* by Wolfgang Amadeus Mozart
- *Flight of the Bumblebee* by Nikolai Rimsky-Korsakov
- *Rhapsody in Blue* by George Gershwin
- Hungarian Rhapsodie no. 2 in C Minor by Franz Liszt
- Hungarian Dance no. 5 by Johannes Brahms
- *Also Sprach Zarathustra* by Richard Strauss (music from 2001: A Space Odyssey)
- "Sabre Dance" from the ballet *Gayne* by Aram Khachaturian
- *Capriccio Espagnol* by Nikolai Rimsky-Korsakov
- *A Night on Bare Mountain* by Modest Mussorgsky (used in the movie Fantasia)
- "The Ride of the Valkyries" from *Die Walküre* by Richard Wagner (the music for the lady opera singers with horns on their helmets)

Classical music doesn't have to be so dramatic to be good. Listen to these pieces that always top the classical music listening polls for kids.

More Classical Favorites

- *Peter and the Wolf* (complete with narrator) by Sergei Prokofiev
- *The Blue Danube* by Johann Strauss Jr.
- "Ah! Vous dirai-je, Maman" by Wolfgang Amadeus Mozart (variations on "Twinkle, Twinkle Little Star")
- *William Tell* Overture by Gioacchino Rossini
- *Peer Gynt* Suite by Edvard Grieg
- *Für Elise* by Ludwig van Beethoven
- *Can-Can* by Jacques Offenbach
- "Dance of the Hours" from *La Gioconda* by Amilcare Ponchielli (the dancing hippos in *Fantasia*)
- *Nutcracker* ballet by Tchaikovsky

Looking into the future, these well-known classical pieces are what you might have at your wedding, but don't wait until then to listen to them.

- Canon in D Major by Johann Pachelbel
- *Bridal Chorus* by Richard Wagner (Here Comes the Bride)
- Selections from the *Water Music* and *Music for the Royal Fireworks* by George Frideric Handel
- *Ode to Joy* by Ludwig van Beethoven
- *Trumpet Voluntary* by Jeremiah Clarke
- *Trumpet Tune* by Henry Purcell
- Selections from *The Four Seasons* by Antonio Vivaldi
- *Ave Maria* by Franz Schubert
- Air from Orchestra Suite no. 3 in D Major by J. S. Bach
- *Jesu, Joy of Man's Desiring* by J. S. Bach
- Largo from *Xerxes* by George Frideric Handel
- Selections from *Eine kleine Nachtmusik* by Wolfgang Amadeus Mozart
- *Bridal March* by Felix Mendelssohn

My Favorite Pieces

Now that you've had a chance to sample some of the world's most popular classical music, I would like to share with you some of my favorite pieces. This is the music I would want on my iPod if I were stranded on a desert island. I think they're all great, but I've put an asterisk (*) by the ones I think are standouts. This list may not have all the important composers or the most important works, but these are pieces I hope you will love as much as I do.

A
Tomaso Albinoni (1671–1750)
Adagio in G Minor (slow, moody music actually composed by Remo Giazotto)

B
Johann Sebastian Bach (1685–1750)
Choral music:
*Magnificat**
All the motets (*Singet dem Herrn ein Neues Lied* and *Komm, Jesu Komm* are my favorites)
Coffee Cantata (yes, it's about the joys of drinking coffee, but it doesn't mention Starbucks)

Keyboard:
Toccata and Fugue in D Minor (this will make you wish you played the organ)
French Suites
English Suites
Goldberg Variations

Instrumental:
Brandenburg Concertos* (no. 3 is especially lively)
Orchestra Suites no. 2
Italian Concerto
Unaccompanied Cello Suites* (the most perfect music for cello solo)
Concerto for Two Violins in D minor
Violin Concerto in E Major
Air

Samuel Barber (1910–81)
Adagio for Strings

Ludwig van Beethoven (1770–1827)
Symphony 5* (you know, the famous ta-ta-ta-taaa
    theme of fate knocking on the door)
Symphonies 3, 6, 7, 9* (actually, all nine of them!)
Egmont Overture
Violin Concerto*
Piano Concerto no. 5* (*Emperor*)
Für Elise
Piano Sonata no. 14 (*Moonlight*)
Piano Sonata no. 23 (*Appassionata*)
Sonata for Violin and Piano no. 9 in A Major (*Kreutzer*)
Piano Trio no. 7 (*Archduke*)
Ode to Joy (from Symphony no. 9) (this triumphant piece
    has been used over the centuries to celebrate)

Hector Berlioz (1803–69)
Overture to *Le Carnaval romain*

Leonard Bernstein (1918–90)
Overture to *Candide*
Fancy Free
West Side Story (Bernstein's answer to *Romeo and
    Juliet* will have you singing along with such hits
    as "Tonight," "Maria," and "America")

Georges Bizet (1838–75)
Carmen (the opera and also the many suites with tunes from the
    opera, including the "Habanera" and the "Toreador Song")
L'Arlésienne Suites

Johannes Brahms (1833–97)
All four symphonies*
Violin Concerto in D Major
Variations on a Theme by Haydn
The piano trios
Hungarian Dances
The "small" piano pieces, such as op. 76 and op. 119
Piano Concerto no. 1
Concerto for Violin, Cello, and Orchestra

Choral music:
Motets (my favorite is *Schaffe in mir, Gott*)
German Requiem

Benjamin Britten 91913–76)
The Young Person's Guide to the Orchestra
A Ceremony of Carols

Max Bruch (1838–1920)
Violin Concerto No. 1

C
Frederick Chopin (1810–49)
24 Preludes
Piano Concertos nos. 1 and 2

Aaron Copland (1900–90)
*Billy the Kid**
*Rodeo**
*Appalachian Spring**
Fanfare for the Common Man

Arcangelo Corelli (1653–1713)
Christmas Concerto

D
Claude Debussy (1862–1918)
*Prelude to the Afternoon of a Faun**
La Mer

Paul Dukas (1865–1935)
*The Sorcerer's Apprentice** (Remember Mickey Mouse in *Fantasia*?)

Léo Delibes (1836–91)
"Flower Duet" from *Lakme*

Antonin Dvorak (1841–1904)
Symphony no. 9* (*New World*)
Cello Concerto
*Slavonic Dances**
String quartets
Piano Quintet, op. 81

E
Edward Elgar (1857–1934)
Cello Concerto

George Enescu (1881–1955)
Romanian Rhapsody no. 1*

F
Gabriel Fauré (1845–1924)
*Requiem**
String quartets

César Franck (1822–90)
Violin Sonata
Symphony in D Minor

G

George Gershwin (1898–1937)
(Gershwin is a great cross between classical and jazz)
An American in Paris
Rhapsody in Blue*
Porgy and Bess (opera)
Rhapsody no. 2 for Piano and Orchestra

Gregorian chant from the Middle Ages
(Written and sung by monks long, long ago but still beautiful today)

Edvard Grieg (1843–1907)
Peer Gynt suites
Holberg suite
Piano Concerto in A Minor*

H

George Frederick Handel (1685–1759)
Israel in Egypt*
Water Music*
Music of the Royal Fireworks
"Arrival of the Queen of Sheba" from the oratorio *Solomon*
Messiah*

Franz Joseph Haydn (1732–1809)
Trumpet Concerto in E-flat Major
Symphony no. 94 (*Surprise*)
Symphony no. 104 (*London*)

Gustav Holst (1874–1934)
The Planets* (*Star Wars* material)
Choral arrangements of English folk songs

K

Aram Khachaturian (1903–78)
Violin Concerto
Spartacus
"Sabre Dance" from *Gayne*

Fritz Kreisler (1875–1962)
Liebesleid violin solo
Liebesfreud violin solo

L

Franz Liszt (1811–86)
Piano Concerto no. 1
Hungarian Rhapsodies

Felix Mendelssohn (1809–47)
Violin Concerto in E Minor
String Symphonies
Symphony no. 4 (*Italian*)
A Midsummer Night's Dream
Octet* (which he wrote when he was only 16)

Wolfgang Amadeus Mozart (1756–91)
Operas:
*The Magic Flute**
The Marriage of Figaro

Choral:
Requiem
Vespers

Instrumental:
*Eine kleine Nachtmusik**
Flute and Harp Concerto
Clarinet Concerto
Oboe Quartet

Symphonies:
no. 35 (*Haffner*)
no. 36 (*Linz*)
no. 38 (*Prague*)
no. 40 in G Minor
no. 41 (*Jupiter*)

Modest Mussorgsky (1839–81)
*Night on Bare Mountain**
Pictures at an Exhibition (piano and orchestra versions)

O

Carl Orff (1895–1982)
Carmina Burana

P

Johann Pachelbel (1653–1706)
Canon in D Major

Niccolò Paganini (1782–1840)
Violin Concertos nos. 1 and 2 (Hear why people
thought Paganini was possessed by the devil)

Giovanni da Palestrina (1525–94)
Missa Papae Marcelli

Francis Poulenc (1899–1963)
Gloria (choral work)

Sergei Prokofiev (1891–1953)
Suites from *Romeo and Juliet*
*Peter and the Wolf**
Sonata in D Major

Giacomo Puccini (1858–1924)
"Nessun dorma" from *Turandot*
"Love Duet," "Un bel di," and the "Humming
    Chorus" from *Madame Butterfly*
"O mio babbino caro" from *Gianni Schicchi*

Henry Purcell (1659–95)
The Fairy Queen
Ode for St. Cecilia's Day

R

Sergei Rachmaninov (1873–1943)
Rhapsody on a Theme of Paganini
Piano Concertos nos. 2 and 3
Symphony no. 2
Vespers
Cello Sonata
Vocalise

Maurice Ravel (1875–1937)
Bolero*
Rhapsodie Espagnole
Pavane for a Dead Princess

Ottorino Respighi (1879–1936)
The Pines of Rome (Respighi's music is a cross
    between Baroque and modern music)
The Fountains of Rome
Roman Festivals
Ancient Airs and Dances nos. 1–3

Nikolai Rimsky-Korsakov (1844–1908)
Scheherazade* (Tales of the Arabian Nights)
Flight of the Bumblebee* (another reason to
    practice those chromatic scales)

Joaquin Rodrigo (1901–1999)
Concierto de Aranjuez (beautiful and lively music for guitar)
Fantasía para un gentilhombre*

Gioacchino Rossini (1792–1868)
The Barber of Seville
William Tell Overture

S

Camille Saint-Saëns (1835–1921)
Symphony no. 3* (*Organ*)
 Carnival of the Animals* (complete with narration and movements
    named "The Fossils," "The Swan," and "The Aviary")

Franz Schubert (1797–1828)
Symphonies nos. 5, 8, and 9
Death and the Maiden (string quartet)
The Trout* (piano quintet)

Robert Schumann (1810–56)
Carnaval
Symphonies nos. 2 and 3
Humoreske
Concerto for Cello and Orchestra

Dmitri Shostakovich (1906–75)
Piano Concerto no. 1
Symphony no. 7 (written during WWII
    during the siege of Leningrad)
String Quartets nos. 3 and 8*

Jean Sibelius (1865–1957)
Finlandia
The Swan of Tuonela

Bedrich Smetana (1824–84)
Ma Vlast (*My Country*)

Johann Strauss III (1825–99)
The Blue Danube

Richard Strauss (1864–1949)
*Also Sprach Zarathustra** (used in the movie *2001: A Space Odyssey*)
Till Eulenspiegel's Merry Pranks

Igor Stravinsky (1882–1971)
*The Firebird**
*The Rite of Spring**

Sir Arthur Sullivan (of Gilbert and Sullivan fame) (1842–1900)
Any of his operettas, such as *The Mikado,*
    Ruddigore, Pirates of Penzance

T

Thomas Tallis (c. 1505–85)
Spem in Alium (Mass for 40 voices)
Canon

Peter Ilyich Tchaikovsky (1840–1893)
*The Nutcracker**
*Romeo and Juliet Overture-Fantasy**
Piano Concerto in B-flat Minor*
Violin Concerto in D Major*
Symphonies nos. 4–6*
*Swan Lake**
*Sleeping Beauty**
*Capriccio Italien**
*1812 Overture**
Serenade for Strings

Georg Philipp Telemann (1681–1767)
Tafelmusik

V

Ralph Vaughan Williams (1872–1958)
The Lark Ascending
*Fantasia on Greensleeves**
Fantasia on a Theme by Thomas Tallis
Choral arrangements of English folk songs

Giuseppe Verdi (1813–1901)
His operas are all big hits with opera lovers:
Aida
Rigoletto
La Traviata
*Requiem Mass**

Heitor Villa-Lobos (1887–1959)
Bachianas Brasileiras

Antonio Vivaldi (1678–1741)
*The Four Seasons**
Gloria

W

Richard Wagner (1813–83)
Tannhäuser
The Flying Dutchman
*Siegfried Idyll**

Charles-Marie Widor (1844–1937)
Toccata from his Fifth Organ Symphony*

Sneak Preview

*Now that you've listened, learned, and loved classical
music played by others, turn the page for tricks
to becoming a skilled player yourself.*

PART SIX

BECOMING A
SKILLED MUSICIAN

TWENTY-EIGHT

Learn the Tricks to Become a Confident Sight-Reader

It was the first orchestra rehearsal of the season, with new parts and new players. The music was rather difficult, but everyone was sight-reading pretty well—except for the new concertmaster. He was confused and lost. He had to keep asking for measure numbers and looking at the fellow sitting next to him for cues. The conductor and other orchestra players were mystified. The concertmaster had a fine reputation as a performer. So what was going on?

A miracle occurred at the next rehearsal. The concertmaster knew every note and played without even looking at the music. What happened? Four days earlier he could barely play the notes.

This is a true story. What happened? The concertmaster had taken the music home and learned it by ear while listening to a recording! Sight-reading would have been a whole lot easier.

Sight-reading is one of the most important skills musicians can have. When I play gigs, I'm often working with musicians whom I've never met. We introduce ourselves, hand out the music, take a few seconds to look it over, note any repeats, set the tempo, and then we're off. People often compliment us, saying, "You play so well. How long has your group been playing together?" We laugh, look at our watches, and then fib, "Oh, we've been playing together for *years*."

Sight-reading is more than being able to read music; it's being able to read music fast for the first time. Good sight-readers are invaluable. Good sight-readers pick up the nuances and phrasing the first time through a piece, instead of focusing only on the notes and the rhythm. You can also learn new music quickly because you'll see it as repeating patterns instead of entirely new material.

Musicians are often called upon to sight-read in ensemble rehearsals and at auditions. You may even be able to fool your teacher when you've had a spotty practice if you can fake it by sight-reading. In addition to its usefulness, sight-reading is fun. Gather a few friends together and sight-read some new pieces and laugh at your mistakes. Sight-reading can become a game. So what's holding you back?

Judy Filibeck, a choral conductor in the Seattle area, was asked to give a sight-reading seminar to high school choir students. She started out her presentation by asking the group, "What is the best thing about sight-reading?" The quick reply from the bass in the last row was, "When it's over." A little nonplussed, Judy continued, "Well, what's the worst thing about sight-reading?" to which a tenor retorted, "When it starts."

The biggest roadblock to sight-reading is *attitude*. Have you ever looked at a piece of music and thought, "Help! I can't play this. I don't know how it goes because I've never heard it, and it's too hard to figure out by myself"? Calm down! If you're old enough to read a book, you're old enough to sight-read music. Take a moment to scout out the music first.

SIGHT-READING CHECKLIST: WHERE DO YOU START?

Key Signature. Say the name of the key and its sharps or flats to yourself.

Key Changes. Scan the piece, and note any key changes.

Accidentals. Accidentals are accidents waiting to happen. WARNING: People often play the accidental correctly where it's marked, but miss it later in the measure. Learn two names for all accidentals (F♯ = G♭) so that either will feel comfortable.

Tempo. Memorize the speeds of the most common tempo markings, especially the variations such as *allegro, allegretto, andante,* and *andantino.* Watch out for tempo changes. Scan the piece and look for the fastest (blackest) notes, because they'll determine your top speed.

Time Signature. Before you begin, mentally mark the beats in the first two measures and in any tricky parts. If the first few measures have divisions of eighth-notes, say, "One and two and" or "tee-tee, tee-tee." If there are patterns divisible by sixteenths, such as dotted eighths and sixteenths, say, "One-e-and-uh two-e-and-uh" or "huck-le-ber-ry" while you're thinking the exact rhythmic patterns of the first two measures. Sure, you know how to count, but matching the rhythm with words helps you stay even and set a tempo. Carefully note any time signature changes and know how the notes relate (2/4 becomes 6/8, but the eighth-notes stay the same).

Tricky Parts. Pay special attention to measures with accidentals, complicated rhythms, hard high or low notes, and notes on many leger lines.

Patterns. Watch out for rhythmic patterns such as syncopation. Use your knowledge of theory to pick out scale and chord patterns and sequences.

Fingerings. Note unusual fingerings. For piano, it might be crossing hands, and for stringed instruments, it might be harmonics or changing positions.

Clefs. Beware of changing clefs in instruments such as the cello, which uses three clefs, or the piano, which can have two treble or two bass clefs.

Repeats. Know the road map before you start. Take note of any repeats, codas, da capos, and signs. If you have the chance, circle them or even draw arrows.

> *Jamie appreciates what it took to become a good sight-reader. "Understanding the basic tenets of music theory was crucial for becoming a good sight-reader and helped me play more musically. Learning the piano first was also very important, because I could read music (treble and bass clef) before I ever picked up a flute, which really helped my sight-reading."*

SCANNING

Good sight-readers and good drivers are very much alike: both scan ahead while playing. How much can you see when reading music? The measure? The whole line? When you play, do you look ahead for tempo changes and complex rhythms? Your eyes should work ahead of your hands.

Try these exercises to build up your speed:

- Read bars, not beats. Keep your eyes moving continuously from left to right and down the page. Practice duets, but look at both parts at once.
- Build up your speed. Use a flashcard or put an index card on the music, revealing just two measures. Look quickly and then look away while you play.
- Practice playing while someone is providing a distraction. Work to quickly scan the score, look at the person, and look back. When playing with a group, look quickly at the music and then directly at the conductor or ensemble members for good communication. (This is a good game to play in band.)
- Do visual exercises. Look at the beginning and end of lines, back to the key signature, from one rehearsal letter to the next, and back to the repeat sign while playing. See how quickly you can jump without getting lost.
- Practice reading piano chords from the bottom up, since the bass clef is the one that usually gives the most trouble.

FAKING IT

There's always music that's impossible to play. It's way over our heads, but we still want to play it. What to do? Fake it!

On the piano, when I try to accompany my students on major concerti, I'm sometimes reduced to playing only one hand and sometimes only one *note*. In the devilishly hard sections, I play my own "chords" and just make sure I have the correct rhythm. I'm not a master of the piano, but I am a "master" at faking. The more practice you get, the less faking you'll need, but in real-life situations it can really come in handy.

If you're still having problems with the music, leave out the extras:

- Given a choice between correct notes and correct rhythm, choose the rhythm.
- Play the outside notes of the chord.
- Play the chord in one position instead of a florid arpeggio pattern.
- Play the chord in a different inversion or in a different octave, whichever will cause the fewest mistakes.
- Leave out trills and grace notes.
- Re-tongue/bow/play ties or slurs to help with the rhythm.
- Play only the first note of a group of sixteenths or a triplet.
- "Sit out" an impossible measure and come back on the next downbeat.
- If you're totally lost, move your hands or pretend that your part has rests!

GREAT IDEAS

Sit straight in front of the music so your eyes can easily track. Keyboard players should sit in the middle to get a feel for the keyboard.

Wear the right glasses and have good light.

Maintain a steady beat. Practice never stopping while playing with a metronome.

"Check your rear and side view mirrors." Don't bury your head in the music and forget to look up at the conductor or other ensemble members.

Count the number of beats, not notes, in each measure. Never count how many G's there are in a phrase, but know what beat every G is on.

Listening to classical music will make you a better player, no matter what instrument or type of music you play.

Always be aware of the downbeat so that, if you mess up a measure, you can easily get back in.

Play musically. Even though you're sight-reading, don't forget that this is music.

If you're playing the piano, a string instrument, or guitar, don't look at your hands. Glancing back and forth from the hands to the music slows you down. Memorize by touch where the two and three black key patterns are, much like reading Braille. Practice scales in the dark or put a newspaper, book, or scarf over your hands to get out of the habit of looking.

Relax and have fun. Give yourself permission to make mistakes. It's just sight-reading!

Sneak Preview

Percussionists and pianists can skip our next chapter, but it is an important one for all other musicians: how to play in tune. Think you're tone deaf or have no idea whether you play flat or sharp? Learn how to listen to yourself and train your ear.

TWENTY-NINE

Intonation

You *Can* Learn to Play in Tune

Bad pitch is like body odor. Nobody says anything to you,
but they talk about you when you leave the room.

—Amy Porter, Associate Professor of Flute at the
University of Michigan

Okay, pianists, you're off the hook. How we wind and string players envy you when every note is in tune—assuming you have a good piano tuner. Life isn't so easy for the rest of us. A few people are born with perfect/absolute pitch (the ability to hear any note and identify it by name). Some people are born with good relative pitch (the ability to know the name of the note when given another reference note). And some people are born being able to tell if a note is too flat or sharp. The rest of us have to work at all of the above. But don't despair! You *can* learn to play in tune.

I remember my first intonation experience all too well. In seventh grade, I had a duet with one of my girlfriends. We both played guitar and sang. We were practicing at her house when she suddenly said, "You're singing flat."

"I am not," I retorted. "Uh, what's *flat* mean?"

Several years later, in college, when I had been playing the flute for six months, I was asked to perform at a church. When the director asked me, "Do you want to tune to the organ now?" I replied, "No, I'm okay." I couldn't tell if I was in tune or not. I just relied on luck. From these very ignorant beginnings, I'm happy to report my listening skills have improved, and so can yours.

There are whole books written on the science of intonation. They talk about "even temperament" and "just intonation." I will leave those explanations to the music scholars and the scientists. In this chapter we are going to talk about how you can quickly learn to hear pitch better and adjust your voice or instrument to play in tune.

Bad joke: Why do violinists always play with good intonation?
Because they are shot if they play out of tune.

Why do violists always play with bad intonation?
Because you can't shoot everyone.

"I have to think about tone, notes, phrasing, and rhythm, and now you want me to think about intonation, too?" Sorry, no matter how great the rest of the package is, playing out of tune is like sticking a dead rat in a present—it's gross and it ends up smelling later. The fastest way to learn to play in tune is to simply be aware and care about intonation.

My student Stan had terrible intonation problems. It always took him *forever* to tune to the piano. One day he became very fast and confident when tuning. I said, "What happened to you? How did you suddenly develop such a great ear?"

He grinned sheepishly. "When I see your shoulders go down, I know I'm finally in tune."

I was giving him the answers without knowing it. Don't depend on your teacher to tell you when you're out of tune. Listen for yourself.

Remember that tuning to the A before playing only ensures that that particular A is in tune at that particular moment. Pre-tuning gives you better odds of being in tune during the piece, but not insurance. Be aware.

PRACTICE INTONATION

- Practice with the piano shadowing you (playing the same notes) and also playing an accompaniment.
- Practice without vibrato to focus on the pitch.
- Play in ensembles to practice listening and tuning up with others.
- Help other members in your ensemble tune.
- Listen to other players and analyze their pitch. Do they sound sharp, flat, or "right on"?
- Sing! Singing helps you think of the pitch before you have to play it. Practice singing scales and arpeggios with the tuner, then transfer that awareness to your instrument.

Bad joke: What's the definition of a minor second?
Two violists playing in unison.

PITCH TENDENCIES

My student Linda consistently played flat. She had a hard time knowing if she was in tune, so I told her, "When in doubt, play higher." The last competition of her senior year was held on a hot, muggy day in a church full of windows. Linda could tell she was out of tune, so she kept going higher and higher. I can still hear her *Concerto in D Very Sharp Major*!

All notes are *not* equal. Both you and your instrument have personal pitch tendencies. If you know them ahead of time, it will be easier to fix a problem before it becomes one. Knowing these tendencies will give you a good guess if you can't tell if you are sharp or flat. But be warned: pitch is ever-changing, and you have to listen constantly.

KNOW YOUR PERSONAL PROBLEMS AND THOSE OF YOUR INSTRUMENT

- What are the pitch tendencies of your instrument? Does your instrument naturally play flat or sharp in the high or low ranges? When you play loud or soft? In the flat or sharp keys? On certain notes? With a temperature change?
- Do you know your own pitch tendencies? Do you always play flat or sharp on a certain note or in a certain position?
- Is your pitch bad because of your posture?
- Is your pitch bad because you are holding your instrument incorrectly?
- Have you memorized alternate fingerings that combat pitch tendencies?
- For strings: Are you flat when reaching with the fourth finger? Are the fifths in tune? If you press the bow hard into the string, does it change the pitch? Do you play out of tune when changing positions?
- Do you always play the same note out of tune? Mark it in the score with an arrow up or down.
- Do you wish you played the piano or drums instead?

Bad joke: How do you get two piccolo players to play in tune?
Shoot one!

An instrument that is not in good repair can ruin the intonation. Wind players, make sure your pads seal. String players and guitarists, change your strings often and keep the tuning mechanism in good shape. Brass players, keep your horns clean.

USE THE TUNER

- Play intervals and slow scales to a constant A. Use your metronome, tuner, a tuning CD, or the Smart Music computer program. Or, if you have a nearby computer or laptop, go online to www.metronomeonline.com, where you will not only get a metronome but also a constant A—and it's free.
- Keep the tuner on the stand when you practice. Check it during long notes, beginning and ending notes, and at dynamic changes.
- Most metronomes have A=440, 442, 444. Practice tuning to each A to begin to hear small incremental changes in pitch.
- String instruments have their own built-in tuner: the open strings. Check fingered notes often with open strings (after you have tuned the open strings as accurately as possible).
- On wind instruments, use the tuner to see how far you

can bend notes. Realize the huge pitch differences
you can make on every note without retuning.

- Play the chromatic scale with the tuner. Armed with
your knowledge of pitch tendencies, anticipate out-
of-tune notes and adjust before you play them.
- A tuning fork is a cheap, portable tuner. Use your ears to tune with
a tuning fork or piano. If you only use the electronic tuner to tell
if you are in tune, you'll be training your eyes, not your ears.

Bad joke: Have you heard about the violist who always played in tune?
Neither have I.

PERFORMING

The pianist should play the A for ensemble members to match their beginning
tuning pitch. Wind players should play their A first, before the piano, so as not
to unconsciously adjust the embouchure instead of the instrument. In a group
of all strings, take the pitch from the cello. Orchestras tune to the oboe.

Do the major tuning before you walk into the room. Make the final adjust-
ments when tuning to the piano.

- String players tune one string with a tuner or piano.
Next, play two strings at once to get the intervals
(a perfect fifth) between the strings in tune.
- When tuning a string instrument, play a few harmonics and listen to the tone quality.
- Step close to the piano and tune quickly. Don't
play an entire concerto on the note A!
- Let your pianist discreetly help you tune if you're unsure. Among
my wonderful accompanist's talents is a fabulous sense of pitch.
If the student is floundering, she looks up to signal to tune higher
and looks down to signal to tune lower. Another accompanist I
know gives the student a subtle cue by playing a D minor chord
under the A to let the student know to play flatter and a D major
chord to tune higher. Hey, we need all the help we can get.
- Don't be afraid to tune between movements or between pieces in a recital. Pitch will change as the instrument or the room warms up.
- (Strings: don't listen to this.) It's all right to tune for a particular piece or section. For instance, the flute is sharp when it's
loud and in the top octave. If the piece is mainly loud and
high, give yourself a break and tune a little flat. (Don't forget to adjust those low, soft notes to correct for the tuning.)

If you practice out of tune, your ears will adjust to the wrong pitch. Soon you'll get into the habit of not hearing and not caring about intonation. Use these practice techniques to increase both your awareness and your ability to adjust.

- Play in unison with the piano or other instruments.
- If you can't decide whether you are sharp or flat, bend the pitch both ways to hear which is closer to the correct pitch.
- Remember that when playing in unison, you should play softer than normal to hear the pitch and to blend.
- Have a clear idea in your mind what the pitch should be by singing. Practice singing the first note of a piece before you play to really get an idea of what the pitch should be.
- Learn to sing scales, arpeggios, and then simple folk songs.
- After a piano interlude, stop and sing the beginning note of the next phrase, then play it.

GREAT IDEAS

Intonation is one of the pillars of good playing. Why? No matter how beautiful your tone, how fast your fingers, or how delicate your phrasing, if you're out of tune, you stink! Bad intonation ruins everything. It's not easy to learn how to play in tune, but it's worth it. Don't give up.

Always be aware of intonation. Know the pitch tendencies of your instrument.

Practice with the tuner and the piano.

Play with other instruments. Learn to hear the pitch by singing.

Sneak Preview

Playing the right notes and rhythm isn't enough, even if they're in tune. In our next chapter, learn how to make music beautiful and expressive with our tips on musicality.

THIRTY

Musicality

The Difference between Playing and Typing

It's easy to play any musical instrument: all you have to do is touch the
right key at the right time, and the instrument will play itself.
—J. S. Bach

Easy for him to say!
—Bonnie Blanchard

MUSICALITY MAKES THE DIFFERENCE

Beginner Alex slumps behind the cello. Slowly sawing away, he nods his head
and puts a big accent on every note. "Twinkle, Twinkle, Little Star" sounds like
"Twinkle, Fizzle, Big Death Star." Then Alex's teacher demonstrates smooth
bow changes, dynamics, and how to connect notes into phrases. "Twinkle"
suddenly transforms into music. With his teacher's help, Alex will gradually
learn how to play musically. Unfortunately, most students never go beyond
pounding out the notes. Music is something mechanical to them, like running
a machine. Because they never learn to play beautifully and express themselves,
they soon quit. Learning to play musically will let you express yourself, keep
you playing, and keep everyone else from running away when you sit down to
play your instrument.

> *Seventeen-year-old Brooke describes how learning to play musically changed
> her life. "For six years I played as all beginners are taught. I read the music,
> fingered the notes, and produced a sound. Then I changed teachers. My new
> teacher changed my playing and, ultimately, my life. She helped me see that I
> had completely missed the essence of music. My music had been dead.*
>
> *"To me, music had been black notes on white paper, and my playing re-
> flected that. I never realized I could play the music and simultaneously feel it.
> A whole new world opened up to me when I discovered phrasing, contrasting
> styles, and emotions. I discovered that music is not just sound; it's a lifestyle
> that completely envelops the listener and performer. People outside a musical
> lifestyle don't understand why we can be so involved. But we have been to the
> other world of music and back, and in doing so we have tasted a little bit of
> heaven."*

Can you tell that Brooke is a very emotional performer? Brooke fell in love with music once she learned to do more than just play the notes. She graduated from college with a music performance degree and is still happily playing.

What is musicality?

Musicality is connecting many notes in one gesture, instead of accenting each individual note. It's playing in sentences that mean something, instead of producing individual syllables with no meaning. It's singing through your instrument instead of speaking like a robot. Playing an instrument is not about how fast or loudly you can play, but what you *say* with the music. When you play musically, you show your audience you're in love with the music. And you convince them to love it, too.

Can musicality be learned?

Yes! All musicians are not created equal, but they can learn to play expressively by imitating others and learning the rules of musicality.

Where do I start?

Say this sentence with no expression: "When he made the winning basket, the crowd exploded in cheers." Spoken in a monotone, the sentence has no meaning and no excitement. Who cares about the game? Well, no one wants to hear you speak like that, and no one wants to hear you play that way, either. Now say the same sentence with normal inflection. "When he made the winning basket, the crowd *exploded* in cheers!" Now you've got their attention.

Notice the natural rise and fall of speech. Do you hear how most sentences settle at the end? Do you notice how your voice rises at the end of a question? You take a breath between sentences, and each sentence leads thematically to the next. The most important word of each sentence gets emphasis. Now apply these things to music, and you'll understand why a phrase is called a "musical sentence." Words and notes mean nothing on their own. It's the way you say them that matters.

• *Listen to good music.* The fastest way to learn musicality is to listen to other people playing musically. Go to live concerts and listen to recorded music. Practice with a pianist, play in ensembles, and play along with computer accompaniment programs.

• *Start with scales.* "What? Scales aren't music!" When you play scales, you're building the foundation to playing real music. Listen for evenness, tone, dynamics, connections, and articulation that will translate into real music.

THE SHORTCUT TO PLAYING MUSICALLY

This chapter is full of ideas and tricks to help you play musically. But it all boils down to these three things:

1. Gradually crescendo and build tension from one note to the next.
2. Give each phrase one destination or climax. Don't accent each beat.
3. Play with emotion. Make your music say something.

Be an independent thinker.

But don't I just have to do what it says in the music? Hasn't the composer already thought of everything?

Composers can't prescribe every nuance.

Composers pass down their written music, but without hearing them play it, we have to interpret their notes.

How can the same written music have different interpretations? Say a simple sentence such as, "Yesterday he gave me flowers." Now emphasize a different word every time you repeat the sentence. "*Yesterday* he gave me flowers. (Why did he wait so long?) Yesterday *he* gave me flowers. (I wish it had been his older brother instead.) Yesterday he gave *me* flowers. (Ha ha. He didn't give *you* flowers.) Yesterday he gave me *flowers*. (But I had been hoping for a diamond ring.)" See how the meaning changes? Music is open to interpretation, too. You may play the same notes as everyone else, but you can play them your way.

Everyone has their own ideas about how music should be played. That's why there are so many recordings and editions of sheet music. How can you put your own stamp on the music? Study the score, listen to recorded music, and consult with your teacher, but use your own creativity. Where do *you* think the music should get louder or softer? What notes should you accent? Should it slow down here? Where does the phrase end? Should you play staccato? Be brave. The only absolutely wrong way to phrase is to do nothing. Try something.

Now let's talk about the "rules" of musicality.

MUSIC HAS A FEELING OF FORWARD MOTION

Every phrase has to go somewhere, and that somewhere is *forward*. Each note must connect to the next. Phrases relate to each other, and sections grow into each other. Music with forward motion tells an exciting story: "Wait until I tell you what happened next!"

For a feeling of forward motion:
- Read notes in groups, not one at a time. Just as beginning readers transition from reading C-A-T as separate letters and sounds to seeing words, progress from seeing one note at a time to seeing chords, scales, and sequences as one unit. (Now aren't you glad you know your music theory?)
- Think horizontally, not vertically. All music has an invisible arrow pointing forward. Mark an arrow above the phrase or between phrases to remind yourself of the forward motion of the music.

- Feel fewer pulses per measure for more of a flow. If the piece is in 4/4, play it in 2/2. Play 3/4 in one big beat per measure, and play 6/8 in two beats per measure. Better yet, play as if there are no bar lines.
- Feel forward motion until the destination is reached. Picture a moving train. You may have to jump off to take breaths or change bows, but you must keep running alongside the train to jump back on.
- Know where the climax of each phrase is. Circle the climax of the phrase. Crescendo and build tension to that climax.
- Keep your eyes scanning ahead to the next phrase to anticipate what will happen next.
- Lighten up! Phrasing should feel like driving a hovercraft, barely skimming the surface and only landing at the climax.
- Don't just practice the notes, play the music. After practicing measures or phrases for accuracy, put them together every day to understand how the phrases and sections relate.

MUSIC IS TENSION AND RELEASE

Think of your favorite movie. The characters and the setting are introduced in the first few minutes, but as the drama unfolds, clouds appear on the horizon. Tension builds to an exciting climax. The problem is resolved in the last few minutes with the good guys living happily ever after (unless there's a sequel). Music is like a good story. In fact, it's a great story! Music has to have both *motion* and *emotion,* not just notes. Each musical phrase, section, and piece must create this same tension and release of a good story line. The most exciting part is never at the beginning, and it isn't necessarily the highest note or the final note, either. Build tension gradually to the most exciting part, explode, and then relax.

Ways to phrase:
- Play every note like a word in a solemn vow, not like reading the lunch menu.
- The end of a phrase is like the last bite of a delicious meal to be savored. Don't chop it off because of a breath or bow change.
- Be aware of what's going on around you in the piano accompaniment or in the other instrumental parts. Be conversational.
- Work on technique so it doesn't hold you back musically.
- Using lots of accents, phrasing, and style can make up for a slow tempo. If your playing is exciting and involved, the tempo won't matter so much.
- Wide intervals are usually expressions of soaring emotions. Use lots of expression in big leaps, and emphasize the bottom note before the leap.

- All instruments (maybe not drums) try to imitate the human voice. Play everything, no matter how simple or boring (yes, even scales), like a song.

MUSICALITY AND BODY LANGUAGE

How you hold your body makes a difference to you *and* to your audience. If you sway too much, you'll look as if you're playing the final concert on the Titanic. If you don't move at all, you'll look like a statue with a built-in recorder. Audiences like *listening* to a performer, but they also like *watching* them move. That's why they come to concerts instead of sitting at home on the couch.

To communicate, body language should reflect phrasing, not random movement. Bobbing on each note or tapping your foot will not only tell the audience that you're accenting every note but it will also force you to accent each note. You can't play a smooth line while moving to every beat.

What if you don't feel the music? Start by moving your body. It may feel silly, but the phrasing will follow. In general, move forward when the phrase becomes more intense, and lift up at the resolution of the tension at the end.

Check your posture and position in the mirror. Musicality comes from the whole body, not just the fingers. If you stand stiff-legged, sit rigidly or slumped over, or have bad hand position, you'll find it harder to express yourself. Videotape yourself to see how you look and sound.

Prepare the first phrase with your body. Pianists prepare with the fingers touching the keys first, followed by a relaxed and slow wrist drop. All musicians should take a big breath in the mood and tempo of the piece. Mirror the emotion of the piece with body language. If it's a sad piece, don't look perky and full of energy.

A body with a firm core is necessary to support long phrases. Tighten up your gut, but not your shoulders. Be careful, however, of becoming too stiff when playing loud, dramatic music. The feeling of the music needs to be expressed in the body. But tightness will ruin not only the music but also your body.

DYNAMICS

If you want to get someone's attention, whisper. Or shout! Dynamic contrast keeps music interesting. When I'm listening to classical music on the car radio with my husband (who likes everything soft), I constantly adjust the dial because of the rapid fluctuations in dynamics. He turns it down when it gets too loud, and I turn it up when it gets too soft. Beethoven keeps us busy with his rapid changes in mood and dynamics.

How do you imagine Beethoven himself might have played? He was a wild and crazy guy, and you must be, too. But playing with big dynamic contrast isn't enough. Dynamics are an expression of emotion, not an end unto themselves. Don't just turn the radio dial up and down; turn the emotion knob up and down, too.

Playing loudly

- Play loud enough to get your audience involved.
- Don't wait until the performance. Practice loudly to get used to projection.
- Are you too timid to play loudly? Do you think you don't have the strength? Pretend to yell to the next house or at your siblings. (Never at your teacher!)
- Adjust your volume to the situation. Soloists (especially flutists and cellists) may have to always play somewhat loudly to be heard in an orchestra.
- Play with support and intensity through the last note of a big forte phrase like running full bore into a wall.
- Don't always play loudly. No one pays attention to someone who yells all the time. Remember, music is about tension and release.
- Never play louder than you can play beautifully.

Playing softly

- Make soft passages just as exciting as loud ones.
- Don't slow down on soft passages and speed up on loud ones.
- When the last note of the phrase is descending, play it softer.
- A pickup note is softer than the note it leads into.
- The cadenza is the chance to play very softly to capture the audience's attention.
- Don't automatically put a diminuendo on the end of every phrase.

Crescendo and diminuendo

- Generally, each note crescendos into the next in a phrase.
- To give a sense of forward motion to a very long note, start very softly with no vibrato, crescendo, add vibrato, and then add volume and widen the vibrato.
- Don't just accent the most important note of the phrase. Crescendo to it.
- Crescendo on repeating notes or phrases like your mother calling, "Come here. Come Here! Come HERE!!"
- Put lots of excitement in ascending chromatic scales.
- Crescendo through the rest to connect phrases in loud passages. Make sure the first note of the second phrase is louder than the previous note.
- A crescendo or diminuendo refers to the next level up or down. It does not necessarily mean to play as loudly or softly as possible.

- When you see the word crescendo, immediately start softer and then crescendo.
- Crescendo like the bell of a trumpet. (This analogy is from Hal Ott, professor of flute at Central Washington University.) Play a gradual crescendo, then flare out at the end. On a wind instrument, use most of your air on the last few notes. On a stringed instrument, use one-third of your bow on the measure run and two-thirds on the last few notes.
- Don't let changing dynamics change the pitch.
- To help you notice dynamics, mark them in different colors.
- Pretend there is a volume meter (or actually pick up one from an electronics store). Play a forte passage. Now make the needle jump up to ff and fff.

Matching dynamics

- Don't play loudly on long notes and automatically play softly on short notes!
- Don't play louder on slurred notes than on tongued or bowed notes.
- Match the dynamics of trills to the rest of the piece.
- Counteract the natural volume tendency of your instrument. (Pianists are lucky here.) The flute is naturally louder in the high register, so crescendo to the bottom to keep the volume the same. The bow is naturally louder at the frog, so work harder at the tip to keep the volume even.

ACCENTS

When I was young, my mother had a mixer with several speed settings and a button called "burst of power" for hitting lumps. Many phrases need a "burst of power" on the climax of the phrase or on a special note that you love. Bring out individual notes with special accents.

Play accents in context. An accent in a *forte* section can mean "Give it all you've got," but an accent in a soft, lyrical phrase can be just a warm bump. Remember, accent important notes, not the notes on the beat!

To accent a note, vary:
- Volume (softer or louder)
- Vibrato (faster or slower, wider or narrow)
- Articulation (a harder or softer attack)
- Length (make it longer or shorter, or play a fermata)
- Tone color (clear, edgy, unfocused, using a harmonic, or playing on a different string)

◀))

Twelve-year-old Anna has a new idol. "I went to Sir James Galway's concert, and it was totally amazing. I could tell what he was trying to say with his music. He didn't sound at all nervous, and by the way he played, you could tell if the song was sad or upbeat. He seemed so happy in his playing, even when he played sad songs. He was totally present in the moment and in the heart of the music. When he played, I could picture it. He almost made the music come to life like it was real."

Music is about feeling, not just moving fingers. If you're not emotionally involved, your instrument is just a machine. You're not a boring person, so don't play like one.

To build excitement:
- Don't let up between phrases. Use a steady air stream or bow tension. As mundane as this may sound, this is very important.
- Vibrato is a measure of emotion. Use more when you're excited.
- Play with your whole body. Support. Use more energy and get into it.
- Enunciate each note clearly. Use a harder attack with the tongue or more distinct finger articulation on non-woodwind instruments. Don't forget to rosin that bow.
- Play more accents and play louder. Use a faster air stream or bow and put "stingers" on accented notes. Pianists, use the natural weight of your arms to get more volume through the power of gravity. Watch videos of great pianists (like Vladimir Horowitz) on YouTube to see how they create accents.
- Don't play any dead notes. Try the "heaven or hell test." If the note is vibrant, you go to heaven, but if it doesn't pass the Excite-O-Meter, you know what happens!

Feel the music.
- Take a cue from the music. Knowing what was happening in the composer's life or why the piece was composed will give you some cues. Titles such as "Silent Night" and "Flight of the Bumble Bee" are obvious images. Obeying musical terms such as amabile, cantabile, brilliante, giocoso, deciso, and maestoso helps set the mood.
- Choose a feeling (excited, nervous, angry, urgent, wistful, innocent, melancholy, etc.) for a piece, a section, or even a phrase. A fun way to get started is to choose one of the Seven Dwarfs for each piece or section. "Does this sound like Sleepy, Happy, Grumpy, Dopey, Bashful, Sneezy, or Doc?" (P.S. Don't have vibrato like Snow White.)
- Imagine a scene from a movie: "What's happening on the screen here?"

- Create scenarios of your own. Angry: your brother just stole your
  diary and is reading it to all his friends. Melancholy: you remember all the good times you used to have with your best
  friend until he moved away. Ecstatic: your parents decided
  that because you had such a great year of practicing, they
  would take you and 10 friends for a week at Disneyland.
- Make up words to sing with solos so that every note has meaning, like
  the words in a song or poem. I sing these lyrics to the first movement
  of Schubert's Arpeggione Sonata: "Oh, I love him. I love his face, his
  smile, his grin. I love his mother and his baby brother. But most of
  all, I love him . . . and his name is Jim." Your friends will think you're
  crazy, but you'll begin to play each note like the word in a song.
- Learn how to conduct. Pretend you're leading an orchestra and show them phrasing with your gestures.

COMMUNICATE WITH THE AUDIENCE

I had a part in my high school play. I quickly learned my lines, but in rehearsals
I felt too shy to let myself get into my part. (I've changed.) I hoped that when
the real performance rolled around, I would suddenly transform into an actress. Needless to say, it was not an Academy Award–winning performance.

Now I realize that it's more embarrassing *not* to get into the role. Good
actors and actresses *become* their roles; they are not aware they're reading a
script. Audiences aren't impressed that actors have learned so many lines or
can say them fast. They get excited when they believe what actors have to say.

Actors exaggerate their speech, movements, and even their makeup. Musicians must do the same (except maybe for the makeup part). If the music is sad,
feel sad. When it's exciting, *be* excited. Decide what character your piece is, and
then play it in that character. Invite your audience in to see the show. If you
love what you do, the audience will share your joy.

To communicate with your audience:
- Take an acting class or work in a restaurant to get
  used to interacting with the public.
- Sell your piece. Make your audience think you have
  all the self-confidence in the world.
- Sometimes in rehearsal, throw caution to the wind. Play with
  wild abandon. Don't worry if all the notes of the run are
  there or if the pitch and tone are perfect. Be an actor.
- Pick someone in the audience to play to. Aim
  your sound right at their forehead.
- Imagine the music flowing to the audience like sound waves rolling forward or like throwing a ball to a point ahead.

- Write a story that accompanies the music, and
    think of each section as an act in a play.
- Practice for someone, even if that someone is a chair. Pretend a judge is in that chair. Play for stuffed animals and posters on the bedroom wall.

Music is theater.
- Play melodies from exciting arias. Pretend you're in full costume onstage.
- Pretend you are your favorite singer or actor.
- Remember that, in performance, you're onstage the minute you walk into the room. Wear distinctive clothing, walk in with dignity, and look like a star.

RHYTHM AND TEMPO

Composers write specific rhythms for certain effects. If you play a triplet like four sixteenths and a sixteenth rest, it won't mean the same thing. At the same time, remember that rhythm can be subtly stretched to emphasize the notes you love.

Tempo changes

- Hold the first note of a run. It will give the note a chance to sound and will make the run sound confident.
- Slow down on the last few notes of a run to counteract the natural tendency to rush.
- Don't be afraid to play rubato in Romantic pieces. But when you play rubato, bend it, don't break it.
- Usually you should ritard at the end of the piece. A ritard should be proportional to the speed of the piece. (No giant ritards on prestos.)
- Impose speed limits. Just because you can play it that fast doesn't mean it makes musical sense or that the audience can even hear it that fast.

BREATHING

Pianists and string players, don't tune out this section. Even though you don't need to blow your instruments to make them sound, you still must make the phrases breathe. Wind players take a breath, string players decide on an upbow or downbow, and pianists let their "wrists take a breath."

I once judged a contest and asked the performer how she decided where to breathe. "At the end of each line on the page, or every four measures," she said. Imagine if we used that rule for writing commas and periods. It doesn't make sense. Where we bow or breathe shouldn't be after a certain number of measures, or where we run out of breath, but where the phrase starts.

- At the end of a phrase.
- Before a pickup.
- Between double notes (two E's in a row).
- When the phrase changes direction (the phrase goes
    from high to low, then starts going up again).
- After the tonic (the name of the key).
- After a long note rather than a short one (breathe after
    the eighth-note, not the sixteenth-note).
- After a low note rather than a high note (the breath won't be so obvious).
- Between members of a sequence (a repeating pattern).
- After an appoggiatura.
- When the main theme returns.

Breathing musically

- Don't cut off the note before the breath.
- Breathe in tempo.
- Take time to breathe. If you have two beats of rest, use them.
- Make the breath part of the piece. Don't apologize for breathing.
- Take silent, motionless breaths. Don't gasp or bounce.

Even pianists and string players should use their breath to prepare an important phrase. Conductors do it, too. If you listen carefully in a good concert hall, you'll hear the conductor draw in a breath before that first downbeat.

MUSICALITY AND MUSIC THEORY

Even if you don't naturally feel the phrases, certain rules can be applied to help you internalize musicality.

What clues does the structure of the piece provide?
- Do sections repeat? Is the form AB or ABA? It's exciting to return to familiar themes. Make a distinction between sections with a slight separation and then more energy.
- A pickup is softer than the note it leads into. Every pickup should have an "up" gesture.
- A sequence is a pattern starting on different notes (CDEC, DEFD, EFGE). If you want to hear examples of sequences, listen to almost anything by Vivaldi, who sometimes sounds as if he used the stencil as a compositional technique. Use terrace dynamics (dynamics in steps as opposed to a gradual crescendo) in a sequence. On the first member of the sequence, play piano, on the second member, play mezzo piano, and on the third member, play mezzo forte.
- Watch the architecture of the piece. Music usually gets louder

and more exciting as it gets higher. (The soprano in the opera never dies on a low note.) But the highest note is not necessarily the most important or the loudest.

- Crescendo on a note tied over the bar line and add vibrato.
- Play an echo (soft) on an exact repeat, then return to the original volume.
- Pick out the main notes of a phrase and play them musically. Now add the supporting (passing tone) notes.
- Different chords serve different functions. For example, the tonic (I) chord has a feeling of rest. The subdominant (IV) and dominant (V) chords create the tension and release of a cadence (ending).

ACCENT NON-CHORD TONES

Enjoy the tension of non-chord notes and lean into the dissonance (two notes whose sounds clash). Crescendo on suspensions (a note held over from the first chord when the chord changes, creating a dissonance). Then relax into the resolution when the note changes to become a chord tone. Don't shy away from trills in the Baroque period that start from above the non-chord tone.

Recognize appoggiaturas. The word *appoggiatura* means "to lean." Appoggiaturas are usually the second to the last note of the phrase and are one step above or below the last note. The real melody goes to the last note, but the appoggiatura delays that melody note and creates tension and dissonance. Crescendo through the phrase to the appoggiatura. Then lean into the appoggiatura by playing it louder and with more vibrato. Lift up and relax on the final resolution note.

Here's a fun trick to experience the emotional and physical feeling of the last two notes of an appoggiatura and resolution ending. Stand in a doorway with the outside of your wrists pressed very hard against the inside of the doorjamb. This tension is like the tension of an appoggiatura. Press for about one minute, then walk away from the door jamb. Your arms, still feeling the tension of pushing (the appoggiatura), will miraculously float up when released in the resolution. Amaze all your friends at the next party.

MUSICALITY AND CONNECTIONS

What do smooth connections have to do with musicality? Everything! Stiff fingers and jumbled connections between notes make disjointed music. But gliding from one note to the next will connect the notes and give forward motion to each phrase.

Keep a gentle touch.

Your instrument is your friend. Don't slap it or fling your fingers off. Take the tension out, and don't squeeze the instrument. Always keep fingers curved and close. Pianists should keep a free wrist and relaxed elbows to gently roll from one finger to the next and create a smooth line.

On the other hand, in your efforts to have a gentle touch, be sure every note sounds. Be careful of ghosting the notes, where the sound isn't clear because the note isn't fingered or bowed strongly enough. Use your ears to make sure every note sounds.

Move fingers together.

Playing perfect connections makes the space between the notes sound tidy, but it can also turn notes into phrases. Think of the notes flowing into each other with no "bumps." Ease one note right into the next, and the notes will be felt in one gesture. When you hear "jungle rot" (those messy fingering slips between notes), analyze what finger didn't move at the same time and then do the opposite. Circle bad connections and treat them as mistakes.

Helpful hints for a steady air stream or bow

Think of riding an escalator or ice skating when connecting notes. Even pianists can think, "Don't take your bow off the string." Keep the tone sounding no matter what the notes are.

For string instruments
- Don't clutch.
- Lift the finger you are sliding when changing positions. If you can hear the intervening note, you are clutching too hard.
- Keep the bow even.
- Don't allow changing positions, changing strings, or different bowings to interfere with connecting notes.
- Don't let playing at the frog, tip, or middle change your phrasing without your permission.

TONE COLOR

A mother croons a lullaby to her baby; a sergeant barks at the recruit; a young man declares to his fiancé his undying love; a woman wails when told her son has been killed. Strong emotions speak in different voices. Tone of voice, or timbre, also conveys emotional meaning in music. A full-bodied open sound declares excitement or confidence, and a round hooty sound conveys mystery. Tone color is especially important on string instruments. Each string has its own sound, and the same note played in different positions or using harmonics conveys different meanings. Imagine your sound as a real color, and play a haunting gray melody or a purple passion piece.

VIBRATO

Vibrato speed and width changes with emotions. If the phrase is exciting, make the vibrato more exciting, too.

Using vibrato:

- Try these forms: narrow and slow, wide and slow, narrow and
    fast, wide and fast. All portray different emotions.
- Use vibrato most of the time (if it is appropriate for your instrument
    and the musical period), unless trilling or playing fast passages.
- Don't "count out loud" with vibrato. In other words, the vibrator
    should not be precisely timed to, say, a sixteenth-note in the music.
- String players should start the vibrato before the note
    and keep it going after the bow has stopped.

Where to use more vibrato:

- Higher notes
- Solos, rather than chamber music
- Music from the Romantic era
- The first note of a slur
- Interesting accidentals
- The note before a skip of a fourth or more
- The highest or lowest note of the phrase
- An appoggiatura
- The climax of the phrase
- The note you love

Where to use less vibrato:

- Music of the Renaissance, Baroque, and Classical periods
- An ensemble (to blend in)
- Fast passages
- Quiet, reflective moments

ARTICULATION

Articulation is about the beginnings and the endings of notes. How hard is the attack, and what is the length of the note? The attack and length of the note depends on the mood you want to convey.

Articulating:

- Use a strong attack (bow/tongue/finger) to add clar-
    ity to runs, especially on the first note of a phrase.
- String players have a huge arsenal of bow-
    ings. Learn the best for each effect.
- The larger the ensemble, the shorter the articulation must be. Staccato
    that is appropriate in band will sound like a woodpecker in a solo.
- Separate a series of the same note with a sliver of si-
    lence so that each note is clearly heard.

GREAT IDEAS

Some of these hints for achieving greater musicality may sound mechanical. But as beginning actors use specific exercises to overcome inhibitions and become expressive thespians, so must beginning musicians learn to unlock their ability to communicate through expressive music.

Soldiers on the battlefield are told that bravery is nothing more than acting unafraid when they are fearful. The same can be said for playing musically. Students learn by acting as if they are musical. Before long you won't need to act. These techniques and exercises will allow you the freedom to express your musicality in any way you choose.

Sneak Preview

Now that you're playing with beautiful phrasing and your audience is giving you a standing ovation because they are so moved, memorization may be the next step in communication. In the next chapter, we'll talk about the pros and cons of playing memorized music and how to learn something so that it is solid under pressure.

THIRTY-ONE

How to Memorize without Having a Brain Freeze

Opening night. The audience is a dark mass offstage, rustling and murmuring. They fade into silence as you walk out to center stage, to the right of the conductor's podium. You bow to the darkened concert hall and take your seat at the piano. As the orchestra soars through the magnificent introduction, you lift your hands to play the first note. Suddenly your mind is a blank. "What note?" you inwardly scream. Your hands hover above the keyboard as the orchestra races on without you. Sweat forms on your brow. The audience titters. The director puts down his baton, and the music stops. You dash off the stage without looking back—never to play the piano again!

Shaking violently, you wake up in a cold sweat from this horribly vivid dream. You don't even play the piano! You're a clarinetist, for heaven's sake! Immediately you panic about forgetting your concerto in next week's concert.

IS MEMORIZING A NIGHTMARE OR A NECESSITY?

Many people perform much better when they play from memory. Playing from sheet music is like reading from a book: the story is there, but reading makes it seem less personal. Playing from memory means you can walk out and play directly to the audience without sheets of mumbo-jumbo getting in the way of what you're saying.

On the other hand, too much emphasis can be placed on memorizing. Professionals sometimes use music, even when playing concerti. If playing from memory makes you nervous, or your memorization skills aren't quite up to par, playing with music is perfectly acceptable. Weeks and weeks of lessons spent on drilling memory can be a huge waste of time. If you play better with the music, play with the music. If you play better with the music memorized, play from memory.

Some musicians play through their piece a few times and it's memorized. They make the rest of us feel bad. If you're someone who struggles, figure out how you can memorize best:

- Aurally. You can listen to how a piece sounds and play it back. (Lucky you!)
- Photographically. You can see the notes in your head and play them without having them physically in front of you.
- Digitally. You let your fingers move through the notes automatically, without thinking about what you're actually playing. This is probably the most dangerous form of memorization, because if you slip, it can be incredibly hard to figure out what note you should start on.
- Theoretically. This is the most analytical form. If you're going to use this method, you'll need a good grasp of scales, chords, and sequences. Despite the required knowledge, this is actually one of the easier ways to memorize, as it's essentially playing digitally with signposts.

Zoë, age 16, is memorizing the Khachaturian Violin Concerto in D Minor. "Most of my memory is finger memory, but now I'm forcing myself to really memorize the notes in case my fingers mess up. I don't want to have to go all the way back to the beginning if I miss something. I try to memorize patterns, and sometimes I depend on my ear if I can't remember a note."

Start Small

Start with a simple piece with lots of scales, arpeggios, and repeating patterns. Be careful to memorize it without any mistakes, as it's hard to fix something that's already stuck in your brain.

Memorize photographically and digitally.

Memorize one bar at a time the same way you would memorize a poem. Play the first bar several times looking at the music, then without the music. Do the same with the second bar, and then add the first bar. Rehearse those two bars before you add the third. Break the piece up into sections. Connect them once they're memorized.

Memorize theoretically.

Name all of the scales, chords and arpeggios, intervals, cadences, key changes, chord progressions, sequences, and repeats. Think out loud or write down as much as possible about the piece without playing it. For example: "Letter B is in G major. Measure 10 is a G major scale starting on the note D. It has a repeating pattern of three notes up then skip a third down. The fourth phrase starts on an E, the next phrase on a G, and the next on an A." Label phrases that are *almost* alike. If measures 10 and 14 are both minor arpeggios, but 10 starts on A and 14 starts on E, give them names. Call one phrase "Big Bird" and another phrase "Oscar." One of my students named a particular phrase "Petunia" because it reminded him of Harry Potter's crotchety aunt! After trying to play the piece without music, analyze every mistake that you made and mark it in the music. Just the act of writing the mistake down will help you remember it.

Time Management

Start memorizing the piece from the moment you start learning it. Divide up the piece and set goals for yourself on your calendar. It's foolhardy to practice the whole piece and then count on memorizing it three weeks before the performance.

Your memory won't be perfect from one day to the next, but if you think you've forgotten something you played just the day before, don't be fooled. You'll probably just be able to check the music once or twice before being able to play it from memory again. Even if you're sure you've got it down pat, go over it again and pay special attention to the connections between different sections.

Once you've totally memorized a piece, put it in the freezer for a few weeks. Thaw it out later to add the final touches.

Test your memory:

- Cut the sheet music into sections and put them in a bag. Pull a section out of the bag and start to play there. This will give you practice in starting anywhere, so if there's a memory slip, you won't need to start at the beginning every time. (I have friends who have told me recital nightmare experiences of going back to the top over and over until they gave up and slunk off the stage.)
- Bring copies of the original score to your lesson and have your teacher mark down each week's memory slips.
- Memorize the letter or numbering system of the music for fast reference. If you get lost, it will be easier to get back on track when the pianist whispers "Letter F."
- Practice singing the piece. Your brain and ears, not just your fingers, need to know the piece.
- Learn to hear the music in your head as vividly as you would in your ear. You're not going crazy when you can't get the piece out of your head.
- Rehearse the music without your instrument. Memorize every note, marking, and fingering.
- Practice with the full score and look for cues to help your entrances and other tricky parts.
- Listen to the recording over and over.

- Play along with the recording or work with the computer accompaniment programs.
- Be prepared to play the piece at a different tempo. If you can't play it slowly, you probably don't really know it.
- Most memory lapses occur during a difficult technical part. Be aware and prepared.
- See chapter 33, "Conquer Your Fear Factor." The more relaxed and focused you are, the less likely you are to have a memory breakdown.

Trick yourself:

- Play with the music to see how far you can read ahead, and then look away.
- Move the music farther and farther away on the stand so that you're barely reading it.
- Start by memorizing the last section to make sure it gets as much attention as the first section. Remember, those are the last notes the audience or judge will hear.
- Photocopy the piece in a reduced size and tape it together. Keep it on the stand as a safety net. Glance at the topography of the piece to recall sections you have already memorized.
- Be patient.

Test it yourself:

- Keep checking the music to make sure all the notes, fingering, bowing, articulation, dynamics, and whatever are right on. If you just play from memory, never looking at the music, your playing will turn into a garbled version of the original. Have you ever played the party games "Chinese Whispers" or "Telephone"?
- Tape-record your playing to pinpoint memory failures.
- Test yourself without your instrument. Write out the music to a difficult section on manuscript paper or play it on the piano.
- If you're not a pianist, play a difficult passage on the piano to make sure your memory isn't just finger memory. This helps you see the note names and intervals in black and white.
- If you are a pianist, play the piece on a table or a keyboard with the sound turned off. Play each hand separately.
- Practice playing the memorized piece at the beginning of your practice session, or space it out during the day to simulate getting only one chance during a real performance.

It's amazing how distracting an audience can be. If your memory's going to slip, have it be at church or a retirement home but not at a contest. Never play by memory for the first time in a stressful situation.

Once you ditch the music, you've gotten rid of your shield. There's nothing between you and the audience now! You probably don't want to stare at the audience, so where do you look?

Closing your eyes is fine if you're at a reflective or emotional part of your piece. But if you do it all the time, you'll look like you're in a trance or hiding from the audience.

If you're a pianist or string player, looking at your instrument is a great strategy. However, this won't work for a lot of wind players, especially flutes.

It's not a good idea to watch your teacher, either. If you try to read your teacher's expression and he burps, sighs, or sneezes, you'll fall apart. If you look at the floor, you'll seem embarrassed or afraid. If you look at the ceiling, it will probably break your concentration, as well as look as if you're asking for divine guidance.

Where *should* you look? The best thing that you can do is to move your eyes around so you don't look like a robot. You can look at the accompanist during important moments and transitions, but it's best to look out over the heads of the audience. You can avoid their stares but make them think you're looking at them.

GREAT IDEAS

Memorization need not provoke fear and a desire to bolt from the room. The goal of memorizing is not to terrify you but to let you connect with the audience more easily. There's an old saying: "A musician should have the score in his head. He shouldn't have his head in the score." Even if you don't feel comfortable playing an entire piece from memory, it's still worth it to have small sections memorized so that your eyes aren't glued to the music all the time. Even if you're afraid to play memorized, the tricks in this chapter will make it easier to add to your understanding of music. Give it a try!

Sneak Preview
Now that you've learned how to sight-read, play in tune, play musically, and memorize, you're ready for your next performance. Or are you? Our next section will guide you in performing your best—and enjoying it.

PART SEVEN

PERFORMING WITH CONFIDENCE

THIRTY-TWO

Put Concerts and Contests into Perspective

"I don't want to play in a contest," 13-year-old Joey protests. "I have to work on the same piece for months just to play it one time. I hate playing in front of a judge. What if he's mean? What if everybody's better than I am? What if I fall apart? Why can't I just play my songs at home?"

Are contests more trouble than they're worth? Even though contests and public recitals have a potential downside, I think the good generally outweighs the bad. Let's look at both sides, starting with the positive.

WHY PARTICIPATE IN CONCERTS AND CONTESTS?

Contests allow to you to accomplish many things:

- Work toward a goal. We always study more before the big test. Amazingly, even though you're focusing on just a few pieces, your musicality and technique will get better on everything because of the performance preparation.
- Work on a timeline. Preparing for a recital in October, a holiday concert in December, and contests in February and April give you goals throughout the year.
- Prepare for the real world. Almost every aspect of life is competitive. Sports, getting into college, and landing a job are but a few examples. Contests help you handle the kind of pressure you will get from taking your SATs and the big final exams in school.
- Gain self-confidence from performing in public. Giving class speeches will seem easy after playing Mozart in front of 100 people.
- Discover there is "life after death." Even though you messed up, no one died. Learning to live through "failures" teaches you how to keep going when the going gets tough.
- Learn from someone other than your teacher. Even if you've already heard a suggestion from your teacher, hearing it from a judge may make you pay more attention.

- Experience the fun of performing. What a natural high!
- Hear other players. You can discover new pieces you might want to play. You can also see how your playing compares with that of your peers.
- Be recognized for all the hard work you've done. You deserve it.
- Be the center of attention. We all love that applause.
- Provide written documentation of awards for use in college applications.
- Get a new outfit and a treat afterwards. (Parents, take note.)
- Share the wonderful gift of music.

ISN'T BEING A WINNER IMPORTANT?

The contest was over and the winners were being announced. "... and third place goes to Barbara Lang." "How wonderful," I thought as I made my way through the crowd to congratulate my student Barbara. But Barbara's mother intercepted me, a distressed look on her face. "Third place is *not* okay," she stated coldly. "We were expecting first. What happened? Why didn't she get first?" Her response shocked and dismayed me. "Barbara played beautifully, and I am so proud of her," I said. "What's wrong with third place?" In fact, I thought, what's wrong with not placing at all?

Winning is a good thing, right? Yes, but not always. When you set your sights only on winning, you take a big risk. The danger here bears repeating. If you only care about winning, you will be disappointed time after time.

Placing too much emphasis on the outcome may even *change* the outcome. If you *have* to win, you'll worry and "psych" yourself out. One mistake can put you into a tailspin. You've seen it happen with ice skaters and gymnasts at the Olympics. Some make a mistake, dust themselves off, and go on to win. Others are visibly shaken by their first misstep, lose their confidence, and then fall again.

FORGET PERFECTION

Have you seen paparazzi pictures of glamorous movie stars wearing baggy sweat suits and no makeup? They don't look so great without all the airbrushing. Don't even try to compare yourself to a famous person unless you get their wardrobe, their makeup artist, and their image consultant. Do you think your favorite singers on the radio sound that good without digital enhancement? Ha. Take the microphone and sound engineer away and listen to the difference. The only perfect performances are in movies or recordings. In real life, notes squeak and get missed, we run out of bow or air, or our brain freezes.

Don't fuel your fears by expecting perfection. When you make the first mistake, be glad you got that one out of the way and go on. I've watched students rush off the stage in tears after a performance. What they thought was a disaster was probably only a few missed notes. But they missed more than just a few notes—they missed the whole point.

The emphasis that the teacher, student, and parents put on the performance and on the preparation is a delicate balancing act. We need to practice our hearts out, but keep in mind that what happens on contest day may be out of our control. So many things can affect a judged situation.

The adjudicators only hear you for that moment in time.

They're not aware of the progress you've made, how long you've studied, how long you've been with your current teacher, or how much effort it took to get where you are. They don't know if you're sick or couldn't sleep the night before. They didn't hear you yesterday when it was perfect at home. They don't know if today's performance represents your best effort.

The judge and your teacher may have different ideas.

Many years in the state competition, I've seen three judges give opposite comments for the same technique. ("Loved your tone"; "Your tone needs work"; "Your tone is awful.") Music isn't math. We love it because it is an art, which means that people's reactions vary. We wouldn't want it any other way.

You can't control your competition.

You may have practiced two hours a day, but the next kid practiced for three, or played the judge's favorite song, or had a better smile. None of us rules the universe. We can only be responsible for ourselves. We have no power over the judge's opinions or how well our competitors perform. If someone does better and your only goal was to win, you'll feel like a failure even if you played well.

The event isn't as important as the preparation leading up to it.

No single day should define our playing. Sometimes we don't play our best, sometimes we're *not* the best, and sometimes the adjudication is just plain crazy. Even Mozart never got a real job! Learn what you can from the judge and the experience and go on.

WHAT MAKES A WINNER?

Performing music is very personal. Playing in front of an audience can be as painful as modeling bathing suits! The more you care about what other people think, or how you compare with other performers, the more you'll feel you come up short. There will *always* be performers who are better and worse. (And people who are richer, smarter, more popular, and cuter, too!) You're "competing" against yourself. If you've improved, then that's what counts. Just because you didn't win first place, or place at all, doesn't mean the effort wasn't worth it. Not everyone's going to be a superstar. *Music is for everyone.*

You are a winner if you answer yes to the following questions:

- Did I put in my full effort in preparing?
- Did I improve on the piece and in my playing?
- Did I learn about my instrument and music?
- Did I enjoy the process of learning and my lessons?
- Did I gain valuable experience performing?
- Did I make music and entertain the audience?

If you answered yes, the concert or competition was a success. If you answer these questions *before* the big day and give some negative answers, your disappointment will be easier to swallow and not so earth-shattering.

WHAT IF I FAIL?

What if you don't win? Welcome to the real world of musicians who vie with many for that coveted first prize or spot in the orchestra. Are you a failure if you go home empty-handed? No!

When your performance is less than perfect, the audience will likely forget in a matter of minutes—if they even noticed. And in the scheme of life, if your performance is off a teeny bit, it's not going to drastically affect your future. Now, if a neurosurgeon is off a teeny bit, someone's future could be cut short. We'll play again, but that spinal cord patient might never walk again.

What if you really bomb? Successful people see their "losses" not as personal failure but as feedback. Take time to lick your wounds, and then analyze what could have helped. Direct your thoughts to "Next time" instead of "What if." Because it didn't go as planned doesn't mean the process of learning was not worthwhile.

Don't let your own performance or a judge's decision undermine your confidence. Anyone who puts themselves through the rigors of performance deserves to feel proud. Failure is about an outcome; it is *not* a personality characteristic. You may have failed to win, but you are not a failure. Even if you are a terrible musician, you are not a terrible person.

IT'S UP TO YOU

When you don't make first chair, get into the orchestra you wanted, win the contest, get into your dream college, or win the scholarship, you have two choices. You can blame something or someone else, or you can decide to work even harder.

When we overreact to life's curveballs, we make ourselves more upset. (I speak from experience.) Life isn't always fair. I've learned the hard way that it does no good to complain to the "authorities" about a judge who seems unfair, arbitrary, or even cruel. Give yourself a day to feel disappointed and then pick up and go on. Say, "Oh, well, there's always next year." Perhaps the judging wasn't right, but get over it. Perhaps you didn't play your best. It doesn't matter.

If you blame favoritism or politics, you will learn to view life as a victim. Victims will never be winners because they feel that no matter what they do, they won't win. Real winners know that it is up to them to make it happen and that the bumps along the road make you stronger.

Musicians who always think, "Me first!" will also never really be winners. "I'm not going to play in orchestra unless I'm first chair" or "Why enter the contest at all unless I go to State?" People with this attitude miss out on what being a musician is all about. It's not all about you and your ego and reputation. It's about the music, remember? Music is not a race but a wonderful gift. We are all winners.

> *"I performed in a music 'festival' (competition) and the judge was unlike any other I had encountered in my seven years of various competitions, master classes, and the like. After I played, he couldn't find one nice thing to say. My mother insists that he gave me one compliment before rushing to the insults, but all my ears heard were put-downs. The purpose of the festival is for adjudicators to give helpful feedback and constructive criticism. Unfortunately, the way this judge presented the criticism was in a condescending, degrading way that made me want to float out the window onto the grassy lawn and cherry blossoms outside.*
>
> *"When the adjudicator was through critiquing me, and I was in the car, my mom asked me if I still wanted to play my concerto for the same judge later in the week. I couldn't think of any reason why I wouldn't. As much as the judge put me down, there was no way I was going to throw away all my hard work and preparation. I would simply go back and play my concerto for the rest of the audience—and for myself. Two days later, when I finished my concerto and took my bow, I felt good inside. I was happy with my playing. Although the judge still gave me deconstructive criticism, I smiled through the entire adjudication. I was so pleased with my performance. Now when I look back at this recent experience, I realize that on those two days, I achieved true success. I gained the rewarding gift of musical maturity—to play for oneself, not to please someone else." (Munya, age 17)*

The advantages of performing in concerts and contests generally outweigh the disadvantages. Focus on the growth you made toward reaching your goals and not just that one big performance. Remember, "It's not whether you win or lose, it's how you play the game."

Sneak Preview

Now that you have the right attitude, what else can you do to prepare for the big day? The next two chapters will show you how to make your best efforts shine through in a good performance.

THIRTY-THREE

Conquer Your Fear Factor

All musicians know the signs: your knees shake, your heart is in your throat, blood pounds in your ears, and your chest feels heavy. Negative thoughts speed faster and faster: "My hands are so sweaty I'll drop my instrument. I can't breathe! I can't hear! I should have practiced more, and now I'm going to make a fool of myself! Why did I ever choose to do this performance? Why didn't I remember my deodorant?"

Some performers are so confident they never worry about stage fright, but for many of us, feelings of anxiety and dread can erase six months of hard practice. It's no wonder we say people suffer from stage fright. Many talented musicians undermine their chances for success when they allow anxious thoughts and feelings to overwhelm them.

Sufferers, take heart. You can learn new habits to help you feel more relaxed and confident playing in front of any number of people. Some people think of stage fright as some deadly demon from a monster movie that appears out of nowhere to terrorize them. But stage fright is not something that happens *to* us. It's something we create with our own minds. Self-created and self-imposed, our fear of missing a note here or there can kick our adrenaline sky high, trigger other uncomfortable physical symptoms, and strip the joy from any performance. Stage fright is not a permanent condition you need to learn to live with; it's a behavior pattern you can change. In this chapter I'll show you how to reduce performance anxiety by preparing your music *and* your mind. You'll learn techniques that will help you in school and later on in your career, whenever you have to perform in public.

PREPARE YOUR MUSIC

"The best defense is a good offense." Everyone has heard this saying as it refers to sports teams and their plan of attack. Since nerves can rob us of a large percentage of our ability, musicians need a plan of attack, too. You might say we need to be prepared 130%. Don't be lulled into a false sense of security if your piece is good enough "most of the time," or if you can play the run on the seventh repetition. During your performance, those funny runs or difficult intervals may come back to haunt you. There's a saying in the military that when a great problem or crisis arises, you don't rise to the challenge, you fall to your level of training. So make sure you are trained well.

"The best way to not be nervous is to practice more! An hour before I perform, I focus on the music I'm about to play. I'm thinking about the tough parts in the music and how to handle them. Onstage I make sure my harp pedals are set right. I'm not afraid of playing in front of an audience because I focus on sharing my music with them." (Keleah, age 15)

PLAN A TRAINING SCHEDULE AND STICK TO IT

We all hate that sense of panic when we realize we've fallen behind and know it will be almost impossible to catch up. Begin practicing early, or you may find yourself praying for a miracle. Like a long-distance runner, use time management to space your practicing so you won't have to cram at the end. Write out your practice goals with a daily practice schedule that allows you to achieve your goals well ahead of performance day.

"I began studying flute about three years ago. I remember that I was so shy, I wouldn't even tune in front of anyone. Over the past three years, I've changed most in my ability to conquer my shyness. Although my attitude has helped this transformation, I am most grateful for my lessons. I didn't have a choice whether or not to perform; I was just thrown out there. This sounds cruel, but it was the best thing that could have happened. Although the first few times were, granted, probably some of the worst experiences I will ever have, they made me more comfortable with performing, and I gained confidence. I also played tons of music. Through duets, concertos, and just sight-reading, I learned to understand the music and know what I was trying to say. This may not seem that important, but once you get out onstage, confidence and experience are just not enough. When you're trying to say something, you don't pay attention to the audience or how you're doing. I can get swept away just by making music, and that combined with the confidence makes performing a cinch." (Perrin, age 14)

PREPARE YOUR PERFORMANCE

Why do some students play perfectly during practice sessions, only to then "fall apart" during pressure situations? Chances are, they've only played their pieces in comfortable, familiar environments and have not learned to adapt to the stresses of performing before an audience or a judge. I have a sign in my studio that reads, "But I could play it at home!" You may think you sound like James Galway, Lang Lang, or Yo-Yo Ma in the privacy of your living room, but can you re-create that superior performance in public?

The path to a stunning performance can seem long. Start small and set progressively more demanding performance goals along the way. Let's say that it takes you 12 performances to go from panicky first-timer to savvy performer. Set goals for each of these performances—even if they start out as small as these:

- Performance ONE: Make it through the performance alive.
- Performance TWO: Make it through the performance alive without fainting or tears.
- Performance THREE: Make it through alive without fainting or tears and remember your own name in the announcement.
- Performance FOUR: Make it through alive without fainting or tears, say your name, and correctly pronounce the name of the piece and the composer.
- Performance FIVE: Make it through alive without fainting or tears, say all the names correctly, and then smile at the audience.
- Performance SIX: Make it through alive without fainting or tears, say all the names correctly, smile at the audience, and then smile at the judge.
- Performance SEVEN: Make it through alive without fainting or tears, say all the names correctly, smile at the audience and at the judge, and really mean it.
- Performance EIGHT: Make it through alive without fainting or tears, say all the names, smile sincerely at the audience and the judge, and look confident.
- Performance NINE: Make it through alive without fainting or tears, say all those names, smile sincerely at the audience and the judge, look confident, and keep playing after you make mistakes.
- Performance TEN: Make it through alive without fainting or tears, say all those names, give the big smile, look great, keep playing after the mistakes, and don't beat yourself up for them.
- Performance ELEVEN: Make it through alive without fainting or tears, say all those names, smile big, look great, make the mistakes, don't worry, be happy, and then smile and bow at the end.
- Performance TWELVE: Make it through alive without fainting or tears, say all those names, smile big, look great, make fewer mistakes, take the bow, and know that although everything wasn't perfect, you did your best, enjoyed the process, shared your music, and look forward to the next time.

Practice playing—even for audiences who can't hear a note!

Imagine if you went out on only one date a year. (Okay, some of you don't have to imagine.) That one date would loom in importance, and you would probably be so nervous that it would be your last. Now imagine going out on a date every weekend. Even if the dates were with different people, you would start to get the hang of dating, and an upcoming date wouldn't seem like the end of the world.

Now imagine if you performed in a concert every week. By the fifth, tenth, or twentieth time you would be pretty confident. Well, it can be a lot easier to set up concerts than to set up dates! Perform as often as you can, taking baby steps if need be. Start with concerts for stuffed animals or even a chair or music stand.

Be your own audience by setting up a voice recorder or video camera. Tape yourself giving your introduction and then playing your piece. Did you get a little nervous when playing in front of the unblinking eye of the video camera? Feeling anxiety when playing alone in a room with a recorder or video camera is proof positive that performance anxiety comes from within.

Gradually increase your audience size.

Desensitize your fear of playing in front of people by building a progressively bigger audience. After your concerts for stuffed animals, progress to the family dog, siblings, parents, relatives, and unsuspecting friends and neighbors who drop by. Don't be shy about asking real people to be audience members; they will appreciate hearing your music. Ask your "audience" for feedback.

Once you feel confident with your in-home audiences, stretch yourself. Play for the person who has the lesson before and after you and anyone else who might be around the music room. Perform at the library, hospitals, church, or retirement homes. Grab your friends at school, perform at one another's homes, or perform in front of the band or orchestra. You may think it's a lot of trouble to have many trial runs to prepare for a concert, but you'll be glad you did when you stride up to the stage and end with a huge smile on your face.

> *"Stage fright: I had it bad. It worked so well for me to take those little steps instead of just thrusting a big solo recital on me. I did small recitals in the studio for just a few people, which helped. By my senior year, I confidently played a solo at my high school graduation. I really had gotten to the point that I had overcome that draining fear and just held on to the adrenaline. I'm so grateful for the confidence that playing an instrument has given me. And I even met my husband in college wind ensemble!" (Kim, who played flute through college and is now an art teacher)*

SIMULATE YOUR PERFORMANCE BY ROLE-PLAYING

Role-playing is practicing a situation in an environment that closely simulates the actual one. Role-playing helps you practice the *performance*, not just the music. Reinvent the atmosphere of an audition. Take time to warm up, then take at least a 10-minute break (while you wait to be called). Next, run up and down the stairs to give you that out of breath feeling of nervousness. If possible, have "judges" on hand to worry you. If you can't find live judges, play to three chairs.

Re-create your real performance as closely as possible by wearing the same clothes you will wear at the actual event. From the moment you walk through the door, you must be "in character." If you stumble up to the front, giggle, wipe your sweaty hands on your clothes, drop pages of your score, sigh, or look distressed, both you and the audience will sense a potential failure.

Learn the walk and the talk.

Your posture and look of confidence "set the stage" for a polished performance. Learn how to shake hands with strangers, look them in the eye, and introduce yourself to gain that aura of self-confidence. Practice walking with your chest lifted, abdomen tight, and chin level with the floor. Performers who walk confidently on to the stage, make eye contact with the judge and audience, and offer a sincere smile have already begun to win them over. Acting with confidence will also make you feel more confident, too. As a bonus, just turning your lips into a smile emits endorphins that help you relax.

Be sure to slowly and loudly announce your piece, take time to get ready, then play your heart out. Acknowledge your audience with a smile and a bow. No matter how the performance went, pretend it was fun. Make your audience feel you are happy to be there—even if you have to fake it. Start the mock auditions at least two weeks before the big day, and the real audition will feel familiar and comfortable.

Know your performance environment.

Why do directors call for dress rehearsals? Because every chance to perform under the same conditions boosts confidence and gives insight into what may falter under pressure. Pilots and astronauts use this technique when they learn to fly using simulators. Just as pilots must become comfortable in the cockpit, you can become more comfortable in front of an audience if you know your performance environment.

If possible, visit the room you'll be playing in even if it is the day of your performance. Note the seating arrangement for the audience and the position of the stage. Notice the position of the music stand, piano, and judges' table. If possible, stand on the stage and mentally place yourself looking out to the audience. Are windows and doors to the sides or in back?

Activate all your senses. Does the room have a particular smell? Is the floor slippery? Does the floor squeak when you walk on it? Do you hear traffic noises? The more specific information you gather about your performance locale, the more successful you'll be with our next suggestion.

PREPARE YOUR MIND

Being prepared is more than knowing your music cold. It's about knowing how to control your body when it reacts to the stress of performance. It's also about training your internal voice to stay positive without judging and criticizing. Most important, it's about learning to stay in the moment so you can share your music and your passion with the audience. Let's tackle the self-defeating habits that can contribute to feelings of stage fright.

Forget perfection.

As we said before, the only "perfect" performances are doctored recordings. You can set impeccably high standards for the practice room, but you should have only realistic ones for the performance hall.

Speak to yourself using positive self-talk.

Once again, attitude is everything. Have you ever heard of a self-fulfilling prophecy? Just thinking about failing can make us fail. If you continually say to yourself, "Everyone is better than I am. I know I'll screw up," your body will be happy to oblige. Imagine if you told yourself every day, "I am a mean and horrible person. I hate everyone, and they hate me." Acting and feeling like a caring, giving human being would be against your beliefs. We become what we tell ourselves. If you tell yourself you're bad, it's going to be hard to be good.

Imagine the worst.

What's the worst that could happen if your performance goes awry? You may feel embarrassed or disappointed. But it won't be life-threatening. Your teacher and parents will still love you. The audience may not even know. A year from now, you'll have forgotten about it. The bottom line is that while it may feel bad, even horrible at the moment, in the end it will add to your experience. It will build character, and you'll recover if you try to learn from your mistakes.

> *"I remember my teacher saying, 'Who cares if you make a mistake? It's a mistake. Big deal! People don't want to feel nervous watching you onstage.' Somehow that clicked for me. Making a mistake, any mistake in life, was a big deal to me. I had never forced myself to think of the true result of my mistakes. Virtually nothing. No one cares. We all make mistakes. So what? Life goes on. People actually feel closer to you sometimes if you make mistakes."*
> *(Meagan, adult)*

IGNORE DISTRACTIONS

Performances aren't played in a vacuum. As the saying goes, "Stuff happens," and aside from an earthquake, "The show must go on!" Ignoring distractions takes effort and practice. Get used to different playing conditions. Practice in every room of the house. Start with the bathroom where the tone sounds wonderful (tone hospital) and the mirror gives valuable feedback on posture, position, and how your announcement looks. Practice in a common room with lots of commotion: people walking back and forth, the radio or TV playing, cupboards banging, someone talking and laughing on the phone.

I've attended contests where sirens wailed outside and a ballet company danced on the floor above, in horribly hot rooms or in freezing rooms with the wind blowing through. Sometimes piano keys stick or you hear performances in the next room. Be prepared.

FOCUS ON YOUR PLAYING

How many times have you read a page in a dry textbook and realized you didn't remember a single word as your mind drifted? Try playing your instrument while doing math problems. How much concentration is left for the music? Our own wandering thoughts can interfere with our performance as much as reading a book can. Learn to bring yourself back on track.

Practice your concentration. Have someone read a book to you. Follow the text and repeat the words right behind them. Listening to the words spoken while you relay the previous words (like a simultaneous translator) forces you to stay focused. As you practice your instrument, make a game with yourself to see how long you can focus on the music without letting other thoughts interfere. As soon as your mind starts to drift, make a conscious effort to pull it back. Ignore extraneous thoughts as you would ignore a 4-year-old trying to disturb you onstage.

FOCUS ON YOUR MUSIC

Remember why you are doing this in the first place: because you love music. When stage fright rears its ugly head, plunge yourself into playing. Gain control of your wandering thoughts first with the technical aspects like correct notes, rhythm, intonation, and tone and then give yourself over to the music. If it is a calm piece, imagine playing it to soothe a baby. If the piece is romantic, tell the world you are in love, and if the piece is exciting, get supercharged. You love this piece, so make your audience love it, too!

IMAGINE SUCCESS WITH VISUALIZATION

Athletes and musicians alike visualize performance situations and how they will respond. Studies have shown that basketball players, for instance, can improve their performance by imagining shooting and making baskets. Visualization, or mental rehearsal, can also help you prepare for a successful performance.

Even if you've never visited the performance room, still try to envision it. Picture where the judges and audience will sit and where you will perform. Imagine every detail of your performance from walking into the room, announcing your name and piece, to playing every note perfectly. When you mentally rehearse the music, play wonderfully and always end with a standing ovation! When performance day arrives, you'll feel more confident having already "experienced" the competition.

Visualization is more than humming the song to yourself. Visualization is like watching a great movie and feeling, hearing, and seeing yourself in a perfect performance. When you practice using imagery, your body will better know what it is supposed to do. A good time to practice visualization is lying in bed in a dark room with no distractions, right before you fall asleep. During this twilight time, your thoughts tend to stay in your subconscious and create a memory as if you had experienced it. Tip: this is also a good time to memorize material for school tests.

Visualize the good, not the bad.

One of the most important aspects of visualization is imagining a positive result, not an embarrassing scenario. On the big day, while you're waiting to perform, imagine the audience clapping and feel your happiness from a job well done. Focus your energy on your feelings of confidence and competence. By banishing negative thoughts and visualizing success, you can learn to think and act like a winner. Later, we'll discuss a proven routine you can put into action that will carry you from the time you're waiting your turn until you've finished your successful performance.

Savor the sweet taste of success.

No, I'm not talking about eating chocolate. Get in touch with the rewards of all your hard work. As you work toward the next concert or contest, remember how your practicing allowed you to play the last piece with ease. Weren't you proud of yourself? Isn't it worth all that practice to make it happen again?

YOUR AUDIENCE, FRIEND OR FOE?

How many of us have gone onstage, heart pounding, asking ourselves, "What will they think when I mess up?" But do *you* sit in the audience thinking, "I can't wait until the performer makes a mistake. There's one. Great!" Of course not. You're there to enjoy the music, and you feel sorry for performers who trip up. The audience is rooting for you. They don't want to see you looking nervous or making excuses. They want to relax in the confidence of your performance, see you succeed, and enjoy themselves. The audience is not the enemy; in fact, we are our own worst enemies.

Many people try to fight their fear by separating themselves from their audience. They might pretend the audience isn't there or imagine them wearing their underwear or even wearing nothing at all. While the underwear trick may work for some people, I don't advise it. When you distance yourself from your audience, you focus even more on your fears. You go into your head and not into the moment. Embrace the audience by remembering your purpose, and you will become "music-conscious" instead of "self-conscious." Think of sharing your music as a service to others; you'll enjoy yourself more and the audience will, too.

> *"Worse than making a mistake is taking away the joy of the performance by making my audience nervous. I started by being nervous that I would get ner-*

vous, then I accepted that I would be nervous and started pretending not to be, and then somewhere several years down the road, I was no longer nervous at all. The people in the audience became friends—people who just needed a moment of nice music or a word of assurance, not people who were waiting to judge or rake me over the coals. When I enjoyed my playing, everyone else did, too. The process of excellence is the same for playing or speaking in front of groups—to remember why you are there and who you are really there for."
(Megan, adult)

Tell the audience your story.

Imagine the minister who concentrates on the sound of his own voice instead of the message of his sermon. His congregation would lose interest quickly. The same thing happens when we focus just on our tone and technique and not on the feeling and expression we wish to convey. Communicate to the audience the beauty of the piece, not just your fingering technique.

Imagine what the composer thought when writing the piece. Picture a scene, a person, an event, even a mood or a color. Treat each piece like program music that depicts a person, place, event, or conversation. Let this picture help you share the drama with your audience.

Now that you have the screenplay, you need the actor, and that's you! Recall performers you've seen who look totally natural onstage. Picture a famous singer performing your piece onstage or in a movie. How would they sing it? Emulate their behavior. Move past the notes to become your character and communicate your story. These stories we create focus on the feelings the music conveys, not on ourselves.

Now that you have your mind "under control," what can you do for your shaking body?

TAME THE PSYCHOLOGICAL ASPECTS OF STAGE FRIGHT

Recognize the physical sensations of stage fright and know which symptoms (such as dry mouth or sweaty hands) you're most likely to experience. Managing your emotions before these symptoms appear gives you power over them.

Try these methods to minimize your body's uncomfortable responses:
- Shallow breathing: Breathe in slowly and deeply for a count of five, hold it five counts, and then breathe out slowly for five counts. Some psychologists call this "square breathing," a technique used to combat panic attacks. Repeat until your breathing feels more normal. If you play a wind or brass instrument, circle the important breaths in a color to remind yourself to breathe deeply.
- Hiccups: Try making snake sounds by hissing to control the diaphragm.
- Dry mouth: Keep hydrated. Don't eat salty foods before your performance. Be careful about drinking too much water, though, because it

can replace your natural saliva. Eating a cookie, a piece of candy, or apples may help increase your saliva. Chew Quench gum or suck on lemon and eucalyptus flavored Hall's cough drops. Try Oasis or Biotene mouth spray or toothpaste. If you are desperate, you can massage the sides of your throat or bite your tongue. Avoid taking cold medicine containing antihistamines, as these can dry your mouth.

- Chapped lips: Try Chopsaver (made just for musicians), Burt's Bees lip balm, Cabello, or Carmex.
- Too much saliva: Tilt your head back slightly to move the spit back. Take an antihistamine before the performance.
- Tight throat: Yawn to relax your throat. Remember that open position when it's time to play. Breathe in with an open throat and keep it open as you breathe out.
- Sweaty hands: Rub unscented deodorant on your hands. Run your hands and wrists under cold water just prior to coming onstage. Keep a loose grip on your instrument.
- Sweaty lips: Put a postage stamp on the instrument or use lip plate grips.
- Cold, shaky hands: Wear gloves to warm them. If you can, immerse your hands in warm water and dry them well before you play.
- The shakes: Shake out the shakes! Get blood out into your hands and away from your heart as it prepares you for fight or flight. If possible, take a short walk and breathe deeply.
- Feeling upset: Think of something funny, or smile at a friend right before you play. Activating your smiling muscles elevates your mood.
- Neck and shoulder tension: Bring your shoulders up to your ears. Count to five and then bring them all the way back down. Roll your shoulders forward, then back. Do neck circles.
- Shaky tone: Concentrate on support, deep breaths, and being in control of vibrato.
- General feelings of nervousness: Concentrate on how much you've practiced and how good you are! Acknowledge nervousness as excitement.

Wow. There's a lot that can go wrong but a lot we can do to combat nervousness.

Try the Alexander Technique.

Under the pressure of performance, our bodies need more adrenaline to perform the task. The difference in tension and a peak performance is how our bodies handle that adrenaline. The Alexander Technique fosters spontaneity and creativity by helping the body move in good coordination. Simply putting the body in alignment can help overcome the tightness and tension from adrenaline and make movement help the performance.

Food

Bananas and turkey have been touted for their ability to calm nerves and aid sleep. The helpful ingredient they contain is tryptophan, an essential amino acid, a substance the body cannot produce naturally and must get from food. Tryptophan helps the body produce niacin, a B vitamin, which in turn produces a remarkable chemical called serotonin, which has been proven to promote feelings of well-being, relaxation, confidence, and concentration. People used to take tryptophan supplements, but we've since learned that the safe way to get this amino acid is by eating foods such as brown rice, nuts, or an apple. Monitor how much of these you eat before a concert, though, or you may feel like curling up for a nap or racing to the bathroom!

Biofeedback

Physical therapists can connect you to a biofeedback machine that will measure where and how much tension you are carrying in your body. With this reinforcement, you can learn to relax specific areas like the neck and shoulders.

Meditation

Unbelievable things can happen through meditation. A friend of mine meditated (not medicated) her way through childbirth! Even if you are not a master at meditation, learn to center and relax before every performance.

Beta blockers

Prescription beta-blocker pills such as Inderal are used in the treatment of high blood pressure, angina, and other symptoms of cardiovascular problems. Because they act to steady heartbeats, they have also proven useful in steadying performers' nerves. Many professional musicians use them before auditions and performances, although some report that while Inderal helped their nerves, it also made them feel more detached from the music and audience.

While beta blockers have been shown to be effective, their misuse can be dangerous, especially in asthmatics. Taking this prescription medication is something you must discuss with your doctor. Never accept medication from a friend or relative. Relying on drugs doesn't address the real problem. The best solution is not medication but focusing on techniques to combat anxiety and self-doubt.

ANTICIPATE PERFORMANCE DAY

Star athletes begin their training months in advance of the big event; we too must train our bodies and our music to prepare for performance day.

Two Weeks before Your Performance

If you can play the trick runs only 5 times correctly out of 50 repetitions, those are not good odds! If you can barely play the phrase in one breath, be assured that under pressure, you will be gasping at the end. Keep your standards high as you learn your piece. Don't allow yourself to leave a passage as "good enough." Keep going back until you can play it with at least a 90% success rate. Aim for a date at least two weeks prior to your performance to be "contest ready."

Prepare yourself with the "first chance" practice method.

How many times have we performed and wished we could say, "Cancel that one!" and then play it again? During a performance, we only get one chance. Test your preparedness with the "first chance" method. For one week, at the beginning of each practice session, play through the piece without stopping. Ask yourself, "Did I play at the level I'll be happy with for my performance?" Be assured that you're ready if you have five good "first chances" in a row. For every mistake you make, give yourself a "penalty" like five minutes extra practice that night, or take one piece of candy from your reward stash. The reward if you perform it perfectly? A boost in your confidence.

Pace yourself.

Athletes alternate strenuous workouts with more relaxed workouts. Likewise, musicians must learn to balance the need for improvement against the danger of burnout. Hours on end spent practicing do not necessarily mean improved performance if your mind is not engaged and your body is tired. Sometimes the best thing you can do to improve a piece is to take a day off. Don't practice every piece every day. Some days lighten your practice routine or don't practice at all.

Dress for success.

What you wear can give people an impression of who you are. One year one of my students showed up wearing an outfit that reflected something other than "talented flute student." She walked on to the stage wearing a tight knit dress with plunging neckline, enormous hoop earrings, fishnet stockings, and strappy high heels. At the same contest, another student refused to change out of her school clothes and came dressed in an old wrinkled shirt and jeans with a hole in the knee! Fortunately, the judge commented on both of their inappropriate clothing choices.

Keep in mind that you're dressing for the judge, not your friends. This is the time to be sophisticated, not trendy. I like my students to dress in distinctive colors because I think judges may be more likely to remember the girl in the red dress or the boy in the bright blue shirt than players dressed in dark, drab colors. Black pants or skirt and a white top are always appropriate, but a little boring and reminiscent of a French waiter.

Sometimes I recommend that my students dress to reflect the piece they are performing. A modern piece could be paired with a sophisticated outfit, and the Doppler Hungarian Fantasie could be paired with an outfit with gypsy flair. My students' ensembles usually match each other in some way, such as all wearing blue, solid tops with floral skirts, or black skirts and red sweaters.

Conquer Your Fear Factor

Keep your hair out of your face, and wear makeup if you think it will help the audience see you better. When you know you look great, your mind will be free to concentrate on more important things—like your playing! Dressing well shows your respect for the event and the judges. Wear something that reflects how you want the audience to see you.

- Strapless gowns may reveal more than the emotions in the music, especially when you bow.
- Practice performing in your dress. Too tight and you can't breathe or move, too long and you might trip, too short or too low and the audience will be distracted.
- Scuff up new shoes on the bottom a little so they don't slip.
- Wear a color that will contrast with the background.
- Wear a slip if material might be see-through in the light.
- Bring antistatic spray so your dress doesn't stick to your legs.
- Carry adhesive tape with you for all emergencies!

Regardless of your age or style of clothing, please cross certain items off your wardrobe list: wild prints and patterns, tippy high heels, extremely short skirts, fishnet stockings, T-shirts, jeans, plunging necklines, and exposed bra straps. And please, no bare bellies! Above all, be comfortable and classy.

Create a routine.

In the days leading up to your performance, arrange for as many mock auditions as possible and keep visualizing yourself performing with confidence. Imagine the smiling faces and loud applause of the audience. Look forward to the event as a time to "show off" what you have learned and to play great music.

Practice your piece slowly, in a quiet, calm room. While you play, focus on relaxing and putting all negative thoughts and emotions aside. This will help you associate relaxation with playing your piece.

If possible, create a routine that can be duplicated on performance day. Getting up at the same time, eating the same breakfast, practicing technique in the same order, even saying a mantra ("I love performing") right before playing every day will help make performance day seem like any other. Instead of a general mantra, you may also pick the two things that you hope to succeed on and make them your mantra: for instance, singing tone, strong breaths, even vibrato, or perfect intonation. Getting in the habit of repeating your mantra right before you play will help you remember what to concentrate on and will calm you down.

Two Days before Your Performance

Practice slowly to retain your confidence. Concentrate on every aspect of playing *except speed*. For at least two nights before the concert, go to bed early and get a good night's sleep. Exercising moderately in the afternoon will help you sleep better, but exercising too close to bedtime may have an energizing effect. Confirm transportation arrangements to and from the performance hall. Double check with friends and family you've invited to attend. Plan what to bring with you on the day of your performance. You might include a water bottle, tissues, snacks, your camera—and, of course, your music and your instrument!

While stage fright or performance anxiety will diminish, it rarely disappears completely. It can return in full force when you are not prepared for a performance. If that happens, review what you did well and what it is in your power to correct, and aim to do better next time. I hope reading this chapter has inspired you to try new strategies for overcoming your fears. Continue to practice overcoming stage fright right along with practicing your instrument. When you consistently apply these methods you'll notice a growing trust and confidence in yourself.

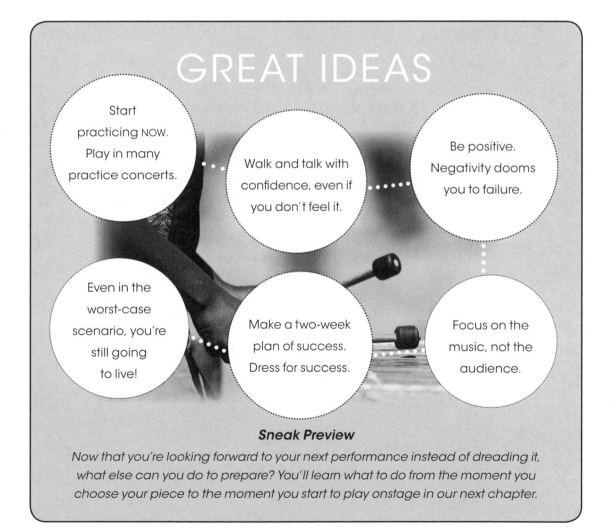

GREAT IDEAS

Start practicing NOW. Play in many practice concerts.

Walk and talk with confidence, even if you don't feel it.

Be positive. Negativity dooms you to failure.

Even in the worst-case scenario, you're still going to live!

Make a two-week plan of success. Dress for success.

Focus on the music, not the audience.

Sneak Preview

Now that you're looking forward to your next performance instead of dreading it, what else can you do to prepare? You'll learn what to do from the moment you choose your piece to the moment you start to play onstage in our next chapter.

THIRTY-FOUR

Ace the Audition

Sara bowed to the sounds of thunderous applause. She looked, sounded, and felt awesome. What a triumph! "I guess it really was worth all those months of preparation," she said. In this chapter you'll learn what it takes to have a successful contest or audition and how to get there.

PLAN AHEAD

- Choose a piece you like. Pick one that showcases your strengths and that challenges you to work. If you suffer from severe stage fright, choose an easy piece to help guarantee success.
- Plan more than enough time to master the material—that means months, not weeks. Set up a timetable. "By next week, play this section with the right rhythm up to tempo. Next month have it memorized."
- Hire a first-rate accompanist for the actual contest or concert. Arrange for ample rehearsals so that you feel comfortable with the ensemble.
- Be overly prepared. Know your piece 130% so that you can lose 30% during performance. Your skills must be so solid that they'll happen automatically under pressure.
- Practice the performance as well as the music. Arrange for as many practice performances as possible before the actual contest.

WHEN YOU STRUGGLE

- Be realistic. If you've played a piece for five months and only learned half, why do you think you can learn the second half in the last two weeks?
- Consider adjusting the program to make it more do-able. Eliminate a movement, slow the tempo, or play with music instead of from memory.
- Ask for extra lessons or rehearsals with the accompanist.

- Don't perform if you don't think your effort will be successful. If you and your teacher are not proud of your playing, stay home this time.
- Set up an alternate performance. Instead of playing at the contest or audition where you will be judged, play at the retirement home where you will be loved.

In chapters 32 and 33, we talked about how to prepare for the big day. Now it's here. *What do you do?*

PREPARE FOR PERFORMANCE DAY

Carol, a former student of mine, thought she was totally prepared for her crucial audition at Juilliard. But the night before the audition, she accidentally set her alarm for PM instead of AM, and she awoke an hour late. With her stomach empty and heart pounding, she raced to her audition. She arrived in the nick of time but feeling a lot less composed than she had planned to be.

The contest routine starts the minute you wake up. Or more exactly, it started when you went to bed the night before. Practicing until 2 AM and then getting up at 7 AM robs you of the energy and defenses you need for the big day. Get your sleep—and set your alarm right!

The focus of the day should be the audition. If you are serious about performing well, make it the top priority of the day. This is not the day to do errands, finish your term paper, or go sightseeing. The plan for the day is to be as calm and focused as possible.

EAT WISELY AND EXERCISE

It was 2:45 PM. Alice and I waited out in the hall to be called for her 3 PM slot in the big contest. Just as she was about to go on, Alice sighed, "I'm so hungry that I feel like I'm going to faint!"

"What have you eaten today?" I asked.

"Oh, I had a doughnut this morning." Needless to say, her performance lacked a certain energy that a well-balanced meal could have provided.

On performance day, eat a mix of carbohydrates and protein. While filling up on only carbohydrates gives you instant energy, your blood sugar may plummet by the time you perform. A mix of two-thirds carbohydrates and one-third protein will give you continuous fuel. Try eating a piece of whole wheat bread and cheese, an apple with peanut butter, or a dish of yogurt and a piece of fruit. Eating some turkey or a banana can help your body produce calming agents. Vocalists, some of you should be cautious about eating dairy products before your performance.

Avoid caffeine and alcohol. (How do those jazz musicians do it?) Keep yourself well hydrated several hours before the event by drinking at least four cups of water in the two hours preceding the performance. You'll avoid being dehydrated—a major source of fatigue—and feel more alert onstage. Schedule a pit stop before you go on.

Our body releases adrenaline when we're nervous, but slows production of adrenaline after exercise. Exercise also releases hormones called endorphins that make us feel relaxed and happy. Take a walk or a run outside early in the day or before you perform. It will get you awake and ready and will clear your mind of cobwebs. If you don't have time for a walk, step outside for a moment. To shake out jitters, some people even run in place or do jumping jacks before going onstage. Remove those high heels first!

AT THE CONCERT HALL

Arrive early and well rested.

It was Jane's turn to play her concerto at the big contest. We had worked for months and planned every detail—but where was she? Moments before she was to play, she blew in the door. Hating to miss her math class, Jane had stayed at school until the last second. She then missed the bus to come to the contest and had no time to change out of her faded jeans, torn sweatshirt, and dirty tennis shoes. Panting and dripping with sweat, she ran up to the stage. Khachaturian was enough to make her sweat, but her late arrival did her in.

Plan on being at the performance hall at least an hour before you are to perform. This gives you a cushion of time to allow for getting lost, being stuck in traffic, finding a parking spot, or getting sick in the car (just kidding!). Arrive early to allow time to size up the room and walk a little to calm your nerves. If you've followed this advice, you'll arrive with your body fueled, hydrated, and refreshed after at least two good nights of sleep and you won't experience the nightmare of my student Anna.

"It was finally competition day. I woke up on time, showered, dressed, and then woke my dad, who was driving me. After our breakfast it was suddenly time to go. That's when things got crazy. Who was riding with us? My mom? My sister? By the time I got my whole family into the car, we were already late. Then I realized I didn't have my music! I frantically searched all over the house, and by the time I found my music, I had that terrible feeling in the pit of my stomach.

"Every red light made me crazy. I pressed my foot on the floor wishing I had the gas pedal. When I got to the contest, I didn't have that precious time to warm up, that time to focus on my music, my goals, and myself. I bolted out of the car and rushed, out of breath, to the performance room. Who was to blame for me being late? When you arrive at the contest unprepared and rushed, you are already finished. I advise other students to tell their parents that they have to be at the contest site at least 30 minutes earlier than is necessary. So there should be no fights in the car or frantic attempts to beat red lights." (Anna, age 17)

Bring a cheering section.

If possible, bring friends and family to give you the "home court" advantage. Even if you're on a college audition tour, it helps to know that your parents are just outside rooting for you.

BEGIN YOUR PRE-PERFORMANCE ROUTINE

You've practiced every nuance of your piece, dressed appropriately, and arrived on time with your music. Now what? Maintain an established routine when you arrive. This makes your waiting time more predictable and productive. Here's how to make that tedious waiting time more productive:

Make a pit stop.

First, head to the restroom and check your appearance. Smile at your reflection—you'll feel better! Make note of where the restrooms are so that you can easily run back if your nerves bring on the urge.

Scope out the performance room.

If you've been visualizing the room for weeks, none of what you see should surprise you. If you haven't been to the room before, check to see where the judge sits, where the music stand is, and where the entrants wait for their turn. Notice how the entrants announce themselves. If possible, listen to a few people to learn the protocol and get a feel for the judge.

Retreat to the warm-up room.

Walking the halls before the national MTNA contest, I heard beautiful sounds coming out of one of the practice rooms. "Wow!" I thought. "That flutist is fabulous. Lauren's really going to have some stiff competition today." Minutes later Lauren emerged from that room. Noting my surprised expression, she said, "I never play my pieces before I play; it only makes me nervous. Instead, I soothe my nerves by playing my favorite pieces slowly."

Once you have scoped out the performance room, take some private time in the warm-up room. Notice that now it's called the *warm-up* room, not the *practice* room. It's too late to practice. Now is the time to perform slow scales as if they were opera melodies and to play tone exercises, your favorite music, and the contest piece at only half-speed. The danger in practicing the audition piece up to tempo is that any mistakes you make will cause self-doubt and anxiety. Take this time to enjoy your instrument and the music, not to test yourself.

Meditate and breathe.

Put down your instrument and take the time to be totally alone and become centered. Sit up straight with both feet on the floor, put your hands on your thighs, or cradle one hand with the other. With eyes half-open, relax and listen to your breathing. Don't let other thoughts intrude. Try isometrics to relax. Tense your body. Squeeze hands, shoulders, and chest tight, then notice the difference when you release them. Maintain that relaxed body.

Breathe in through your nose and exhale through your mouth. (Mouth breathing can be drying.) While you exhale, say a mantra, like the word *Ohm* or *sky*, or chant, "I'm calm. I'm calm." Breathe in on the count of five beats, hold your breath for five, and then exhale for five. As you wait for your turn to play, keep your breathing slow, deep, and even. If you begin to feel lightheaded, take more shallow breaths.

DON'T LET THEM SEE YOU SWEAT

Many performers believe that the hardest time to control anxiety is right before they play. When you're waiting your turn, force away any negative self-talk and visualize only positive outcomes. Remember happy times and successful performances. I sometimes pass around cartoons at contests to help break the tension. Close your eyes and hear the thunderous applause of an appreciative audience. See their smiling faces as you take a gracious bow after a winning performance.

Be prepared.

One year at an important contest, I witnessed the most complete lack of preparation imaginable. When 14-year-old Jaclyn's name was called, she remained seated, calling out, "Wait a minute!" as she rummaged through her backpack for her music. Finally she pulled out a pile of photocopies and trudged up to the stage dressed in jeans with shiny zippers running down both sides and embellished with metal hoops and studs. Wild red-streaked hair framed her face. Her top, a tie-dyed T-shirt, was adorned with several home-made beaded necklaces that swung as her sturdy hiking boots clunked up to the music stand. Immediately she dropped her straggly bundle.

Sighing, she then turned to the piano to tune with her accompanist. After she tuned, she shrugged, as if to say, "I guess that was good enough." Her pianist said, "So what order are we playing these pieces in?" The order was decided, and then she asked the pianist, "How fast should we play the first one?" When the girl finally played, she stumbled on the runs and her body slumped along with her flute, dragging toward the floor. The saddest thing about this whole scenario was that even through the badly chosen packaging, it was obvious this girl had talent and personality. She moved her fingers quickly, and she sparkled when she spoke to the judge, yet I knew she would never get anywhere without the guidance of a good teacher and a trip to "charm school." Remember, you are onstage from the moment you walk into the room.

YOU'RE ON!

You hear a name called. It's yours! Now you must make your entrance. All your planning and preparation will now begin to pay off. To avoid that feeling of "My gosh, now what?" memorize this routine, which you can put into action once your name is called. Above all, take your time.

- Tune before you go into the room.
- Take a deep breath and tell yourself, "Remember to breathe." Exhale as slowly and quietly as you can. Remember, you've practiced diligently, and you're prepared.
- Rise from your chair and walk confidently toward the stage, making brief eye contact with the judge.
- Announce your name slowly and loudly. Use this time to get used to being onstage. Stand still while you talk. Don't fuss with your clothes, rock from side to side, push your hair back, or scratch yourself—anywhere!
- Make eye contact with a few people in the audience. Imagine you are playing for these few people. Some students have a ritual of smiling at their mom right before they play.
- Present yourself to the audience with confidence. They have no idea what you're thinking, and your nervousness will not show as intensely as you feel it. Show them that you're happy to be there and that you have a wonderful story to tell.
- Before you begin to play, quickly recheck the pitch to be sure you are in tune. Take time to get it right.
- Adjust the piano bench or music stand to the proper height. Don't hide behind the music stand; let the audience see your face. Try putting the stand down low and flattening it to make it less obtrusive.
- Take a moment to think about the first few phrases of the piece and get into character or say your rehearsed mantra, "Beautiful tone and dramatic dynamics." There's no rush. Gather your thoughts and give the audience a moment of anticipation. Remember to share your passion!
- Breathe deeply. Shallow breathing can lead to nervousness and bad playing, especially on wind instruments.
- Don't clutch your instrument; maintain a relaxed grip. You should feel it resting loosely but firmly in your hands.
- Keep balanced on both feet. Most people feel secure with feet about shoulder width apart and one foot slightly in front of the other. Don't tap your foot along with the music! If you must keep time, wiggle only a toe in your shoe. Keep your knees bent to help get a deeper sound on wind instruments and prevent fainting (that's a good thing).
- Begin playing that opening line you've memorized to perfection. Often your stage fright will disappear as you keep playing and get into your piece.

- Keep in character. It breaks the spell if you smile (or look scared!) at the audience in the middle of the piece.
- Keep an upright posture. Don't bend over when the going gets tough. Don't look like you're reeling in a fish when you're out of breath.
- Remember, you are a performer and this is all part of your act.
- Don't let the audience know your mistakes by your facial expressions. Don't grimace or sigh when something goes wrong. Even if you make a mistake, maintain a positive impression. Fake it. Move on.
- It's over. No matter how you feel you performed, don't grab your music and charge off the stage. Bow graciously; acknowledge your accompanist and the audience's applause. Smile! You did it!

GREAT IDEAS

Careful planning can bring success.

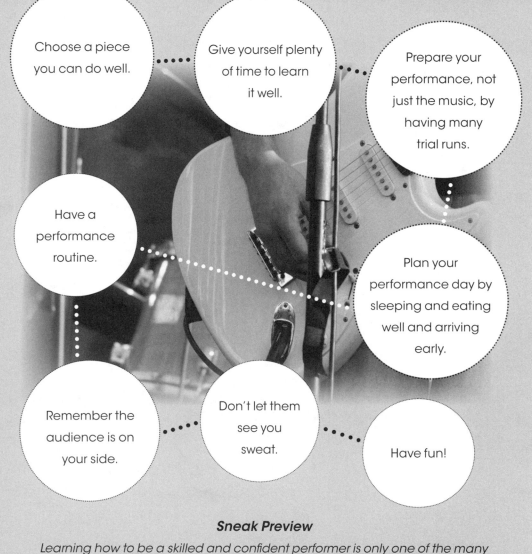

Choose a piece you can do well.

Give yourself plenty of time to learn it well.

Prepare your performance, not just the music, by having many trial runs.

Have a performance routine.

Plan your performance day by sleeping and eating well and arriving early.

Remember the audience is on your side.

Don't let them see you sweat.

Have fun!

Sneak Preview

Learning how to be a skilled and confident performer is only one of the many challenges we face as musicians. Part 8 has tons of tips and tricks for getting along with your parents, teachers, and other students, and for dealing with setbacks. You'll find solutions to your own problems in the many stories and advice from other students. So don't get stressed— turn the page and keep reading!

PART EIGHT

AVOIDING STUMBLING BLOCKS
ALONG THE WAY

THIRTY-FIVE

Finding the Middle Ground

A Guide for Frustrated Students and
Their "Helpful" Parents

When music students talk about their biggest challenges, conflicts with parents often top their list:

- "Before I can hang out with my friends, my mom forces me to practice for 30 minutes!"
- "My parents jump in and correct me at my lessons. I don't need TWO teachers."
- "My parents don't know a thing about music. What makes them think they can help me?"
- "My mom stays in the kitchen while I practice, but the second I make a mistake, she yells what I did wrong or runs in to correct me."
- "My parents try to organize my practice sessions. I don't need their help."
- "I just want to play cello well enough to play in chamber groups. My parents are trying to make me the next Yo-Yo Ma!"
- "If my Mom doesn't get off my back about practicing every day, I'll show her and just quit."

Do you think I've been eavesdropping at your house? Don't worry. I've heard all of these complaints, plus hundreds of variations, from my students *and* my own two sons. As irritating as they may seem, your parents can be your best tool to help you improve on your instrument. Before I try to convince you of that idea, let's talk about another event where teens often rely on parents for help. I'm talking about a new skill that terrifies parents and makes kids froth at the mouth: *getting your driver's license!* Both kids and parents see this milestone as a major step toward independence and becoming an adult.

Like learning to play an instrument, learning to drive a car can be exciting, yet sometimes hard and confusing, especially at the beginning. When you get your driver's permit, your parents don't toss the keys at you, wave good-bye, and say, "Have fun! Come home when you need more gas money!" If you're lucky, they may do that someday. But first you've got to learn how to stop suddenly, merge onto interstate highways, and achieve everyone's favorite challenge, parallel parking.

When you begin to drive, do you pull out of the driveway with your parents curled up in the trunk where they can't bug you? Of course not. The two of you are sitting side by side as you learn the written and unwritten rules of the road.

Learning how to get a sound on your instrument, read music, and practice can be equally as exciting, difficult, and frustrating—although hopefully not as dangerous. Learning a new skill takes time, but you'll progress faster when you allow your parents to help you. The trick is to find common ground where you each have a role and don't step on each other's toes.

MESSAGE TO PARENTS: COMMUNICATING WITH YOUR TEEN

How well your support is received will have a lot to do with the way you communicate. For a positive learning relationship, stay calm, patient, and positive. Easier to say than do sometimes, and I speak from experience. I'll give parents more specific suggestions soon. First let's answer teens' specific questions about parental involvement.

SHOULD MY PARENTS COME TO MY LESSONS?

A parent at the lesson can help you understand and remember what the teacher said. If you're confused or have just had a hard week, a parent can let the teacher know. "But my mom keeps butting in!" My son Scott knows the feeling. I have to admit that his viola teacher asked me not to go to the lessons because I would involuntarily groan and grimace when he played out of tune. (I swear I couldn't help it. I really *was* trying to be a good parent!) My other son, Kyle, wanted me to come to every cello lesson so I could remember the assignment and help him with his practice. With me as part of the team, he could learn faster and get done earlier. My sons also took piano lessons, and I would only drop in for a few minutes when I picked them up. Each kid, teacher, and parent relationship is different. See if you can work out something mutually beneficial to all three of you. If you feel your parents interfere too much in your lessons, show them this list.

Good parent behavior:
- As hard as it may be, let the teacher have the role of teacher. Your role is that of an interested and supportive mom or dad. If you contradict or question the teacher, your child will feel confused and conflicted, and the teacher will be unhappy.
- Avoid complaining about your child during lessons. The teacher doesn't need to know your daughter left the bathroom a mess. If things are happening in your child's life that would affect her music, contact the teacher before the lesson, if possible.

- Refrain from chastising your child if she doesn't perform
    well. Show your child love and respect during the les-
    son. Leave the critiquing up to the teacher.
- Watch your facial expressions and body language (note to self).
- Don't steal the teacher's attention away from your child. Even though
    the teacher seems like your best friend, this is your child's time.
- Do your best to remain quiet. Don't crinkle paper, talk on
    your cell phone, or click your knitting needles.
- Try not to interject unless you're asked a direct question or you want
    to rave about the great performance. (Or the studio is on fire!)
- Keep siblings occupied if they must attend the lesson. Bring them
    something to read or color. Your child can't have a good les-
    son if your other children are demolishing the music room.
- When your child does something extremely well or over-
    comes an obstacle, show your pride. Compliment,
    clap, or celebrate with an after-lesson treat.
- If you are an accomplished musician, it may be hard to rein yourself in
    and to remember that the focus of these lessons is on your child and
    his teacher. At home, if you suggest playing a duet, remember that
    your child may see this as competition. Make sure you're not show-
    ing off (even inadvertently). If your child is studying an instrument
    that you don't play, make sure you say something like "I certainly
    can't play the oboe as well as you are playing it!" or "I love the sound
    you make on that cello." If your child is playing your instrument,
    be careful not to make uncomplimentary comparisons ("I could
    play that same étude when I was three years younger than you").

MESSAGE TO PARENTS: ENJOY BEING
A MUSIC STUDENT'S PARENT

Enjoy this special time with your child. Driving to lessons may be the only time
all week you have a private time to talk. Lessons are a time when your child can
be the center of attention and you can show your support and appreciation. Sit
back and enjoy the wonderful gift you are giving your child (whether he or she
appreciates it now or not). Your enthusiasm for the lessons and support of the
teacher will be contagious.

Sitting in on lessons has a benefit to you, too. You get to hear some beautiful music and learn more about music yourself. We're all busy, but take some
time to attend some lessons, help your child practice, and go to concerts and
performances. Don't miss out on this wonderful bonding experience with your
child.

Now back to the student.

At home, your parents can help you set up a schedule, remind you to practice, and be your cheerleaders. They can reinforce what your teacher said at the lesson. Even if they know nothing about music, they can help you learn faster just by offering structure and encouragement. And the faster you learn, the better you get, and the better you get, the less you'll need them! Pretty soon you can take over your own practice. And someday you'll be driving to lessons on your own.

Besides attending lessons and monitoring practice, parents can support you in many ways.

Parents help by:
- Answering your questions: If you can't remember what your teacher said, or you didn't understand your assignment, your parents can help.
- Being your advocate: If you practiced lots, but it still sounds bad, or if you had such a busy week that you couldn't practice, the teacher will believe your parents.
- Explaining your concerns to your teacher: If you're having a problem with your lessons or with your teacher, they can intervene and be a buffer. They can put your feelings into words to the teacher and brainstorm possible solutions.
- Keeping you company and making learning fun: Your parents can help make learning more fun by playing practice games, playing duets, or taking you to concerts. Practicing can sometimes feel boring and isolating. A parent sitting next to you or even calling out from the next room can keep you on track.
- Supporting you when you face disappointments and failure: Your parents will love you no matter how you play. (Your teacher will, too!)

REWARDING GOOD WORK

Now here's a great idea: talk to your parents about setting up a reward system. Parents can acknowledge your improvements with compliments and even tangible rewards such as new music, concert tickets, video games, or an outfit for the recital. Some parents of my younger students use prize boxes with different levels of rewards that correlate with how good the lesson was.

Better yet, you could work to do something fun: a sleepover, choosing the next vacation destination, a parent-and-child outing, a shared activity like ice skating, a bike ride together, or a "get out of jail free" card for your most hated chore for a week (like taking out the garbage). You should practice because you want to get better. But sometimes these little motivators can give you a jump start.

Spontaneous rewards are fun, too. Ice cream on the way home or permission for a sleepover or a movie after an extremely good practice session or lesson are great motivators.

ADVICE FOR SPECIFIC PROBLEMS

"They expect me to do too much at home."

For some students, family and church obligations may leave little time for practice and free time. Try to work with your parents to create a time for practice, homework, and some free time every day. Remind them that they're not getting their money's worth out of lessons unless you practice regularly. My husband, Don, still remembers how his sister got out of doing dishes to practice the piano. Maybe you can make the same kind of deal with your parents to trade chores for practice.

"They put the whole burden of practice on me."

Do your parents say things such as, "I already have to tell Rick to do so many other things, I don't want to have to remind him to practice"? or "If Jessica really wanted to learn music, she would practice all on her own"? I'll bet they still remind you to brush your teeth and do your homework because they feel that's important. Let your parents know you do want to improve but that some days you just forget to practice or need help getting started.

"They make practicing difficult because there's no quiet place to practice."

If the TV is always on and your siblings are running around, it's going to be hard to concentrate. Ask your parents to provide a quiet environment and a scheduled practice time.

"They put too much pressure on me to be perfect."

Do your parents jump on every mistake? Do they only approve of the finished product instead of the small accomplishments along the way? Help them change their tune by saying, "Practice does not make perfect. Practice makes better." If you're doing your best, they should be proud of you every step of the way. Show them when you've learned something new, and ask your teacher to let them know when you've had a particularly good lesson.

"My family life is chaotic."

Maybe your parents are divorced and you have to divide your time between two houses. Perhaps your parents have to spend lots of time away at work or just aren't available to you. Maybe your parents aren't supportive of your music and don't really care if you quit or not. Perhaps they're struggling with their own problems and don't have the strength to help you with music.

It's tough feeling that you're on your own, but you have two choices. The *easiest* choice is to blame your parents (which some people do for their entire lives). You can think that if you don't make it in music, it's all their fault. The *mature* choice is to realize that your destiny is your own responsibility. If your family life is chaotic, then you need music even more. Music can be the stabilizing force in your life, but it is up to you. Reach out to your teacher for guidance. Set up your own practice schedule, keep track of lessons and rehearsals, and order your own music. Handel, Tchaikovsky, and Debussy all become famous musicians *despite* their parents. You are the one who decides whether you let your past ruin your future or you retain control over your life.

"When my parents tell me to practice, it makes me NOT want to practice."

If you're a beginning student, you need your parents to help structure your practice time. As you get older, they need to give you more "subtle" reminders that don't make you want to rebel. Instead of saying, "Sit down at the piano right now and get your practicing done!" they can say things like, "What's your plan for the day?" "Would this be a good time to play the piano?" "When are you going to practice today?" "Would you rather practice this morning or in the afternoon?" Have you played your guitar yet today?" "You probably won't have time tonight after we go out to dinner, so do you think you could practice before we leave?" "You'll be tired after your sleepover on Friday, so is there another good time you could practice?"

"Every time my parents help me, we get into a huge fight!"

Who usually starts the fight? Do they start yelling at you, or do you act mad every time they give you a suggestion? Promise me, the next time you and your parents are practicing together, see how long you can go without getting mad or irritated. Getting upset takes so much more effort than just practicing.

Try these compromises:
- Let them help you practice (and hold your temper) for 10 minutes, then ask them to leave. Practice, and then let them come back for the last few minutes.
- Try letting them help you with the first and last practice of the week.
- Only ask for their help when you have a problem.
- Promise to use the metronome if you can practice by yourself.
- Ask your teacher to give you a daily practice assignment. Ask your parents to come hear you when you think that assignment is good. The amount of time you practiced doesn't matter, just your accomplishment

BUT I DON'T NEED MY PARENTS TO HELP!

If you turn down your parents' help, you may be trading your independence for not learning as fast. Is it worth getting them out of your music if it means you won't improve? The more time and energy you spend getting into fights with them, the less time and energy you'll have for learning your instrument.

You don't need your parents to help you? Prove it! Have four excellent lessons in a row (critiqued by your teacher) where you practiced all by yourself. Your parents and your teacher will be thrilled and proud that you have matured enough to take over your own practice. Yeah!

USING YOUR PARENTS AS A CRUTCH

Instead of being resentful of their parents' help, some kids depend on their parents' help too much. "My lesson's not good today because my dad was out of town and couldn't help me" or "I can't play this part because my mom didn't understand the rhythm."

One of my sons didn't like me in the room when he practiced, missing out on my help. My other son wanted my help almost daily. When we practiced together, I pointed out all the mistakes and helped him with the rhythm, so he got finished with his practice faster. I became his "ears" and "music conscience." With me as overseer, his pieces got better faster, but he didn't learn how to practice on his own and become his own teacher. Once he was in high school, he became an independent (though not as effective) practicer.

IT'S YOUR LIFE

When you've had a few years of lessons, it's time for you to take over your practice. If you require your mother or father to be a "Helicopter Parent," you'll never grow up musically or emotionally. When you're a teenager, you may still need reminders and rewards, but it must be largely up to you to determine where, when, what, how, and how much you practice. If you practice only when your parents force you to practice, music will be just another chore and something you give up once you leave home. Your parents may have to accept a lower level of involvement, but that will be up to you. Please base your decision on how involved you want to be in the music. Don't stop practicing because you want to show them who's the boss, you want to have no responsibilities, or you want to spend all your time playing video games or hanging out. Try to work out a compromise. Invite your parents to some lessons, ask for their help when you need it, share with them your accomplishments, but become independent. Music is your thing.

Finding the Middle Ground

GREAT IDEAS

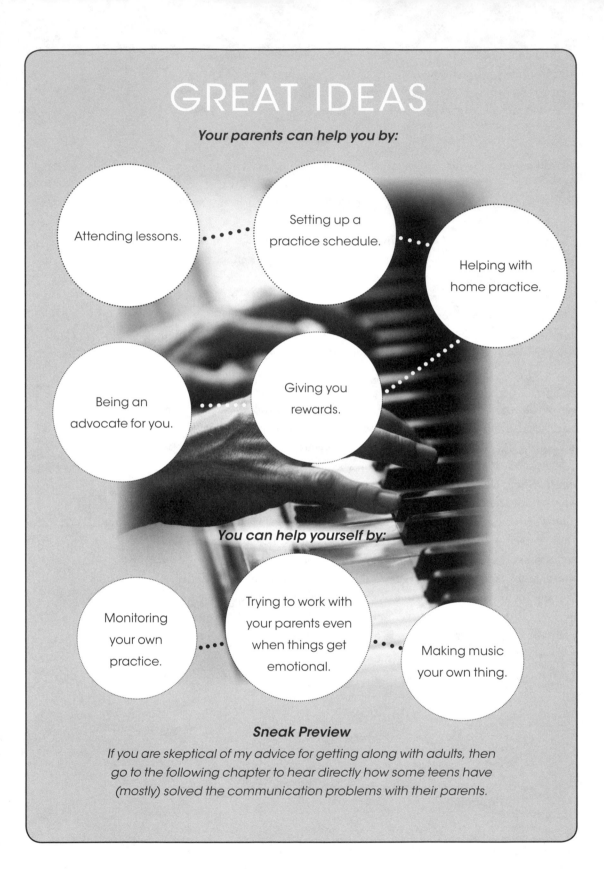

Your parents can help you by:

Attending lessons.

Setting up a practice schedule.

Helping with home practice.

Being an advocate for you.

Giving you rewards.

You can help yourself by:

Monitoring your own practice.

Trying to work with your parents even when things get emotional.

Making music your own thing.

Sneak Preview

If you are skeptical of my advice for getting along with adults, then go to the following chapter to hear directly how some teens have (mostly) solved the communication problems with their parents.

THIRTY-SIX

Student to Student

Advice from Teens

Now it's time to hear from the *real* experts on how to get along with your parents. Two of my 16-year-old students, Simon Berry and Lydia Walsh, helped edit my book while I was writing. They were brutally honest about the content and even more so about the writing style. (Ouch!) Now it's their turn to write a chapter. (See, it's harder than you think, guys!) Simon and Lydia will share with you their own experiences and perspective about getting along with their parents, and some of my other students will chime in, too.

PARENTAL INVOLVEMENT IN PRACTICING
(FROM SIMON AND LYDIA'S PERSPECTIVE)

Many people blame disagreements on "personality conflicts." That's true—*some* of the time. But more often than not, disagreements are not about personality; they're about who is controlling whom. A lot of your problems with your parents are probably because you want to do something *your* way, and they want you to do it *their* way. It becomes a power struggle, which is usually resolved when you either exert what control you *do* have and leave the argument, or give in to your parents and do what they want.

Practicing is an area where the issue of control comes into play. We frequently get into fights with our parents about practicing: how much, when to do it, and certain privileges that can only be obtained through practice first. We've heard of some students whose parents control their practicing to the extent that they can't drive the family car or spend time with friends until they practice.

I would bet that *your* parents have tried to make you practice recently. Did it work? Maybe, maybe not. If you're like us, you have found it somewhat irritating that your parents think that you can't practice on your own. On the other hand, it might be helpful for your parents to remind you if you're always forgetting to practice. The trick then is to remind yourself that your parents are only trying to help; they're not trying to be annoying or pushy.

An equally important issue is parental *involvement*. Some students say they like it when their parents help them practice. Others say that they find it distracting and like it much better when they concentrate on their own. What you decide depends on both you and your parents. If your parents are musicians, it might be worthwhile to hear what they have to say. Even if they're not, they might be able to point out a mistake you didn't hear or offer an outside perspective. This is where you must execute a delicate balancing act. If your parents are truly helping you, and you feel receptive, then by all means allow them to help. You can even ask them for help. They'll think that it's great you want their input! If they're pushing you too hard, or you feel like it would be easier and better to practice alone, tell them that. You can also try setting up a schedule so that *you,* not your parents, decide when you practice.

🔊 *Simon says, "My mother loves to butt in on me when I'm practicing and make 'helpful' contributions. She's a musician, too, and what she says is usually really good. But I just don't want to hear what I'm doing wrong or how I could improve. I can figure it out for myself. On the other hand, if I ask her for help instead of her forcing herself on me, I can learn music extraordinarily quickly and easily.*

"That's the big difference. At this point in my life, I really want to do things for myself. By having some control over when my mother helps me, I feel like I'm doing what I want, instead of being forced to go back and play a section again, play the whole piece slower, work on long tones, or go through countless other long, boring processes. But when I do ask her for help, she can make practicing fun with encouragement and sly little tricks that will help me remember what I'm learning. My mother can be an amazing resource, but only when I want her to be."

🔊 *Lydia says, "When I first started playing flute, my dad would come to every single lesson and remind me to practice every single day. He isn't musical (and often sings off-key), but it was comforting to have a familiar presence in the lesson space. As I grew older, however, I found that I didn't need him to sit in on every lesson, and I found the constant practice reminders annoying. I asked him to stop nagging me to practice, and while that took care of the irritation factor, I realized that I wasn't practicing as often as I used to. Because of this, my dad and I have come to a new agreement where he asks me if I'm going to practice once every day. That way, I have a friendly reminder to fit practicing into my schedule, but I don't feel like I have to go on the defensive against constant nagging."*

PARENTS AT LESSONS

Having your parents observe your lessons is another opportunity for conflicts to arise. Some parents don't just *observe;* they actively jump in with comments that are designed to be helpful but are actually annoying. Eventually you just want to scream that it's the *teacher* who's supposed to teach you, not your parents. Conversely, some music teachers *require* parents to attend all lessons because the parents can be a useful resource at home in remembering assignments or explaining tough musical concepts.

If your parents are the type who like to make unsolicited comments at your lessons, try politely asking them to leave the teaching to your teacher. After all, that's what they're paying for. If that doesn't work, try asking your teacher to speak to them on your behalf.

Now let's hear from some other students who have found how to get ahead in music and get along with their parents:

Eighteen-year-old Anna has played in many ensembles, won awards, gone to summer camps, and performed many places. She credits her parents with part of her success. "One of the most important factors in becoming a successful musician is getting support from your parents, not by pushing you to become a professional, or forcing you to practice, but by helping you. Your parents can help you work lessons and practice into the family schedule by allowing you to practice instead of studying or doing chores when something big is coming up. They can also show their support by giving you rides, funding your lessons, competition fees, and group trips, and coming to all your concerts. And most important of all, valuing what you do. Congratulating you on your accomplishments because they think music is important and you're important too means everything."

Andrea, age 18, knows about the pros and cons of having musician parents. "My parents are both musicians. Talk about pressure! Okay, so maybe it's not that bad, but when I'm practicing something I just can't get right, it can sure feel that way. The only way we coexist is by staying out of each other's musical life. It works best if they only give me help when I ask for it. Luckily, my parents play different instruments than I do, so it's not incredibly hard. The plus side is that I can talk to them about auditions, tough rhythms, and fears, and they're always there for me."

Leslie, age 18, can sympathize with Andrea. "My father is a professional musician, and he has always been my clarinet teacher. I take piano and flute lessons from other teachers. We bonded through music, although sometimes it was hard having him as my teacher. If we argued about something else, then that tension would carry on into the music. Most of the time I would try to forget he was my father and respect him as much as I respect my regular teachers. I did ask him not to come in when I practiced, because I didn't want him always critiquing me. I want music to be my own thing, not just something we share."

Rana, age 13, appreciates her parents' help. "Nagging makes me dread practice. I think, 'Okay, fine, I'll do it!' But I don't put my heart into it. I do better with a gentle reminder or with consequences. My parents will say, 'What's your plan for getting homework and practice done today?' Or 'This would be a good time to practice.' Or 'You need to practice before you go to your friend's house.' If I miss a day, I try to make it up the next day. Otherwise, missing a day becomes a habit. I also do a better job of practicing if I practice where my parents can hear me. If I practice in my bedroom, it may take me a long time just to get the books on the stand and get my instrument out of the case. But if they hear me, then I'm more focused. Most of the time I practice without being told because it feels so good to walk into your lesson when you're prepared."

Lucy, age 16, has figured out that fighting doesn't work. "Playing an instrument was my idea when I was in fourth grade. But once I realized what a big commitment it is, my parents had to step in. My mom would help me practice, but when I got frustrated with myself, I would get mad at her.

"I still need my parents' help because sometimes I have a hard time making myself play exercises and scales. I just want to play the fun stuff. It was also hard to force myself to practice when I got braces because my tone got so bad. Through the tough times, my parents helped me see the long-term benefits of practice. Now that I'm in high school, we have a contract that I practice half an hour five days a week to keep my cell phone and have permission to go to my friends' homes. They don't let me watch TV on school nights, either, so that makes it easier for me to get my practice and homework done. We gave up fighting about practice. If my parents had had to fight with me the six years I've played an instrument, they would have given up."

GREAT IDEAS

As much as it may seem that your parents love to nag you and use music to make your life miserable, they can be an important part of your music team.

Sneak Preview

One of the stumbling blocks of learning for brass and wind players is getting braces. Ouch! Our next chapter has lots of ideas for how to have beautiful teeth and a beautiful tone too.

THIRTY-SEVEN

Brace Yourself for Braces

"Braces? You've got to be kidding. I don't need braces. My teeth don't stick out that much. Braces are ugly. They hurt. Braces make you talk funny. I can't eat popcorn with braces. Worse yet, how will I play my instrument with braces?"

Calm down. Look around you. How many kids do you see wearing braces? They still eat, drink, and smile. They still play their instruments, and, hey, some of them are pretty darn good. You, too, can live through braces, and it will be worth it for years to come with your perfect smile. Braces may not be a big deal to pianists and string players, but to wind and brass players, some advice is definitely in order.

THE SCHEDULE

When should I first get braces?

Although it's not always easy to have your dentist work around your schedule, summer is a good time to get braces. If you can't wait until the summer, at least wait until any big concerts or contests are over. Schedule your braces for a time without pressure and deadlines. If just the top braces are put on first, then another adjustment will be necessary when the bottom braces are put on, so ask your orthodontist if both sets can be put on at the same time.

When should I schedule other orthodontist appointments?

Braces are usually tightened once a month. The day or two after they get tightened, there is usually some discomfort, so schedule those appointments as far away as possible from concerts or private lessons.

How long will it take me to get used to playing with braces?

Woodwind players, and particularly those who play clarinet, oboe, and saxophone, usually get used to playing with braces within a month or two. Flutists can take longer. Brass players have a tougher time, with an average range of between one to three months, because brass mouthpieces are pressed against both the upper and lower lips. Some trumpet players temporarily shift to a brass instrument, such as trombone, baritone horn, or tuba, with a larger mouthpiece that's easier to play.

Unless you play strings or percussion, braces will hurt your sound. High notes and low notes are especially trying. Since braces change your embouchure, they change your tone. Here again, brass players have a particularly tough time of it, but almost everyone goes through an adjustment period.

"Getting braces is definitely a mental shock! When I got braces, my tone died. The notes I could get out were airy and completely unsupported, my low notes took ages to get to in connections, and the high notes were thin if they were there at all. I had to rearrange my mouth and lips around the braces." (Perrin, age 16)

"Getting braces affected my tone, but more than that it affected my motivation. When you play and it hurts and you can't get a decent sound, you don't want to practice. You have to constantly adjust because your teeth and jaw keep moving. Getting new rubber bands, a chain, or head gear also forces embouchure changes." (Lucy, age 15)

THE PAIN

"I had heard about the cut lips, sore jaws, the snapping bands, and dislodged wires from friends with firsthand experience and the scratches to prove it. But I wasn't worried about that. I could deal with braces if minute pains were to be my only problems. I wasn't worried at the thought of what braces could do to my career as a flutist—I was terrified! As it turned out, the pain was manageable and not so much to worry about." (Angela, age 17)

THE FIRST DAY

"When I tried to practice the first time, I burst into tears, since half my notes sounded horrible and the other half wouldn't come out at all. It's better not to practice that first day, since the effects are rather damaging to your confidence. Do something else to occupy your mind. I had friends come over to make cookies, and their laughter and all that sugar put me in a much better mood." (Perrin)

Relax. It's not going to sound good, so accept it. Give yourself a few days off and then gently ease into practicing. The most important thing to do is to believe it will get better and give yourself time to adjust and heal.

HOW TO PRACTICE

Concentrate on your tone. The more you focus on your sound, the sooner you'll get the sound you want. Start by playing very slow, soft notes in a middle register. Practice half-step slurs from your best note and gradually work your way up and down to the top and bottom registers. Don't become so focused on the metal in your mouth that you forget to blow.

Next, practice articulation exercises. Your aim is for the tongue to move as little as possible. You may have to tongue in a different place on the mouth or teeth to avoid the braces and wires.

Listen to professional musicians to focus on their great sound and tone. Now listen carefully to your sound, comparing it in your head to the sound you want. Your muscle memory has been disrupted by braces, so you'll have to experiment. You sound like a sick cow, and you want to sound like a pro? Make your way through the beginning books, starting on lesson one. Give it time!

Make your practice sessions short (10 to 20 minutes at most). If you try to play longer, your mouth will hurt and your temper will flare. When you feel tired or stressed, stop.

"It was devastating to me when the braces were put on. I had planned quite a bit for my sophomore flute year, State Competition and All State Band being the most prominent. Upon setting foot in the house after getting bits of metal glued to my teeth, I put the flute up to my lips, blew, and received a wispy rasp. Needless to say, I was horrified, but my dreams weren't about to escape my grasp.

"I began to practice like never before. At first it seemed remedial, blowing and listening hard to improve tone and pitch, then experimenting with different embouchures to see which suited me the best. It's something I should have done before, and I intend to keep up when I get my braces off. Hours and hours went into perfecting my fallen tone. More time was spent on preparing audition pieces and ignoring throbs of pain emitting from my cut lip. I was driven by competition and a thirst to emerge victorious. Over time I got used to the feel of braces, my lip healed and hardened, and my tone improved with much determination." (Angela, age 16)

MECHANICAL AIDS

Braces tend to give instrumentalists an overbite, making it hard to have a focused air stream and thus splitting the tone. Some people find these mechanical aids helpful, and others decide to do without and rely solely on good practice.

To help ease the pain, try some of these:
- Wax to put over the sharp parts of the brackets.
- Ezo denture cushions.
- Braceguard and the Morgan bumper available through Giardinelli.
- Ask your dentist for a 3" × 3" sheet of polymer material to be affixed with dental adhesive powder. Cut a strip with scissors to place in front of the lower teeth (or both upper and lower) to even them up.
- Brace Relief from Pro-Tech Medical Health Supplies.
- The Lip Protector, which is available through the Brasswind.
- Over-the-counter pain relievers in pill or gel form.

For flute:

Cut masking tape into small strips to fit the lip plate. Play for a minute or two with one layer of tape, and then add one by one, more layers (usually three to six layers) of masking tape until your tone gets better. You can keep these layers of tape on until your embouchure adjusts to the braces or the braces come off.

For trumpet:

Try a bigger mouthpiece with a wider rim for more cushion on the outside of the lips and a V-shaped cup. Try the BP mouthpiece created for those who wear braces or the Mad Max polycarbonate mouthpiece. Don't press the mouthpiece too hard against the lips.

GETTING YOUR BRACES OFF

The day finally arrives when you get your braces off. But wait. What happened to your tone? You've figured out how to have a good tone with all that metal in your mouth, and now you have to figure out how to sound good without it. It's another adjustment, but this one is shorter and more fun. This adjustment will come more naturally. Congratulations! You've lived through braces.

THIRTY-EIGHT

Help! I Want to Quit

"I've had it! I'm never playing this thing again!" (Crash!)

Hold on . . . before you make a rash decision, step back, and think. Did you flub your last performance? Are you overloaded with homework or exams? Are you at odds with your parents? Do you *really* want to quit playing an instrument? Quitting might seem like an easy cure, but it might be a long-term and unfortunate solution to a short-term frustration.

You're not the only one.

Almost every music student feels like quitting at some time or another. I've talked to plenty of students who said they wanted to quit taking lessons—including my own sons. After talking it out, many soon realize quitting lessons wouldn't solve their true problem. Talk through your feelings with your parents, teachers, and friends to better understand them. The more specific you are about what's bothering you, the more specific a solution you can find.

Most reasons for quitting fall into a few main categories, including teacher, parent, practice, and performance problems. To learn what's bugging you, review the following list of "typical complaints" from students who want to quit. Do any look familiar?

THE STUDENT-TEACHER RELATIONSHIP

Having the right teacher can make all the difference. If you think your teacher is the problem, first read chapter 8, "How to Be a Great Student." Assuming you're doing your best to be a great student, is your teacher's personality a good match with yours? What about his teaching style? If your teacher speaks too harshly or lectures you, he may not realize how his words affect you. Do you feel encouraged when you stumble? Do you have fun together?

Would a new teacher renew your interest?

Are your playing assignments as dull as dirt? Have you seen everything in your teacher's bag of tricks? If you've been with your teacher for at least three years, a new teacher might reenergize you. Do you need a teacher who can challenge you more or one who understands your busy schedule? New ideas and different music might give you the jump start you need. If you're not sure this teacher is for you, find a better match using the suggestions in chapter 7, "Finding the Perfect Teacher."

LESSONS AND ASSIGNMENTS

Are you loaded down with "heavyweight" pieces?

Have you ever thought, "How will I ever memorize this whole piece?" or "This song is so long and complicated, I don't know where to start?" Everyone enjoys the satisfaction of mastering a difficult piece, but if it takes you months to reach the finish line, you may lose the motivation to get there. Ask your teacher how to break monster songs into smaller, doable sections or give you pieces that you can more easily accomplish.

Do you have only long-term goals?

Smaller, achievable goals keep you motivated. If your only practice goal is the year-end recital, shorter performance goals will give you progress checkpoints. Learn how to set big and small goals in chapter 12, "Get in Gear with Goals."

Have your parents or teacher set the bar too high?

Do your parents or teacher expect you to be best in the studio? Thirteen-year-old Sarah decided to pull back. "High expectations were good for a while. Then as they got higher, I wasn't ready for them. I know it would be more fun if I put more effort into it, but that's not what I want to do right now."

Do you feel pressured to become a music major?

Do your parents or teacher have you on the "fast track" and playing in every competition, recital, or music event that comes along?

You alone must decide what role music plays in your long-range plans. Music may become your reason for living or just one of your hobbies. If you feel pushed to choose the alternate path, express your concerns to your parents and teacher. Map out your long-range goals together.

Do you want to quit band or orchestra?

Is your music so easy that you memorize it after playing it one time? Students join band and orchestra with varying skill levels, and classes often start from the lowest level. If boredom is your problem, check out chapter 42, "What Can I Do If I'm Bored in Band or Orchestra?" Are you having trouble keeping up with your section? If you don't take private lessons, a few lessons or extra coaching will move you ahead quicker.

Is the problem with your section or with the director's teaching style? You can't switch schools, but can you share your concerns with the director? If your teacher just doesn't like clarinet players with curly hair and names starting with *J*, tough it out for the time being. Some day you'll move on, glad that difference didn't stop you.

PRACTICE PROBLEMS

You don't like to *practice*? Good. That means you're normal. Thirteen-year-old Breanna can always think of reasons not to practice. "I'd rather just practice band music or Disney music. After I do my homework, I want to relax and watch TV, not practice."

Not wanting to practice may be your biggest reason for wanting to quit. But not having practiced may be what got you there in the first place. It's a vicious circle: you hate to practice—you don't practice—you sound bad—you want to quit.

Let's make a deal. If you promise to put in a half hour of concentrated practice every day for three weeks, I promise you the results will shock you and encourage you to do more. You practice—you sound better—it gets easier—everyone says you're good—you want to practice more. And then you're hooked!

Sure, practicing can be a drag sometimes. So can brushing your teeth and flossing, studying for the math test, or putting your money in the bank. But all those things pay off later. Do you want to have cavities, flunk out of school, or go broke? Practicing will be worth it in the long run, too. Really.

Have you fallen into a practice rut? It's time to climb out.

Who wants to practice the same way every day? Make it fun. Read chapter 15, "Shake Up Your Practice Routine" to learn 75 ways to practice differently every day. Are you spending more time than you need to get the job done? Find practice tips and tricks in chapter 14, "Quit Wasting Your Practice Time."

Do you need to reorganize your practice sessions?

If you feel overwhelmed with practice, ask your teacher to help you set up a daily practice plan. Having a different practice assignment for each day of the week takes out the guesswork of knowing where to start. You'll feel good when you check off items on your list or write down the amount of time you spend on daily assignments.

Do you have fun with music?

Take the last 10 or 15 minutes of practice to mess around. Make up songs, improvise, and play easy songs or old favorites. Sight-read beautiful or fun pieces to relax. Schedule an impromptu family concert to show off your progress. Goofing off doesn't waste practice time. It helps you see practice as fun, not just homework. I promise that once you've put in a few weeks of concentrated practice, your results will surprise and encourage you to do more. Why not call practicing "playing" your instrument?

Now that you're a teenager, do you wonder where your time goes? Keep track of your activities for a week. You might be surprised to discover how much time those phone calls, TV, games, and shopping eat up.

Is your schedule slammed? Do you have a hard time saying no? Even teens run out of energy. Growing teens need more sleep than when they were children. Is your schedule packed with volleyball practice on Mondays and Wednesdays, violin lessons on Tuesdays, youth group on Thursdays, family night on Fridays, and volunteer work on Saturdays? Do you need time to earn your driver's license, study for SATs, search for colleges, and still enjoy after-school activities and your friends? Don't even think about that part-time job! Where will you squeeze *practice* into your already overloaded schedule?

Katlyn took three flute lessons and felt so overwhelmed that she wanted to quit. Her mom told me in an e-mail: "Katlyn feels she doesn't have the drive to meet your expectations. She feels stress instead of enjoyment when she plays. In her words, 'My orchestra teacher doesn't care at all, and Bonnie cares too much!'" Katlyn's parents finally realized that her schedule was much of the problem. "I never imagined such emotion and tears tied to music!" her mom wrote. "I realize now that part of the problem was our poor timing. We had her dive into the flute while juggling not one but three spring sports. This summer her biggest wish is to 'restart' lessons and focus entirely on the flute. When school starts, she will limit herself to one sport at a time. We look forward to a brand-new start and years of fun." Don't you love happy endings?

Have you set priorities for your after-school life?

If you have too much to do, first block out enough time to succeed at your main job: school. Decide what else is important to you, and drop low-priority activities or spend less time on them. Watching TV is relaxing, but if you're not planning a career as a professional trivia player, how much will you remember even a year from now? I know your parents must have been ecstatic when you finally made level 60 on World of Warcraft, but how will that triumph support your future goals? Sports and music are great ways to spend time with friends. Will you still be playing football when you're 50? Music will be in your life forever.

You *can* juggle sports and music. Limit yourself to one sport per season or one sport per school year. Compensate for missed music practice with practice sessions before school and extra practice on weekends. Ask your teacher to ease practice requirements during sports season or heavy homework times—as long as you promise to work harder when your schedule eases.

P.S. Don't forget to put sleep high on your list of important activities.

Even teens who love music don't always put music first.

Tenth-grader Anna agonized over her decision to quit. "It was a hard choice to stop taking music lessons. My teacher and my music have been a big part of my life for the past five years. Between tougher high school classes, homework, and sports, I don't have enough hours in the day to put in the time and effort I need to play well. Now I need to put other things before music." Anna didn't leave music completely behind. "I'm not turning my back on music forever," she adds. "I won't always have school and homework and team sports, but I will always have music."

MIDDLE-SCHOOL STUDENT DANGER ZONES

The early teens are tough transition years. People expect you to act more mature, yet you're not ready to give up being a kid. You're also starting to test your independence, and you want to make your own choices. You're worried about what other kids think, and you wish you had more self-confidence. Sometimes you feel alone or that no one understands you. Wow, that's a lot to handle.

As weird as it may seem, music can help you. Want to be your own boss? You can show your parents your independence by taking over your own practice schedule and choosing the instrument, music, and teacher you want.

Feel inadequate? Being good at your instrument will make you feel good about yourself. You'll get attention and respect from other kids, too. Worried about your social life? If you participate in school music, you'll make a bunch of friends. And don't forget your private teacher, who can be your port in the storm.

Poet Maya Angelou knows just how you feel. "Music was my refuge. I could crawl into the space between the notes and curl my back to the loneliness." When things go wrong, music will always be there for you.

Are you uneasy about moving to a new and bigger school?

Many teens decide to quit when they move from middle school to high school. Do you wonder if you'll meet the demands of having several teachers and more homework? Ask your music teacher to lighten your assignment load for the first three months while you adjust to your new school.

HIGH-SCHOOL STUDENT DANGER ZONES

When you enter high school, your life changes drastically. One minute you were reigning supreme over the younger grades, and the next you found yourself at the bottom of the pile as a freshman. Your social life becomes more important, and with new demands on your time you may have trouble balancing school, hobbies, family, and friends.

Many students want to quit when they go to high school, but here again the advantages of playing an instrument outweigh the disadvantages. This is the time when you can really enjoy the progress you've already made. You're not a struggling beginner anymore. You can play better music and have more playing opportunities. There are lots of good times ahead in band and orchestra, too, with better music and fun group trips.

As sad as it may be, this may be your last time playing an instrument, at least for a long while. After you graduate, college, careers, and family all get in the way of playing, and your instrument may go in the attic for a long time. The more skilled you become now, the greater the chance you will want to return to playing. Appreciate this precious time you have now to be a musician.

Are you having trouble coming back after a break?

After taking the summer off, it can be hard to gear up for a practice schedule again. If you're thinking about quitting when school starts in the fall, sign up for lessons anyway. If you still want to quit after fall semester, you'll have given yourself three more months of playing experience.

Are braces slowing you down?

Zoe advanced quickly for three years. Then at 15, her teeth got in the way. "When I got braces, I wanted to quit. I just couldn't get a good tone. My mouth hurt, and it seemed like too much trouble. My teacher gave me three weeks off to settle down, and I gradually came back to loving playing, but it was a close call."

Hang on through high school.

The middle school and high school years offer you plenty of excuses to quit. Kristin, age 15, suggests that you remember the reasons you started playing. "When you start, you start with a purpose," she says. "Don't forget that purpose when you get to that point when you want to quit." The hardest time to keep going in music may be when you're about 14 or 15. If you can hang in there through tenth grade, you'll probably keep playing through your high school years and even beyond.

FAMILY MATTERS

Is sibling rivalry distracting you?

Sibling rivalry can be a powerful force. Does your sister play piano better than you do? Her playing has nothing to do with your playing. If you both play the same instrument and you're tired of the comparisons, let her continue playing classical and you switch to jazz or even add a new instrument.

Are you missing family fun?

Are you the only musician in the family? Do lessons or practice keep you from enjoying family activities? Do you compete with the TV while you practice, or envy your siblings' free time? Do you feel overworked and underappreciated? Your parents might not even realize it. They can create a home life that shows everyone in the family the importance of your music and practice time. Ask them to schedule family activities around your lesson and practice times. You could earn special treats like a new outfit or game to reward your hard work. To even the playing field, suggest that while you practice, your siblings can finish your chores!

Do you need more support from your parents?

Your parents' guidance and encouragement can keep you motivated. If you feel lonely practicing, ask a parent to keep you company. You won't feel stuck in solitary confinement with a parent listening or calling out praise from another room. They can notice improvements and cheer you after disappointments. Music can be tough to learn alone. Their support can keep you going.

Has your family experienced serious problems?

If your parent lost a job, your family may face uncertainties, and you might feel guilty for spending money on music. Talk to your parents before you volunteer to quit. They may be able to work out a money solution. If your parents are getting a divorce, it's normal to have trouble coping with sadness, fear, or anger. It's hard to keep your old schedule, much less fit in practice, when you're not sleeping well and you're moving or splitting time between two homes. Allow yourself time to recover. You may need months to adjust. Playing music can help you feel better and can take your mind off your troubles.

Is life difficult for you right now?

Personal problems can affect your outlook on life and your music. Are you falling behind in school? Facing a major assignment or test? Suffering an attack of "Senioritis"? Upset over a breakup with your boyfriend or girlfriend? At odds with your best friend? Hurt feelings and worries spill over into your music. Quitting your lessons or instrument will not remedy the situation. Music can help you feel better about almost anything.

PEER PRESSURE AND OTHER PEOPLE CONCERNS

Are musician friends passing you by?

Are your friends making great strides on their instruments and you feel left behind? They may practice more faithfully. Are you willing to put in that extra time to keep up with them?

> *Fourteen-year-old Fiona says that not being first chair is no reason to give up. "Quitting because you're bad is never a good reason, because you can always get better. If you think you want to quit, then you should think long and hard about it."*

You don't quit the basketball team if you're not the star forward or drop out of school if you're not on the honor roll. If your friends are better players, you can still enjoy playing. Your true friends will be your friends, no matter where you sit in orchestra.

Have nonmusician friends encouraged you to quit?

Are your friends sports players and you're the solo music player? People, especially teens, feel more secure around people who are like them. Your friends may give you a bad time, but deep down they're probably jealous. Kids who earn top grades often get the same treatment. Would your sports-minded friends turn down a straight-A report card or the ability to read music and play an instrument? Doubtful. Most people aren't willing to put in the time and effort. The best revenge is to smile. They don't know the fun they're missing.

Has someone teased you about being a musician?

Being called "weird," "geek," or "nerd" is no fun. Neither is being ridiculed for playing a "girl's" or a "boy's" instrument. If it happens again, remember this: people's putdowns reflect who *they* are, not you. Insecure or unhappy kids try to lift themselves by putting someone down. They may envy your special skill. They may feel inferior because they don't understand music and think they'll never be good at it.

When people make a mean comment, don't react. If you jump to defend yourself, they win. Look them in the eye, stay calm, and *you* win. Sam, 18, plays sports and French horn. "I was late to math class a couple of times when orchestra rehearsal ran overtime. When I said I'd been in orchestra, a couple of kids made smart remarks like, 'Orchestra? You play in orchestra?' I just said yes in a matter-of-fact tone, and they quit bugging me."

If you still get teased, laugh right back. One high school orchestra had T-shirts printed with "Orchestra Geek" on them. It's hard to make fun of someone if they've already anticipated you!

Has solitary practice replaced group friend fun?

Practice can feel boring and isolating. You may practice alone, but music should be a social event. Join an ensemble, or start one of your own. Play duets written for Piano Four Hands. Make a "playdate" that starts with ensembles and ends with a sleepover or video games. Joining a studio broadened 16-year-old Lydia's social circle. "Music is an important part of my life," she explains. "At times, I feel like quitting after a hard lesson. I know I won't because the students in the studio are my friends, too."

YOUR GROWING NEED FOR INDEPENDENCE

"But it was never my choice to play an instrument!"

I understand your frustration. When some students threaten to quit, it's not really about the music. It's an attempt to gain more control over their lives. When you were young, you didn't mind so much that your parents chose your wardrobe, instrument, teacher, and practice times. You're probably not so willing to go along now.

Do you need more decision-making power?

Sometimes we challenge rules and resist just to show that we can.

Fifteen-year-old Julian observes, "Some kids quit because all they think about is 'My parents are making me play.' If you enjoy it even a little, then work with your parents. Tell them you want to keep playing, but you want to practice at your own rate and on your own time. Soon you may start liking it more. When you enjoy doing something, you'll find it pretty easy."

Think twice about giving up something you like just to show your parents that you're in charge. Proving "you can't make me!" only hurts you in the end.

Do your parents enforce rigid practicing requirements?

If you resent their control, remind your parents that you're the one putting in a gazillion hours of practice and that to stay motivated, you need more say in where, when, and how. Ask them to ease up and let you skip practice or reschedule a lesson if it means you'll miss a special party or class trip. Ask for a practice vacation over the holidays or a few weeks off during the summer to refresh your interest in music. Better yet, show them how faithfully (and cheerfully!) you can practice without their help. How's that for a dose of shock therapy? Let your progress prove they can leave you alone.

Does a parent attend every lesson?

If you want them to bow out and let you work alone with your teacher, suggest they attend lessons only once a month or join you for the last five minutes. If you really want to go it alone, ask them to write the check, drive you to lessons, and leave the rest up to you and your teacher.

If your parents aren't willing to set you free, they might be surprised to learn their demands could cause you to reject music altogether. Talk with other teens. See what works for them. If you and your parents can't agree on a musical balance of power, find help in chapter 35, "Finding the Middle Ground." Even if playing was your parents' idea, it's okay to keep playing for your own reasons. If you still want to rebel, shave your head, walk with a slouch, or refuse to eat your vegetables.

PERFORMANCES AND CONTESTS

Did you recently have a "painful" music experience?

Are you upset you didn't win the prized spot in jazz band? When you work hard for an event and don't place well, or you perform less than your best, your disappointment looms large. Don't let your recent upset color a long-term decision.

Karen, a sophomore, almost made that mistake. "One year I practiced to get into the youth symphony, and I didn't make it. I felt like quitting lessons. I spent all my time practicing and felt I got nothing for it. I decided to spend my time doing something else. When my mom called my teacher to say I was going to quit, my teacher told her to give me two weeks without a lesson to cool off, then bring me to a lesson so that we could talk."

In chapter 32, "Put Concerts and Contests into Perspective," you'll find advice on how to get over disappointments, keep your confidence, and find the motivation to try again.

What happened at Karen's lesson after her two-week cooling off? "My teacher and I laughed about how bad I was when I started lessons, and she pointed out how much better I had gotten in only a year. I realized that with only one year of playing I wouldn't be good enough to play ten years from now. If I quit, that whole year would be a waste." That lesson happened five years ago. Karen is now first chair in her youth symphony. What does she say today? "I'm sure glad I didn't quit!"

Do you feel pressured to perform?

Alisa, age 15, considered quitting after a contest. "I had a bad experience with a cold judge. I felt pressured to perform and wanted to quit. Then I talked to my friends who play sports and things like chess club or debate team. They said they all went through that phase, too. I realized that all through life I would have pressure and people who were hard on me. I decided I might as well learn to deal with it now. Facing my fears and sticking with it made me grow up."

Do you fear you'll "fail" when you perform?

Fear dampens anyone's spirits. To boost your confidence, get a few successes under your belt. Choose easier pieces that you can play with confidence. Find stress-free ways to show off your musical skills. Share your music at casual family parties. Offer to play at a local retirement home—always an appreciative audience! Play at the mall, or accompany hymns at your place of worship. As a bonus, you'll earn community service hours. If you feel you need more time, skip a few months of performances. Prepare for any event following the systematic plan outlined in chapter 33, "Conquer Your Fear Factor."

THE FASTER PACE OF EXPERIENCED LEARNERS

Has reality set in?

By now, the novelty of your instrument and lessons has worn off. You may have had unrealistic expectations about how soon you'd get to the more interesting repertoire. You may no longer get by playing every song at the *largo* (very slow) tempo marking. Twelve-year-old Kurt has played tenor sax for several months and is still catching up. "Jazz has some really fast notes. Sometimes I feel like I won't ever be able to play a piece, but it just takes time." Even adults like Japanese translator Sayoko get discouraged. "As an adult, I can quit any time I want to. I know I am making progress, but progress has some steady inclines and sharp curves. Sometimes I feel I don't have any talent. Other times I just want to skip the hard parts."

Are you challenged by more advanced techniques?

"How can I ever learn double stops and *six* sharps? There's no way I can play the third octave. It's impossible!" Does your progress on seemingly impossible techniques only inch forward? Sayoko explains how she made it through: "I recently hit a brick wall learning a hard new technique. I thought I would never be able to play it. It was a perfect time for me to say, 'I quit!' Instead of quitting, I looked at it as a goal. I knew I wouldn't be able to quickly get the tough technique, so I decided to practice it only 10 minutes a day or 10 times throughout a day. I decided not to worry if I got it. I just put in the time knowing I was building toward success. It really helped with my frustration level."

When some people say they're bored or don't like music, they're really saying it's too hard. When you hit a plateau, instead of giving up, now is the time to buckle down and practice more. Dieters who reach a weight loss plateau add extra minutes of daily walking to shed their final pounds. Add extra minutes of daily practice to get over the hump that much faster.

MUSIC MONOTONY

If your music is putting you to sleep, ask your teacher if you can learn technique through real pieces instead of études. Perhaps you need more emotional music or music that tells a story. Maybe venturing into different styles would give you a life. What would you like to play? The blues? Pop music? Classical music created by real composers, not method book companies? Classical pieces by contemporary composers? Television or movie themes?

Classical guitarists, do you want to improvise your own melodies and rhythms? Then model the powerful riffs of rock legend Carlos Santana. Singers, have you sung one too many Italian arias? Try singing in a different language—the nonsense syllables made famous by Ella Fitzgerald's jazz "scat." Bring in sheet music you like. Broadening your music makes learning more fun.

INSTRUMENT ISSUES

Many famous musicians were unhappy with their first instrument and only later found their "lifelong partner." After seven years of piano lessons, Kyle found his "true love" in the electric guitar. "If you don't love your instrument, you'll never play well. Finding the right instrument made a big difference to me. The sound of power chords reverbs in my head. I keep on hearing it, and I love the sound. Besides, the guitar gets you more girls!"

Finding the right instrument made all the difference for 18-year-old Stephan. "I started playing clarinet in sixth-grade band. I really wanted to play drums, but too many kids had signed up for drums. The teacher chose clarinet for me. I played it in band from sixth grade through eleventh grade. I wasn't really into it in high school. I liked the teacher and the class and being part of a group, but I didn't like the bass clarinet parts. They weren't challenging, and I didn't like marching."

Spend time exploring. If you play piano, try the organ, keyboard, or challenge yourself by playing clarinet or drums in band or orchestra. If you take lessons on the cello, add the guitar for fun. And don't forget about singing. Take voice lessons or join a choir.

Learning a second instrument is always easier. Stephan didn't quit; he kept searching. "I picked up the guitar in my sophomore year. Without a teacher, I had to push myself and find a way to play. It was good for me to learn how to focus and discover it on my own. When I started taking lessons, it was a lot easier and more fun."

Playing on a clunker instrument is discouraging. If you're not making much progress, perhaps it's not your fault. Blame it on your instrument!

BEFORE YOU MAKE YOUR DECISION, CONSIDER

It's easy to storm out of a bad lesson, hard practice session, or fight with your parents and scream, "I quit!" But before you make such a rash move, please calm down and give these ideas some thought.

Have you kept your teacher and parents in the loop?

No teacher likes to be blindsided. Give your teacher the chance to fix things, especially if you've kept quiet until now. If your teacher doesn't understand the problem or isn't willing to work with you, consider changing teachers before you throw in the towel.

Have you talked to your parents about quitting? Okay, have you talked to them about quitting when you weren't mad at them about something else? Give your parents a chance to help you find a solution.

Will you regret quitting some day?

Quitting is a big decision, and many people regret it for the rest of their lives. I've never heard an adult say, "I'm so glad my mom let me drop piano lessons!" (Notice it's always the mom.) High school student Selina plays flute, but still regrets dropping out of piano lessons. "I played piano for five years, then I quit because I didn't like to practice. When I quit, I felt free. Now I see people playing piano solos, and I feel jealous knowing I could have played that well, too."

Other teens miss it much later. Eighteen-year-old Joe is a "former" trumpet player. "I played trumpet in school from fourth to ninth grade, but never took it seriously," he recalls. "When I got to high school, I had to be in marching band. I could never march and play at the same time, and the band director always yelled at me. He's a good director and a cool guy, but still I could never get the hang of it." That year was the end of playing for Joe.

"Last week I walked home from school past the marching band practicing outside. I went home and dug out my trumpet from the basement. I felt good knowing I could still play scales and a couple of pieces. I think learning music is a valuable skill, like learning a different language. Now when I see someone play well, I know what it takes. I'll never regret my time as a musician."

Are you giving up when it's time to cash in?

No matter what your age, if you've been playing for years, don't toss your hard-earned successes away unless you know that quitting is the best solution. You've already made it through the hardest part. You know how to read music, position your instrument, count rhythms, and do things easily that you never thought you could. It's downhill now. Enjoy the rewards of your time and effort. It's payback time!

CHOOSE MUSIC FOR YOU

Are you playing because you have to?

Music isn't something you choose because it's good for you, might help you get into college, or your parents are making you. Fifteen-year-old Julian agrees. "Teens should only play music if their hearts are really into it. If someone is forcing you to play, don't do it. The point is to enjoy it—not to please your parents but to please yourself." Anna, a graduating senior, says, "Above *all else*, music should always be for you and not for someone else." You need to choose your music every day: "It's up to *you* to decide when you're going to practice. Think, 'I choose to practice right now. I'm playing this piece because I enjoy it.' You have to do it for yourself."

Even skilled musicians need to choose.

High school student Fiona played well but never for her own pleasure. "I really didn't like music that much. I liked the people I performed with and my lessons, but I never found any particular joy in listening or playing. I started taking lessons to keep up with my friends in band. I practiced only for the good feeling of being prepared, not for any good feeling from music. I quit because I was doing so many different things and felt I wasn't doing well at any of them."

Gifted musicians have the skill but not always the passion to continue. Their parents can find it hard to accept. "As painful and unbelievable as it is to hear, violin has no place in Janet's world," Janet's father wrote to her teacher. "We're sad about her lack of interest in developing her God-given musical talent." Both of Janet's parents are professional musicians, yet they didn't hound her to continue. "After a year of honest reflection and discussion, we understand Janet and need to be her advocate. A passion for classical music and violin needs to grow from within, from a spark to a flame to the glowing embers of a refined, beautiful artist. My wife and I were born with that spark. Janet was not. We accept her decision."

Anna wrote this beautiful poem to illustrate why she plays the flute:

The Test

I lift the silver flute,
I lift the pencil to take a test,
I lift my toe to the starting line.
Adrenaline rushes through my veins.
Am I nervous?
I am prepared.
I close my eyes, visualizing my goal
Perfect, flawless performance
Confidence builds.
Negative thoughts drift in
Smashed by my love for competition.
People are watching, waiting.
Breathe.
This is for me and no one else.
The rhythm escapes my veins like electricity.
I play for the love of playing.
This race is for me.

CONSIDER A COMPROMISE

If you're still lukewarm about lessons, your decision doesn't have to be all or nothing. Call it a "temporary extension." Take just two or three more months of lessons. With a new approach, your teacher might change your attitude toward lessons and practice. Compromise kept 14-year-old James going for years. "When I first started taking piano lessons, I didn't like it. It was different and hard. My parents told me, 'Stick with it, and you'll like it eventually.' They always encouraged me to keep playing. They told me to just play one more week or one more month and see if it gets better. I do it, and then I always keep liking it."

If playing was mostly your parents' idea, they might consider offering you an incentive to continue lessons, at least until you play well enough to inspire yourself. Sign a contract that specifies how long you'll commit to lessons and a reward that matches your commitment. A one-month promise might earn you a game rental. Rewards for longer promises might be getting your driver's license, going to sports camp, or choosing the location of your next family vacation. If you still want to quit, take a three-month break and reassess with your parents before you make a final "now or never" plan.

THE FINAL CHOICE IS YOURS ALONE

Have you tried other solutions to your problems, thought through your decision and the consequences, and you still want to quit? I believe you. Quitting doesn't mean you're bad, stupid, selfish, or unmusical. It means you have other priorities, find it too stressful, or lack the motivation to continue. I will never become a ballerina. I like to watch ballet, but I don't want to dance, and no amount of lessons will change my aptitude or my attitude. I have no interest in being an accountant or a professional garage organizer, either. I admire them and appreciate their skills, but I don't want to be them. (And don't try to make me!)

THE MECHANICS OF QUITTING

The best time to quit

If you decide to stop taking lessons, the best time is in the summer. Summer is a natural transition time and most convenient for your teacher's schedule. Be as honest as possible in explaining why you want to leave. Your teacher can use this information to improve her teaching style. She may assume she's the reason you decided to channel your efforts elsewhere. Please explain your reasons in person or at least over the phone. Make the transition easier by following my advice in chapter 9, "Is It Time to Change Teachers?"

With her permission, I have quoted a letter written by Susan, a cello student, to her teacher.

> DEAR ANITA,
>
> It's been a privilege and honor to have studied with you. I've learned so much in the past year. You are a fabulous teacher, but I am not a fabulous student. Wanting to quit is not about you. It's about me. I start dreading my lesson two days before because I hate being unprepared, but I still don't want to practice. It's gotten so bad that you could take away everything I own and I would trade if for not having to take lessons. I don't even like the sound of the cello anymore.
>
> It's hard telling my parents I want to quit because they are both musicians and love music so much. But music is their dream, not mine.
>
> Please know that I appreciate everything you have done for me. I have many good memories I've shared with you. But now it is time for me to quit.
>
> Thank you for understanding.

Leave the door open.

You may say good-bye today, but leave the door open for tomorrow. It doesn't have to be a lifetime decision. If you quit lessons, stay active in music at school. If your timing isn't right now, it may be in a year or two. Simon suggests that teens who get discouraged should take a break and then pick it up again. "Give yourself another chance in six months or a year," he suggests. Seventeen-year-old Aureli returned after a break. "A few years ago I tried to play 'Under the Bridge' by the Red Hot Chili Peppers. It has some weird fretting and strumming parts. I just couldn't get it, so I gave it up. A year later I came back and I could do it."

Music isn't for everybody. Neither is playing paintball, square dancing, or owning a potbellied pig. Find another fun and challenging project. Join the chess club or the tennis team.

If you do quit, your friends will still like you, your parents will still love you, and your teacher will understand.

GREAT IDEAS

Everybody wants to quit sometime. Before you do, take a deep breath and consider all of your options.

Sneak Preview

Deciding whether to quit or stay is only one problem music students may face. In our next chapter, I offer solutions to other problems weighing on students, from how to handle jealousy to how to get used to the new band director. Turn to the next page to learn how to handle your own dramas and dilemmas!

THIRTY-NINE

Thorny Questions from Students

You're Not Alone!

Gabrielle worked hard on her instrument all summer, and by fall she was eager to move up in high-school band. Her plans were stymied, however, by older girls who sat in the top seats but weren't as good as Gabrielle. Marie loves her new teacher and private music lessons. At least she *thought* they would be private, until her mom insisted on attending every week. Daniel wants to quit lessons because he is so bored with the music that his teacher assigns. How can he convince her to give him a choice? Read on and you just might recognize a sticky situation from your own music life.

Q: *I'm 15, and I've played the cello for four years. Now I really want to play the electric guitar. My mom says, "No, electric guitar is not a 'real' instrument like the cello." How can I persuade her to let me?*
A: This is a situation calling for compromise. Would your mom consider letting you play both instruments? Here are some possibilities: you could take cello lessons and play the guitar on your own. You could take guitar lessons and play cello in the school orchestra or in chamber music. You could play both instruments with no lessons, or play both instruments with lessons on both. Perhaps your mom would be more willing to let you give up the cello if you took guitar lessons from a teacher who teaches both classical and rock/jazz.

If you continue to play both instruments, you'll have the best of both worlds. If your love for the cello is completely gone, have a heart-to-heart talk with your mom and convince her you're serious about the guitar. Then practice like crazy. Just remember that all the skills that make playing the guitar easier you owe to your years of cello practice.

Q: *I just don't think I have what it takes to be a good musician. I'm not the type who can sight-read fast, memorize easily, or even play without lots of mistakes. My parents aren't musical, and I don't think I am, either. Should I give up because I'm not talented?*
A: You have typecast yourself as a musical loser. When you see yourself as a failure or try to place the blame on someone (your parents) or something (that elusive thing called talent), you will be a loser. Do you attend all lessons with

an open mind? Do you pay attention to your teacher? Do you put in the practice hours? Do you practice with concentration?

Next, take a look at the rest of your life. Do you feel negatively about how you do in school? Your relationship with friends and family? Other talents such as sports? Perhaps the problem is not with music but with your self-image. Stop the negative self-talk. You can only become what you believe you can become. Every time you tell yourself you're not good enough, you've taken a step toward failure.

Find a mentor who believes in you. It can be a family member, teacher, someone skilled in music, or even a friend. Their support can help you begin to see your strengths and give you courage to keep trying. If you want to be a musician, then be a musician.

Q: Our neighbor wants me to give piano lessons to her 7-year-old. I've taken piano lessons for eight years, and I'm a pretty good pianist, but I don't know if I should teach. What should I tell her?

A: Every child deserves a good teacher. Even though your neighbor's daughter is just a beginner, learning correctly from the very beginning is so important. Perhaps the neighbor girl can take lessons from your teacher. If that's not an option, then ask your teacher to help you choose books, make lesson plans, and be your mentor. If you're serious about becoming a great teacher, read the first book in the Music for Life series, *Making Music and Enriching Lives: A Guide for All Music Teachers.*

Q: I practice about four hours a day. Lately my hands have been going numb. Is this common?

A: Talk to your teacher and videotape yourself to make sure you're holding your instrument and your body correctly. If you're tense and tight, you can damage your body—and your playing won't sound so great, either.

See if you can cut down on your practice time with more concentrated practice. If you need to put in the time, stretch often and be sure to take several breaks. If the numbness in your hands persists, see your doctor.

Q: The orchestra director at my school also teaches private lessons. He clearly favors the students who study privately with him and always awards them the top chairs. He has an ensemble at school made up entirely of his students, and he even threatens to let only his students sign up for competitions because "they are the best." How can we make him be fair to the rest of us?

A: It is unethical for the teacher to teach privately and charge for the lessons unless there is no other teacher available, especially if he favors those students. You and your parents should first talk to him, then to the principal and even to the school board.

Q: During the week, I keep forgetting what my teacher told me at the lesson. I know what songs I'm supposed to work on, but I can't remember what she said to make them sound better, and I keep making the same old mistakes. Is there a better way?

A: You need a memory aid to take home with you. Try these ideas: Invite a parent to help listen and take notes. Ask your teacher to make notes in the music or to write suggestions in a separate notebook. Tape the lesson so you can review it at home. Practice right after your lesson or at least the very next day. Make a copy of your music, and each week choose a different colored pen or pencil to make notes on the music of things your teacher wants you to correct.

Q: There are way too many flutes in my band, and most of them don't take lessons. I get bored waiting for them to learn the music, and my director keeps telling us to play quieter. It's no fun playing this year. How can I make it until June without going crazy?

A: During band, you need to follow your director's lead. In the meantime, how about playing the piccolo? You could surely be heard there! Can you switch to another instrument like the oboe or bassoon in band? Suggest to your director that perhaps some of the "excess" flutes could double an oboe part. Ask your director if you can form a small ensemble of the top flutes that meets once a week to give you a break from the band music. If you're still frustrated, talk to your band director to see if he has any suggestions. Be sure to check out chapter 42,"What Can I Do If I'm Bored in Band or Orchestra?"

Q: I'm a junior and play in our high school band. My problem is the two girls who sit in front of me. I play better than both of them, but because they're seniors they always take the good parts and solos. It's not fair. I feel upset when I have to sit and listen to them show off. What can I do?

A: No one feels good when their playing skills are not recognized or appreciated. Are there any other reasons besides age that led your band teacher to choose the other two girls for solos? Have they earned the privilege? Did the solos require a technique you haven't quite mastered? Does your director feel the two seniors are good section leaders and should get to play the solos?

If you answer no, ask to speak to your band director privately. Thank him or her for meeting with you and then say something like, "Could you please tell me your policy for handing out solos? Do you go by skill or seniority? I'm asking because I've noticed you've given the solos to the same people all the time."

If the director's reason is only seniority, you've got another year to wait—there's not much you can do about it. If you're certain you play better than those chosen, politely ask your director to hold a "blind" audition where he or she doesn't know who is playing. The three of you could take turns playing in front of the band with your director's back turned away from the performers.

You could also play behind a screen or he could listen to anonymous audition tapes. Blind auditions reveal who plays best and eliminate the impression of the director "playing favorites."

Q: I thought I had what it takes to become a professional musician, but lately I've lost some contests, and some other kids got seated ahead of me in orchestra. Is this a sign I'm not good enough to become a pro?

A: Every professional has disappointments; they lose a contest, don't get the job, or play a concert not up to their standards. Did you know that Mozart never could find a good steady job? See, you're in good company! If you are consistently not doing well, then talk to your teacher about your progress. You need to be a top performer to make a living playing music. If your dream is to become a professional, work hard to make yourself better and don't worry about your "competition."

Q: My mom teaches piano lessons. I want to learn how to play piano but not from her! How can I persuade her to get me a "real" teacher?

A: Has your mom tried to teach you? Give it a chance. If you still want another teacher, talk to your mom. Tell her you understand that she has a lot she can teach you. You know it would be a lot more convenient and cheaper for her to teach you, but you don't want your relationship to get in the way of the music. It's easy for kids to confuse rebelling against the music as rebelling against their parents. One of the big advantages of taking lessons is the wonderful relationship that you can build with an adult outside of the family. Tell her you'll probably learn more with an outside teacher because it's a lot easier to listen to and obey an adult outside of the family. The ultimate goal should be for you to learn the piano and stick with lessons, not to save money.

Q: I'm definitely not the best student in my teacher's studio. I do practice, but playing clarinet isn't the most important thing in my life like it is to some other kids. I enjoy my lessons, but I have a social life, too. When my mom hears how well other students play in recitals, she gets mad at me because they're so much better. Should I give up trying to please her?

A: Music plays a different part in everyone's life, and that's okay. What if every clarinet student wanted to become a professional? The world would be overrun with clarinetists! There's room in the world for students who want to be professionals and those who just want to have fun with music. Are you and your mom on the same page? Does your mom feel you need to practice a certain number of hours per day for her to "get her money's worth"? Talk to your teacher about a practice plan. If your teacher is happy with your progress, she can tell your mother. Make sure your mother hears you practicing at home, so she knows you're putting in effort.

Q: My teacher wants me to play in a contest this spring. I played in it last year and didn't do very well. I don't want to play in any more contests because I know I won't win. How can I persuade my teacher to let me off the hook?

A: While I can't give you any guarantees that you will win the contest this year, I can tell you one way you will lose for sure: don't enter! Did you learn anything from your experience to help you play better this year?

But wait! Not everyone who enters a contest wins. Does that mean it's only worth it if you take the prize? No! The preparation for the contest is the reason for doing it. You're a winner already if you learned to practice hard, had fun learning the piece, enjoyed your lessons, and became a better musician because of your effort. Your success is not dependent on others losing but on you becoming better. If you really want to win the contest, write down your goal and all the things you will have to do (and sacrifice) to get there. Then get to work.

Q: *I think my new high school orchestra teacher is weird. He's not anything like my old teacher, who made jokes and laughed a lot. This new guy says things about our playing he thinks are funny, but they just come out being mean. He's really picky and points out people who can't find their place. He even names the ones who played the wrong note. I miss my old teacher—but I have to admit our orchestra does sound better this year.*

A: It's hard to get used to a new teacher after your favorite teacher leaves. Give the guy a break and some time to settle into his teaching style. Soon you may get used to his approach and higher standards. Remember that this is a class and you're there to learn. He needs to be a good teacher, not your best friend. Appreciate the improvements he's making in your band. If your new director is more organized and accomplishes more than the last one, you'll be grateful at the end of the year when you've advanced that much more.

Q: *I'm sick of doing scales and études. My teacher says I have to play lots of them before I can play real songs. I want to play real music instead of exercises. Is she right, or is she just trying to trick me into doing more boring stuff?*

A: Learning scales and études is like learning the alphabet and grammar. Every solo will sound better with this solid foundation. Instead of rebelling, perhaps you can make a compromise with your teacher. Try saying something like, "When I'm through the 10th lesson in the étude book, can I choose a piece to play?" You could ask your teacher to give you one "fun" piece for every four pieces assigned. Or how about a piece in every key of the scales you mastered? Politely ask if there are any songs that could teach you the same skills as the études. In her zeal to make you better, your teacher may have forgotten that we play for the joy of music, not just to master the instrument. If the "carrot" of real music inspires you to practice your scales and études better and without complaining, I bet your teacher will be all for it.

Q: *Two of my friends and I started taking voice lessons at the same time. Now both of them are better than I am. Will I ever catch up?*

A: Everyone learns at their own rate. The student who catches on quickly at the beginning may not be the one who is out in front in the end. Most voices don't mature until you are well into your twenties, so you have lots of time. Being worried and tense will only make you sound worse. Relax and enjoy the process of learning, not just the end goals. You can also try asking your friends to coach you on the side. Have them come over and sing duets or trios with you. They can be extra pairs of ears to help you improve your singing.

Q: *I'm taking viola lessons from a really well-known teacher. I feel lucky that he accepted me as a student, but I don't think I'm good enough to be in his studio. I'll never be able to play the way he wants me to, and I feel I am just wasting his time. Should I switch to a different teacher?*

A: Who says you aren't good enough? Your teacher had faith in you, and now it's your turn to have faith in yourself. You owe it to your great teacher and to yourself to practice hard and realize your potential. You're worth it.

Q: *I like to play my trombone at school, but I hate to practice. It's fun to play in jazz band, and I like my lessons, but after I do all my homework I'd rather play video games, not practice. Should I quit taking lessons?*

A: Practicing is the tough part of learning an instrument. It wasn't always fun for me either. Video games may be more fun at the moment, but the great times you will have with your instrument will last a lifetime. If practicing has gotten you to the point of wanting to quit, why not make some compromises? Can you play an hour of video games for every half hour of practice? Can you practice before school or right after school before you do your homework so you are still fresh? How about a snack before you practice as an incentive to get going and to give you an energy boost? Can you ask your teacher to lighten the load, or even find a less demanding teacher? At the very least, please stay in jazz band. You'll still be learning and having fun.

Q: *I play in two orchestras and a chamber group; I take lessons from a really tough teacher and practice about three hours a day. I've been winning contests, and I enjoy the attention I get. Everyone says I can make it as a professional in the future, but right now I feel burned out. I'd like to be a musician, but some days I just want to give it all up. How can I keep up this grueling schedule and keep my joy in playing?*

A: Have you ever heard of "having too much of a good thing"? We all need a chance to refresh and renew ourselves no matter how much we love what we do. Take one day off every week with no practice. How about asking your teacher to go easy on you during tough weeks at school or ask to have a week now and then where you just sight-read or play old favorites at your lesson instead of having to prepare new material. Take a break from the normal routine this summer, and keep your chops up by attending music camp. Schedule in a couple of weeks for vacation away from your instrument. Your batteries will be recharged when you return.

But what can you do right now? Nurture yourself on a daily basis if possible. Sometimes all it takes is a few minutes of solitude to calm down. Before you get up in the morning, when you go to bed, or for a couple of minutes during the day, have some alone time to think about your goals and give yourself a pep talk. Exercise can also give you those endorphins that make you happier and healthier. Listen to your favorite CDs and luxuriate in the beauty of the music. Strive for a balance in your life so you can keep music and your sanity.

Q: My teacher brags about another one of her students at every lesson. "David plays at a conservatory level even though he is just in ninth grade. David is playing the Tchaikovsky. David won the contest. David, David, David." I'm sick of hearing about him. How can I get her to stop?

A: Your teacher is being insensitive, but perhaps she is bragging about David to give you a role model or a goal to work toward. She is probably so proud of David that she doesn't know she is bragging. Who knows? Maybe she's bragging about you, too. If it's too hard for you to say, "I'm really happy that David is doing so well, I'm doing my best, too," perhaps your parents could diplomatically talk to your teacher.

Q: I hate performing, and I especially dread playing in contests! I turn red as a beet, and my hands sweat so much I'm afraid my trumpet will fall on the floor! Can you help me?

A: To learn to be comfortable playing in front of a group try these suggestions: Gradually work up to performances in front of a full, live audience. If you need to, play for stuffed animals at first. Then practice on your dog, your parents, and friends. Play a duet or trio instead of a solo at the recital or contest. It helps to "share the pain." Play a recital piece that's so easy you could play it in your sleep. Ask your teacher if you can only play in recitals and not in contests. For more ways to gain confidence while performing, see chapter 33, "Conquer Your Fear Factor."

Q: I like playing the cello, but I have a hard time finding the time to practice because my friends want me to hang out with them all the time. They say that playing the cello is for geeks, and they want me to play computer games or go to the mall instead. How can I balance my music and my friends?

A: It's hard to face peer pressure, but think of what they're asking you to do. How do you feel about yourself after you've wasted eight hours playing video games or hanging out at the mall? Do your friends ever think about the future, or is their idea of long-term goals making it to the next level of Zelda or Mario? Now think of how you feel when you've had a productive practice, great lesson, or performance. We all want to belong (that's why peer pressure is so hard to resist), but you have to be true to what you want, not just go along with the crowd. Sure, you should have time for video games and relaxing. But keep your eye on what's really important.

Q: I'm a 13-year-old boy and I play the flute. Kids at my bus stop tease me and say it's a sissy instrument. I like playing flute, but I'm thinking about switching to something more macho like saxophone, trumpet, or drums. What can I do so the other kids will stop bugging me?

A: The best thing you can do is to ignore them. I know it's hard, but the more you react, the more they'll want to keep getting that reaction. One way to respond is to make a joke of it yourself, saying something like, "Hey, real men don't have to play big instruments to prove themselves." "The flute has the best range when it comes to shooting spitwads." "Have you noticed that all the best-looking girls are in the flute section and I'm surrounded by them?" "I only chose the flute because I can keep it up my sleeve when it rains." "Did you know that many of the world's greatest flute players are guys, too?" The second best thing you can do is to get so good they'll quit bugging you because they're all so jealous. Keep a smile on your face, and eventually instead of bugging you they'll look up to you.

Q: I don't think my piano teacher likes me. She's a good teacher, but she always acts so strict and businesslike, never like a friend. Should I change teachers?

A: Your teacher may not realize the effect of her sternness. Instead of changing teachers, why don't you think of how you could get her to lighten up? Walk into the studio with a smile, say hello, and ask how her day has been. Give her a compliment or bring her flowers, chocolates, or a small gift. Write her a short note or give her a card showing your appreciation. Pay attention during the lesson, always act respectful, and thank her when you leave. Showing your appreciation of her as a teacher and a person may do wonders.

Q: My mom is a music teacher, and she comes to all my lessons. I dread having her there. When I don't do something right, she points it out, even before my violin teacher has a chance to. Or she talks about me as if I'm not there, saying things like, "I already told him that at home!" How can I get her to stop butting in?

A: It's a tricky situation when you're the "pickle in the middle." Have you talked to your mom about her actions? Do you think she realizes what she is doing and how it affects you? Say something like, "Mom, I want to talk to you about my lessons. It's nice that you want to be with me every time, but I've noticed that you often correct me or say things my teacher was about to tell me." Tell her how you feel when she jumps in. Then tell her what you'd like her to do. For example, you might say, "It's confusing to have two people correcting me, and it's not very respectful to the teacher. How about if we make a deal? You can talk at the beginning or end of my lesson, and the rest we'll leave up to my teacher." If you don't want her to come at all, say, "I feel I could play a lot better if I wasn't distracted with you in the room." Or suggest, "How about coming to my lessons once a month?" If you don't want her there at all, maybe it's time for you to take more responsibility for your lessons and practicing.

Perhaps you can have your teacher talk to your mom. Your teacher can very diplomatically say, "I would like you to stay outside during the lesson because I want to focus on your daughter."

Q: *I don't like the music my piano teacher gives me. I want to play fun songs like the ones I hear on the radio. How can I get my teacher to let me?*
A: Listen to recordings or the radio and come to your lesson with ideas of something you would like to work on. Ask your teacher if you can choose one piece that's not in the regular books every week/month/ten pieces, etc. After playing more popular music, you may realize that you're not learning as much from easier pieces, your teacher has a very narrow taste in music, or you want to study with a teacher with taste more like yours. If you do choose to change teachers, make sure you're doing it because the new teacher has more to offer than easier assignments.

Q: *My teacher is a professional violinist and has played all over the world, so everyone wants to study with him. I finally got into his studio, but all he does is talk about how great he is or tell me stories about his concerts. When I ask for help on a technique, he just says, "Just play what comes naturally" or "Play it like this." He demonstrates but doesn't really show me step by step. I guess I'm learning by imitating him, but I need more help. What can I do?*
A: Many famous performers are also fabulous teachers. But knowing how to play an instrument doesn't mean you know how to teach it. You're probably not going to change his teaching style, so you might want to change teachers. Stick with this teacher for six months or a year, assess your progress, and then make your decision.

Q: *I love playing violin, and I practice a lot. I'm way better than the other kids in my grade who play violin. They're jealous and talk behind my back and say I'm stuck up. How can I keep playing and have friends, too?*
A: Why not invite some of these kids to play in an ensemble after school with you? That way they could get to know you better and realize you don't think you're too good for them. With your parents' permission, you could invite them over to play and then finish with pizza. At school or at home when you're playing with other kids, be careful not to be bossy or tell them what they're doing wrong; that's the teacher's job. Never brag about how good you are or even how much you practice. You can also try to find some other players at your level who attend different schools and play in other ensembles, or you could audition for a youth symphony or honor band.

Q: *My friend is always criticizing other players and talking about them behind their backs. It makes me uncomfortable and also makes me wonder what she says behind my back. How can I get her to stop without seeming critical of her?*
A: Putting someone down doesn't make you better. It puts you down, too. The next time your friend starts to cut other kids down or gossip, do your best to change the subject, say something nice about the person, or just refuse to join

in. She'll soon find it's pretty boring talking about someone if you have no audience.

Q: *My parents don't understand how much I like music. They say, "You'll never make a living as a musician!" They think being a music major in college is a waste of time, and they want me to go into the medical field instead. Help! I hate the sight of blood and love the sound of Beethoven!*

A: Perhaps your music teacher could talk to your parents. You can also show them the many career opportunities musicians have. Not everyone is a starving artist. One of the greatest successes we can have in life is doing a job we love. On the other hand, just because you have a different major or career doesn't mean you can't also take music classes and lessons and keep playing. One of my friends was a music major in college, and then became a doctor and retired early. Now he has time to do what he really loves: taking piano lessons and practicing three hours a day. There are many ways to follow your dream.

Q: *I love my piano teacher. We laugh, and I learn so much from her. She's almost like a second mom to me. We have good talks, and my hour with her is the best part of my week and maybe my life. Now my parents tell me we're moving to another state! I don't want to go!*

A: It's hard to leave favorite friends, places, and teachers behind when you move. It's especially tough saying good-bye to a teacher you love and respect. You might feel as sad as if you were breaking up with a boyfriend or girlfriend, and you might be afraid of losing your music, too. But remember, like dating, there are a lot of fish in the sea.

Before you leave, you and your teacher should list all the theory and repertoire you have learned. Perhaps she can also make a list of the repertoire she feels you should tackle in the future. I'm sure your teacher will be happy to stay in contact with you through e-mail or phone calls after you leave. Believe it or not, you might find a teacher you like as much or even better. You are lucky you've had such a great teacher. Now you know what qualities to look for in the next one. When you're settled into your new home and are ready to look for one, read our chapter 7, "Finding the Perfect Teacher."

Don't forget to tell your teacher what she has meant to you over the years. A thoughtful gesture like a memory book with some photos and your own drawings or a gift of flowers from your garden would mean the world to your teacher.

Q: *I'm jealous when my friends get a higher chair in band or a better grade at contests. I smile on the outside, but it just eats me up on the inside. How can I be happy for them when it means I lose?*

A: Having your self-worth depend on how you compare with others will never make you happy. No matter where you live or how good you are, there will always be someone who can sight-read or play faster, has a more beautiful tone, can memorize without trying, or has a more expensive instrument. But if you're working as hard as your friends, then you're making progress, too. Although they may be ahead of you, it's still a win-win situation. There's always going to be somebody at school who scores higher on the test or makes varsity before you, so you might as well get used to dealing with the success of others. If you quit wasting your time on jealousy and learn to be a good sport, you'll have more friends, and that's worth a lot!

Q: I get so frustrated when I practice because I keep making the same mistakes. How can I keep from throwing my saxophone out the window?
A: Mistakes, as maddening as they are, are part of learning. Try these hints to nip those mistakes in the bud: look at the music before you start to play it for the first time. Mark the beats if the rhythm is hard and sing the rhythm. Play the scale of the key signature so you have it in mind. Circle any accidentals or anything unusual. Read it like a book before you even start.

Start each piece very slowly to avoid making mistakes in the first place. Take one small section at a time and work on it. Remember, playing slowly gets faster results. Mark all your mistakes the very first time you make them.

When you start a practice session, keep in mind that what you learned yesterday may not be perfect again today. Review pieces at slower tempos than when you left them. Be patient with your progress. When you start to get upset, take a deep breath. All the energy you put into yelling, moaning, and groaning will just make playing harder. During your practice session, if you're really trying and your mistakes are still coming, leave it for tomorrow. Remember, if you weren't making mistakes, you wouldn't even need lessons! If you need more help making your practice time count, look for lots of ideas in part 3.

Q: My teacher is nice sometimes but mean other times. If I don't practice, she makes faces and gets mad at me. I am afraid to go to my lessons because I don't know how she'll treat me that day. Should I quit?
A: Invite your parents to sit in and observe a lesson or two. Do they agree with you, or do they think you're being overly sensitive? Are you mistaking your teacher's intentions? Is she strict because she demands high standards, or does she seem to be mean for no reason? Sometimes teachers use a stern tone of voice to get their point across, especially if they think you haven't been listening. If you're learning and would like to stay with this teacher, ask your parents to talk to her. She may be unaware of how her actions affect you and will treat you differently if asked. If her moods seem random, it may be time to switch to another teacher who is more consistent and has better people skills.

Q: I think music should express your feelings and you should be able to play the music the way it makes you feel. My violin teacher says I have to play exactly what is written on the page. He dictates to me the dynamics, tempo, and rubato. I feel my music isn't my own. Whose way is right?
A: You're both right! Understand that you must follow certain musical traditions. If you didn't, it would be like making cookies and trying to toast them

instead of baking them. Music has changed styles over the centuries, and each period has its own distinct feel. Playing Bach like Tchaikovsky would have seemed as startling as a guest wearing short shorts to visit Queen Victoria's palace. Certain pieces also have traditions that have been passed down and should be acknowledged.

On the other hand, each person should put a personal stamp on the music. Move your body in the way the music makes you feel. Make up your own story line to the music and play out this story. Perhaps you can concentrate more on music from the Romantic period, which allows more freedom of expression. If you still feel too confined by the conventions of classical music, try exploring rock or jazz. But please don't give up those violin lessons!

Q: I want to practice a lot so I can get into a good college music program or conservatory and maybe even earn a scholarship. I have so many demands on my time in high school; I can't find the time to practice my violin as much as I should. How can I find 25 hours in each day?

A: If you want to achieve your goals, you have to make practice a priority over everything else. You might be surprised at how much free time you're filling with phone calls, shopping, internet chats, or watching TV.

Can your parents help? Can they ease up on household chores? Can they give you rides to school to save time on the bus? Would they be willing to help you get a car so you're less dependent on others for transportation? Perhaps you can take one less class at school, or use a study hall for practice. Can you take classes that demand less homework to free up time at home? Can you get up even 30 minutes earlier to practice before school? It sounds inhumane, but it's possible!

But remember, to gain admission into a good college or earn that scholarship you must take the required classes and keep up that grade point average. You'd never want to resort to asking your parents to do homework for you, but could they run to the library, print something out from the internet, or help you type your finished report? Consider other options for high school. Would your parents be willing to home school you? Could you participate in an early college entrance program that allows you to finish your last two years of high school at a junior college? Could you postpone college for one year to devote the year after graduation to honing your skills?

One last thing to keep in mind is your focus. Remember that spending hours a day practicing doesn't count as much as concentration. Focus during your practice and lessons, and you will progress more quickly even without those extra hours in your day.

Q: I wasn't getting anywhere with my old teacher, so I switched to one who is more experienced and much more demanding. My new teacher tells me everything I learned before is wrong. I'm mad at my old teacher for not teaching me right, and I feel so discouraged.

A: Take heart. It is always hard to switch to another teacher, especially one who has much higher standards. Teachers each have their own values and methods, so you're probably being treated like every other transfer student. Talk to your teacher and explain your frustration. Perhaps in your teacher's zeal to correct all the wrongs, she is forgetting to let you know what is right. Analyze your playing as it was on the day of your first lesson with the new teacher and then today. Have you improved? If so, then it was worth relearning a few things. Learning an instrument is a long journey, and you're lucky you now have a good teacher to guide you. Give it time. If the teacher is good and you're trying your best, it will all be worth it.

Q: *My parents are both professional musicians. My mom teaches piano, and my dad plays the viola. Ever since I was little, they always assumed that I was going to be a professional musician, too. But music is their thing, not mine. What can I do to make them see my side of the story?*

A: Professional musicians who love music want their children to experience that same love and joy, and it's hard for them to face the fact that their child may not feel that same spark. Do some soul-searching. Are there times you enjoy playing an instrument? Would you miss it if you didn't play? Has this difference in expectations weighed heavily on your mind for a long time, or do you think this might just be a difficult bump in the road? Could you compromise with less of a commitment to music but remaining involved? Don't give up playing just because it's not going to be your profession. Have a heartfelt talk with your parents. You may disappoint them at first, but they'll appreciate your honesty and ultimately want you to have a career you love as much as they love theirs.

Q: *I play clarinet and just started taking private lessons so I could get better in my middle school band. My new clarinet teacher is teaching me notes and rhythms that we don't use in band. I don't think the stuff she's teaching me is going to help. I don't see how I can work on band music and her assignments, too. How can I get her just to teach me the band music?*

A: Even though your first goal is to improve in band, your clarinet teacher sees farther down the road and is giving you the building blocks you need to be a good musician. Ask her if she'll help you with your band music every week, but please be open to the new material she is giving you. I think you'll be surprised at how fast you improve. In only a few months you probably won't even have to practice the band music because what she has taught you has made you so advanced.

Q: *I've played piano for five years, and now I have a chance at school to play a band instrument. Should I quit piano so I can play something new?*

A: Here are some of the pros and cons of playing the piano versus another instrument: The piano is a good basis for learning any instrument. It makes learning music theory easier and is always a good first instrument. Lots of music has been written for the piano, so you'll always find music you love to play. Many people own a piano, so you can often play at friends' parties if you want to. You can practice and perform without needing anyone else, or you can accompany a solo instrument, play chamber music, and play four-hand piano duets or two-piano duets. But opportunities to play piano in a large ensemble are limited.

The main advantage and disadvantage of most other instruments is that they're not really complete without accompaniment by a piano or some other instrument. They offer opportunities to play in an ensemble, which is a fun way to meet new friends, and playing in a large group can be a thrill.

Have you considered keeping the piano and adding another instrument? Do you have the time and the interest to keep up two instruments? Will you be able to add on practice time, or will each instrument get only half of the time it needs? Can you find a teacher who would let you consider one instrument a main instrument and the other more of a hobby? Playing both instruments will give you a busy practice schedule, but it will also make you a well-rounded musician and be double the fun. If that's too much commitment for you, try the band instrument. After five years, you have a solid basis in piano that can help you learn a new instrument easily.

Q: I'm 16, and every time we have company, my parents force me to play for them. I feel like a trained seal act. How can I get out of it?
A: As much as you hate being the star performer, you should be happy your parents feel so proud of you. Your playing is a wonderful gift for guests and gives you valuable performing experience. Plus, it makes your parents happy! Music is meant to be shared. If you truly hate it, ask your parents to make a deal. Ask your parents to give you plenty of warning before you have to perform so you'll be prepared, or ask your parents to give you a choice about whom you play for. They should also keep it short so your company's eyes don't glaze over. While it might not feel like it now, having all this performance practice will benefit you in later contests and recitals.

Q: It's my senior year, and I'm swamped. I have college essays to write, the SATs, honor classes, community service, and the list goes on. My violin teacher wants me to play in a string quartet, audition for colleges, try out for All-State Orchestra, participate in master classes, and enter three contests this year. I'm really stressed. How can I get her to back off?
A: It's natural for your teacher to want you to have these great musical experiences, but you won't enjoy them or do your best if you're overloaded. These activities are even more valuable if you plan on becoming a music major. At the same time, your sanity must come first. The job of a good teacher is to help you fulfill your goals, not to demand that you fulfill hers. Tell her you love

music and your lessons, but need some space. Ask for help in choosing which activities are most important. Streamline your assignments to focus on building new techniques and working on performance pieces instead of any "busy work" so you have time to prepare.

LOOKING AHEAD

In this chapter of questions and answers, we aimed to solve common problems music students face in communicating with their teachers, directors, parents, and friends. You might have noticed that nearly every solution centered on the idea that success stems from strong relationships. Whether the problem was a parent's conflicting goals, rivalries between students, or feeling overloaded by teacher demands, the solution almost always involved effectively communicating to reach a solution.

If you have a problem we didn't cover, perhaps an honest heart-to-heart talk will lead you to solving it. And if you don't currently have a problem to solve, remember that the stronger your relationships are with your parents, teachers, and music friends, the less likely it is that you'll have a problem with them in the first place.

FORTY

Is All This Hard Work Worth It?

Being a musician is a big commitment. First, there's the *money* spent for music, instruments, lessons, ensemble fees, and music camps. Then there's the *time,* probably thousands of hours, spent practicing, rehearsing, and traveling. And don't forget all the *sacrifices* when music interferes with TV, playing video games, reading, hanging out with friends, social occasions, sports, family, and sleeping. Even if you love music, do you ever think it's just too much money, too much time, and *way* too much work?

I've been teaching for 35 years. Some of my students have become professional musicians who are glad of every second they spent preparing for their future. But the vast majority of my students never become music majors or professional musicians. Sadly, many rarely pick up their instrument once they've graduated from high school. So many times I've wondered if these students, who are adults now, were glad of their accomplishments or resentful of all the time they had "wasted." I've also talked with kids who are currently taking lessons and asked why they're willing to give up their free time for music. When you're feeling down about your commitment to music, read some of their answers:

REFLECTIONS FROM STUDENTS TAKING LESSONS NOW: IS IT ALL WORTH IT?

"A lot of my friends don't play an instrument. Whenever I play songs, they don't know what I'm doing and they always say that's really neat. I think they're a little bit jealous." (Daniel, cellist, age 14)

Anna, *a recent high school graduate, expanded her circle of friends by playing flute. "Through music, I've met many people I would never have met anywhere else. Even if they have different interests, racial backgrounds, families, and personality types, if we have music in common, at times my connection with that person can be stronger than to someone who's almost a clone of me.*

"It's as if the music person and I are two chocolate chip cookies. And even though I'm a star shape and they're round, I will still have more in common with that chocolate chip cookie than any star-shaped sugar cookie.

"My band went to New York to play at Carnegie Hall. On the bus one day, I sat next to a kid who is a fabulous drummer and trumpet player but who has a reputation for being a troublemaker. I would never have thought to talk to him at school, and he would never have thought to talk to me because he thought I was a geek. But once we started talking about our passion for music, we realized we had more in common than with anyone else. Music is a connecting factor between different personalities."

My son Scott is now studying to be a pilot, but he appreciates the fringe benefits of being a musician. "Being in music can help your social life. In fifth grade I wore a music camp T-shirt to school, and one of the kids in my class was wearing one, too. From then on we've been best friends.

"Girls really are attracted to musicians. You hang out with them on a field trip or start playing the piano, and girls sit down on the bench next to you."

Leslie is going to be a clarinet major next year. "I've met every one of my closest friends through music. I can list dozens of amazing people I never would have met without music. I still keep in touch with many of them, even though we met years ago. Once you join a group, you're rehearsing and practicing and you're together often. Music is a big community, and you see people everywhere you know. Once you're in the music community, you're in.

"I love music so much, and once you master a piece, it's so much fun. It's a great feeling to make something so beautiful yourself."

Andy, age 15, likes being the center of attention. "Being a musician is fun because you get attention you might never have had from your parents and friends. And you get to show off to people who are learning to play. My friends ask me to demonstrate, and it makes me feel good."

Alisa, a high school junior, says music has helped her understand who she is. "During high school you find yourself in situations that aren't good for you. People know the dangers of drugs, but they still use them to fit in and be noticed. Drugs give people a false sense of confidence.

"Music gives you a healthy sense of confidence. Instead of trying to find your identity from potentially harmful sources outside yourself, music helps you look inside yourself. It allows you to find your own identity instead of letting other people choose it for you. Healthy peer pressure is playing in a group and not wanting to let anyone down.

"Music gives you attention for all the right reasons. I never felt I needed to get pulled into the drug crowd and do stupid things to prove I'm cool to other people. I had already proved to myself that I'm a worthwhile person.

"Playing music helped me set higher standards for myself. I learned to practice and push myself. I saw the results of my efforts. It didn't take me long to realize that the more time I spend on things like playing music and studying for the SAT, the better results I get.

"Music helped me become a confident speaker. Making school presentations no longer freaks me out because I'm used to being in the spotlight. I've played for big audiences, and they're strangers! Making a presentation to 30 kids I already know isn't scary at all.

"Music is a stress reliever. When I'm having stress from school or I'm frustrated with friends, I can play my music. It's a personal thing just between me and my instrument."

REFLECTIONS FROM STUDENTS LOOKING BACK: WAS IT ALL WORTH IT?

Jamie won many contests in high school, took music classes in college, and is now a physical therapist. "Sorry if this sounds cheesy, but I think that music lessons prepared me well for a career and life in general. Although I'm not in a musical field, the discipline, commitment, practice, teamwork, leadership, following a leader, skillful listening, ability to explain concepts, presentation of yourself to others, being prepared, arriving early, and loving what you do have stayed with me all my life."

Anna quit lessons in her junior year to help keep up with the rigors of a private school and to play sports. She continued in her school ensemble until she graduated. "Is it worth it? To answer that, I have two questions: Are you dedicated to it? Do you love it? If the answers are no to these questions, then the answer is also no to the first. If you make only a half-hearted attempt, then you may end up wasting your money and your teacher's time.

"Musical knowledge is priceless. It's like being fluent in an international language. It also cultivates a lasting appreciation for listening to classical music. The time I spent working on pieces, practicing, and performing gave me experience in time management, determination, patience, and stage presence that most people never get. Don't struggle on with something you no longer have time or appreciation for. But all that you've given and all that you've received? That is worth every minute!"

Debbie was my very first student ever. Now she shares music with her own children. "As an adult, I now recognize that the lessons I took laid the foundation for me years ago, which I now rely on to enjoy music with my own children. I've got the background and knowledge to communicate musically with my children, as well as realize how important music education and appreciation are for my family. We're all having a great time, and it began when I first started lessons in fourth grade."

Bob is a city attorney now with four children of his own. "Sometime about age 14 or 15 it occurred to me that (a) I did not want to spend my life in a practice room and (b) I would starve if I became a professional musician. This resolved, I took cello lessons until age 21. I've been very fortunate to know some wonderful, inspirational music teachers during high school and college. My best advice to anyone wanting to learn an instrument is to find teachers you can love and trust to develop your talent, and then find opportunities to play for others alone or in a group.

"What did I do with music in adulthood? I made wonderful friends and memories, and also met beautiful women, including my wife of 25 years. Music was always a part of me. The first thing my new law partners knew about me was my cello arriving by crate mail at the law firm. By the time I arrived, everyone already thought I was cool. I played and sang in the local college orchestra, the symphony chorale, a church choir, and a piano trio. When our kids came along, it became more difficult to maintain practice, but somehow I managed.

"It has been a great source of happiness to continue to play good music. Music is better than a hobby; it's a key to spiritual and emotional renewal. I'm very blessed with this gift and would want anyone with musical ability to be able to realize what a huge personal benefit it has been."

Music was a huge part of Janna's life in high school. Now she is a college senior majoring in Japanese. She still takes private lessons in college and plays in the wind ensemble. "Even though flute doesn't play the same prominent role in my life these days in college, I still look back on all of my music memories fondly. In fact, I still consider classical music and playing the flute to be major passions.

"The discipline that I learned through my practice, lessons, and ensemble participation easily carries over into different aspects of my life, because it is now part of my character. I certainly learned skills specific to the flute, but I also learned the more overarching lessons of working toward immediate and long-term goals, building self-confidence, dealing with stress, and preparing to perform in front of crowds. I also learned life lessons on how to get over the occasional but inevitable disappointment that will accompany any worthwhile challenge. I'm so grateful that I kept music a constant in my life! Music will not be a career for me, but I hope to continue playing flute recreationally."

🔊 Dan returned to music after having another career. "I was a piano performance major in college, but did graduate studies in another field and never pursued a career in music. I had always hoped to keep my playing up and perform as a serious amateur. Unfortunately, my profession demanded so much time and energy that I never seemed to find time to consistently practice and keep up my playing skills. It was very frustrating to play at a lower level than I had when I was studying full-time, and often I chose not to play at all. Eventually I realized that I would never play as well as when I was a student, just as I would never run as fast as when I was on the track team. But I could still find immense pleasure and intellectual satisfaction in learning and playing pieces from the vast chamber music repertoire, and enjoy the music as it was meant to be enjoyed—in an intimate setting with friends."

🔊 Irene moved frequently, and this meant changing teachers. But everywhere she went, she sought out music. "Not everyone has the chance to experience music. I'm glad I was one of the lucky ones. I value all the lessons, performances, the competitions, and the ensembles, despite the fees and hassling rehearsals, because they are precious experiences."

🔊 Leslie looks back at her high school band experiences as one of the best of her life. As an adult, she finds it hard to keep playing. "After a tough beginning in middle school, my experiences started to get better. When I look back on everything, I'm so glad that I stuck with it. Even with the bad moments, I wouldn't have changed anything, and I would do it all over in a moment. I think you have to go through some tough times, and if you continue with it and survive them, it just makes it all the more rewarding. It can be hard work, work you don't always want to do, but it's an awesome feeling of accomplishment when it's all done and over with.

"As an adult now, I haven't picked up my flute in a few years, and recently a friend suggested I should sell it on eBay and make some money. She just couldn't understand my forceful response when I told her she was crazy. I may not play as often as I used to, but that was a great part of my life. My flute has sentimental value, and I don't think I'll ever get rid of it. After all, who knows when I will get the sudden urge to start playing again?"

🔊 Kristin teaches preschool and has three young children of her own. "Looking back on it now, there was really no way of knowing all the amazing gifts that music would give to me throughout my life. I loved being able to transform the notes on the page to beautiful music. There are also the more complex rewards such as learning the value of practicing and working hard at something, and the gift of being able to pick yourself up and dust yourself off after a 'not-so-

great' performance. Playing an instrument has helped me try things I may not have tried, had I not received such intensive training in music. I truly believe that practicing, entering competitions, learning how to memorize, and hearing critical feedback about my playing gave me the strength and the desire to push through difficult and nerve-wracking situations.

"Even though I don't play regularly anymore, I believe that being a musician has also allowed me to hear music in a way that a nonmusician might not be able to. Anyone can pop in a CD and appreciate the sound of the instruments or voice. But when you really 'know' music, when you've worked at it, and you understand how hard it really is to create a passionate and sincere sound, the experience of hearing music—all different types of music—can become richer and more meaningful. So even if (God forbid!) you should actively stop playing, know that throughout your life you will continue to reap the benefits of having once dedicated yourself to the practice of making music."

Jennifer knows how valuable being a musician is in the job market. "A music performance degree really prepared me for the real world. I have a high-intensity job at a prestigious company. My music is what got me in the door! The CEO was impressed that music was something that made me stand out. He felt that if I put that much energy into my playing, that focus would translate into the corporate world.

"Although I'm not currently using my degree, I feel the skills still get used. Musicians make great employees in the real world because we're used to working in teams from chamber music and we understand attention to detail. We're great at giving presentations to important people, we understand the need to be professional when presenting, and we know how to block out distractions when necessary. PowerPoint presentations are easy. I know how to calm myself when being challenged. I can crank out a project in an office with a hundred distractions, which comes in handy in an office with cubicles. Even though I don't work as a musician, being a musician is part of who I am.

"My parents said playing an instrument made me an easier child. Sure there were lessons and rehearsals to drive to, but they didn't have to worry about me sitting in front of the TV rotting my brain. I had practicing to do. When I eventually have children, I hope they can enjoy music the way I did.

"There are times when I had to give up things for music. In high school I was at a party in the evening after a competition. I got a phone call telling me I had to come home because I had won and had to play the next day. There were weekends in college where my buddies were going out of town, and I had to stay behind for a rehearsal or performance. But I wouldn't give it up for the world."

Is All This Hard Work Worth It?

Music opened many doors for Meighan. "I started flute lessons at school in fourth grade and have been playing on and off now for 32 years, sometimes seriously and sometimes just for fun. Along the way I've picked up the recorder, tin whistle, hammered dulcimer, and hand bells, as well as a music education degree.

"I now work in the Education Office of the Seattle Symphony, having taught elementary music for four years. As part of my current job, I visit elementary schools, bringing string, brass, and woodwind instruments for the students to try. When I visit schools and put instruments into the hands of children, they make that first sound and a light turns on in their eyes. What an honor it is for me to be part of that magic moment.

"I tell the students how music has enriched my whole life. It has given me a creative, spiritual, and emotional outlet. I have come to know and love masterpieces and composers throughout history and around the world. I have met and made music with people of all ages and abilities. Music permeates everything I do. I can't imagine my life without it."

Christina learned how to deal with the ups and downs of music. She is now an interior designer. "To be able to pick up an instrument and play, and I mean really play a piece, is magical to me. The thought that my fingers, my breath, and my mind are somehow working together to create this wondrous sound still amazes me to this day. Although I spent so many years of my young life practicing and sometimes slaving over musical notes and rhythms, I don't consider my ability to create music more rewarding than the ability of a beginner. You can achieve the enjoyment that music has to offer at any level.

"Music is a gift. However, I do believe that through the journey of music lessons the fulfillment of the musical gift can sometimes be lost. I can remember many times when I felt discouraged or disappointed because I couldn't play the music the way it was written. Maybe I was having difficulty with the articulation or with the fingering, or maybe my playing lacked dynamics and emotion. Whatever it was, I always told myself to remember why I played an instrument and how it made me feel to produce such a beautiful sound.

"When times really got rough, I would return to the music that I could play. Whether it was something simple, like a folk song, or something more powerful, like a concerto, being able to play the piece reassured me that I was indeed still an able player. More important, it made me realize that I still had the gift of music.

"Even though I haven't taken a lesson in many years, I turn to music to find that magic feeling that I'm creating something special. Through it all, I remember just how great music is and how fortunate I am to have been given this gift."

Ann never had lessons, but that didn't stop her. "Although I never had lessons, I played violin in school groups through high school but gave it up to pursue a different career in college. Then I got married, and the time commitments of a job and children got in the way of playing. When I retired, it was an amazing epiphany when I came back to playing the violin after 25 years. Only then was my soul turned on again."

GREAT IDEAS

When the contests and recitals are over, when there's no parent around to tell you to practice, when a real-life job and family take priority over music, you still have a gift that no one can take away. Music can be a hobby, friend, comfort, and joy for your whole life.

Sneak Preview

Double your pleasure, double your fun, when you make music with others. Part 9 is all about playing with friends. You'll learn how to get an ensemble started and hold effective rehearsals, what to do when you're twiddling your thumbs in band, and even how to not make a fool of yourself at a classical concert or a rock concert.

PART NINE

MAKING BEAUTIFUL MUSIC
TOGETHER

FORTY-ONE

Have Fun and Make Friends When You Play Music Together

Music is meant to be shared. Playing with other kids can be exciting and challenging, and it can also improve your social life! Join your school band or orchestra or a community youth orchestra. Form a chamber music ensemble on your own. Even playing piano duets will be more fun than you've had in a long time. If you've never played in an ensemble, you're missing out on a wonderful learning experience *and* a great time.

WHY PLAY IN BAND OR ORCHESTRA?

Band is a good beginning. Many kids would not even think about playing an instrument if they weren't introduced to music in their school band or orchestra program. School instrumental programs plant that seed in their minds. Parents love the school programs because they give beginners a start and are free and convenient. If you don't have private lessons, your band director can show you the basics.

Being in band or orchestra is like being a member of a special club. It's fun to be part of something bigger than yourself, to feel that sense of community and power in a large group. Lauren, age 16, agrees: "I love to play with other people because you can often create something greater than you could alone. Being in a group creates a sense of belonging and is also a good way to support your school and show school spirit."

Unlike other classes, you're usually with your band members three or four years, so close friendships form. Because you're with your fellow musicians during class but also for concerts, outside rehearsals, and even field trips, the friendships you form may last a lifetime.

Andy, age 14, is glad he plays in school band. "You make more and different friends in band, the kind of friends you can trust to help you out. We get to travel to places like to the high school for a competition or on longer trips, and we even played during eighth-grade graduation." Zoe, who plays in band with Lauren, likes the social aspect, too. "You meet a lot of great people when you join band, and the band keeps you together. You bond with the other band members, especially those in your section. And when you get a substitute teacher, you get to fool around and play each other's instruments. It's also really fun to go on huge band trips with so many people."

Your conductor can play an important part in your life as a role model and mentor. Eighteen-year-old Anna appreciates her band and orchestra conductors. "It's encouraging to see adult figures who have worked through the tough times and come out the other side enjoying themselves. Seeing someone who loves it so much sparks your interest. Some kids don't even want to go to school, but a band, orchestra, or choir teacher gives you a reason to listen to them and stay in school."

GET CLOSE WITH CHAMBER MUSIC

It's often exhilarating to play in a large group, but there's something magical about playing duos, trios, quartets, and other small ensembles, one on a part. Chamber music, especially that written for strings, is some of the best music ever written.

Being on your own makes you an independent musician. Each member contributes musical ideas, and decisions are made within the group. Without a conductor, ensemble players learn to both lead and follow. Like a good sports team, they cooperate for the good of the group—no prima donnas allowed. Like the lessons you learned in kindergarten, chamber music teaches you to play well with others.

The musical skills you gain are priceless, too. When you're responsible for your own part, you learn to listen to other parts, play in tune, and play musically. This makes your solo performances better, too.

Tired of playing by yourself all the time? Don't miss out on the fun of chamber music. Music won't seem lonely when you're with friends. Afraid of performance? There's not so much pressure when you share the stage. Want a social life? Playing music in an intimate setting gives you more chances to interact and become friends. Tired of the music you play? Chamber music gives you a whole new repertoire. Wish you were a better sight-reader? Sight-reading together can seem like a game as you force yourself to keep going and laugh at your mistakes.

Zoe's flute duet won first in state when she and Lauren were freshmen. Zoe says, "I love playing in smaller groups. It's something completely different than playing in an orchestra. Because it's a smaller group, you have to listen to each other, know how everyone's part sounds, and you play with one another more. You communicate through the way you play, the way you move, when you nod and cue one another, and through eye contact."

Learning the skills to play in ensembles may be the one thing that keeps you performing past high school. Once you become a good sight-reader and know how to play well with others, you'll have the tools and desire to join music groups and just get together with musical friends the rest of your life.

Rosemary is getting her master's degree in woodwinds from New York University. "Because I play the flute, clarinet, and the saxophone, I've performed with many different ensembles. I find great freedom that I can play Bach in one rehearsal and Count Basie in the next. This has helped me to appreciate music in all its diversity. An open mind has helped me become a more diverse musician. After all, every classical flute player needs to play the blues once in a while.

"Playing in an ensemble gives you an overwhelming sense of unity. It's a fun social event, but it requires responsibility, dedication, focus, and cooperation. Ensembles benefit all the performers, from the principal violinist to that guy in the back who whacks the triangle with a stick. My high school ensembles have taken me to Mexico, Spain, the Netherlands, France, Switzerland, Belgium, Luxembourg, and China. I also got to perform a concerto with my flute quartet with the Seattle Symphony. The experience I shared with fellow musicians is priceless."

STARTING A CHAMBER MUSIC GROUP

Find the players.

If possible, play with students who attend your school so you can hold extra practice sessions before, during, or after school and perhaps even be featured in a school concert. Ask the other kids in your section or the best players in the other sections to form a group.

Playing with other students in your teacher's studio is an easy way to start. If one student stays 15 minutes after the lesson and the next comes 15 minutes early, you have an instant duo or trio, if you include the teacher. Students in your ensemble can also trade giving up their lesson for ensemble practice so there is no extra time or money spent.

Organize the sheet music.

Buy the original sheet music, but make copies for each player. Paste the copies on cardboard so they can be written on and won't fly off the stand. Be sure all parts are from the same edition. Number the measures in the margins, and always come armed with a pencil.

THE REHEARSAL

Tune up.

Take ample time to tune at the beginning and retune during the rehearsal when everyone has warmed up. Let one person play the tuning A (cello in a string quartet, first clarinet in the clarinet ensemble, always the piano if it is part of the ensemble), and the others take their A from him. Younger players may need to tune one at a time and then try it all together. It's much easier to hear a pitch when someone else plays, so take turns helping each other.

Count rehearsal measures.

When you go back to rehearse a section, begin by counting off your place out loud, "Before letter B—1, 2, 3, 4, 5, 6 measures." That way the whole ensemble is right there with you at the same time. When counting after letter B, count letter B as measure 1. Say, "After letter B, 1, 2, 3, 4," and you're all ready to play.

Make decisions.

The ensemble, rather than just the teacher, should help make decisions. Which piece do you want to play? Who really, really wants to play first? Which tempo do you think is best? How short should the pick-up note be? How loud is the part at letter D? Should we take the repeat? This is your chance to put your personal stamp on the music.

Be independent.

It's up to the ensemble to figure out attire, transportation, copying music, and rehearsal scheduling. Don't leave all these jobs to your teacher or your parents.

Create a group identity.

Decide on new members and which pieces you want to play. Get creative with an ensemble name: Flirty Flutes, Beethoven's Boys, or Tom's Tubas give the group character. Encourage every member to contribute ideas and to verbalize them. Rehearse occasionally without the teacher.

Be responsible.

If you make a mistake, you have to "pay." If Alex needs to miss a rehearsal, it's his job to reschedule. If Sean comes to the rehearsal late, he brings the cookies next time. If Mary Beth plays G♮ in A major for the fifth time or plays during the rest, she brings cookies. If Holly doesn't look at the leader at least at the beginning and the end, again her fine is to bring cookies. Anything for cookies and to make the point.

Decide on group goals.

Do you want to sight-read new material every week? Look for performance opportunities? Prepare for a contest or concert? How often do you need to meet to reach these goals?

AVOID SCHEDULING NIGHTMARES

The most difficult thing about playing in ensembles is getting everyone together.

- Never let group members leave until you've planned the next rehearsal.
- When trying to decide on a schedule, ask group members to say when they are free instead of getting into a litany of all their other activities. ("I am free Monday, Wednesday, and Friday from 4:00 to 6:00, and Tuesday after 7:00.")
- Set up a phone tree so each person takes responsibility for notifying someone.
- If one person has to miss a rehearsal or wants it scheduled for another time, that person is responsible for calling everyone. Ensemble members may suddenly become free if they have to make all those tedious phone calls.
- Enlist your parents' help. Ask them to monitor the rehearsal schedule, make phone calls, provide transportation, and offer their home and help for rehearsals.
- Try trading off lesson times for ensemble rehearsals. Week one, the trio meets at Owen's lesson, week two is at Melinda's, and week three at Maren's.

BE A TEAM PLAYER

Have you ever seen the U.S. Navy jet pilot team, the Blue Angels? This precision flying team epitomizes teamwork. When flying in formation 18 inches apart, solid teamwork is critical. When the Blue Angels take off in unison, their flight leader sets the pace. The pilots don't measure how fast to go or when to turn; they follow his lead. Even their narrator on the ground follows, matching the rhythm and timing of the leader's choreographed moves.

Playing chamber music is like flying with the Blue Angels. Well, maybe not quite so dramatic or dangerous. We follow the leader and collaborate to play as a team. Ensemble playing is great conversation among friends, all of equal status. Someone once said, "It's amazing how much you can accomplish when it doesn't matter who gets the credit." In ensembles, playing the fastest, the loudest, or with the most unusual tone and vibrato won't win you any points. Ensemble players keep their nose and ears out of the music and tune in to each other. They learn to think and sound as if they're one player. This ability to listen makes you a better musician. Enjoy a musical laugh. Learn to hear and think as a cohesive group, and enjoy the high energy of ensemble playing!

LOOK

Watch one another to begin and end sections together. Look at the other players when you pass off a melody to another instrument and when you play a melody with another player. In a large ensemble, if you're looking at a conductor, position the stand so you can see him or her over the top.

Ask for a cue from another part on a tricky entrance. "Look at Ellen" written in your comrade's score can give you added insurance for an unsure entrance.

Recording with a video camera is an invaluable tool to let members hear their performance and to show whether they're really leading and watching. It even points out those members who might be a little too theatrical. The camera never lies.

LISTEN

Match tone and tone color.

If Sue has a wispy sound and Clare, the leader, has a solid tone, then Sue must try to match Clare by playing firmer and louder. Match amplitude and vibrato speed: if the leader has a wide vibrato, then the other players must blend or keep out of the way, avoiding the attack of the killer vibrato bees.

Match articulation attack and length.

Whoever plays the theme first sets the stage. If the leader plays the eighth-notes short, then all the eighth-notes have to be short. If the first player with the theme uses a sharp attack, then the others must follow suit. If the violins play pizzicato, the woodwinds need to play staccato to match. Give careful attention to first notes and cut-offs; don't come in early or stick out at the end. What happens in the middle isn't as important as starting and stopping together.

Match the pitch.

The only thing worse than one person playing out of tune is four people playing out of tune! Mark places in the music where there are unisons or octaves to tune up. The more players on one pitch, the softer they should each play for blend and pitch.

Match emotional playing styles.

Cecilia, the violin player in my quartet, is Hispanic and plays with wild personality and passion. I have to listen hard to match her rubato and glissandos when we play tangos. To really match each other's style and articulation, practice playing the same theme together.

Match dynamics.

If the leader plays the opening forte, everyone else should, too. Be careful about taking dynamics too literally, though. Sometimes inner parts or lower parts must play louder than their dynamic marking to be heard, or they must play softer than marked to allow the melody to stand out. To do this you must understand the limitations of each instrument in mixed ensembles. A trumpet playing with a flute should adjust all dynamics down at least one notch. And remember, the most impressive effect can be when the ensemble plays extremely softly.

Watch the balance.

Give as much care and attention to supporting parts as you would to playing a solo. Every part and every note is important. Even if you have "boring whole notes," follow the melody players' lead in phrasing and dynamics and always play musically.

Always know who has the melody or the most important material. Try color coding your music so you remember who the star is at that point and who has a supporting part. The balance can be affected by placement of players, so experiment with seating for better projection and blend. Make sure the player on the first part is positioned so that his sound points out to the audience. Have someone go to the back and middle of the concert hall to judge balance and volume.

Become a team.

To sharpen listening skills, practice facing away from each other so each player must depend entirely on his ears and not his eyes.

HOW TO START AND STOP

One year I judged a trio of junior high clarinetists. They burst into the room just in time to play. Sweaty and dressed in torn jeans and T-shirts, they jostled to see who would stand where. When they were finally ready to start, the leader shouted, "One, two, three, four, ready, set, go!" I don't know if I heard the rest of the piece because I was (quietly!) laughing so hard. Here's a more subtle approach.

How to lead:
1. Tell your ensemble what kind of note gets the beat. If you are in 4/4, does the quarter-note get one beat, one half beat, or two beats? Before starting, make sure everyone is watching you with instruments in the ready position.
2. Start with your head (if you are a pianist) or your instrument in a neutral "home" position. I tell my flute students to imagine the flute resting on a shelf.
3. Mentally think through the first measure before you play it.
4. All instruments use their breath to begin the piece (even pianists and string players). Breathe on the beat before the entrance and make the breath the length of a beat and in the mood of the piece. Your audible breath and eye contact will assure the ensemble that this is the time to start. For example, in 4/4 time, with the music starting on the downbeat, you would silently count: 1, 2, 3, breathe on beat 4, play on beat 1. While breathing, lift the instrument a few inches above the "shelf." The cue for the rest of the ensemble to start is when the leader's instrument (or head) returns to the shelf/home position. You're giving a visible downbeat, just as a conductor does.

Have Fun and Make Friends When You Play Music Together

5. To cut off at the end, do the opposite. Start out with the instrument on the shelf, bring the instrument below the shelf, and when it is returned to the shelf, stop playing. Make both of these motions fairly small and up and down, not in big circles, so you don't look like a drum majorette.

FOLLOW THE LEADER

We'll use the term *leader* to refer to the person in charge at the moment in the music. Even though there may be a designated leader such as the first violin, the clarinet with the highest part or the piano in the piano trio, these roles change throughout the music as the important line shifts from person to person.

What Is the Leader's Job? Listen!

Know what's happening in all the parts. Look at your ensemble members and expect them to look back. Make the beats very clear, especially if you hear something amiss or feel a ragged tempo. When things get unsteady, it's the leader's job to look at the ensemble and nod until everyone is playing together again.

The leader makes musical decisions, too. What's the tempo? What's the articulation? Where do we start and stop? But being a leader isn't being a dictator. Be open to suggestions. Ensembles with input from everyone make for good company.

What Is the "Follower's" Job? Look!

Watch for tempo changes, dynamics, and other cues. Try to be the leader's "clone." Match the leader in style and articulation. Quickly memorize the first and last measures so you can look right at the leader for clean beginnings and endings. If you're not the leader at the moment, don't try to set the tempo, tap, or beat time with your instrument.

What if the leader isn't doing his job? Diplomatically use "I" terminology when asking for something. Instead of saying, "You're not giving a clear beat on measure 12, and there's no way I can follow you," it would be better to try: "I'm not clear on my entrance at measure 12." Or "Could you give us two preparatory beats instead of one?"

INSURANCE AGAINST GETTING LOST

Check out the road map. Where are the repeats, is there a da capo, and where is the coda? If the sheet music is your own, you can draw lines and arrows to help you remember your way, or at least circle the coda and signs.

Number the measures in every margin or every five measures. It makes rehearsals go faster and is a great safety net. (Measure 39 whispered when you are floundering makes you glad you could easily find it.)

Be extra cautious during long rests, which are dangerous traps. Use your fingers if you need to (held down low, of course), to keep track of measure numbers *and* beats. Count *1234, 2234, 3234.* The first number denotes the measure of rest, and the others denote the beat.

Plan meeting spots if you get lost (for example, meet at letter B where we all have the same rhythm).

Check out the score so you see how your part fits in and know what's happening in the other parts. "I know what the clarinetist has at letter H, so if I'm lost at least I can join back there."

Train your ears. Always know where beat 1 of each bar is. No matter what happens during a complex bar or an inconvenient page turn, get back on beat 1. Listen to how your part fits in. If something sounds wrong, even if you felt you counted correctly, be willing to adjust.

FAKE IT!

You're lost. It happens to everyone. How do you recover? Keep going. If you make some mistakes, probably no one will even notice. But if you quit playing, the whole group may grind to a halt. It won't be a pretty sight. Keep beat 1 in your head at all times, and try to stick it out through the rough patches.

How do you get through the hard parts? Listen to the other players. If you can't figure out that tricky rhythm, there's a good chance it appears in someone else's part and you can copy their counting. When a flurry of notes is too hard, play what you can catch. Play the first note of each group of four sixteenths and come back in on beat 1.

Ask for help. If you're playing in the wrong place for more than two measures, look to someone else for help and a whispered measure number. But above all, *never let them see you sweat.* Act as if you have the longest rest or even just move your fingers. Keep your facial expression calm and your body serene; you'll soon find your place again, and 99% of the audience will never know you had any mishap.

ENSEMBLE ETIQUETTE

Ron Patterson, professor of violin at the University of Washington, once played in an orchestra where the violinist sitting next to him kept almost hitting him with the tip of his bow. His wife, Roxanna, also a gifted professional, remembers a violist one chair below her who would "accidentally" tip over her music stand. Another friend recalls sitting first flute and hearing the second flute snidely say, "How did you get this job? Do you know the conductor?" One of my students had to deal with the jealousy of other girls when she played solos in her band. To unnerve her while she played, the two girls who sat below her glared and made faces. These players needed to learn some manners! Even if you are not friends, be musical friends when you play together.

Support Your Team Members

- Whether you play chamber music or perform in an orchestra, you're in this together. Everyone shares the result, good or bad. If this is an ongoing ensemble, the number one rule is to come with music prepared. Mark any mistakes you make and fix them.
- Help each other out. If you and another player have the same difficult entrances after long rests, look at each other and silently name the measure number for reinforcement. If someone is lost, point to the place in the music or whisper the measure number.
- Make page turns easy. If two players share a stand, the player on the inside (farthest away from the audience) turns the pages. Turn soon enough so you don't miss any notes on the next page. Turn quietly and, if possible, wait to turn your page until after someone else's important solo.
- In an orchestra, if you have a question, the first person you ask is the section leader. Usually it's best not to ask a question directly of the conductor unless it is an emergency. It's better to wait until after rehearsal.
- Don't practice the first chair player's or the visiting soloist's solos within earshot before the concert. Avoid doing anything that would indicate disrespect, even if you don't admire their musicianship.
- Quit whining about your boring part. Work hard to become a better player, and you'll get better parts.
- If you must carry your cell phone, make sure it's turned off before the performance. (I'll never forget the look of embarrassment on the face of the cello soloist when his cell phone rang in the middle of the concerto with the Seattle Symphony!)
- Never turn around and look at the person who made the mistake in the ensemble or dropped his trumpet mute on the floor. Don't wince when things go wrong or give any other negative visual cues to your listeners.
- If you play a different part than your neighbor, don't read over his shoulder.
- Don't eat, chew gum, read a book, talk, or do anything that distracts you, your colleagues, the conductor, or the audience. Whether you are sight-reading with your friends, performing in a student ensemble, or playing in the New York Philharmonic, be professional.

MAKE FRIENDS

- Getting along socially makes a huge difference in getting along musically. Plan some social occasions to get to know each other and solidify the team.

- If there is a personality problem with a member of the group, try to work it out away from the rehearsal. Start the conversation by pointing out all the things that are right before discussing the things that are wrong. Most personality conflicts boil down to different interpretations of members' goals, roles, and how things get done.
- Look upon your fellow members as colleagues, not competition. Don't be afraid to ask for help and pay compliments.
- If you'll be even five minutes late, call.
- Try to schedule rehearsals with more than 24 hours' notice.
- Come with everything you need: music stand, pencil, music, extra strings, water, etc. Your mother's not going to show up to help you out.
- In small ensembles, learn to discuss musical phrases, dynamics, and articulation. Try things different ways and agree as a group on your interpretation. Even if there is a leader in a small group, democracy can work.
- Be diplomatic about offering suggestions. Instead of saying, "you," try to substitute "we." For example, say, "We always seem to slow down at letter D," "We're out of tune in the soft section," or "It's hard to hear the melody in measure 12."
- Every moment you're onstage, you're on display. No frowning, no flirting, and no fighting. Use your best posture and smile to look like you're having the time of your life.
- Have fun!

GREAT IDEAS

Playing in band, orchestra, and small chamber music ensembles is a fun way to become a better musician and make friends. Learning the rules of playing and etiquette will make for better music and better friends.

Sneak Preview

As much as you may love playing in your band or orchestra, sometimes rehearsals can be a drag. Our next chapter tells you how to beat boredom and make rehearsals valuable for you and the group.

FORTY-TWO

What Can I Do If I'm Bored in Band or Orchestra?

"My band director is really dull. We play the same pieces over and over, and he works with the trombones because they never know their part, so the rest of us just have to sit there, and the drummers just goof around all the time, and the music for the flutes is really easy because we are the best section, but even half of the flutes don't know which end to blow in, and I want to quit, but my mom says I have to stick it out because the band needs good players, and I made a commitment because I love music, but I don't love this because it is so boring, and then I start talking to the kid who sits next to me, and then I get in trouble. What can I do?"

Okay, okay, enough complaining. This is the reality of ensemble playing, but there are ways to make it a rewarding experience and to grow as a musician.

When you're bored, try these tips:
- Play "Extreme Music." Follow the dynamics to the extreme and see how loudly and how softly you can play and still be in tune.
- Try Velcro fingers. Can you play with your fingers never leaving the keys?
- See how long you can play in one breath. When everyone else breathes every two measures, try to go four or six or eight measures in one breath.
- Work for your best tone. Pretend you're a contestant in the $1 Million Tone Contest.
- Make a game of sight-reading far ahead. Look at the music and see how far you can play without looking back. Unnerve your conductor by looking right at him all the time.
- Practice memorizing the music. Even though your band or orchestra music isn't something you need to know, memorizing it will help you memorize other pieces more easily.

- When the band director is working with another section, look at your watch and see how long you can hold your breath. Make it a silent game in your section.
- Bring a solo piece you're working on and silently finger it while the director is working with the other sections.
- Practice hard so you can be first chair and get all the solos.

So now you are transforming band rehearsal into your own private practice session. What else can you do? See if you can "get out."

Ask your director if one day a week you can:
- Practice on your own in a practice room.
- Take the other instruments out for sectionals.
- Have a coach come for sectionals.
- Help the clueless player in the last chair.
- Form an ensemble.
- See if you can audition to get into the next level band.

Remember, your band director has a tough job dealing with all those instruments and all those kids playing at all those levels. Give him a break. Sit up. Shut up. Be cooperative, and be a good example. Who knows, you may be in his shoes someday.

FORTY-THREE

Concert Etiquette, or Dude! When Do I Clap?

In chapter 26, "Why Listen to Classical Music?" you learned about the benefits of listening to a variety of music. Attending concerts is a great way to introduce yourself to new styles of music. For little more than the cost of a movie, you can buy tickets to most college, community, and small group concerts. You can attend free concerts at your school and find plenty more listed in your local paper. The thrill of seeing and hearing excellent musicians may inspire you to get on the stage yourself!

Classical music has survived for hundreds of years, and so have its traditions. Sure, men in the audience no longer wear curled wigs and lace ruffs, and women don't wear corsets tight enough to cut off their oxygen supply, but certain etiquette "rules" still apply. Did you attend your last concert in a huge stadium with tens of thousands of raucous, crazed fans? Did performers magically appear in a fog cloud illuminated by colored strobe lights? Even if you attend country, Christian, or Celtic concerts, if you're not used to going to classical concerts, you may want to brush up on your classical concert etiquette.

Libraries cater to a quiet, more studious crowd. Not so at the Hard Rock Café. Just as you change your behavior between those two venues, concert-goers act according to the culture of the venue and the music they're hearing. You know the saying: "When in Rome, do like the Romans."

Have you ever watched toddlers bouncing, singing, and dancing to music they enjoy? Little kids naturally translate their love of the music into their body movements. Like most rock concert-goers, they don't care what anyone else thinks—that is, until they get "civilized" and act more like classical concert-goers.

Classical music is about structure and form. Okay, let's be honest. Acting like a happy toddler can be a lot more freeing than acting like a serious classical concert-goer. Is it boring to act the latter way? Do classical audiences feel restricted, unable to naturally express their emotions? Do you have to check your personality at the door? No way! It's all part of what makes classical music unique.

Classical music lovers feel every bit as enthusiastic about superb performances; they just show it in more subtle ways. Like anything else, once you're in on the secret handshake or the special rules of the group, you want to play right along with them. If you loved golf and football, would you avoid golf tournaments because you have to whisper and can't do the "wave"?

In this chapter we'll compare two very different traditions of audience etiquette: classical concerts versus rock concerts. Whether you're attending a classical concert in the community, at a private recital, or a band or orchestra concert at your school, these guidelines apply!

Where to buy tickets:

Classical: Buy tickets online or at the door.

Rock: Buy tickets online or from scalpers at the door.

How much to spend:

Classical: Spend three days' pay on tickets to New York City's Metropolitan Opera.

Rock: Spend your life savings on tickets for a final concert tour.

What to wear:

Classical: You don't need to rent a tux or wear your satin prom gown to a classical concert, but keep your torn jeans, door knocker earrings, and tube tops at home. Dress in clothes you would wear to visit your grandma or to attend worship services. If you're going to the opera, wear semiformal clothes or the clothes you'd wear to convince your "special someone's" parents those rumors about you are not true. Shoes and deodorant are mandatory.

Rock: Wear your usual weekend clothes. Anything goes if it's comfortable! If you're going to a big-name concert, wear clothes to convince your friends those rumors about you *are* true. Shoelaces and deodorant are optional.

Who not to bring:

Classical: Your whiny, wiggly little sister.

Rock: Your wide-eyed innocent little sister.

Getting a good seat:

Classical: If open seating, choose one of the many good seats available.

Rock: If open seating, camp out on the sidewalk for days in the rain.

Getting to your seat:

Classical: Audiences usually sit in formal rows of chairs. Arrive early and seat yourself *before* the concert begins. If you walk in late, wait to be seated between pieces, and find a seat at the back. If you're at the opera, an usher may seat you after the overture, but once the opera starts you'll have to wait until intermission. Many theaters close their doors when the program is about to begin.

Rock: If you're in an open space concert venue, squeeze your bod in wherever you can. Get there early or get there late, but at two dollars per minute of concert time, you might as well get your money's worth!

Concert programs:

Classical: Be sure to read the program. You'll find descriptions of the music you'll hear, learn about the composers, and know how many movements to expect.

Rock: It's too dark to read the stinkin' program. You're already a big fan. Who needs a program?

Proper audience behavior:

Classical: Don't distract the performers by talking, whispering to friends, laughing, giggling, wiggling, or unwrapping noisy candy wrappers. Never whistle or call out names of performers—even if they are your friends!

Rock: Talk, laugh, yell, whistle, jump up and down. In a dark cavernous room with 10,000 fans screaming and amps on full blast, who cares what *you're* doing!

What to do with your cell phone:

Classical: Turn your phone off! If not, you may have to slink out the door after the elite solo performer stomps off, upstaged by your *Für Elise* ring tone.

Rock: Keep your phone on! Your cell provides light and a way to locate your friends. Call the ones who couldn't come and brag about how great the concert is. Never mind you can't hear a word they say and all they hear is someone shouting with crowd noise in the background. Take pictures of tiny dot performers your friends will never recognize.

How not to become part of the performance:

Classical: Avoid drawing attention to yourself. Don't sing, hum, or beat time with your hands or feet, or clap in time to the violins. If you fall behind (and you will), your syncopated claps will not add to the string section.

Rock: Clap when you want to, in or out of time with the music. Better yet, scream and body surf over other sweaty fans—anything to get the attention of friends and performers!

Eating and drinking:

Classical: Eat and drink only in the lobby. No security guards are needed, only kind ushers.

Rock: Eat and drink whenever you want. Who cares if someone spills beer on your cell phone or you're sitting in the sticky pool of a spilled drink. Security guards are roaming the place—and for good reason. Don't bring in drugs or alcohol. That doesn't mean the two lovebirds in front of you haven't already imbibed.

Taking a break:

Classical: Don't stand up and leave during the performance. Most classical concerts give you a 15-minute break.

Rock: If you need to use the facilities, plan on leaving an hour before you need to. Round-trip, it will take you that long to push through the crowd, climb 75 steps, wait in line 25 minutes (45 if you're a woman), and then return to where you were sitting.

When to applaud:

Classical: Only at the very end of a piece. There is no applause sign. Long classical works are sometimes divided into movements or parts of music with pauses in between like acts in plays. New classical concert-goers often see the pause as their signal to applaud. If a piece has five movements, clap only at the end of the fifth movement.

Hint: A few seconds after the last notes are played, you'll see the director's arms lower and performers put their instruments in a relaxed position. Now you can clap! If you're not sure when, follow people who look like loyal concert-goers. (They're not too hard to spot!)

Rock: Clap anywhere anytime. Whistle. Sing. Shout. Whatever.

Other ways to show your appreciation:

Classical: If you loved the performance, honor the performers with a standing ovation.

Some people say *Bravo!* Or *Brava!* if the soloist is a woman. (Good job! in Italian) or *Encore!* (Play it again). If you really appreciated the performers, throw flowers onto the stage!

Rock: If you loved the performance, you're probably already standing. Were you ever sitting? Yell anything you want, and let's not even get into what audiences toss to performers at rock concerts! Use good judgment and no personal clothing items, please!

How you'll feel the morning after:

Classical: You wake refreshed and feeling a warm glow, the blissful night before a happy memory.

Rock: You wake just before dinner time, head throbbing and ears ringing, the insane night before a blur. You also may have incurred permanent hearing loss. If your ears are ringing hours later, it's a sure sign of damage to your eardrums.

A word to the wise:

You've heard it before, but it's true: the high decibel levels at rock concerts can damage your hearing. The risk of damage depends on the sound level and how long you're exposed to it. A very loud sound of 120–150 decibels can damage your hearing immediately. Rock musicians hear music at 100–115 decibels.

Many rock musicians and orchestral musicians often wear special earplugs that evenly filter all frequencies so they can still hear themselves and the group.

Final advice:

Classical and ROCK: Have fun!

Rock audiences and classical audiences may seem worlds apart, and traditionally they have been. But does it always have to be the classical world's "rules" versus every other kind of music? Not at all! That imaginary line between classical and other styles of music is slowly blurring. More classical musicians are finding alternative lives as musicians in rock bands and other genres. Rock groups use classical players to back them up.

Internationally renowned classical cellist Yo-Yo Ma, for example, ventured into unfamiliar territory to play duets with the improvisational a cappella singer Bobby McFerrin of "Don't Worry, Be Happy" fame, winner of ten Grammys, and one of the most creative singers ever. A trip to YouTube will let you see and hear Yo-Yo Ma and Bobby McFerrin combining their classical and improvisational styles. Check out other crossover artists such as Wynton Marsalis, Renee Fleming, Mark O'Connor, and Edgar Meyer.

Crossing over the classical rock divide wasn't always that easy. Classical purists traditionally saw rock as a threat to classical and off-limits to serious classical musicians. Judith Kogan in *Strad* magazine says, "A classical musician who also plays in a rock band was once considered to have crossed over to the dark side—to the devil's playground." Now that is harsh! Today classical purists are softening to the idea of classically trained musicians playing both rock and classic cello. Symphonies offer concerts for less traditional audiences. Setting aside tradition is often controversial, but today you'll find more imaginative and experimental classical music, an interest in making classical concerts less stuffy, and more people saying, "Let them clap!"

So what do rock concert-goers and classical concert-goers have in common? They're all connected through the power of music! For people passionate about music, there are no boundaries. Now go buy those tickets! Don't let the few extra rules for classical music audiences discourage you from adding classical concerts to your musical menu.

Sneak Preview

Now you're ready to attend concerts in any musical style you choose. In our next section, part 10, we'll look at much bigger choices: deciding whether a career in music is right for you. In this section you'll learn about everything from what you need to do if you want to be a music major and how to choose a college and career, to lessons that seasoned musical professionals have learned the hard way.

PART TEN

DECIDING IF A MUSIC CAREER
IS RIGHT FOR YOU

FORTY-FOUR

So You Want to Be a Music Major?

"What do I want to be when I grow up?" If you're a high school junior or senior, you've probably been spending a lot of time thinking about that question. If music figures into your future, now is the time to start making some decisions, especially if you want to be accepted as a music major. In many other areas of college study you can go in as a rank beginner and learn from the bottom up, but for music, you have to already be skilled and highly motivated to gain acceptance. Almost all schools allow students to take some music classes, but if you want to graduate with a music degree, you'll need to declare a music major and start preparing now.

HOW DO I DECIDE WHETHER I SHOULD MAJOR IN MUSIC?

Being a music major is a big decision. It's not only about the classes you take in college, but a commitment to an art and a lifestyle. You should NOT be a music major just because your parents want you to major in music or because your parents were musicians and everyone assumes you will be one, too. Majoring in music takes a lot of dedication. DON'T do it if you're just pretty good at your instrument, or you can't think of anything else to major in. You should NOT become a music major just because your friends are going to music school, and you think it would be fun to go together. You have NO IDEA what it takes to be a music major or a professional musician if you think it would be easier than taking "real" classes. You are WRONG if you think a music degree will be something to "fall back on," the life of a musician sounds fun and exotic, or you expect to become rich and famous.

There is ONE and ONLY ONE reason to be a music major:

YOU LOVE MUSIC, YOU CAN'T IMAGINE DOING ANYTHING ELSE WITH YOUR LIFE, AND YOU'RE WILLING TO DO WHATEVER IT TAKES TO MAKE YOUR DREAMS COME TRUE. AND NO ONE (NOT EVEN YOUR PARENTS), CAN TALK YOU OUT OF IT.

Do I have what it takes?

If you're near the top of your performing groups, winning contests, receiving high grades in adjudications, and playing difficult pieces well, you may be ready to major in music. If you're not sure how you compare, especially if you live in a remote area, travel to hear other students your age. You may find out you're a big fish in a small pond now, but you might be swallowed up by the bigger fish when you move to the ocean.

What are my chances?

Many top schools accept only a handful of students for each instrument every year, so competition is fierce. You may be competing against dozens of other students for one or two spots. But if being a musician is your dream and you really want it, go for it.

WHAT DEGREES IN MUSIC ARE USUALLY OFFERED?

Every school has its own programs and requirements. Here is a sampling of what you may find:

- Bachelor of arts degree with a major in music. Required classes are usually 60% music and 40% in other liberal arts. With a bachelor of arts, you can specialize in instrumental or vocal work, music theory, music history, and sometimes ethnomusicology. Typical credits for this program might be 48–54 in music, 15–20 in a minor area, 45 or 46 in liberal arts core curriculum courses, 12–15 in academic electives, and 6 credits in upper-level free electives.
- Bachelor of music degree. This degree puts more emphasis on performing and requires more music classes than the bachelor of arts degree. This degree can also include composition.
- Bachelor of music education with a teaching certificate. This degree usually has an instrumental or choral emphasis, as well as a focus on primary or secondary grades. You will be taking classes in both the music school and the education department and need at least one quarter of student teaching.
- Music minor. This degree is for those whose main interest is outside of music but who take a required number of credits including music history, music theory, and performance.
- Double major in music and another field. Students need to fulfill all requirements of two majors. Plan on adding at least one more year of college. (A double major in music and business can give you more options. You may be able to make enough money to support your "music habit.")
- Other degrees offered might include music engineering with an electrical engineering or a computer science minor, music therapy, musical theater, or a degree in music business and the entertainment industry.

In addition to the bachelor of music degree, conservatories may offer additional programs. For example, the Colburn School Conservatory of Music offers:

- Bachelor of music. Students take 134 semester units to complete.
- Performance diploma for students who have not yet completed the baccalaureate degree program before they come to Colburn. This program includes no humanities and requires 74 semester units to graduate in about four years.
- Artist's diploma. This program is for students who have already completed the baccalaureate degree program, and it takes two to four years to complete.
- Professional studies certificate. This program emphasizes professional and pre-professional activities outside of Colburn and requires 24 semester units.

Specialized schools such as the Berklee College of Music may also offer a degree or diploma in contemporary writing and production, film scoring, jazz composition, music business/management, music synthesis, and songwriting. Some schools such as the Hartford Conservatory offer degrees in jazz and popular music as well.

COMBINED COLLEGE/CONSERVATORY PROGRAMS

Some colleges such as Oberlin have both a college and a conservatory. Oberlin College offers a four-year undergraduate program leading to the bachelor of arts degree. The Conservatory of Music offers a four-year undergraduate program of professional and academic studies leading to the bachelor of music degree. In addition, Oberlin offers a five-year double degree program leading to both baccalaureate degrees. The Conservatory also offers five-year integrated programs leading to the master of music (opera theater, conducting, and historical performance in six private-study areas).

WHAT YOU CAN EXPECT AT ALMOST ALL SCHOOLS

Almost all music programs will require piano proficiency, instrumental or vocal instruction, chamber music, humanities, large ensembles, music history, music theory, and aural skills.

HOW LONG WILL IT TAKE TO GRADUATE?

According to a study done in 2006 by the National Center for Education Statistics, less than 35% of students at four-year colleges graduate in only four years, and about 56 percent take six years to graduate.

When I was a music major at the University of Washington, my friends would ask me what classes I was taking. I would reel off a long list. Thinking that I must be a genius to take so many credit hours they would say, "Wow, I'm impressed. Just how many credit hours is that?" They were astonished that so many classes could add up to so few credits. So was I, considering how much work I was doing.

Many music majors have a tough time graduating in just four years. A music program has many small credit hour classes with lots of homework. Private lessons may be only a couple of credits, but they require many hours of practice per day. Music history classes demand hours of reading and listening, and music theory classes require studying and composing. Performance classes such as orchestra or choir also take up many hours for few credits.

Timing is also a factor. No matter what year you are in school when you declare a music major, you'll probably have to stick around four years from that date to finish all the performance and theory requirements. Many classes are only offered once a year, so if you miss out on Theory 101 in the fall, you'll have to wait until next fall to take it.

Each school has different requirements and expectations. For example, the Curtis Institute of Music predicts students in the diploma program will graduate in two to four years, bachelor of music students graduate in three to five years, and professional studies certificate students graduate in two or three years. So the short answer is that it takes about four years to graduate—but don't count on it.

WHAT DO I HAVE TO DO NOW TO PREPARE?

You know the old joke: New York tourist to taxi driver: "How do I get to Carnegie Hall?" Taxi driver: "Practice, practice, practice." You should practice every day no matter what. Remember, if you're not practicing, someone else is, and they can win that audition. Most conservatory and university-bound seniors practice two or more hours per day.

How can I find the time to practice?

Organize your school schedule to allow for more practice time. Think outside the box. Can you practice during study hall, be a teacher's assistant for a music class and practice part of the time, or take fewer classes? Can you finish your last one or two years of high school at a community college to allow for less in-class time? What about being homeschooled? Can you take the year off after graduation just to study your instrument?

Your instrument must become your priority. This may be the year you give up some outside sports, an after-school job, hanging out at the mall, playing hours of video games, and watching TV. Quit whining—it's worth it!

Will knowing more instruments help?

Play the piano. Most schools require a piano proficiency, especially if you are a music education or voice major. Learning the piano also helps you understand music theory and gives you valuable accompanying skills.

Learn all the variations of your instrument. Can you play oboe and English horn? Violin and viola? Flute and piccolo? Learning more instruments is a plus, but don't spread yourself too thin.

HOW CAN I PREPARE FOR MUSIC CLASSES?

Get a head start in music theory. Complete the music theory section in this book. Practice analyzing chords. Know your scales backwards and forwards and upside down.

Sing to prepare yourself for ear training classes. The first thing you will need to learn is how to recognize intervals by ear. What's a perfect fourth? Can you sing it? Can you recognize it in writing and by ear? To get a start on sight-singing classes, learn solfegge. Solfegge is what Julie Andrews taught the kids with "Do-Re-Mi" in *The Sound of Music*. Ask your teacher to give you rhythmic and melodic dictation. Can you write the music to a hymn played on the piano? To a song on the radio? Can you play it by ear?

Familiarize yourself with the composers to prepare for music history classes. What are the dates of the musical periods, and who are the most prominent composers from each period? Can you recognize the styles of Bach, Beethoven, Mozart, Brahms, Tchaikovsky, and Mendelssohn just by hearing their music? Listen to the classical radio station and quiz yourself. Do you know the performance practices for each period? Read music history books and biographies of the composers. We've included several chapters in part 5 of this book to teach you music history and familiarize you with the most famous classical pieces. Also check out *The Idiot's Guide for Music, Classical Music for Dummies,* and *Bach, Beethoven, and the Boys,* which are great fun.

PLAY, PLAY, PLAY

Take advantage of every possible musical opportunity. Participate in your school and youth music programs. Play in the school musical. Perform at church. Enter as many competitions and master classes as possible. Give a senior recital or go to summer music camp. Perhaps you need two lessons a week. Build your résumé of pieces learned, master classes, ensemble and orchestra playing, and competitions. Now let's hear from my former student Christina.

Christina auditioned at five conservatories and colleges before making the Manhattan School of Music her choice. She recalls what prepared her for the exciting new world of studying at a conservatory.

"New York, New York! Hundreds and hundreds of aspiring musicians flock to the city with a desire to achieve musical success. And after almost 11 years of hard work and practice on my flute, I was one of those hopefuls.

"From almost the time I began to study flute, I knew I wanted to devote my life to music. There was no question of whether or not I would put in the required time and effort. I knew I was competing against hundreds of other

young flutists for only one or two openings per school. To really 'make it' in the music world requires absolute discipline in practicing and dedication to perfection. When it was hard to keep that discipline, my parents and my private flute teacher pushed me, and I did it.

"In my junior year of high school I had two lessons a week. One day of lessons for solo literature and the other for études, ear training, music history, and theory. In my senior year, because of heavy time commitments, I had only one lesson and focused almost completely on the music for my auditions.

"By entering contests and participating in master classes, I gained from the criticism of amazing musicians. I also made more permanent connections and relationships with those teachers and learned to feel comfortable performing."

Do I have to be a music major to take music classes?

Each school has its own rules. There are schools that allow you to sign up for music classes the same way you sign up for other classes. You may not have to audition or major in music. A few small schools may even let you learn an instrument if you are a beginner. You may also find schools that allow you to be a music minor, take music education classes, or even take some music major classes without auditioning on an instrument. In addition, there are "partner schools" that allow you to be enrolled in one school but take lessons or be in an ensemble in another school.

Larger schools or those with a well-known music program will likely require you to audition to become a music major before you can take private lessons or other music classes. There are usually many applicants for each opening, so expect lots of company at the auditions.

If you aren't accepted as a music major, or you declare another major, there still may be playing opportunities. Most schools have large ensembles such as marching bands or 100-voice choirs that have open enrollment. Search out ways to have music be a part of your college experience, no matter what your major is.

HOW AND WHEN SHOULD I START PREPARING FOR THE AUDITION?

Start thinking about colleges and preparing audition music one year before you plan to apply. As you look at different schools, you'll see that they have some of the same repertoire requirements. These are the pieces you should start learning now.

Study with the best teacher.

Make sure you're studying with one of the best teachers in your area, someone who can take you to your highest potential. If you're serious about majoring in music, study with someone whose students have become music majors.

If you can't or don't want to change teachers, enter contests and participate in master classes for feedback.

Keep your grades up.

Some schools may admit you on the basis of your audition, but most schools require that you be accepted to the school based on your academics first.

Be a well-rounded person as well as a well-rounded musician.

Participate in student government, service clubs, and sports teams. The student who only knows music is not an interesting person. Involvement in many activities shows you have energy, enthusiasm, and a work ethic for the world, not just for your instrument.

GREAT IDEAS

Wow! And you thought filling out the college applications and writing the essays was going to be the hardest part. Being a music major is a big decision and should be made for the one and only right reason. If you decide to major in music, the time to start to prepare is now.

Sneak Preview

So you've made your decision: you want to study music in college. But which college? Our next chapter will help you choose between a college and conservatory, small or large school, and even give you some ideas on how to pay for it. So turn the page and start planning your future.

FORTY-FIVE

Choosing a College or Conservatory

Now that you've decided you can't live without being a musician, it's time to think about college. Begin investigating schools, programs, and teachers during your last two years of high school. Imagine your future. Would you like to be a public school teacher? Private teacher? Band director? Chamber musician? Soloist? Orchestra member? Jazz musician? Sound engineer? Arts administrator? Your career path will help determine your educational path.

But how do you choose a school? There are 700 accredited NAMS (National Association of Music Schools) schools. That's a lot of choices. (You can get a complete list of school names and contact information at nasm.arts-accredit.org.)

Start with the basic choice between attending a college or a conservatory. Let's compare what conservatories and colleges have to offer.

THE CONSERVATORY

Most students who choose to attend a conservatory have hopes of becoming performers. They dream of playing in an orchestra or having a solo career. Thus the playing standard for admission into conservatories is usually higher than that of some colleges where music is less of an emphasis. Because of this focus on performance, the conservatory curriculum includes more music classes and fewer academic requirements in other subjects. Some conservatories offer a teaching degree and many kinds of music such as jazz, popular, and ethnic, while others may only offer a strict classical performance-based curriculum.

🔊 *Clarinetist Leslie likes the atmosphere at a conservatory. "The focus at a conservatory is completely on music. Because of that single center of attention, the students are very dedicated. Of all the music students I know, almost all the conservatory students practice twice as much as the college students. Being surrounded by a school full of students who share your passion for music is an experience that can't be matched by some academic institutions."*

Flutist Katy writes from the Eastman School of Music: "The most important thing at any school is the teacher, but there are definitely differences between a college and a conservatory. A college is better for someone who is very interested in other subjects, although many conservatories have arrangements with local colleges that allow double majors as well. Personally, I like the conservatory atmosphere because there are fewer distractions, and it keeps me focused."

THE COLLEGE

Your world reaches beyond music when you meet people and take classes in other disciplines at a college. In addition to your music classes, you're required to take a certain number of credits in other areas such as science, language, and math.

Colleges offer a range of options. If you're interested in two fields of study, you can major in two subjects or have a music major and another minor. You might even choose to major in some other field but still take some music classes.

College offers more flexibility than conservatories. If you decide that majoring in music is not for you, you can easily switch to another major without changing schools. The music credits you have earned at a college will be easily transferred to the general distribution credits required for any major or to another school.

Melissa graduated from Central Washington University. "I'm so happy I decided to double major at a college instead of going to a conservatory even though that meant I was in school for five years. It was hard keeping up both my math classes and music classes, but I learned so much. I was able to play in the orchestra and take private lessons while getting the knowledge and experience for my present job in the government."

HOW DOES THE TEACHING COMPARE?

Don't make any assumptions about music programs until you find out more. The fact that the institution has the word *college* in its title does not mean its music programs are inferior to those of a conservatory. Many colleges such as the University of Michigan and Indiana University have top-rated music programs. Admission can be as competitive as at most conservatories.

The level of teaching you receive depends on the teachers, not the name. The conservatory teacher may be a master teacher used to having a higher level of applicants, but the excellent college teacher can attract those same students and provide the same enrichment. The conservatory teacher might be a big name performer but not a good teacher, and the college teacher may have more experience teaching. The music program at a college may be weak and thus not attract top teachers or talent. You never know. Investigate the individual programs and teachers before making your choice.

🔊

Ana had a hard time deciding on her school and her future, and she is now happy at Dartmouth. "I was shopping and I found two shirts. The blue shirt came from Banana Republic, and the red was Gucci. Both were the same price. As much as I wished choosing colleges was as easy as shopping, I found that making my college choice was one of the hardest decisions I'd ever faced. In my college shop, I narrowed down my choices to two colleges: the well-respected local state school and the well-known East Coast Ivy League school. These two schools were different in every way possible. East and West Coast, public and private, strong music professor against strong academic program, smaller versus large classes. Because of a scholarship, the cost was the same.

"Because I wanted to do an undergraduate double major in flute performance and another academic subject and I couldn't do that at the East Coast school, I had to make my career decision four years earlier than I expected. As I was choosing between my two 'shirts,' was it music or academics? I laid out all the pros and cons for days upon days and talked to as many people as I could. In the end, something in my gut told me to go to the East Coast school and choose academics over music for my future. I probably won't know whether I made the right decision for another four years. But for now, I have a new shirt, and I'm completely satisfied."

THE BEST OF BOTH WORLDS

Can't choose between a college and a conservatory? Choose both! Many conservatories and colleges have a reciprocal agreement with a partner college. For example, the New England Conservatory has a five-year double degree program with Harvard University and Tufts University. This program allows you to be a student at one school and take classes at the other.

Other colleges, such as Rice University's Shepherd School of Music and Indiana University's Jacob School of Music, have a world-renowned "conservatory" program that allows students to take a broad spectrum of academic classes. Taking so many classes can be a heavy workload but may pay off in the end.

Consider these questions when deciding whether a conservatory or a college education is right for you:

The conservatory:

- Can a conservatory provide more performance opportunities?
- Will I have more time to practice at a conservatory without the requirements of many nonmusic classes?

- Can I study more than one instrument?
- Will I be able to take more in-depth music classes?
- Will I be happier and more stimulated being "with my own kind"?
- Will I make more contacts at a conservatory?
- Will the level of teaching be better?
- Will the performing groups be at a higher level?

The college:

- Will I benefit from taking classes in other areas instead of focusing only on music?
- Do I like the diversity of interests and students at a college?
- Will the classes I take at a college give me "something to fall back on" if I can't get a music job?
- Will I be able to find the same level of teaching and student performance in a well-known college music program?
- Is the college more affordable than the conservatory?
- Will I have more playing opportunities and be able to stand out more with less competition?

Kasumi attended junior college for her last two years of high school. She is graduating from the Eastman School of Music this year and will start the application process all over again for grad school. "I chose to study in a conservatory setting because in music you need ample time to focus on your main area of study: practicing. College academic requirements take away from the time in the practice room.

"At Eastman I got lucky because there's a college campus nearby where I can take classes. There are also some wonderful humanities professors here who understand our needs as musicians.

"I'm very happy with the decision I made to attend a conservatory. I've heard musicians say, 'Why be a jack of all trades and a master of none?' I think music deserves a great amount of mastery. For now, that is what I am aiming to do."

THE "FAMOUS" SCHOOL

If you want to attend a well-known school, consider:

- Will doors open for me if I study with the "I've performed everywhere and everyone knows my name" teacher or at "Wow, you must be good if you went to Famous Name School"?
- Will just the mention of the big name school or teacher give me instant credibility?
- Will my own standards rise when I'm surrounded by superstars?

- Will studying with other top performers help me make
    lasting friends and professional contacts?
- Will the big-name teacher have more information and teaching
    skills than someone from a school that is not as well known?

Or:

- Is the big-name teacher only known for performing and not teaching?
- Will the big-name teacher be away concert-
    izing for many weeks at a time?
- Will the teacher be more interested in his or her career than mine?
- Will I have enough money left over for graduate school
    if I attend "Big Mega-Bucks" school now?

Leslie tells of her dilemma choosing schools. "I got accepted to the University of Rochester and the University of Washington. My dedication to music and academics made it hard to choose, so I put deposits down on both schools.

"The University of Rochester is connected to the Eastman School of Music. I had an amazing lesson with the clarinet teacher there. I would be among first-class performers and have the benefits of a conservatory and a better chance of transferring to the conservatory after a year.

"The clarinet teacher at the university had credentials rivaling those of the conservatory teacher, and the university is well known for its high academic standards.

"In the end I chose to go to the University of Washington. Although the University of Rochester would offer me some of the perks of a conservatory, there would be more competition and less chance to perform. I also got a full scholarship plus living expenses to the U of W, which helped make my decision. This may not be my final decision for the four years of my undergraduate degree, but for now I am happy."

LOCATION, LOCATION, LOCATION

Attending college is more than just going to classes. It's the experience of living away from home and experiencing a new lifestyle. If you go to school in a large city, you can hear world-class concerts, have a wide choice of restaurants, have more options for travel to and from the college, and experience more diversity in the population. But being in a big city may also mean dealing with city problems such as bad traffic and a higher cost of living.

There are trade-offs in a more rural setting, too. It's easier to find time to practice if your college is in the middle of a field in the middle of nowhere. If you attend college in a small town, the college becomes your focus (rather than the city); you probably have a better chance to meet people, too, in a smaller

tight-knit community. You can also explore the outdoors and live a more relaxed lifestyle. But you have a better chance to be bored, too, when your only
entertainment for four years is ordering out for pizza and renting a movie.

BUILDING A REPUTATION

Wherever you go to college, you will begin building your reputation. The contacts you make can later lead to job opportunities after you graduate. Leslie
took this into consideration in her college choice. "Going to school in the city
where you want to live eventually will help you make connections that are essential in any career, especially music."

Will this school help build my future?

- Will the people who attend this school and the profes-
    sors be able to help me after I graduate?
- Will this location give me playing opportunities?
- Is this a place where I would like to live?
- Are there many job opportunities here?
- Will I become so good here that it won't matter where I live be-
    cause the world will be clamoring for my services?
- Will I be going on to graduate school, and can
    I think about my future then?

CHOOSING A LARGE OR SMALL SCHOOL

Being part of a crowd of 3,000 or 30,000 can make a big difference.

The small school:

- Will I benefit from the extra experience and personal atten-
    tion I'll receive in smaller programs and smaller classes?
- Will it be easier to make friends and contacts in a smaller school?
- Will there be less competition for performance opportunities?

The large school:

- Will graduate students at larger institutions fill all
    the choice spots in performing groups?
- Will a large college or conservatory be too impersonal?
- Will I have more choice of teachers and classes?
- Will I study with the main teacher, or be assigned a graduate assistant?
- Will I be able to meet more people?
- Even though I'm part of a larger school, will the music pro-
    gram itself become my "small school within a school"?
- Will I be able to continue to graduate school here?

This is going to be your home away from home for the next four years. What's life going to be like?

- Is the campus or surrounding area beautiful? Dull but acceptable? Who has time to see the campus?
- Do you have a choice of dorms? Is there a dorm for music majors? A quiet dorm? A dorm for nondrinkers and nonsmokers? A dorm for video game addicts?
- Do the dorms feel like a luxury hotel? A prison? A space capsule?
- Is the dorm food haute cuisine? Passable? Unrecognizable?
- Can you easily get a practice room? Do the pianists hog all the practice rooms? Do you have to call Ticketmaster to reserve a room?
- Are the practice rooms in the dorms? Across campus? In the next county?
- Is there a large library? Is there a listening library? Library? Who goes to the library when you have the internet?
- Are there many school clubs and activities? Are all the clubs connected to the Future Farmers of America? Is Facebook a club?
- Are the students happy and proud to be here? Do they duck their heads when asked where they go to school? Are they all waiting to transfer to another school?

Leslie says, "I chose a school based on its music opportunities but also on the atmosphere on campus. The students at the University of Washington had more school spirit, a stronger sense of community, and shared more values and goals with me than the students at some other schools I visited. It's important to find a school where you'll fit in with the student body and have a good time while you're working on your education."

GET ORGANIZED

Keep a notebook with information about prospective schools. Compare teachers, locations, costs, and required classes. Research on the internet and call the admissions office yourself. It's your future; you should be the one planning it.

Being organized helped Kasumi with her decision process. "I recommend keeping one organized notebook where you keep checklists and record information regarding applications, e-mail addresses, audition dates, times, and items needed for the application. Anytime you need a piece of information such as a deadline or audition date, you can refer to your notebook. It's no fun ripping apart your room trying to find that one piece of paper that had the really important piece of information you needed!"

Unless your Aunt Edith left you a big wad of cash, money will play a role in choosing a school. What is the tuition? How much is normally spent on books? What is the room and board? Are private music lessons extra? What is the cost of travel to the school?

Loans and Scholarships

Research scholarships well in advance. Talk to your school counselor about any money available through your school music program. Ask your private teacher and band and orchestra director for ideas. They may have contacts or have had previous students who have been successful at getting money. Research scholarships offered by community groups such as the Rotary Club. Check out the scholarships offered by the schools you're interested in. Some schools offer music scholarships, and some offer need-based scholarships. Most offer academic scholarships, so keep studying for those SATs.

Be sure to ask your guidance counselor, and check on the internet, about a huge spectrum of special-interest scholarships available in very specific categories—from ethnic (are you $\frac{1}{16}$ Native American? Norwegian?) to geographic (some scholarships are limited to residents of a particular state or city) to professional (does your parent work at any of a long list of certain companies?).

Apply to several schools. If you've been accepted into more than one school, you may get a "bidding war" going. If you're a top-notch student, you may be surprised at how much money may be available. Often there's more money at smaller schools, with less competition for scholarships. You may be the best musician they've heard all year in a school in a smaller music program.

Keep practicing, keep studying, and keep applying for scholarships. Investigate student loans. How much financial aid can you get, what is the interest rate, and when does it need to be paid back?

Before you take out a large loan, ask yourself if it's worth being saddled with a big debt when you graduate. Cost factored into Leslie's decision: "How much you pay for college should strongly influence your decision. If you later want to go to grad school, you don't want to be saddled with huge debts and student loans, especially since music is not a high-paying profession." I agree. Do you want to pay more for college per year than you will be earning as a working musician?

So you still don't have enough money to go to "Big Bucks School"? Think of alternate ways to earn or save some cash. Can you live off-campus and share an apartment with other struggling students? Are there work-study programs? Can you get an off-campus job? Work in the music library or file music and stack chairs for the marching band? Get a church job? Be on a stage crew? Be a teaching assistant? Teach private lessons? Grade papers? Scrub floors?

So far we've talked about factors to weigh when you choose a school. But the most important consideration is the teacher who will give you private lessons. Who is going to be your taskmaster, role model, mentor, and friend? Learn who the top performers and teachers are for your instrument. Listen to recordings and attend concerts. Network to get the inside scoop on teachers. Attend summer camp, a convention, or master classes to have the chance to "try out" other teachers. Ask other students about their experiences. Talk to local teachers and performers. Contact students who are currently studying with college and conservatory teachers. Ask them about their workload and their teachers' expectations. Find out the truth about the rapport between the student and teacher and between the students within the studio. If you're looking at the big schools, find out how graduates of the schools are faring in the real world. Are they being accepted in graduate school? Are they getting jobs?

Hal Ott, professor of flute at Central Washington University, gives this advice on choosing a college teacher: "Students should look for a teacher who will follow through with kids. When they are in college, they need lots of guidance. Every victory seems to indicate to them that they will definitely lead a charmed life. Every defeat, even if it is minor, often sends them into a depressive state, and they question their very existence! They need someone who is there for them on a regular basis, someone who has been through the ups and downs that life as a musician brings, someone who will help them find that delicate balance in their lives so they can be successful at whatever they pursue."

Brooke, one of Hal's students, has something to add: "I chose where I went to college based on the flute teacher. How I liked the teacher's playing style, teaching style, and general personality were probably the most important questions I took into consideration. I found a teacher who has not only been a wonderful role model on the flute but a person I greatly respect and admire. Four years later, I am 100% satisfied with my past decision and don't regret a single lesson I've learned from him."

HOW MANY SCHOOLS SHOULD YOU APPLY TO?

You can picture yourself at many schools and be tempted to apply to them all. But remember that with every application you will have to fill out forms, pay a fee, write an essay, practice that school's required audition music, and play a regional audition in a major city or travel in person for the audition. That's a lot of work. Keep your list of applications to no more than 10 and include one "in my dreams" school and one "for sure" school to make sure you really will be going to college!

Now that your head is full of questions, let's hear from my former student
Rose. She received her undergraduate music degree from Vanderbilt Univer-
sity and master's degree from New York University as a multiple woodwind
major. She offers these great suggestions for scouting out colleges.

"The best way to find out about a college is not on the internet or through
glossy brochures, but from real people. Start with your high school counselor
or SAT tutor. Ask your school music directors, your private teacher, and any
college friends. Talk to everyone you can about their college experience.

"Once you've picked a variety of small and large schools, find people who
have gone there or know someone who has gone there. If possible, arrange
to visit your top choices. You will immediately get a vibe when you meet the
students. Have coffee with some of them, or just go to the campus center and
strike up a conversation. Is it easy to meet friends? What do they do on week-
ends? Are there fun on-campus activities? Do teaching assistants teach most
undergraduate classes? Is there a relationship with the professors? Are there
many performance opportunities in the school and in the community? Is this
a place you would like to end up staying? The more information you have, the
more informed your choice will be."

This is but a partial list of some of the top colleges and conservatories in
the United States:

Berklee College of Music

Cleveland Institute of Music

Colburn School Conservatory of Music

Curtis Institute of Music

Eastman School of Music

Indiana University

Juilliard School

Manhattan School of Music

Mannes School of Music

New England Conservatory

Northwestern University Bienen School of Music

Oberlin (conservatory within the college)

Peabody Institute of the Johns Hopkins University

San Francisco Conservatory

Shepherd School of Music at Rice University

UCLA (University of California, Los Angeles)

University of Cincinnati College–Conservatory of Music

University of Michigan

GREAT IDEAS

Choosing a college or conservatory is a big decision. You must weigh the advantages and disadvantages of a conservatory versus a college, a small school versus a large school, a big city versus a small town, and most important, the instrumental or vocal teacher. Don't rely only on the school's reputation. Do some investigative reporting so you can make the right choice. You can also check out collegeconfidential.com and the U.S. Department of Education's site, the College Navigator, www.nces.edu.gov.

Sneak Preview

Now that you've decided on a list of potential schools, turn to the next chapter where we'll give you some insider tricks and tips on how to get in!

FORTY-SIX

Getting into the School of Your Dreams

You've chosen your dream school. Everything is perfect. But wait—100 or more other students who play your instrument have the same idea, and there are only a few openings. How can you get the audition committee to choose you?

PREPARE EARLY AND PRACTICE A LOT

Your college audition can literally change your life, so do everything possible to ace the audition. To play perfectly and remain calm under pressure, start preparing your pieces and scales six months to a year in advance of the audition. Preliminary tapes are usually due in the fall, and auditions are usually held in the winter, so plan your timeline accordingly. It goes without saying that if you're headed toward a career in music, this is the time to practice. If you don't have the desire or fortitude to put in a lot of practice time, you probably don't have the desire or fortitude to make it as a musician.

> *Leslie focused like a laser as she prepared for her college auditions. "I showed my clarinet teacher a list of the schools I wanted to audition for, and she told me which had the best clarinet programs. All of my schools required specific pieces. I had to prepare six pieces totaling 13–15 pages of music. Clarinet became my main focus, and I spent all my free time practicing for four months. I had two teachers giving me feedback. They advised me to play certain pieces for certain schools. I recorded myself once a week and listened with score in hand to take notes on what I thought needed work."*

ARRANGE A TRIAL LESSON WITH A PROSPECTIVE TEACHER

A trial lesson will not get you a promise for a spot at the school. It can even work against you if you are a slow learner, resistant to change, immature, or have an attitude problem. But a trial lesson provides an opportunity for prospective students to accomplish several things:

- Visit the school before making a commitment to apply. The glossy brochure may be beautiful, but did you realize that the school sits in the middle of a cow pasture or an urban gang turf war?

- See if you and the teacher hit it off. Does the teacher
seem encouraging and offer helpful advice, or does
the teacher seem joyless or condescending?
- Experience the professor's teaching style. Does the professor use words and examples or only demonstrate? Do you
value expression, while he or she is tied to the metronome?
- Show how "teachable" you are. You may not be perfect now, but if you learn quickly and are open to suggestions, the teacher may take a chance on you.
- Receive coaching on what needs fixing. What you learn
at one lesson will help you with other auditions.
- Receive realistic feedback on how competitive you are, depending on
how encouraging the teacher is about coming back to audition.
- Offer the teacher your résumé and tell him or her a little about yourself.
- Stand out in a crowd in the forthcoming audition. "Great to
see you, Derek," will make you feel a lot more relaxed.
- Gain more confidence in the forthcoming audition,
which will seem like "the second time around."

🔊

*Christina thinks finding the right teacher is most important. "I always con-
tacted the professor at each school ahead of time and requested a lesson. Sure,
getting into a famous conservatory is wonderful, but if the teacher is not right
for you, you will be miserable. Get to know as much as you can about the
school, the programs offered, and the professor. Only then will you be prepared to make your choice."*

SCHEDULE THE TRIAL LESSON

If possible, make arrangements to take a trial lesson a few months before the
real audition. This will further help you stand out from the pack and give you
more time to implement the suggestions before your real audition.

Call the school or get the professor's name or e-mail address off the school
internet site. Most professors are happy to give a trial lesson. It is their way of
getting to know you, too. Some professors will give a discount to prospective
students, while some may require you to pay full price. Most trial lessons will
be held at the school, while some teachers may invite you into their homes.

Ask questions during trial lessons.

Arrive at the trial lesson armed with a written list of questions for the
teacher. Show your interest in learning and in the curriculum. Know something about the program and the teachers at the school. After each lesson,
write down everything you remember so you can compare these comments
with other schools and teachers.

Kasumi compiled these questions for her own audition tour. You might want to e-mail some of these questions to the professor to save time at the lesson. If you ask *all* these questions, you might never have a chance to play!

Questions to determine school opportunities and requirements:

- Will I have a choice of teachers? May I change teachers during the course of my four years of study? If I am accepted into the program, is there a chance I would be studying with a graduate student instead of the teacher for whom I auditioned?
- What orchestra opportunities are available?
- Will I be in chamber music groups?
- How big are the classes?
- Are certain programs limited to upperclassmen or music majors?
- What are the requirements to graduate? How many credits per quarter should I take? What is the graduation GPA requirement?
- How many students will be accepted into the program this year? Do undergraduate students compete against graduate students for admission?
- What careers have students from this school moved on to?

Questions about the lessons:

- What is a normal lesson like? Do you focus on tone exercises, scales, études, solos, or orchestra repertoire?
- What are the normal lesson requirements? Do you require a certain number of études or orchestra excerpts? Is memorization necessary? Do I have any choice in repertoire?
- What do you expect your students to know before they begin lessons with you? Are there certain études and pieces that should already be learned?
- How much emphasis do you place on modern music or early music performance practices?
- Does the studio plan activities outside of class?
- How do you arrange lessons when you have to travel or perform?
- Am I qualified to return for the auditions?

PLANNING FOR THE COLLEGE AUDITION

Compile a list of audition requirements:

- When are the auditions?
- Will there be a representative from the school traveling to my state, or do I have to audition at the school?
- What audition pieces are required?

• Is something from each musical period mandatory? What about orchestra excerpts?
• Is a preliminary recording required? Do they require a CD or DVD?
• Is memorization a requirement? Will there be sight-reading?
• Do I need to be accepted academically to the school before I arrange an audition?

Kasumi will graduate in one year and is already planning her graduate school auditions. She knows the value of starting early. "I would highly recommend beginning the application process as early as possible to save money on application fees and to keep organized. Sometimes if you submit your applications early enough, there are reduced application fees. Ask for letters of recommendation from your teachers early on. Don't wait until the last minute!!"

THE AUDITION RECORDING

If sending in a video is an alternative to auditioning in person, consider what will work best for you. Does your magnetic personality come through best live, or will a video or recording give you the confidence to perform without jitters? When sending in a preliminary audition recording, make sure it is a recording of the highest quality. Hire a great pianist, dress well, and send it by FedEx, UPS, or another delivery service that can track your delivery. And no midnight runs to the post office the night before.

Leslie thinks a live audition at the school gives you an advantage. "I recommend going to the school itself to audition. People tend to be more forgiving toward mistakes when you're playing in person. If you play at a regional site or record your audition, not only do you have fewer excuses for mistakes in your audition, but many professors will see this as a sign that you're not truly committed to their school. In addition, going to the school provides you with a valuable chance to interact with faculty and students and tour the campus. Many professors will allow you to set up a private lesson so you can get a feel of whether their teaching style is right for you. Some even give free/reduced lessons to prospective students!"

When auditioning for schools, don't set your sights on just one. Pick several schools you're interested in. Choose some "in my dreams" schools, some "I sure hope I can get in" schools, and some "they would be lucky to have me" schools.

TRAVEL AND SCHEDULING HINTS

Plan ahead not only for the audition but for the trip itself. Some of my students and their friends tell horror stories about their college trips. One girl traveled alone to audition at Juilliard. She was so stressed by the travel experience and the time change that she mistakenly set the hotel alarm for PM instead of AM and arrived late to the audition. Another student's luggage was lost on the first day of her college tour. Her suitcase contained not only her audition clothes but her flute, too! A student cellist arrived at the big city for an audition only to discover her cello had arrived with three big cracks. The moral of these stories: bring an adult to help you deal with travel. If possible, never let yourself be separated from your instrument in travel. If anything happened to it in the luggage, you would get only a fraction of its value back from the airline. If you have to ship a big instrument such as a cello, get a sturdy travel case.

In case you haven't heard enough audition horror stories, here's one more from Sasha. This chilling story happened as she searched for schools in which to get her master's degree in flute performance. She's now looking to continue on to get her doctorate degree, but this time things will be different.

"Driving rain battered the crumpled bus schedule in my hands. I had no idea how to find the bus to the University of Arizona. I brushed the rain off my watch. Where did the time go? I had less than 45 minutes to get to my audition. Then I remembered I had forgotten to bring bus money.

"The distance looked short on the map, so I started out on foot. An hour later, I reached the music building as a sweaty, soaking mess. I trudged down the hall, my shoes leaving soggy footprints on the carpet. I finally found room 102, but it was empty and dark. Did I have the time wrong? Had the committee given up on me? I frantically ran up and down the long hallway and stairs, and minutes later I found the audition committee waiting for me in room 201! I raced into the room, still panting from my hunt, wet hair dripping down my smelly wool coat. Standing before the committee, I must have looked like a lost dog rushing in from a storm.

"I had no time to compose myself. It was too late to mentally rehearse techniques I had worked to perfect. I dove into playing. My wet fingers stumbled on notes. Where was my tone? I wanted it to be over. When it was, a professor asked me, 'Why do you want to go to this school?' 'I want a challenge,' I said, 'and a stimulating learning environment.' Coming from a miserable wreck dog-person, the statement sounded ridiculous.

"Did I pass the audition that day? No. Did I learn something? Oh, yes. Now before I leave, I check the weather, print out bus routes, pack for all circumstances, and keep change for bus rides. Most important, I allow myself more time. You can be musically prepared, but if you sabotage yourself on the way there, you'll never take the journey."

Plan ahead so your audition trip doesn't turn into a nightmare:

- Arrange to travel to several schools on the same trip.
- If possible, audition at the school that's on the top of your list after you've had a few auditions at other schools.

- If you're in high school, bring a parent along to deal with the details.
- If you're traveling to a different time zone, gradually "bend" your sleeping and eating to coordinate with the schedule you will have at the audition.
- If possible, arrive one day before to rest.
- Dress appropriately. Pants are okay for girls, but look "pulled together." And please, no belly buttons or bra straps showing. Guys don't have to wear a suit, but choose whatever you would wear to take your girlfriend out to a nice dinner. No denim, no sweats, no T-shirts, no tennis shoes.
- Schedule plenty of time for the audition.
- Leave parents outside during the trial lesson to give the teacher the chance to see you as an adult and relate only to you.
- Don't exhaust yourself by sightseeing before the audition. Remember, the focus of the trip is the music. Save the Statue of Liberty for later.

Kasumi has learned from her first round of auditions. "There are certain things I'm going to do differently now that I'm auditioning for grad school. For instance, instead of going to each school prior to my audition to take lessons with the teachers, I'll be attending the National Flute Association convention to take lessons from all the teachers I will be auditioning for. It will save me lots of money in plane tickets! Other money-saving options include taking lessons with the teachers within a few days of your audition to save trips; however, I prefer to get it out of the way now. I've also formed relationships with teachers at summer music festivals I've attended. Already knowing them will make it easier to audition for them, and they'll seem like old friends."

WHAT TEACHERS LOOK FOR IN THE AUDITION

At most schools, many more students will audition than can be accepted. Teachers look not only at your musical skills but also at related factors such as your personality, test scores, and even your appearance to determine your future success as a student at their school and as a musician out in the world. Teachers at the top schools may not want to take time to change a bad technical problem, such as a bad bow arm or poor hand position. However, if you're really interesting, you may convince them you're worth it.

Hal Ott, professor of flute at Central Washington University, knows the trial lessons help the student and the teacher. "A private lesson prior to an audition helps the student audition the teacher and make the final decision whether or not to go to that school. The student is auditioning the teacher, and the teacher is auditioning the student. From the teacher's standpoint, teachability is far more important than talent or achievement. A private lesson, more than just an audition, gives the teacher that insight."

What does the teacher look for at the trial lesson and audition? We've touched on some of these attributes already, but they bear repeating here.

Increase your chances of winning the college audition by having:

- A command of the instrument. Knowing the notes is not enough. You must have a beautiful tone and play with musicality, emotion, and excitement. Put an individual stamp on the music.
- Several years of lessons with a good private teacher and experience in school, youth, state orchestras and bands, solo and ensemble contests, summer camps, master classes, and recitals.
- A desire to go to that particular school. Learn everything you can about the program and have some questions for the committee.
- Good grades. Remember that usually you must first be accepted to the school through your academics before you will be accepted into the music program.
- Curiosity. A well-rounded education, love of literature, and interests outside of music such as sports, school clubs, church, and volunteer activities make you a more interesting person. Show the audition committee that you are disciplined and have a life outside your instrument.
- A work ethic and an openness to change. Show respect for the music and a desire to excel. This is where a trial lesson can really give you extra points.
- Love of performing. Audition committees can overlook a few wrong notes if the music is presented with enthusiasm. Being overcome with fright during the audition doesn't bode well for a career spent performing. If you look as if you're afraid to play in front of others, the committee may wonder why you've chosen a profession you hate.
- An ability to communicate well. Be polite and respectful. Use proper English. No "Me and her goes to school," or "He goes like wow!" Never say, "Yeah, whatever." Look everyone in the eye and answer each question with a full sentence. Correctly pronounce the names of the composers and pieces you play. Most important, always smile and remember to say, "Thank you," no matter how the audition went.
- Maturity. Have self-confidence, but don't brag about yourself. Dress conservatively.
- A fire in the belly. Those who "make it" in the music field aren't necessarily the most talented; they are the ones who want it the most. Show you are willing to work and unwilling to make excuses.
- A sense of humor. Lighten up. Of course, the audition is serious business, but the teacher wants to know that teaching you will be fun, too.

Kasumi knows the music is not the only important thing in an audition. "Be courteous and polite at your audition. Teachers aren't just looking for the best player; they're looking for someone they will have fun teaching and who will fit into their studio. And remember, if you don't get in somewhere, the reason may have been out of your hands. Many times, like in real orchestral auditions, they already know who they want before the audition takes place. This is why taking lessons, networking, and just being polite in general can be so important.

"And one last piece of advice: When you're at your audition, and you come into contact with the other auditioning students, be friendly. You will most definitely be running into these people for the rest of your life."

QUESTIONS YOU MAY BE ASKED DURING THE TRIAL LESSON OR AUDITION

- Why have you chosen this school?
- What do you know about us?
- What can you bring to this school?
- What are your goals in music?
- How do you picture yourself in 10 years? In 20 years?
- What other pieces are in your repertoire?
- What is your solo and ensemble performing experience?
- Have you studied music theory and history?
- What other interests do you have besides music?
- If you couldn't be a musician, what would you be?
- What's the last book you read for fun? (Mention this book!)

Other hints: Bring a repertoire list and know something about your former teacher and the teacher for whom you are auditioning. If you really want to make a good impression, send a "thank you" note when you return home.

FIND OUT THE TRUTH FROM THE STUDENTS

All teachers will paint a rosy picture of their college and studio, but the students will give you the straight facts. Knock on every practice room door, talk to students in the elevators and in the hall, and approach them at lunch. Students will be happy to share their experiences and that of their friends with you. Talk to everyone you can to get the "insider information" about the rigors of the curriculum and the teaching style of the teacher. Teachers may be entirely different when they are recruiting than in daily life. Get a feel for whether students in the studio seem to compete or to cooperate with each other. Is this a happy place to be?

Some teachers never know a thing about you before the audition and base their decision solely on that moment. Other schools (and jobs) may require a written résumé. Your job is to sell yourself on paper and in person. Include a cover letter. List your most recent accomplishments first. Be concise. Make the résumé easy to read and free of mistakes. (One of my friend's sons, when applying to multiple schools, put the name of the wrong school on his application!) Ask for input from other professionals. Proofread your résumé. When applying to be a music major, include all music-related activities. Bring your résumé to the audition.

Shelly Collins, assistant professor of flute and music history at Delta State University, offers these tips on the aspects to cover when writing a college résumé:

Education

Include high school and, for transfer students, any universities attended. List anticipated date of graduation, current GPA, and SAT/ACT scores.

Private study: List names of private music teachers and the dates you've studied with them. If you've studied a secondary instrument, include this information as well.

Intended Major/Minor

Many schools require you to be a music major to audition for private lessons, while other schools don't limit the options open to nonmajors. If you are considering becoming a music major, let them know.

Music Experiences
(include dates for each item)

- School ensembles
- Youth or community music ensembles
- Honor bands/orchestras
- Solo and ensemble contest/festival participation
- Other ensembles
- Music camps
- Master class participation (specify whether you were a performer or auditor)
- Recitals
- Major repertoire
- Theory/history classes taken
- Musical employment/volunteering: Have you taught private lessons? Volunteered with a grade school band? Accompanied the school choir?

- Awards, scholarships, etc.
- Nonmusical accomplishments: class valedictorian? National Merit Finalist? Speech team?

Other Activities

This is where they find out if you have a life outside of school and music. Don't list everything you've done since you were 3 years old. But if you were class president, spent a year as an exchange student, or found a cure for the common cold, let them know! You might include:

- Work experience
- Offices held
- Church involvement
- Volunteer activities
- Hobbies

ADDITIONAL RESOURCES FOR INVESTIGATING COLLEGE AND UNIVERSITY UNDERGRADUATE AND GRADUATE PROGRAMS

These sources are from the informative website of the National Association for Music Education (www.menc.org).

College Board (www.collegeboard.org)

College Music Society (www.music.org)

Excel-ability Learning (www.excel-ability.com)

MusicSchoolSearch (www.musicschoolsearch.com)

MusicStaff.com (www.musicstaff.com)

National Association of Schools of Music (www.arts-accredit.org)

GREAT IDEAS

It's a competitive world out there. But if you prepare well, you can increase your chances of attending that perfect school.

Start planning your auditions early.

Find out if you need to audition in person

Practice A LOT

Choose audition music you can use for several schools.

Build a résumé.

Arrange a trial lesson.

Plan your travel so unexpected problems don't sabotage your audition.

Arrive armed with questions.

Remember, teachers are looking for more than a finished product. Personality and passion count.

Always say, "Thank you."

Sneak Preview

Now that you've chosen your school, built your résumé, and planned your audition trip, the next step is the actual audition. What should you play? What should you wear? How can you play without fainting? Our next chapter will walk you step by step through college and professional orchestra auditions with concrete advice for real-world situations.

FORTY-SEVEN

Preparing for the College or Professional Orchestra Audition

In the previous chapter you learned how to prepare your music, arrange for a trial lesson, and schedule your audition. Now the big day is here. You're an old hand at playing in front of an audience in concerts and contests, but today the stakes are high. The results of your college or orchestra audition will affect your future as a musician. What should you play? How should you play? How should you act? What should you do if you mess up? In this chapter, I'll share tips I've used to help many of my students succeed in the college and conservatory audition process. You'll also learn from the advice of professional musician friends who have been on both sides of the screen.

HOW TO PREPARE BEFORE YOUR COLLEGE AUDITION

Although we touched on some of these topics earlier, remember these things before your college audition:

- Start six months to one year in advance to choose and learn pieces. Assemble and compare the requested repertoire lists from many schools. Choose pieces required by many schools so you can get the most mileage from each piece you prepare.
- Know your scales from memory. Major and minor in all forms. All of them!
- Be prepared to play something from memory.
- Practice sight-reading. You may also be asked to play something by ear.
- Attend master classes, compete in competitions, and perform as much as possible.
- If you are auditioning for a particular teacher, listen to recordings of that teacher.

Christina remembers the unreal world of the auditions. "The auditions were different from anything I had ever experienced. Every one was unique. I flew into each city a few days before the audition and had to quickly adapt to the unfamiliar place and its weather. Though suffering from jet lag, I had to play my absolute best. And in those same two days, I had to evaluate the school to see if I wanted to spend the next four years of my life there. Quite a daunting task!"

WHAT TO PLAY FOR YOUR COLLEGE AUDITION

- You will probably have to prepare three pieces. Play pieces you know inside out rather than reaching for something that might be technically too difficult. No one is impressed by the virtuosic piece played poorly.
- Play contrasting pieces from different musical periods that show all aspects of your technique and musicality. Include something lyrical and something technical.
- Choose pieces that will stay within a limit of 10–15 minutes, or play portions of pieces.
- Choose pieces that aren't too slow, aren't too repetitive, that don't have lengthy piano interludes, and that build quickly to a climax. (You never know when they will cut you off!)
- If you have a choice, start out with your easiest piece to gain confidence.
- Select pieces that show off your fantastic sound. Pay close attention to vibrato.
- Never dismiss Bach and Mozart as being easy.

Being prepared helped Leslie relax and do well at her college auditions. "Weeks before my audition, I had a 'dress rehearsal.' I performed my pieces and scales for an audience while wearing the same thing I planned to wear at the actual audition. I even did practice interviews with friends and family.

"The night before, I made a list of everything I needed to do or bring. Auditions are stressful, and writing everything out gave me one less thing to worry about.

"On audition day, ARRIVE EARLY. I tried to arrive at least 45 minutes early to scope out where I would be playing and to give myself a chance to calm my nerves. I don't recommend listening to other auditions if they are of the same instrument. (That's a really good way to scare yourself.) But if they are of a different instrument, it can be helpful to listen for a moment to get a sense of the room's acoustics so you can modify your tone and dynamics accordingly."

Anna played three auditions and each was different. "My first audition, for the Peabody Institute of the Johns Hopkins University, was held in a Seattle church. I only saw one other student at the audition. The admissions representative talked to me, but it was less of an interview and more just to learn about the school. I'm not sure if he had input into the selection process, but he recorded me, and I was told the results weeks later. (I didn't get in.)

"The next was for the University of Washington. There were many people

milling around in the halls beforehand, and I played in a room with many tiers. The five members of the woodwind faculty were scattered around the room, which made it hard for me to reach out with my music to them and even harder to know where to look. But I played my best and was accepted.

"My next audition was for the University of Michigan. It was the most comfy, as it took place with the teacher in her office. She had between 60 and 80 flutes trying out for just six spots, so I was very nervous. I listened to my iPod beforehand, so I couldn't hear any of the other amazing players. I'd had a lesson the day before with her, so we had talked then and she asked me some questions during the audition, too.

"In the end I chose to go to Dartmouth. My audition was a CD, and I never had to audition in person. You never know what will happen."

THE VOCAL AUDITION

"The issue of good audition pieces is a difficult one," says vocal coach Nancy Zylstra. "Each school has different requirements about how many pieces, how many languages, art song, opera aria, oratorio, something before 1800, something after 1950. How to choose those pieces is a very, very individual thing. Everyone I've helped audition for college music programs has had a different puzzle to put together depending on how long they've sung, how mature their voices already are, how technically advanced they are, how much they've sung in other languages, and how good their musical skills are. I highly recommend that singers be working closely with their teachers well in advance of the deadlines, with requirements in hand (I can't stress this too many times or too much), and to carefully choose pieces that suit them and fill the requirements of the schools. Each school has slightly differing requirements. One student had to learn twice as much repertoire as usual just to audition for three of those schools.

"The biggest mistake students typically make is to leave finding out deadlines and requirements until it is too late. This can be a very costly misjudgment on their part. They also need to make sure they don't leave the recording of the audition CD until too late, because they often catch colds and then they're stuck with a recording that doesn't show their voice at its best. They need the deadlines and requirements early, early, early, and plot backwards from the deadline. This includes mailing or e-mailing the DVD or file to the school, reproduction of the DVD if necessary or transfer to file, one or two recording dates (in case of illness or other untoward occurrence). Vocalists need to make arrangements for the recording and even sometimes video setup. Where are they going to do this? Who will their accompanist be? Will they have to hire someone to do the recording/video? The motto? Be prepared!"

Once your college days are over, your next dream may be to play in a professional orchestra. The competition here is unreal. There might be 200 applicants, all of them qualified, who show up for one job. Do absolutely everything you can to prepare.

(Many of these tips will apply to your college orchestra audition, too, so don't wait until you graduate to read them.)

Before your orchestra audition:

- Study concerto and orchestra excerpts until you know them inside and out. Listen to the CD and study the orchestra score to see how your part fits in, so you can play in context. Perform as if you hear the orchestra playing along with you.
- Ask an orchestra musician or conductor to listen to you play prior to the audition. Ask an orchestra member if he/she will coach you for the audition. They know how the process works locally and what is likely to be required.
- Practice with the Orchestral Musicians CD-ROM library. Print out the full orchestral part and start with Beethoven.
- Use actual orchestra parts, not excerpt scores, which might not have all the right markings.
- If the audition will be behind a screen, practice behind one or facing away from your audience to learn how to communicate without the visual impact.
- Although the audition requirement may be only one movement of a concerto, learn all three.
- You may be asked to play the whole piece. Study the orchestra you are auditioning for and learn what they value. For example, the Philadelphia Orchestra is known for its luscious and fat sound.
- Check blogs and orchestra-related websites for anything you can find about the specific orchestra's audition process and history.

What is the orchestra looking for?

- Practice makes perfect. Most orchestras opt for the competitor who makes the fewest mistakes. With competition so high, you can hardly afford to make even one error.
- Orchestras are looking for someone who can play as a soloist but who can also blend in. Their number one priority is rhythm, followed by pitch and sound.
- If auditioning for an assistant job, work to be able to blend your sound and vibrato with the principal player.

- Realize that orchestra auditions may seem to have nothing to do with the actual job opening. Violinists are asked to prepare solos from Don Juan and Capriccio Español to audition to play in the middle of the second violin section. A better audition would be for finalists to sit in the section on probation, but most people who audition never get that chance.
- Orchestras are also looking for someone who is both a leader and a follower; they want someone who will be part of the team. Personality counts. So does appearance. This is not the place to flaunt your multiple tattoos, your extreme hairstyle, or the bizarre side of your wardrobe. Even scent is important: most orchestras have regulations against wearing perfumes or colognes because you will be working in close proximity with people who might have allergies.

Additional hints for both college and orchestra auditions:

- Play lots of chamber music to learn to listen to others in a group and to refine musicianship.
- Don't be so busy practicing excerpts and audition pieces that you forget to study music.
- Recognize the odds. Music school and orchestra positions are now international competitions, with players from around the world auditioning.

Although Leslie prepared well, auditions were still a challenge. Leslie found the anticipation of the auditions was worse than the auditions themselves. "Auditions were the hardest (and scariest) part of the college application process. I had to start preparing months ahead of time: choosing my repertoire, setting up audition dates (most schools have many to choose from), and filling out all the paperwork that you often have to bring to the audition.

"However, at each audition I was surprised at how laid-back the atmosphere was. Because most schools audition multiple instruments on the same day, I was never surrounded by competing applicants on my instrument, which made the atmosphere much more relaxed. Still, make sure to stay away from anybody who seems overly nervous or competitive, because that can affect your own nerves. The people running the auditions and listening were also very friendly. Their job is to help and to make things run smoothly, not to make you nervous."

THE AUDITION

Auditions for orchestras and for some conservatories are unique. With a callback system, you are never sure of when you'll have to play and what you'll be asked to play. You may draw the number to play first or fortieth. You may have been asked to prepare 30 minutes of music and be asked to play 5. You may have no time to eat or no place to warm up. The whole system gives you no sense of time or normalcy. Sounds like fun, huh?

SUGGESTIONS TO GIVE YOU A COMPETITIVE EDGE

Before the audition:

- Bring something to read, or something mindless to do like knitting or Sudoku, so you're not preoccupied with the audition and can keep a handle on your nerves.
- Bring something light to eat and drink. Complex carbohydrates and vitamin B help to counter stage fright.
- Give yourself quiet time. Talking too much can tire your embouchure and take away from time to inwardly prepare. Talking to the person who is busy freaking out or who is busy showing off can ruin your concentration.
- Be careful about how much you eat and how much water you drink. Go to the bathroom (and check your zipper!) before you go onstage.
- Be communicative and pleasant. Work on your reputation for being kind and cheerful.

On the stage:

- Try to simulate normalcy. Check your watch before you walk out. Look around to get your bearings.
- Take an extra few seconds to take a few calming breaths.
- Repeat an affirmation such as, "I'm going to play my very best" as you walk out onstage. Imagine a successful completion.
- Make a connection with your audience. Remember that you're onstage the moment you walk into the room.

HOW TO PLAY

- Every note counts. The first 10 seconds of the piece count the most. Many judges form their opinions quickly.
- Adjust your sound to the room. In a very dry room, play staccatos longer and add more vibrato.
- Because so many players are now so technically proficient, the key (especially with strings) may be vibrato and warmth.
- If you are playing behind a screen, go for even bigger dynamics and dynamic contrasts, as the screen deadens the sound.
- Be a human metronome.
- Fast fingers are not everything, although in some auditions it may seem that way. Tone and phrasing should count as much or more.

- Colleges and orchestras are looking for some-
    one who looks like they love what they're doing. If
        you enjoy the music, the committee will, too.
- If you make a mistake, show your matu-
    rity and concentration by going on.
- Knock 'em dead!

🔊

Leslie agrees that each audition was a little bit different. "At Eastman's re-
gional audition, a single member of the faculty spent as much time interview-
ing me as he did listening to me play. He also made a recording to send back
to faculty at the college. My regional audition for Northwestern was recorded
by the dean of admissions, who knew next to nothing about music. There was
no interview, but I had to provide a résumé and detailed information on my
instrument, reeds, and other equipment. For both Eastman and Northwest-
ern, I had to warm up in a room full of other applicants. My best experience
was at the University of Washington. I got one of the few individual practice
rooms to warm up in, and an entire panel of woodwind professors listened to
and interviewed me. I also brought the scores to my music to every audition,
even when they didn't ask for it."

THE (UNREAL) WORLD OF PERFECTION

Students receive conflicting advice from teachers on how best to play an orchestra audition. Because of the intense competition for orchestra jobs, technical perfection has almost come to be the baseline. Because there is no room
for error, many musicians have decided to "play it safe." They play with a safe
tone to avoid a cracked note and to fit in. They play with a safe interpretation
so as not to offend anyone. Ron Patterson, professor of violin at the University
of Washington, has taken and adjudicated many orchestra auditions. "A bad
sound, out of tune note, or imprecise rhythm will get you eliminated in the
first or second rounds of an orchestra audition. It's in the third round where
you have the freedom to start showing what you can do artistically."

But if everyone is perfect and everyone sounds the same, how can they
choose a winner? Some teachers advise students to exaggerate tone, dynamics,
tempo, and phrasing to stand out in the crowd or even to prove that it's possible. Other teachers say to play what is on the page and no more. Many teachers
advise students to follow their hearts and play the music as they think it should
be played and hope the judge on that day agrees. What's going to win you that
audition? Who knows? It depends on the school, the judge, the orchestra, the
day, the alignment of the stars, and luck.

After each audition, take stock of what went right and what went wrong. If the audition was not successful, what did you learn? Were you taken off guard by the questions or format? Were there any surprises? Did you prepare well? Did stage fright rear its ugly head? Did you play less than your best because of physical problems related to travel? Or did you play your best, and your style was not what the judges were looking for? Were you great, but was someone else greater?

VIEWS OF A VETERAN AUDITIONER

Lois Bliss Herbine, flutist with Orchestra 2001, has recorded for CRI and Albany labels and for radio and television. I appreciate her sharing her experiences and philosophy with us. Her extensive experience has given her an invaluable perspective on auditioning.

"I believe the orchestral audition process has no correlation to the actual job. As an orchestral musician, when do you ever stand onstage alone, save one person sitting and listening to you at your back? Where you have no accompanying musicians? No conductor? No audience? Where else do you need to play better than the musicians performing the selections before and after you, or you are out of a job? A sports team would not hold tryouts without seeing what the player does on the field with the other players. I'm not sure why we continue to hold auditions this way.

"In the audition there is nothing to look at, nothing to listen to, and if the judges don't ask for something differently, nothing to respond to. I personally play better for an audience than I do alone. I liken the process to a gunfight at the O.K. Corral. I'm standing in the center of town with my pistols drawn, and I'm sure there is more than one gunfighter hiding behind the saloon gauging the right time to make their move. Since I can't see or relate to them, I can't engage or disarm them. In the end, I get blown away.

"My worst audition experience started with my first exposure to a 'cattle room,' a place where all auditioners are sent to warm up together. It's the prime spot to become the victim of mind games. This was such a bad experience for me that it helped me stay away from auditions for years. As I warmed up for my audition in a large room with at least a dozen other piccoloists, I ran through the excerpt from the Semiramide Overture. *This excerpt was not difficult for me, nor did I feel threatened by any of the players in the room. But I flubbed the first run-through. Concerned and a bit embarrassed, I played it again and made the same mistake. Instead of stopping and slowing the music down to correct the problem, I continued to play it in succession, getting more frantic and making the same mistake every time. Going through my head was a mixture of "How can I be missing this? I know it cold. I don't need to slow down to get this" and "I hope no one here recognizes me!" At the point when*

I finally gave in and slowed it down to clean it up, the damage had already been done. By the time I exited the room, I was a bundle of nerves and had set myself up for the worst audition experience I ever had. I had prepared for over six months and driven 1,000 miles. Five minutes and 28 measures later, it was all over.

"The best audition experience I had was for one of the top 10 American symphony orchestras. The preliminaries were by invitation only and were held on the stage of their largest concert hall. I was awestruck standing for the first time on this stage with the elegant crystal lighting. It was so inspiring that I pretended to play for a packed house of 2,500 eager audience members, instead of a committee of judges behind a screen. It was the best I had ever played for an orchestral audition. I took something else valuable home with me from this audition—the judging sheets. From these sheets I learned the reasons I was elevated as well as ways to improve my performance. I've become a better performer by acting on these suggestions.

"Sometimes the judge's comments can be revealing in a different way, and we need to ask a trusted teacher or colleague to look over the comments and verify their suggestions. After my audition for a regional symphony orchestra 15 years ago, one of the judges told me my opening to the Vivaldi Concerto in C Major was not 'even.' The committee was interested in hearing the opening sixteenth-note passage metronomic and straight, while I was emphasizing the first of the groups, which were the melody notes, by elongation and volume. The committee did not ask me to play it differently, so I was eliminated from the onset.

"From years of experience I've learned:

1. Even the top auditioner has room to improve.

2. No one should overlook the auditioner who is quickly eliminated from the start.

3. Last but not least: There are other ways to have a satisfying career in music other than winning an orchestral audition."

IS IT ALL DEPRESSING NEWS?

Every year, musicians are getting teaching and orchestra jobs. Take the case of Joshua Roman, a 22-year-old cellist right out of school who decided to make the rounds of orchestra auditions to get some good experience. He was very surprised to win the first audition he took, with the Seattle Symphony, where he became principal cellist for two years, prior to his departure to start a solo career. It just goes to show you that you never know about these things.

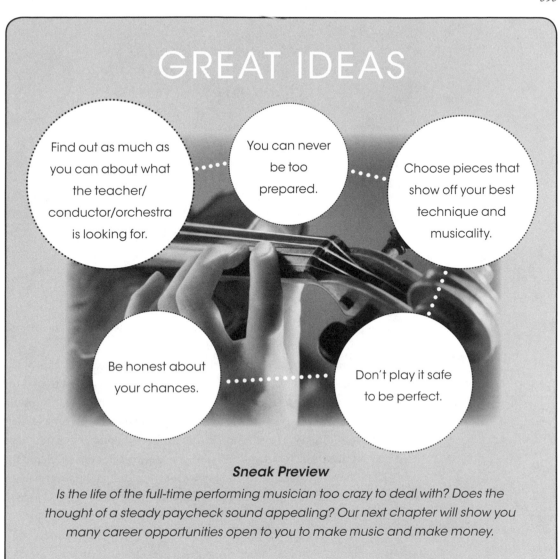

GREAT IDEAS

Find out as much as you can about what the teacher/conductor/orchestra is looking for.

You can never be too prepared.

Choose pieces that show off your best technique and musicality.

Be honest about your chances.

Don't play it safe to be perfect.

Sneak Preview

Is the life of the full-time performing musician too crazy to deal with? Does the thought of a steady paycheck sound appealing? Our next chapter will show you many career opportunities open to you to make music and make money.

Preparing for the College or Professional Orchestra Audition

FORTY-EIGHT

Music Professions

Ways to Live by What You Love

We musicians are so lucky to have our passion be our profession. But how do we turn that love of music into dollars? In this chapter we'll talk about the reality of the job market and how to support yourself. First we'll start with the bad news.

THE REALITY OF JOBS IN THE MUSIC WORLD

I know I already gave you some pretty depressing statistics about winning orchestra auditions in the previous chapter, and I need to be honest again with you here. There are a lot of jobs for musicians, but there are even more musicians wanting those jobs! Imagine the thousands of music students at the hundreds of colleges and conservatories around the country. Add to that the professionals with degrees searching for more work. Compound that with people coming from all around the world to get their training and make their mark. The result? Sixty string basses try out for one symphony position. One mistake and they're out of the running. And sometimes not one is offered the job! The Juilliard graduate lands a one-year contract with an orchestra; when the contract expires, he can't find any other work and has to sell his bassoon to make ends meet. The conservatory student with a master's degree earns as much money teaching as the person with no degree at all. The volunteer community orchestra is full of conservatory graduates. The student with the doctorate finally lands the orchestra job in the small city, and his salary per year is half of what he used to pay in tuition.

Life in academia is not much easier. Most college professors must have a doctorate and be able to teach music theory, history, pedagogy, and sometimes even the history of rock 'n' roll as well as teach their instrument. There are scores of ready, willing, and able applicants for every college teaching job, but few job openings every year.

Having a hard time finding a way to make money? You won't have that same problem spending it. You'll need money for additional lessons, summer festivals, a quality instrument, sheet music, and instrument maintenance. Not to mention the hours of practicing needed to prepare for these jobs.

Can you make it as a musician? Of course, there are a few people who make it big and give us dreams of becoming famous, but they are 1 in 1,000. The amount of money, training, and time you put into becoming a performing musician would make you a millionaire in most other fields. As depressing as these facts are, there are ways to beat these statistics, so don't give up hope!

ARE THERE TOO MANY MUSICIANS IN THE WORLD?

Although finding a job may be tough, the world is a better place because of musicians. Musicians have a connection to the past, they keep culture alive, and they make the world a more beautiful place. And they're such fun people, too. The world needs musicians!

Junko lives in Tokyo, where she teaches English. She has come to terms with not being a professional musician. "After graduating from college with a degree in performance, I was searching for my ideal job in a semiprofessional group. How naïve I was. I looked on the internet, watching for possible auditions. I finally settled for a job in a music store, but felt I wasn't getting anywhere in life and quit after two years. Well, life is a board game.

"During depressing times, I thought, 'What a waste of time and money I have spent in four years of college. I should have studied law!' Now, however, I don't regret not having a job currently related to music. I knew from the start that making a living through music would be tough. I've concluded that college was just a fun part of life for me. It allowed me to grow in different ways and realize there is no right way to live your life. Enjoy the time you have in college. Experience competition and the recognition. Allow yourself to fail. If you choose to be a music major, just remember you chose to study music because it's beautiful. There's nothing wrong with not getting a music job with your degree. Keep learning and go for life."

THE GOOD NEWS

Someone is getting those music jobs, and that someone could be you if you are highly talented, educated, committed, hardworking, personable, and *lucky*. Even then expect to start at the bottom of the ladder with a small college or orchestra job and work your way up. However, there are a few ways to increase your chances of landing a job.

Tips for making your career:

Don't wait for a job to come knocking on your door.

Create a musical life for yourself. Most musicians don't have one job but a medley of musical jobs. Brainstorm ways you can make yourself more salable.

Be flexible.

You may never play in the "No One's as Famous as Us Orchestra" or teach at "Snobby Conservatory U," but you can still have a wonderful life as a musician. Perhaps you can play for a small community orchestra or sub for the big city orchestra. Just because you don't have a full-time contract doesn't mean you can't be a full-time performer. If you don't get a university job, you can still have a wonderful private teaching studio, teach part-time at a small college or community college, or teach in the public schools. Singers, choral conductors, and organists find fulfilling jobs in churches, where there often is very high-level musical activity (Seattle's St. James Cathedral is the city's second-largest music contractor after the Seattle Symphony). Where there is a thriving branch of the film industry, freelance instrumentalists find many opportunities to play in orchestras organized to perform soundtracks. (Seattle, where so many movies are shot on location, is a good example.) Musicians who master a number of musical styles can build a lucrative business playing weddings and parties. There are many opportunities out there to explore.

Get a college degree.

There are many famous performers who never finished college, but having a degree is usually the first step to becoming a professional musician. A degree will give you knowledge in the basics of music and skill on your instrument as well as a chance to meet and work with other musicians. These contacts can provide leads and job opportunities in the future. Will having more than one degree help? Getting a master's degree will give you more skill and opportunities to network. If you want to teach college, you'll be more marketable with a doctorate. But more important than your degree is how you perform, how you teach, and how well you get along with people.

Be willing to play different styles of music.

Become an expert in a "unique" style such as early music or ethnic music. Can you compose or improvise? The more versatile you are, the better your chances. Can you play more than one of these genres: African, alternative rock, big band, blues, Cajun and Zydeco, Celtic, classical, country, disco, easy listening, ethnic, folk, gospel, heavy metal, hip-hop, jazz, jazz fusion, jazz rock, klezmer, Latin, marching, Middle Eastern, polka, pop, progressive rock, punk, reggae, religious, rhythm and blues (R&B), show tunes, swing, techno, world beat? You never know what will land you a job.

Find a mentor.

Get to know someone who has the type of job or lifestyle you would like. Ask their advice and model their behavior.

Develop friendships with other musicians.

Your musician friends can play in ensembles with you, recommend you for jobs, and commiserate with you when times are tough.

Treat music as a business.

Of course you're an *artiste,* but you're also looking for a job, so be businesslike. Dress professionally, return phone calls, speak courteously, send "thank you" notes, and be on time for appointments—all the things your mother told you to do.

Know your worth as a musician.

You have a valuable commodity and need to be paid. Be selective about playing free gigs. Playing for "exposure" usually gives you nothing but an empty pocketbook. Find out what other musicians and groups are charging and model your prices on theirs. Do not try to undercut other musicians, or you will devalue our profession and make enemies.

Advertise.

Give business cards to everyone you know, including your hairdresser and the neighbors. Use blogs, MySpace, and YouTube. Create a website. Work every day to become "famous."

MANY MUSICAL CAREER PATHS

Many people, especially parents, think there are only two ways to make money: teaching or being a world-famous performer. I'm here to tell you there are as many ways to make money in music as there are musicians. If you really want music to be your vocation, you *can* make it happen. Most musicians lead very busy and fulfilling lives by doing a variety of things in the music field. Consider these ideas:

Perform.

It would be wonderful to become a world-class artist, but not many people earn a living performing solo literature. Most are in professional ensembles or symphonies. Many community orchestras have paid principal players, and some choirs have paid soloists. Maybe your rock band will make it big—or semi-big. You can also supplement your income by recording your music and selling it.

Teach private lessons.

The most common supplemental job for performers is private teaching. As my beloved college choir director Rodney Eichenberger says, "Knowing that the joy one has experienced as a performer and a teacher passes on to one's students and enriches their lives is nearly as gratifying as the musical experience itself."

Being a music teacher isn't just a profession, it's a passion. You must be committed and work incredibly hard, but it feels amazing to have music in your life and to change the world through your students. As with other music jobs, the price you're paid is determined by both your experience and your success with students. But when someone asks you how much you make as a music teacher, tell them, "I make a difference!"

For creative ideas on how to start a successful and lucrative teaching studio and have happy students, read my first book in the Music for Life series, *Making Music and Enriching Lives: A Guide for All Music Teachers*.

Coach.

Coach your instrument section of the local school orchestra, band, or youth symphony. Be a coach at a chamber music or band camp, or coach soloists and ensembles preparing for contests or concerts.

Accompany.

If you're a pianist, offer your services at local schools. Perhaps the choir needs someone to accompany the spring concert or kids need an accompanist for solo and ensemble competitions. They might need someone to play for the school musical. Play for other accompanists or accompany someone for free to get your name known.

Freelance.

You're on your own here. To be a good gig musician you must be technically and musically excellent on your instrument and be a great sight-reader or improviser. Knowing the standard literature of the ensemble will make sight-reading and improvising a lot easier. To become known, contact established groups and offer to audition or play a gig for free. Find out if the musicians union in your town gives referrals and if it will be worth the dues for the number of jobs you may get. Contact churches, theater groups, schools that do musicals, recording studios, orchestras, and anyone else that might hire you.

Form your own group.

Decide on the type of music you want and find musicians who are willing to share the responsibilities of running a business. You'll need a website, cards, brochures, photos, and a demo CD. Once you've rehearsed and put together a gig book, you'll need to advertise. Network with event sites, businesses that hold events, schools, event planners, nightclubs, churches, and talent agencies. Be creative about where you might perform. Weddings and receptions, art galleries, store openings, farmers' markets, and business holiday parties are just a start.

Again, be very business-minded and remember that the customer service you provide is as important as the music. For ideas on promotion, check out the website of my performing groups, www.silverwoodmusic.com.

Work as a church musician.

Churches need song leaders and cantors, children and adult choir conductors and accompanists, organists, composers, and worship musicians.

Share your expertise.

Give master classes, offer to substitute teach for other teachers when they're away, give music lectures, play at libraries, write a handout (or even a book), or teach online theory or history classes.

Orchestras, choirs, and bands need new music. Perhaps you will land a more glamorous job writing TV and radio ads or movie scores.

DO IT ALL!

Most musicians don't depend on one job but build a career doing many things. Teaching, playing gigs, giving concerts, and having a church job will give you a very busy life, but can also give you a living wage. Just as every other waitress in Hollywood is an aspiring actress, many musicians combine their love of music with their day job. It doesn't have to be an all-or-nothing profession. It's up to you to decide the role you want music to play in your life, to sell yourself, and to make that dream a reality.

As tough as the music profession might be, if music is what you love, then follow your passion. Perhaps you won't make as much money as you would in a different career, but you can wake up every morning looking forward to your day—and that feeling is priceless.

CREATING A LIFE IN MUSIC

I'd like to share with you insights from a recent college graduate looking for a job and ideas from other successful musicians who have made wonderful lives for themselves through their music.

Let's hear first from Christina Sjoquist. "Having recently received my master's degree in flute performance at the Shepherd School of Music at Rice University, I'm now facing the challenge of starting my professional career as a flutist. Obviously, there is no secure nine-to-five job to easily step into. I believe the three most important aspects for success in my job search are organization, networking, and excellence in performance. It's easy to get caught up in day-to-day activities and to forget to spend time promoting your career. I plan to set aside a fixed amount of time each day to make calls, to prepare my press kit, and to network. Classical music is such a small world, your relationships with other musicians may lead to the best opportunities that open for you. Of course, no matter how much time I spend working on promoting my career or on networking, my musical performances must be excellent or no one will want to hear me play! I want to be known as a player who knows her part and commits fully to the music.

"My long-term goal is to practice and audition for orchestras around the country, so I will keep practicing and create opportunities to perform. I also enjoy the challenge of helping younger students get excited about music, so I'm starting a teaching studio. I've already made personal contact with a few local band teachers, taught master classes to students at their schools, and helped coach the flute sections. As a young professional musician, it's important to pass along what I've learned to the next generation.

"A musician must always be an entrepreneur. Stepping into the freelancing lifestyle can be scary, but it also allows for freedom of expression and a chance to do what I love. Above all, I must always remember the passion for the music that first drew me to this career."

Now let's hear from some working musicians.

Lonnie Mardis is the wonderful guitar player in my Silverwood groups. "When I first graduated in guitar from a conservatory, I needed to find work. I bought a cheap bass and started playing in musicals. I learned all sorts of music—New Age, blues, barrel house, jazz, rock, classical—you name it. Now I sub in lots of bands and play in recordings. I've built a recording studio in my downstairs and now record other musicians as well. Recently I took several classes in composing music for video games and just received a commission to compose some movie music. I teach at jazz camps and work in recording studios. I would advise any guitar player to go beyond playing tabs and learn how to read music well. Make yourself marketable by being versatile."

Paul Elliott, the violinist in my jazz trio, agrees with Lonnie. Paul used to work for Microsoft, but retired to make music his career. He's making less money now but having a whole lot more fun. "Though jazz is my main style, I'm in groups that play Latin-Cuban, bluegrass, tango, French cabaret, and classical. I teach private lessons and at jazz summer camps. I'm having a great time."

Valerie Coon has done an amazing job in just two years to make a career in music. "I graduated from conservatory just over two years ago. Since then, I've been surprised at the variety of careers in music. My one-credit course electives (beginning dance and choir) were immediately put to the test when I made it to the finals of a singing, dancing, violin-playing touring troupe. I play in two community orchestras in leadership roles (even soloing with one), play as part of a local semipro orchestra, played for a few soundtracks and CD projects, have substituted with a major symphony orchestra, and regularly as a coach for a local elite musical prep program. I teach 20 students per week, formed a duo and organize chamber concerts, and play for and manage an indie rock band. I had no idea how many types of music I was going to be involved in. It's definitely been an adventure.

"My regrets? I wish I had taken improv and more jazz classes, and I really wish I had taken some business-related classes (which weren't offered at my conservatory)—so much organization is involved in a career in music. It would have been helpful to get more guidance for taxes, billing, all that sort of thing. We are artists, but we are still entrepreneurs."

Flutist Sarah Bussingthwaighte has a doctorate in music and keeps very busy. "When I was in high school, I never dreamed I'd be doing so many different things with music. In an average week, I might teach at the university in the morning, give private lessons at home in the afternoon, and then do a movie-soundtrack recording in the evening. The next day, maybe I'll compose before organizing rehearsals for my chamber ensemble. Over the weekend, I could finish writing that article about vibrato, call to get the piano tuned for my next recital, then head out to play at a fancy wedding. Never a dull moment! And for me it's just the right mix of time with other people and time alone."

Spencer Hoveskeland, string bass, and his wife, Tracy Hoveskeland, cello, are the Bottom Line Duo, a highly entertaining group that defies definition. They play jazz, classical, folk, rock, and world music in arrangements written by Spencer. Spencer recounted how he has many full-time jobs.

"To be a successful musician, you must have multiple income streams. I spend as much time creating jobs as playing them. My main job as a performer in the Bottom Line Duo is only possible because of my other jobs. Being a performer also means giving great customer service: returning phone calls, learning new music, and fulfilling contracts. Most important is to always play my best, no matter if I am playing at the state capitol or for a classroom of 5-year-olds.

"My second job is research and development: scheduling our gigs and arranging all travel. My third job is composition: arranging and writing for our group and others. I advise composers to make sure their tunes are registered with BMI and ASCAP so they own their own intellectual property and can get royalties.

"Being a writer is another big job. I write our marketing materials, programs, and website. My next job is marketing. We perform at wedding shows, and play for banquet managers and catering sales meetings to get known. I contact community colleges, art centers, and schools about performances. We work to build a fan base and keep them informed through the web, e-mail, and newsletters. We sell our CDs and DVDs through the web and CD Baby. I also write grants and am working on three children's music storybooks.

"My job as a freelancer is very diversified. I'm in groups that play klezmer, swing, world music, and tango. Tracy and I both perform with chamber groups and symphony orchestras.

"My most important job? Being a homeowner, husband, and father."

Spencer has more advice:

- Find a mentor. The first famous bass player I approached to be a mentor just brushed me off. He said that coming to him for help was like someone who has seen football once on TV and asks the coach to be the quarterback. Thankfully we found another mentor who saw our passion and gave us great career advice and support.

- You are a business. Make a 2-, 5-, and 20-year plan. What do you want to do, and how are you going to get there?
- Don't put yourself out there until you're ready. People will remember.
- Get playing experience with people who are better than you and always work to grow in your art.
- Face the reality of where you live geographically. If you want an inexpensive house with a picket fence in the country, you may not be able to make it as a recording artist.
- Take advantage of every opportunity.
- Make your own music. Take the pop music you love now and put it into classical music. Your voice will make it grow.

Now you can see why every musician is so busy! We work seven days a week, but we wouldn't have it any other way. I wish you the best of luck getting that teaching or orchestra job, but if it doesn't happen, with a lot of work and talent you can have a wonderful life in music.

OTHER OPPORTUNITIES MAY AWAIT YOU IN THE MUSIC COMMUNITY

Does the thought of being self-employed without a steady paycheck make you break out in a cold sweat? Do you have other talents such as teaching or writing skills that you'd also like to use on a professional level? Many exciting careers can provide the security you seek and allow you to merge your music skills with your other talents and training. Your first step is to explore other career fields.

Here are some possibilities to get your brain ticking:
- Performing arts manager or development specialist
- Arts administrator in colleges
- Orchestra, opera education specialist
- Composer
- Conductor
- Arts critic
- Film editor
- Grant writer
- Music editor
- Music magazine staff
- Ethnomusicologist
- Government arts advocate/worker (e.g., National Endowment for the Arts)
- Instrument maker

- Accessory maker (music bags, jewelry, etc.)
- Instrument repair person
- Instrument sales representative
- Performer (solo, orchestra, chamber music, freelance)
- Musicologist
- Music librarian
- Music book author
- Music publisher
- Music therapist
- Piano bar or club musician
- Recording engineer
- Sound reinforcement specialist (setting up sound systems for pop/rock)
- Studio musician
- Pit orchestra musician
- Cruise boat musician
- Arranger
- Radio announcer
- NPR/PBS employee
- Recital soloist/concerto soloist
- Chamber musician
- Church or temple musician
- Private teacher
- Early music education specialist
- Elementary school music specialist
- Elementary school through secondary school band, orchestra, or choir teacher
- College professor
- Booking agent
- Business manager
- Community choir director
- Jingle writer
- Music arranger
- Music attorney
- Music consultant
- Music promoter
- Music publicist
- Music store manager
- Piano tuner
- Recording technician
- Recreation director
- Staff or freelance songwriter
- Studio musician
- Transcriber

GREAT IDEAS

There are so many ways to make a living as a musician. If something sounds interesting, find someone in the profession; talk to them or shadow them at work for a week. I hope that these ideas and suggestions will help you choose your path and start your career on the right note!

Sneak Preview

Music may seem like a glamorous job—and it sometimes is—but our next chapter will let you in on what the life of a professional musician is really like.

FORTY-NINE

Life as a Professional Musician

Is It for You?

Our group of eight musician friends talked and laughed as we ate the lunch I had prepared to celebrate one of our birthdays. Our lively conversation drifted to a discussion of the ups and downs of life as a self-employed musician. Louise, a music major and a bassoonist in college, had recently left her chamber orchestra job to become director of development for a natural history museum. "How's your new job?" I asked her.

"It's a great job, with a lot of advantages," Louise said. Then she added, a little wistfully, "I do love it, but I'll never feel the passion I did when I worked in music."

"At least it's a nine-to-five job with benefits," said Karen, a former member of the Philadelphia String Quartet. "You'd never get those hours in the arts." As director of a successful program for teens, Karen worked many evenings and weekends.

The other members of our lunch bunch are Eileen, who plays viola in the ballet orchestra, freelances, and teaches piano, violin, and viola; Nancy, who is a professional singer, renowned Baroque specialist, and vocal coach; Mary Kay, who is the accompanist for my studio as well as community and school choirs and who teaches beginning strings at a school; Page, who teaches and plays cello in the symphony, ballet, and opera orchestra; and Melinda, who is a composer and music critic.

As we talked that afternoon, I realized that life is sometimes a trade-off. Musicians enjoy rewards unsurpassed in other professions, but also some downsides; underpayment is a prime example. I pictured a comic drawing you may have seen, called *If other professions were treated like artists*. The illustration shows a homeowner pointing to his broken toilet and talking to a plumber. "I need you to fix this today," the homeowner says. "I can't pay you, but I promise to give you great exposure." Every musician, at one time or another, has been taken advantage of as free entertainment, and we all know that such "exposure" doesn't pay the bills.

Even as a professional, the life of a self-employed musician can be tough. A banjo player in a bluegrass band once told me, "I didn't go into music thinking I would make a lot of money, and so far that's really working out!" Then there's the joke: What's the definition of an amateur musician? Someone with a day job. And, What's the definition of a professional musician? Someone whose spouse has a day job. Or, What's the difference between a pizza and a guitar player? A pizza can feed a family of four. Ouch! Unpredictable paychecks, unusual hours, and the need to build a good reputation are a few of the downsides of this business. But don't let those discourage you. Career experts suggest we find our perfect job by first determining our passion. They say if you can find a job so interesting that you lose yourself in it, you'll never want to retire. Many musicians are in this enviable position. If music is where your passion lies, consider following in their footsteps.

Choosing a career can be daunting. To help you choose, let's look at some of the positive and negative aspects of life as a self-employed musician or studio teacher. Let's start by getting the negatives out of the way:

THE DOWNSIDE OF LIFE AS A SELF-EMPLOYED MUSICIAN

- *You have weird hours.* Musicians typically perform at night and on weekends. Even if you're teaching, you will still need to mainly work after-school hours and on weekends.
- *You can't take a break; there's no office to leave behind.* As a self-employed teacher, your life is not your own. Teaching is not just a job that you can leave at the office. Students phone seven days a week, and some assume that you're "always on call."
- *Your paychecks fluctuate.* It can be feast or famine. One month you get four extra playing jobs and two new students, and the next month there's a weeklong school holiday, and all your students desert you for Hawaii or Disneyworld.
- *You might need two or more jobs.* If you don't have steady work, you must supplement your playing with extra jobs, sometimes unrelated to music, causing you to realize the value in the advice: "Don't give up your day job."
- *You might experience dry spells.* Even established musicians have them, especially during an economic downturn. Only musicians with long-term contracts such as symphony players can count on seasons of steady work. The stress of always needing to find more work leads some musicians to seek permanent, full-time positions and then play music to supplement them.
- *Your car may become your second home.* I now know all the shortcuts, back roads, and potholes in the Greater Seattle area. I've learned to eat in my car as I scan vague directions to obscure locations during rush hour traffic. Some jobs require overnight stays.
- *You'll turn into a quick change artist.* Many afternoons I've finished teaching, raced upstairs to pull on a sparkly outfit, and been out the door in two minutes to play a job until 10 PM.
- *Your "benefits" may not be monetary.* If you're self-employed or you work part-time for many employers, you won't be eli-

gible for unemployment compensation and typical benefits such as sick leave or paid vacations (unless you factor vacation days into your payment schedule). You'll also have no retirement plan with matching funds, no employer-sponsored health plan or life insurance, and no automatic pay raises.

- *You will always be busy.* Even when you're not performing, you'll spend much of your remaining time practicing, in rehearsal, promoting your groups or yourself, making phone calls, finding music, preparing for students, and doing bookwork.
- *Your reputation must be earned.* And, yes, that includes sometimes offering your talents for free. Not everyone knows you're the next Joshua Bell. At some point you'll need to play for paying customers, or you'll resent having worked too hard for too little money to become better known.
- *You are your own promoter, marketing department, and publicist.* You can never stop "selling" yourself and your business to prospective clients. Being a self-employed musician is like perpetual dating!
- *You may feel taken for granted.* Some clients treat you like royalty while others treat you like a babysitter, a servant, or even a potted plant. Students may love you or take advantage of you.
- *You are your own boss.* Along with a sense of freedom, you'll recognize that your career will not advance unless you make it happen. (Although I always give myself a great job performance review!)

While I may have painted a gloomy picture of life as a professional musician or studio teacher, let's be fair and look at the unrivaled rewards that may also await you.

THE PLUS SIDE OF LIFE AS A SELF-EMPLOYED MUSICIAN

Who can put a price on the joy of music? That feeling you get of being in love when you hear or play a romantic piece. The goose bumps from a phenomenal composition. The pride of accomplishment when you overcome technical difficulties and finally get it. The intense communication and joy in sharing a special secret when playing with others. The sense of awe from a stellar performance. The comfort of having a lifelong friend to turn to through better or worse, in good times and in bad, in sickness and in health, 'til death . . . whoops, you understand the analogy. Your job is both your passion and your hobby. You may make sacrifices, but how many people get to spend their days (and nights) working with something so near and dear to their hearts?

- *You're always learning.* There is always one more piece to practice, one more topic to study, one more student to figure out, and one more teaching trick to learn. Being a musician has even been shown to stave off Alzheimer's disease.
- *You meet wonderful, educated, creative, and inspirational people.*

A great reason to have my sons in orchestras is the kids they meet. Their new friends play instruments, and they're usually intelligent and hardworking. The same holds true for my own musician friends. I'm stimulated by their interesting conversations and impressed with their accomplishments. It's a treat being around them.

- *You're never totally out of work* if you're a musician. Unlike "regular" jobs where you can be fired or laid off, musicians can always advertise themselves and get some work. And since you will probably have several ongoing jobs, it's unlikely that they would all end at the same time.

- *You contribute to society.* As a musician, you connect to the past and give to the future of civilization.

- *You can set your own hours* to some extent. If you don't want to teach on Fridays, you don't have to. If you only want to teach 15 hours every week, that's your choice. When you want to take a vacation, you don't have to ask anyone—just don't forget to tell your students.

- *Enjoy lifestyles of the rich and famous,* at least while you're at the gig. Sometimes being a musician includes you in the "glamorous" life when you play in fancy places or meet celebrities or other interesting people whom you would never otherwise have the opportunity to know.

- *You are admired by people in the community.* When new people I meet ask me my profession—after they ask, "Do you play for the symphony?" or "Can you make a living doing that?"—they are always intrigued by what I do. Many times I even detect a bit of jealousy.

- *The pay per hour can sometimes be fairly good.* Okay, it's not as much as a doctor or a lawyer, but, hey, no blood or lawsuits!

- *You are your own boss.* No time clocks, no performance ratings; upper management is you.

- *You can literally change people's lives.* The beauty you bring your students and your audiences can lift them up.

- *You can't live without it!*

Life as a performing musician or self-employed studio teacher can be crazy, but it's also well worth the rewards.

Sneak Preview

Now that you know what you're getting into, let's go to the final chapter to learn how to create a life with balance, friends, and music.

FIFTY

Lessons about Life You Can Learn from Professional Musicians

If you've read the 49 preceding chapters, you already know that music is a wonderful and demanding profession that will teach you many life lessons: discipline, responsibility, self-actualization, and the art of having fun while you work. (No wonder the verb for making music is "to play.") Here we have compiled a list of the best advice our contributing professional musicians have to offer. Whether or not you become a musician, these are lessons that will make you a finer person—in whichever future you choose. Here goes:

It's up to you.
- The life of a musician requires taking risks. You may not win the audition, but you will always lose if you never try.
- Don't wait for opportunity to knock. Seek it out. Be proactive and learn to promote yourself.
- Just because you went to the best school and studied with the best teachers doesn't make you a fine musician. People care more about how you play than where you studied.
- You are responsible for yourself personally and musically. It is not your parents' job or your teachers' job to make your life easy. No one owes you anything; you have to earn it.
- Believe in yourself, or no one else will. Don't let anyone talk you out of your dreams.
- There is no substitute for hard work, not even talent.

No job is perfect.
- Even players in the best orchestras in the country (and sometimes *especially* the players in the best orchestras in the country) can be dissatisfied with their profession.
- Teaching is not second best to performing.
- You may need several jobs to make it as a musician.

Stay balanced.
- It's not worth it unless you are having fun. That's why
    you became a musician in the first place.
- There is a difference between loving music and making it the cen-
    ter of your existence. You want to be dedicated but not driven.
- Be a well-rounded musician with interests other than music.
- Your self-worth is not based on how you play. You may have
    bombed the concert, but you are still a good person.
- Keep your body healthy so you can play music for years to come.

Life's not fair; get over it.
- The best person does not always win the audition or get the job. The
    great violinist Joshua Bell played famous solo works for 43 min-
    utes in the Washington, D.C., subway and hardly anyone even no-
    ticed. Mozart never got the perfect job, and you may not, either.
- Sometimes it really is politics or who you know.
- Knowledgeable people have high respect for what it takes
    to be a musician, while some others think it's just
    a "fluff" major or career. Music *is* a real job.

Develop resilience.
- Think outside the box. You didn't make it into the Big Bucks
    Prestigious Orchestra, so get over it and get real. You can al-
    ways audition again or for other orchestras; even the very
    top young players audition again and again before they get
    a job. And be sure to look beyond the traditional orches-
    tral jobs. There are lots of ways to be involved in music.
- It may take years to build a good reputation and finally reap the rewards.
- Use your "failures" as learning experiences, not as dead ends.
- The path is not always smooth. Roadblocks are put in your
    way so you can prove how much you really want it.

Be a good person as well as a good musician.
- Music is important, but people are more important.
- How you treat your peers and your students is
    more important than how you play.
- Don't try to win at the expense of others. You
    won't win anything except enemies.
- Never try to "psych out" competing musicians at an au-
    dition by playing mind games, and never let any-
    one do this to you. Smile politely and walk away.
- Network with other musicians. They will be the ones to rec-
    ommend you for jobs, but also become your friends.
- Share your talent with your community, schools, and family.

- You have no right to treat others poorly just because you are a famous musician.
- Use the Rotary Club 4Way Test: Is it the truth? Is it fair for
  all concerned? Will it build goodwill and better friendships? Will it be beneficial to all concerned?
- Become a teacher so the dream can live on.

There's nothing better than being a musician!
- We meet interesting people.
- Our career is our passion.
- We are always learning.
- Our music brings joy to us and to others.
- What we do really matters.
- We are so lucky!

I hope this book has given you lots of tricks to help you become happier
and more musical. Music has the power to lift your spirits, ease your fears,
calm your nerves, connect you with friends, and be there for you in the fun
times and the tough times. It's one of the greatest gifts you will ever be given,
so appreciate it and use it well. I wish you a life filled with the joy of music.

BONNIE

APPENDIX A

Music Theory Review

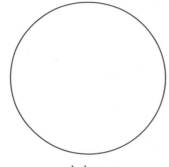

whole note

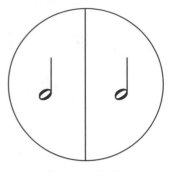

whole note = 2 half notes

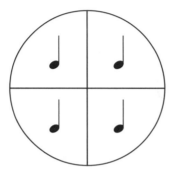

whole note = 4 quarter notes

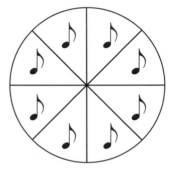

whole note = 8 eighth notes

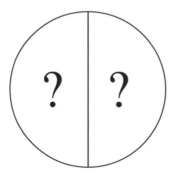

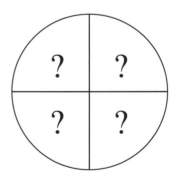

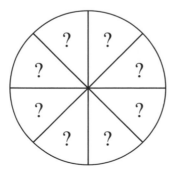

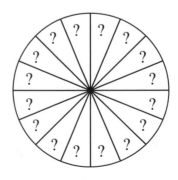

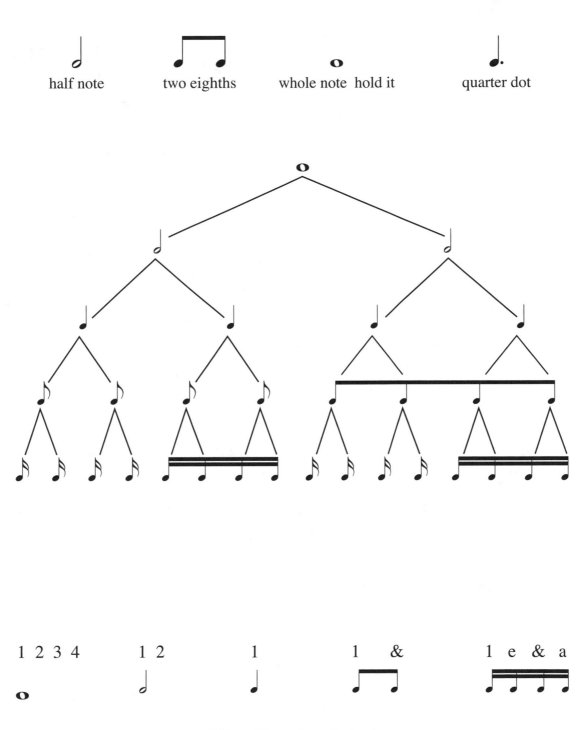

Different Ways to Count Out Loud

418

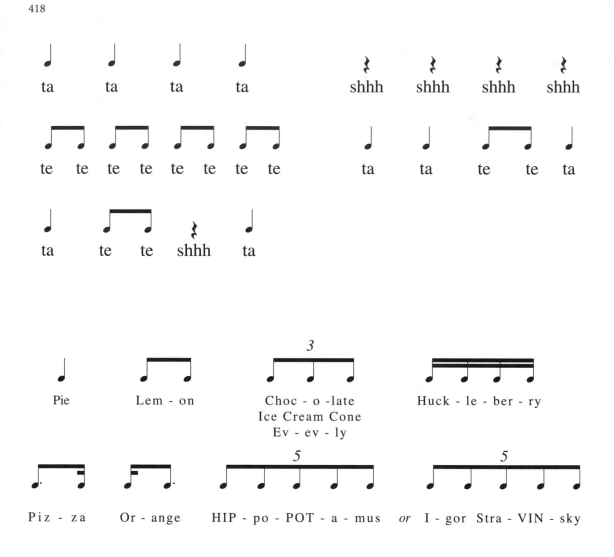

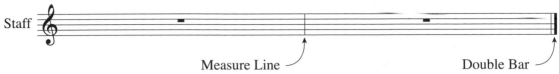

Staff

Measure Line

Double Bar

Examples:

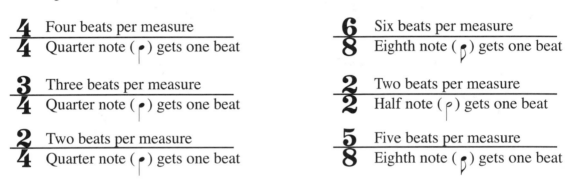

4/4 Four beats per measure Quarter note (♩) gets one beat	**6/8** Six beats per measure Eighth note (♪) gets one beat
3/4 Three beats per measure Quarter note (♩) gets one beat	**2/2** Two beats per measure Half note (♩) gets one beat
2/4 Two beats per measure Quarter note (♩) gets one beat	**5/8** Five beats per measure Eighth note (♪) gets one beat

Time Signatures

tonic   supertonic   mediant   subdominant   dominant   submediant   leading tone   tonic

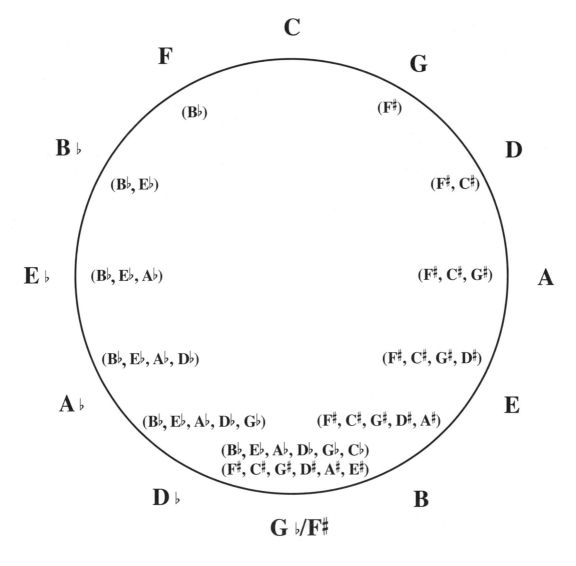

The Circle of Fifths

APPENDIX B

The Musical Periods

The Middle Ages
Before 1450
Hildegard of Bingen, Guillaume de Machaut, Guillaume Dufay, Josquim
Desprez

The Renaissance
1450–1600
Giovanni da Palestrina, William Byrd, Giovanni Gabrieli

The Baroque Period
1600–1750
Johann Sebastian Bach, Bach's sons—W. F., C. P. E, and J. C. Bach—
Arcangelo Corelli, François Couperin, Christoph Willibald Gluck,
George Frideric Handel, Claudio Monteverdi, Henry Purcell,
Domenico Scarlatti, Georg Philipp Telemann, Antonio Vivaldi

The Classical Period
1750–1820
Bach's sons again (see the Baroque period), Luigi Boccherini, Franz Joseph
Haydn, Wolfgang Amadeus Mozart, Franz Schubert, Ludwig van
Beethoven

The Romantic Period
1820–1910
Ludwig van Beethoven, Johannes Brahms, Frédéric Chopin, Antonín
Dvorak, Gabriel Fauré, Franz Liszt, Fanny Mendelssohn, Felix
Mendelssohn, Nikolai Rimsky-Korsakov, Clara Schumann, Robert
Schumann, Peter Ilyich Tchaikovsky, Giuseppe Verdi, Richard Wagner

The Impressionists
1860–1910
Claude Debussy, Maurice Ravel

The Contemporary Period
1911–1945

Samuel Barber, Béla Bartók, Amy Beach, George Gershwin, Paul Hindemith, Charles Ives, Francis Poulenc, Sergei Prokofiev, Sergei Rachmaninoff, Arnold Schoenberg, Dmitri Shostakovich, Igor Stravinsky

The Late Twentieth Century
1945–2000

Leonard Bernstein, Benjamin Britten, John Cage, Aaron Copland, Philip Glass, Joaquin Rodrigo, Joan Tower, Ellen Taaffe Zwilich

GLOSSARY OF MUSICAL TERMS

Music is a universal language, but the words written in music are usually Italian or French. Composers use these terms to tell you how to play. If you don't know what *largo, sostenuto,* and *dolce* mean, you may play a piece like a march instead of a lullaby. Instead of trying to memorize this long list, memorize the terms in each of your pieces, and you'll soon have a big vocabulary.

A

a cappella	Unaccompanied.
à la	In the manner of.
a piacere	At pleasure.
absolute music	Music that is not descriptive.
accelerando	Becoming faster.
accent	Emphasis or stress on one note.
accidentals	A sharp or flat in the piece that's not in the key signature.
adagio	A slow tempo between andante and largo.
affettuoso	Affectionately, with tenderness.
agitato	Excited.
air	A song or an aria.
al fine	To the end.
alla breve	In cut time, 2/2.
allargando	Slowing down, usually with an increase in volume.
allegretto	A little slower than allegro.
allegro	Lively and happy.
alto	Second highest part in four-part singing.
amabile	Lovingly.
andante	Walking speed.
andantino	A little faster than andante.
animato	Getting faster.
appoggiatura	To lean: a nonchord tone on a strong beat that resolves to a neighboring chord tone on a relatively weaker beat.

arco	With the bow.
aria	Vocal song from an opera.
arioso	A piece with a singing quality.
arpeggio	Chord that is "rolled," one note at a time.
art song	Song of a serious nature.
articulation	Tonguing and slurring, or the exact length of the note.
assai	Very, extremely.
atonality	Not in a particular key.
attacca	Go immediately on to the next movement.

B

bagatelle	A short light piece.
bass	Lowest part in four-part singing.
berceuse	Lullaby.
bourrée	A quick seventeenth-century dance.
brio	Vigor, spirit.

C

cadence	A chord progression at the end of the phrase giving a feeling of rest.
cadenza	In a concerto where the orchestra stops and the soloist shows off.
cantabile	Singingly.
coda	A short additional passage at the end.
common time	4/4 time.
con	With.
concerto	A piece for soloists and orchestra.
concerto grosso	A piece for two or more soloists.
consonance	Two notes that sound good together.
crescendo	Getting louder.
cut time	2/2 time.

D

da capo	Return to the beginning.
dal segno	Return to the sign.
decrescendo	Getting softer.
diatonic	Major and minor scales.
diminuendo	Getting softer.
dissonance	Two notes that clash.
dolce	Soft and sweet.
dominant	Fifth scale degree.
duet	Composition for two performers.
dynamics	Volume.

E

elegy	Piece with a mournful character.
embouchure	Position of the lips.

Glossary of Musical Terms

enharmonic	Two names for the same note.
ensemble	A group of performers playing together.
étude	A study piece.
exposition	Introduction of the theme in sonata form.

F

falsetto	Singing above the normal male range.
fantasy	Composition with a feeling of improvisation.
fermata	To hold a note longer than its value.
finale	Last movement of a piece.
flat	To lower a note one-half step.
forte	Loud.
forza	Force.
fugue	A polyphonic composition with the theme stated in three or more voices.

G

gavotte	A French dance in the Baroque period in modern 4/4 time.
gigue	A dance in a fast triple meter (usually 6/8).
giusto	Just right or in a strict tempo marking.
glissando	A slide of distinct notes.
grazioso	Gracefully.
Gregorian chant	Choral chants named after Pope Gregory (c. 540–604) used in the early Roman Catholic Church.
gross	Large.

H

Habanera	A Spanish flamenco dance.

I

improvisation	Creating your own spontaneous music.
intermezzo	A small work written between larger movements.
interval	Distance between two notes.
intonation	The act of playing or singing in tune, neither sharp nor flat.

J

jazz	Twentieth-century American music that includes ragtime, blues, swing, and bebop.
jig	Sixteenth-century English dance; known in France as a gigue.

K

key	Pertaining to a scale or tonal center.
key signature	Sharps or flats in a piece.

L

ländler	German popular dance, probably the origin of the waltz.
larghetto	A little faster than largo.
largo	Very slow and broad.
leading tone	The seventh scale degree; also known as the subtonic.
legato	Smooth.
leger lines	Short lines under or over the staff.
leggiero	Light.
lento	Slow.
lieder	German songs of the eighteenth and nineteenth centuries.

M

ma non	but not (ma non troppo = but not too much).
madrigal	Secular unaccompanied Renaissance vocal music for two or more voices.
maestro	Conductor.
maggiori (majeur)	In a major key.
mano	Hand.
marcato	Marked, accented.
martellato	Hammered.
marziale	Martial.
measure	The space between two bar lines.
mediant	Third scale degree.
melisma	Long melodic passage sung on one syllable.
meno	Less.
meter	The grouping of notes in a time signature.
mezzo	Medium.
mineur (minore)	In a minor key.
minuet	French dance in triple meter.
moderato	Medium tempo.
modulation	Change of key within a piece.
moll	Minor.
molto	Very much.
monotone	On one note.
mosso	Moved.
moto	Motion.

N

natural	Neither a sharp nor a flat.
neoclassicism	A movement in the twentieth century to imitate the Classical period of Haydn and Mozart.
nocturne	Night piece.
nonet	Music for nine instruments.

obbligato	An accompanying part.
octave	Interval of an eighth, such as from C to the next C.
octet	Music for eight instruments.
opera	Musical drama with singing throughout.
opera buffa	An Italian comic opera.
opera-comique	French opera that includes spoken dialogue.
operetta	A short, light opera.
opus	A numbered work.
oratorio	Music for solo voices, chorus, and orchestra on a religious theme performed in a concert setting without sets or costumes.
ornaments	Embellishments of the melody such as trills, turns, mordents, and appoggiaturas.
ostinato	A repeated melodic phrase.
overture	An introduction to an opera or oratorio.

P

passepied	A lively French dance in 3/8 or 6/8.
pastorale	Music depicting a pastoral scene (the outdoors).
pavane	Slow sixteenth-century dance.
pentatonic scale	Five-note scale.
pesante	Heavy.
phrase	Musical sentence.
piano	Soft.
piano trio	Ensemble of piano, violin, and cello.
più	More.
pizzicato	Plucking the strings rather than bowing.
plainsong	Gregorian chant.
poco	A little.
polonaise	Polish dance in 3/4.
polyphonic	Two or more interweaving melodic lines.
portamento	Sliding between notes.
presto	Very, very fast.
presto possible	As fast as possible.
program music	Music suggesting a person, place, event, or mood.

Q

quartet	Piece for four voices or instruments.
quasi	Almost.
quintet	Piece for five voices or instruments.
quintuple meter	Five beats to a measure.
quintuplet	Five notes to one beat.

R

rallentando	Slowing down.
refrain	Recurring section of music.

relative pitch	The ability to recognize one pitch after being given a first pitch.
replica	Repeat.
resolution	Going from a dissonance to a consonance.
retrograde	Going from the last note back to the first.
rigaudon	French seventeenth-century dance in 2/4 or 4/4.
rinforzando	Sudden accent.
ritardando	Gradually slowing down.
ritenuto	Slowing down.
rondo	Piece with a repeating theme (ABACA).
root	Note upon which a chord is built (C is the root of a C chord).
rubato	Freedom in tempo; taking time from one note and giving it to the next.
rumba	Cuban dance.

S

sarabande	Slow French dance from the Renaissance and Baroque periods.
scherzo	Joke.
scordato	Abnormal tuning of a stringed instrument for the purpose of producing some unusual note or changing the general tonal effect.
secco	Dry.
segno	Sign.
segue	Something follows.
semi	Half.
sempre	Always.
senza	Without.
septet	Music for seven voices or instruments.
sequence	A repeating pattern starting on different notes.
serenade	Evening music to be played outdoors.
sextet	Music for six voices.
sforzando	Sudden accent.
sharp	To raise a note one half-step.
shift	To change positions while playing a string instrument or trombone.
sight-read	To play without having seen the music previously.
simile	Similar.
sinfonietta	Small symphony.
slentando	Slowing down.
solfeggio	Using syllables for notes (do re mi fa sol la ti do).
sonata	Piece with three or four movements of contrasting speed.
soprano	Top voice in four-part singing.
sordino	A string mute.

sotto	With a soft sound (sotto voce).
staccato	Shorter than the rhythmic value of the note.
staff	Five parallel horizontal lines on which the notes are written.
stretto	Strain forward.
string quartet	Ensemble of two violins, a viola, and a cello.
string trio	Ensemble of violin, viola, and cello.
subdominant	Fourth scale degree.
subito	Suddenly.
submediant	Sixth scale degree.
suite	Set of Baroque dances played together.
supertonic	Second scale degree, or the note above the tonic.
syncopation	Accents on normally unaccented beats.

T

tacet	Silent.
tango	A modern Spanish ballroom dance.
tempo	Speed.
tempo giusto	Normal speed or a strict tempo.
tenor	Third highest part in four-part singing.
tenuto	Hold the full value of the note.
ternary	A musical form of three sections.
tertian	Harmony built on three-part chords.
tessitura	Vocal or instrumental range.
timbre	Tone color.
tonic	First scale degree.
transcription	Piece originally written for other instrumentation.
transition	Passage connecting two sections.
transposing instruments	Instruments for which music is written in a different key not in its real pitch.
transposition	Changing keys.
tremolo	Alternating rapidly between two pitches.
triplet	Three notes that get the same amount of time as two notes of the same value.
tritone	Augmented fourth.
troppo	Too much.

U

una corda	In piano, to use the soft pedal.
upbeat	Pickup. The first note of a phrase starting on any beat other than beat one.

V

valse	Waltz.
vespers	Evening church service.
vibrato	Small fluctuation of the pitch.

virtuoso	A person extremely skilled on the instrument.
vivace	Very fast.
vivo	Lively.
voce	Voice.

W

waltz	A dance in triple meter.
whole tone scale	A scale of whole steps.

READING, BROWSING, WATCHING, LISTENING

A List of References

Books Especially for Teens

Bachel, Beverly K. *What Do You Really Want? How to Set a Goal and Go for It*. Minneapolis: Free Spirit Press, 2001.

Benson, Peter L., Pamela Espeland, and Judy Galbraith. *What Teens Need to Succeed: Proven, Practical Ways to Shape Your Own Future*. Minneapolis: Free Spirit, 1998.

Bluestein, Jane, and Eric Katz. *High School's Not Forever*. Deerfield Beach, Fla.: HCI Teens, 2005.

Bolles, Richard Nelson, Carol Christen, and Jean M. Blomquist. *What Color Is Your Parachute? for Teens: Discovering Yourself, Defining Your Future*. Berkeley, Calif.: Ten Speed Press, 2006.

Canfield, Jack. *Chicken Soup for the Teen Soul: Real Life Stories by Real Teens*. Deerfield Beach, Fla.: Heath Communications, 2007.

Canfield, Jack, with Janet Switzer. *The Success Principles for Teens: How to Get from Where You Are to Where You Want to Be*. New York: Harper Collins, 2008.

Carlson, Richard. *Don't Sweat the Small Stuff for Teens: Simple Ways to Keep Your Cool in Stressful Times*. New York: MJF, 2009.

Covey, Sean. *The Seven Habits of Highly Effective Teens: The Ultimate Teenage Success Guide*. New York: Simon and Schuster, 1998.

Leslie, Roger. *Success Express for Teens: 50 Activities That Will Change Your Life*. Houston, Tex.: Bayou, 2004.

Meyer, Stephanie, and John Meyer, eds. *Teen Ink: Our Voices, Our Visions*. Deerfield Beach, Fla.: Heath, 2000.

Books Especially for Teen Musicians

Marsalis, Wynton. *Marsalis on Music*. New York: W. W. Norton, 1995.

Nathan, Amy. *The Young Musician's Survival Guide: Tips from Teens and Pros*. 2nd ed. New York: Oxford University Press, 2008.

Pinksterboer, Hugo. *Tipbook Music for Kids and Teens: A Guide for Parents and Caregivers*. The Netherlands: Tipbook, 2006.

Books on Music Performance

Bruckner, Susan. *The Whole Musician: A Multi-Sensory Guide to Practice, Performance, and Pedagogy.* Santa Cruz, Calif.: Effey Street Press, 2004.

Bruser, Madeline. *The Art of Practicing: A Guide to Making Music from the Heart.* New York: Bell Tower, 1997.

Goode, Michael I. *Stage Fright in a Musical Performance and Its Relationship to the Unconscious.* Oak Park, Ill.: Trumpetworks Press, 2003.

Gordon, Stewart. *Mastering the Art of Performance: A Primer for Musicians.* New York: Oxford University Press, 2006.

Green, Barry. *The Mastery of Music: Ten Pathways to True Artistry.* New York: Broadway Books, 2003.

Green, Barry, with W. Timothy Gallwey. *The Inner Game of Music.* Garden City, N.Y.: Anchor/Doubleday, 1986.

Greene, Don. *Audition Success: An Olympic Sports Psychologist Teaches Performing Artists How to Win.* New York: Routledge, 2001.

——. *Fight Your Fear and Win: Seven Skills for Performing Your Best under Pressure—at Work, in Sports, on Stage.* New York: Broadway Books, 2001.

——. *Performance Success: Performing Your Best under Pressure.* New York: Routledge, 2002.

Havas, Kató. *Stage Fright: Its Causes and Cures, with Special Reference to Violin Playing.* London: Bosworth, 1973.

Ristad, Eloise. *A Soprano on Her Head: Right-Side-Up Reflections on Life and Other Performances.* Moab, Utah: Real People Press, 1982.

Salmon, Paul G., and Robert G. Meyer. *Notes from the Green Room: Coping with Stress and Anxiety in Musical Performance.* New York: Publish America, 2005.

Schneiderman, Barbara. *Confident Music Performance: The Art of Preparing.* St. Louis, Mo.: iUniverse, 2008.

Westney, William. *The Perfect Wrong Note: Learning to Trust Your Musical Self.* Pompton Plains, N.J.: Amadeus Press, 2003.

Books especially for Singers

Adams, David. *A Handbook of Diction for Singers: Italian, German, French.* 2nd ed. New York: Oxford University Press, 2008.

Cook, Orlanda. *Singing with Your Own Voice: A Practical Guide to Awakening and Developing the Hidden Qualities in Your Own Singing.* New York: Routledge, 2004.

Hong-Young, Arabella. *Singing Professionally: Studying Singing for Singers and Actors.* Rev. ed. Portsmouth, N.H.: Heinemann, 2003.

Marquart, Linda. *The Right Way to Sing.* New York: St. Martin's Press, 2005.

Peckham, Anne. *Vocal Workouts for the Contemporary Singer.* Boston: Berklee Press, 2006.

Sheil, Richard F. *A Singer's Manuel of Foreign Language Dictions.* 6th ed. New York: YBK, 2004.

Books on Sight-Reading

Bona, Pasquale, and Th. Baker. *Bona: Rhythmical Articulation.* Milwaukee: Hal Leonard, 1997.

Hess, Gary. *Encyclopedia of Reading Rhythms: Text and Workbook for All Instruments.* Hollywood: Musicians Institute Press, 1997.

O'Reilly, Sally. *String Rhythms: For Classroom or Individual Study.* San Diego, Calif.: Neil A. Kjos, 1992.

Richman, Howard. *Super Sight-Reading Secrets: An Innovative, Step-by-Step Program for Keyboard Players of All Levels.* 3rd rev. ed. Tarzana, Calif.: Sound Feelings, 1986.

Sources for Music Theory

Alfred's Essentials of Music Theory (book and computer program). Van Nuys, Calif.: Alfred Pub. Co., 1998–2004.

Kolb, Tom. *Music Theory for Guitar: Everything You Ever Wanted to Know but Were Afraid to Ask.* Milwaukee, Wisc.: Hal Leonard, 2006.

Miller, Michael. *The Complete Idiot's Guide to Music Theory.* New York: Penguin Group, 2002.

Pilhofer, Michael, and Holly Day. *Music Theory for Dummies.* Indianapolis: Wiley, 2007.

Sueta, Ed. *Rhythm Vocabulary Charts.* N.p.: published by author, 1986.

www.musictheory.net.

Books on Making Music

Bernstein, Seymour. *With Your Own Two Hands: Self-Discovery through Music.* New York: Schirmer, 1981.

Cannel, Ward, and Fred Marx. *How to Play the Piano Despite Years of Lessons: What Music Is and How to Make It at Home.* Garden City, N.Y.: Doubleday, 1976.

Holt, John Caldwell. *Never Too Late: My Musical Life Story.* Reading, Mass.: Addison-Wesley, 1991.

Johnston, Philip. *The Practice Revolution.* Canberra, Australia: PracticeSpot Press, 2002.

———. *Practiceopedia: The Music Student's Illustrated Guide to Practicing.* Canberra, Australia: PracticeSpot Press Pearce ACT, 2007.

Johnston, Philip, and David Sutton. *Not Until You've Done Your Practice: The Classic Survival Guide for Kids Who Are Learning a Musical Instrument but Hate Practicing.* Pearce, Australia: PracticeSpot Press, 2004.

Jordan, James. *The Musician's Walk: An Ethical Labyrinth.* Chicago: GIA, 2006.

Jourdain, Robert. *Music, the Brain, and Ecstasy: How Music Captures Our Imagination.* New York: William Morrow, 1998.

Judy, Stephanie. *Making Music for the Joy of It: Enhancing Creativity, Skills, and Musical Confidence.* Los Angeles: J. P. Tarcher, 1990.

Kogan, Judith. *Nothing but the Best: The Struggle for Perfection at the Juilliard School.* New York: Limelight Editions, 1989.

Shockley, Rebecca Payne. *Mapping Music: For Faster Learning and Secure Memory—A Guide for Teachers and Students.* Middleton, Wisc.: A-R Editions, 2001.

Werner, Kenny. *Effortless Mastery: Liberating the Master Musician Within.* New Albany, Ind.: Jamey Aebersold, 1996.

Books on the Music Business

Beeching, Angela Myles. *Beyond Talent: Creating a Successful Career in Music.* Oxford: Oxford University Press, 2005.

Butler, Mimi. *The Complete Guide to Making More Money in the Private Music Studio.* Haddonfield, N.J.: published by author, 2002.

——. *The Complete Guide to Running a Private Music Studio.* Haddonfield, N.J.: published by author, 2001.

Newsam, David R., and Barbara Sprague Newsam. *Making Money Teaching Music.* Cincinnati, Ohio: Writer's Digest Books, 2002.

Books on Music History

Barber, David. *Bach, Beethoven, and the Boys: Music History as It Ought to Be Taught.* Toronto: Sound and Vision, 1996.

Krull, Kathleen. *Lives of the Musicians: Good Times, Bad Times (and What the Neighbors Thought).* San Diego, Calif.: Harcourt, 2002.

Levine, Robert. *Story of the Orchestra: Listen While You Learn about the Instruments, the Music, and the Composers Who Wrote the Music.* New York: Black Dog and Leventhal, 2001.

Libbey, Ted. *The NPR Guide to Building a Classical CD Collection: The 350 Essential Works.* New York: Workman, 1999.

Pogue, David, and Scott Speck. *Classical Music for Dummies.* Foster City, Calif.: IDG Books Worldwide, 1997.

Sherman, Robert. *The Complete Idiot's Guide to Classical Music.* New York: Alpha Books, 1997.

Stanley, John. *Classical Music: The Great Composers and Their Masterworks.* Birkenhead, Auckland, New Zealand: Reed Consumer Books, 2004.

Motivational Books

Carnegie, Dale. *How to Enjoy Your Life and Your Job.* London: Cedar, 1989.

——. *How to Win Friends and Influence People.* London: Vermillion, 2006.

Covey, Stephan. *The Seven Habits of Highly Effective People: Restoring the Character Ethic.* New York: Simon and Schuster, 1989.

——. *The Speed of Trust: The One Thing That Changes Everything.* New York: Free Press, 2008.

Lowndes, Leil. *Good-bye to Shy: 85 Shybusters That Work!* New York: McGraw-Hill, 2006.

——. *How to Talk to Anyone: Ninety-two Little Tricks for Big Success in Relationships.* Chicago: Contemporary Books, 2003.

McGinnis, Alan Loy. *Bringing Out the Best in People: How to Enjoy Helping Others Excel.* Minneapolis: Augsberg, 1985.

Peale, Norman Vincent. *The Power of Positive Thinking.* Running Press, 2002.

Scott, Steven K. *Simple Steps to Impossible Dreams: The 15 Power Secrets of the World's Most Successful People.* New York: Fireside, Simon and Schuster, 1999.

Urban, Hal. *Positive Words, Powerful Results: Simple Ways to Honor, Affirm, and Celebrate Life.* New York: Fireside, Simon and Schuster, 2004.

Books on Keeping Healthy while Playing

Dawson, William J. *Fit as a Fiddle: The Musician's Guide to Playing Healthy.* Lanham, Md.: Rowman and Littlefield Education Publishing Group, 2008.

Horvath, Janet. *Playing Less Hurt: An Injury Prevention Guide for Musicians.* Rev. ed. Minneapolis: J. Horvath, 2004.

King, Vicki. *Playing the Piano Naturally.* Natchitoches, La.: Conners, 1999.

Llobet, Jaume Rossett. *The Musician's Body: A Maintenance Manual for Peak Performance.* Ed. George Odam. London: Guildhall School of Music and Drama; Burlington, Vt.: Ashgate, 2007.

Strings Magazine. *Healthy String Playing: Physical Wellness Tips from the Pages of Strings Magazine.* Milwaukee: Hal Leonard, 2007.

Jazz and Blues Books

Hunt, Chris. *Blues by the Bar: Cool Riffs That Sound Great over Each Portion of the Blues Progression.* Milwaukee, Wisc.: Hal Leonard/Cherry Lane Music, 2002.

Marsalis, Wynton. *To a Young Musician: Letters from the Road.* New York: Random House, 2005.

Ratliff, Ben. *The Jazz Ear: Conversations over Music.* New York: Times Books, 2008.

Szwed, John. *Jazz 101: A Complete Guide to Learning and Loving Jazz.* New York: Hyperion, 2000.

Magazines

Acoustic Guitar	*Grooves*
All about Jazz	*Guitar One*
American Harp Journal	*Guitar Player*
American Music Teacher	*Guitar World*
American Songwriter	*Harp Column*
Bass Player	*Harp Journal*
Bottom Line	*Instrumentalist*
Brass Player	*Keyboard*
Clavier Companion	*Keyboard Player*
Clavier's Piano Explorer (for young people)	*Modern Drummer*
	Opera News
Computer Music Journal	*Performing Songwriter*
Double Reed	*Piano Today*
Downbeat	*Sheet Music Magazine*
Electronic Musician	*Songlines*
Fiddler	*Songwriter*
Flute Talk	*Stick It!*
Flutist Quarterly	*Strings*
Future Music	*Windplayer*

Visit http://library.music.indiana.edu/music_resources/journals.html to see a listing of hundreds of music journals and magazines, newspapers, and other periodicals.

Especially for Singers

www.classicalsinger.com
www.harmetz.com/soprano/singing/links.htm
www.operabuffs.org/
www.operatoday.com:
www.vocalimages.com

Electronic Music

http://audacity.sourceforg/e.net: Free cross-platform sound editor
www.copyright.gov/circs/circ50.html Copyright reg-
   istration for musical composition
www.freesound.iua.upf.edu
www.mfiles.co.uk.mp3-files.htm: computer simulated music
www.purevolume.com: Post songs and discover new music and artists
www.splicemusic.com:/makemusic/intro

Jazz Websites

www.Allaboutjazz.com
www.jazzimprov.com
www.jazz.com

Rock and Rhythm & Blues

www.classicbluesradio.org
www.garageband.com:/htdb/popup/tour.html
www.mudcat.org
www.rockonthenet.com

World Music and Beyond

www.futuremusic.com
www.globalrhythm.net
www.icebergradio.com
www.jambands.com

Orchestras and Instruments

www.bbc.co.uk/orchestras/play/musical games
www.bsokids.com (Baltimore Symphony Orchestra)
www.classicsforkids.com:/stations
www.dso.kids.com (Dallas Symphony Orchestra)
www.kennedy-center.org//nso/orchestra
www.msokids.homestead.com (Memphis Symphony Orchestra)
www.nyphilkids.org (New York Philharmonic)
www.philharmonia.co.uk/thesoundexchange
www.playmusic.org (League of American Orchestras)
www.sfskids.org (San Francisco Symphony)
www.tucsonsymphony.org//kids

Music Video Websites

www.video.google.com
www.metacafe.com
www.YouTube.com

Music Subscription Websites

www.napster.com
www.naxosradio.com
www.rhapsody.com

Classical Music Websites

http://classicalwebcast.com
www.classicalarchives.com
www.classiccat.net
www.bbc.co.uk/radio3/classical/index.shtml
www.contemporary-classical.com
www.kdfc.com (San Francisco)
www.king.org (Seattle)
www.kmozart.com
www.mymusicstream.com/music
www.wcrb.com/html/index.html

Music Collaboration Websites

http://creativecommons.org/
Imusicscene (also known as MIXposure): www.imusicscene.com/
Kompoz: www.kompoz.com/compose-collaborate/home.music
Musicians Collaboration Studio: www.musicianscollaboration
    .com/forum/index.php
V-Band.de www.v-band.de/

Music Associations and Their Websites

American Guitar Society: www.americanguitarsociety.org
American Harp Society: www.harpsociety.org
American Pianists Society: www.americanpianists.org
American String Teachers Association: www.astaweb.com
American Viola Association: www.americanviolasociety.org
Dalcroze Society of America: www.dalcrozeusa.org
Guitar Foundation of America: www.guitarfoundation.org
International Clarinet Association: www.clarinet.org
International Horn Society: www.hornsociety.org
International Society for Bassists: www.isbworldoffice.com
International Society of Bassists: www.isbworldoffice.com/
International Trombone Association: www.trombone.org
International Trumpet Guild: www.trumpetguild.org
Internet Cello Society: www.cello.org
Music Teachers National Association: www.mtna.org
National Flute Association: www.nfaonline.org
National Guild of Community Music Schools: www.nationalguild.org
National Piano Foundation: www.pianonet.com
New Directions Cello Association: www.newdirectionscello.org
North American Saxophone Alliance: www.saxalliance.org
Percussive Arts Society: www.pas.org
Tuba Universal Brotherhood Association: www.tubaonline.org
Violin Society of American: www.vsa.to

Teen Radio Show

www.fromthetop.org/

Movies with Wonderful Music

Almost Famous	*Phantom of the Opera*
Amadeus	*The Pianist*
August Rush	*Rattle and Hum*
Baton Bunny	*Ray*
The Blues Brothers	*The Red Violin*
Coal Miner's Daughter	*Rent*
De-Lovely	*Rock 'n' Roll High School*
Don't Look Back	*The Rose*
Drumline	*Round Midnight*
Fabulous Baker Boys	*Saturday Night Fever*
Fame	*School of Rock*
Fantasia	*Shine*
Gone with the Wind	*The Soloist*
High School Musical	*Sound of Music*
Immortal Beloved	*Standing in the Shadows of Motown*
Jazz Singer	*Super Fly*
Krush Groove	*That Thing You Do!*
La Bamba	*Thing Called Love: Stand*
Lady Sings the Blues	*by Your Dream*
Light of Day	*This Is Spinal Tap: A Rockumentary*
Mama, I Want to Sing!	*Walk the Line*
Mr. Holland's Opus	*West Side Story*
The Music Man	*What's Love Got to Do with It?*
Music of the Heart	*The Who: The Kids Are Alright*
Notorious	*Why Do Fools Fall in Love?*
Peter and the Wolf	*Yellow Submarine*

Movies Featuring Classical Music

2001: A Space Odyssey	*Philadelphia*
Ace Ventura: Pet Detective	*Platoon*
Ace Ventura: When Nature Calls	*Pretty Woman*
Alien	*Primal Fear*
Fabulous Baker Boys	*Psycho*
George of the Jungle	*Rollerball*
Godfather	*Romy and Michele's High*
Goodwill Hunting	*School Reunion*
Kill Bill: Vol. 2	*Room with a View*
Lorenzo's Oil	*Schindler's List*
Master and Commander: The	*The Shining*
Far Side of the World	*Sleeping with the Enemy*
Misery	*Somewhere in Time*
Mrs. Doubtfire	*Sophie's Choice*
My Dinner with Andre	*Sour Grapes*
My Favorite Martian	*Star Trek: Insurrection*
My Geisha	*Titanic*
Out of Africa	*Truman Show*
Patch Adams	*V for Vendetta*

INDEX

Italicized page numbers indicate figures.

accents, 229, 230, 234
accidentals, 214, 236
accompanists, 266, 400
acting classes, 231
adjudication. *See* auditions; contests
adrenaline, 268
advice from students, 285–88, 324–31
air stream, 230, 235, 291
Alexander Technique, 261
Amadeus, 182
American Idol, 68, 83, 195
Annie, 70
anxiety. *See* stage fright
appoggiatura, 234
arias, 232
arpeggios, 3, 153–60, 216, 222, 239
articulation, 110, 115–16, 229–30, 236, 340, 345
asthma, 262
attitude:
    believe in yourself, 79–81
    positive self-talk, 80
    sight-reading, 214
    take responsibility, 80–81, 250–51, 338, 411
audiences:
    communicate with, 231–32, 238, 250, 260
    concert behavior, 350
    eye contact, 242, 271
    friend or foe, 254–55, 259–60
    practice and rehearsals, 231–32
    response, 18, 71–72, 75, 259–60
auditions (*also see* goals; performances), 266–73
    be prepared, 266, 375, 377–78, 386–87, 389
    blind auditions, 311–12

choice of material, 387
conservatories, 361–62
experience of, 393–94
instant replay, 393
instrument quality, 22, 24
judges and adjudicators, 249, 251
orchestra, 386–95, *394*
performance day, 266, 267, 269, 391
pre-performance routine, 269–70
by recording, 378
role-playing, 255–56
sample questions, 382
tips for success, 269–72, 377–81, 386, 390–93
vocal, 388
what is looked for, 380–82, 389–90
when you struggle, 266–67
you're on, 270–72

Bach, Beethoven and the Boys (Barber), 361
Bach, Johann Sebastian, 172, 178–79, 223
bananas, 262, 267
bands. *See* marching bands; rock music/musicians
Baroque period, 178–80, 236, 421
barter system, 47
Beatles songs, 193, 199
Beethoven, Ludwig von, 10, 171, 183–84, 198, 229
beginners:
    practice tips, 15, 114–15
    top mistakes, 12–19
beta blockers, 262
biofeedback, 262
blues music, 195, 435, 436
body and body language (*also see* health; physiology; posture):
    cold and shaky hands, 261

body and body language *continued*:
    musicality, 227, 230
    neck and shoulder tension, 261
    pain from braces, 290–92
    protect voice, 72–73, 75
    self-confidence, 256
    singers, 68
    stage fright symptoms, 260–61
boredom:
    in bands and orchestras, 311, 344,
        346–47
    classical music, 192
    monotonous music, 303
    during practice, 192, 300, 313
    questions from students, 311, 313
    quitting because of, 294–95
    tips for overcoming, 346–47
braces, 289–92, 298
brass instruments, 34, 289
breathing, 75, 116, 232–33, 260, 269–71
burn out, 314–15, 322–23

cadences, 165, 234, 239
caffeine, 72
calendars, 93, 100
calming agents, 260, 262, 269–70
Catholic Church music, 173–76
CDs/DVDs, 44, 48, 69, 108, 119, 193, 389
cell phones, 344, 350
cello (*also see* instruments), 214, 221, 309,
    315, 337–38, 378–79
chamber music, 336–37
chapped lips, 261
chess, 188
children, 70
choral groups, xii, 70, 193, 358, 398
chords, 142–44, 153–60, 162–65, 215–16,
    234, 239
chromatic scales, 130–31, 221, 228
chunking, 84–85, 106–107, 118
churches:
    church choirs, xiii, 68, 74, 241, 255, 361
    job opportunities, 371, 398, 400, 401, 405
    music history, 173–77, 192
clarinet (*also see* instruments), 17, 21–24, 47
classical music (*also see* music history),
    171–208
    learning to love it, 18, 193–96, 198
    mood music, 198–99
    movie list, 438
    soundtracks, 191, 195
    stereotypes, 191–93
    traditions, 348–49
    websites, 198, 437
    why listen, 191–97

Classical Music for Dummies (Pogue and
    Speck), 361
classical music lists, 199–208
    composers, 201–208
    dramatic music, 200
    favorites, 200
    movie scores, 199–200
    wedding favorites, 201
Classical period, 181–82, 236, 421
clefs, 214, 215
clothing, 263–64, 349, 380
colleges/conservatories, 364–85
    applications, 372–73
    auditions, 375, 377–78
    college programs, 365–68, 373, 379,
        392, 401
    conservatory programs, 359, 364–65,
        366–67
    credit hours, 359–60
    facilities, 368–70
    loans and scholarships, 371
    music majors, 357–58
    "partner schools," 362
    preparation for, 362, 370, 377
    resources for choosing, 384
    resumé, 383–84
    school visits, 375
    teacher-student relationship, 372,
        375–76
    teaching quality, 365–66
    tips for success, 361–62, 363, 370
    trial lesson, 375–77, 380
commitment:
    instruments, 25–28
    music, 6, 324–31
    practice, 28, 79–81, 101–103, 110, 117–19,
        281, 314–15
community colleges, 47, 48, 360
community musicals, 74
community orchestras, 398
competition. *See* contests
composers:
    Baroque, 180
    Classical, 182
    Contemporary, 188–89, 190
    Middle Ages, 174
    Renaissance, 176
    Romantic, 185
concertos, 178
concerts:
    audience behavior, 350
    classical and rock compared, 349–52
    concert etiquette, 247–51, 349–50
    concert programs, 350
    crossover artists, 352

decibel levels, 351–52
family concerts, 295, 322
food and drink, 350
history, 181–82, 184
tickets/seating, 349–50
what to wear, 349
when to applaud, 351
who not to bring, 349
why participate, 247–48
conducting/conductors, 231, 233
confidence, 12–13, 231, 247, 255–57, 271,
    309–10, 314
conservatories. *See* colleges/conservatories
Contemporary period, 187–90, 422
contests (*also see* performances; stage
    fright), 247–51
    college applications, 248
    dress for success, 263–64
    feedback, 49
    importance of, 49, 247–48
    judges and adjudicators, 249, 251
    living through failures, 312, 313
    preparing for, 249, 250, 313
    questions from students, 312, 313, 315
    rehearsals, 60, 266
    stage fright, 315
    time management, 247
    what makes a winner, 249–50
counting:
    beats per measure, 419
    measures, 338, 343
    notes, 50, 417–18
country music, 18
crescendos, 225, 226, 228–29, 233, 234
crossover artists, 352

dairy products, 267
dance suites, 178
day-planners, 93
deadlines, 100
decibel levels, 351–52
diminished chords, 157
diminuendo, 228–29
dissonance, 234
distractions, 257–58
driver's license, 277–78
dry mouth, 260
DVDs/CDs, 44, 48, 69, 108, 119, 193, 389
dynamics, 116, 117, 227–29, 233, 340, 345

ear, nose, throat doctors (ENTs), 72, 74
ear training, 361
Eastman School of Music, 365, 367, 368, 392
eBay, 30, 32–33
electric guitar, 309

electronic games, 92
electronic keyboards, 22, 24
electronic music websites, 436
electronic tuners, 221
embouchure, 290
emotion:
    dynamics, 227–29
    ensembles, 340
    musicality, 225
    playing with, 230–31, 235
enharmonics, 127–30
ensembles (*also see* marching bands; or-
    chestras), 335–52
    balance and tone, 236, 340–41, 345
    be a good team member, 338–44
    be professional, 344, 345
    boredom, 311, 344, 346–47
    chamber music, 336–37
    dynamics, 340, 345
    fake it, 343
    how to start and stop, 341–42
    know the music, 342–43, 345
    mistakes, 344
    number the measures, 338, 342, 343
    phrasing, 345
    pitch, 340
    rehearsals, 337–38
    schedules and goals, 338–39, 345
    tips for success, 346–47
    tuning, 221, 337–38
ethnic music, 364
etiquette:
    concerts, 348–52
    ensembles, 343–44
études, 3, 107, 303, 313
expectations (*also see* frustration), 13–14,
    16, 53, 294
"extreme music," 346

failures, living through, 247–48, 250–51,
    257, 301–302, 312, 313
faking it, 215–16, 343
family life, 280–82, 295, 312, 322
fear factor. *See* stage fright
feedback, 49, 251, 255
fermatas, 119, 229
figured bass, 164–65
fingering, 3, 46, 116, 214, 220, 235
flow charts, 100
flute/flute players (*also see* instruments; les-
    sons), 3, 8, 220, 229, 292, 316
focus:
    goals, 82–83, 87
    practice sessions, 59, 60, 102–104, 116,
        320

folk music, 174, 184, 195, 222
food and drink, 72, 262, 267, 350
forte, 229
French horn, 17, 23–24, 177
frustration (*also see* guide for parents and students):
    changing teachers, xi–xii, 320–21
    discouragement, 13–14
    impatience, 101
    lack of progress, 15–16
    learning pace, 302–303
    making mistakes, 310–11, 319
    quitting, 12–14, 293–308, 314

glossary of musical terms, 423–31
goals:
    10 action steps, 82–89
    anticipate obstacles, 87–88
    auditions, 83, 86
    chunking, 84–85
    ensembles, 338
    goal-setting mistakes, 86–87
    long-term/short-term, 83–84, 93, 100, 294
    memorization, 240
    musical goals, 85
    outcome goals, 83, 88
    performance goals, 83, 86, 247, 254
    plan for success, 82
    practice goals, 93, 95–96, 100, 102
    priorities and deadlines, 87
    technical goals, 85
    write them down, 84, 87
gospel music, 195
great ideas (*also see* tips for success):
    auditions, 273, 395
    buying an instrument, 28, 38
    college preparation, 363, 374, 385
    help from parents, 284, 288
    performances, 265
    practicing, 97, 112–13
    setting goals, 89
    sight-reading, 216–17
greatest hits:
    Baroque, 180–81
    Classical, 182
    Contemporary, 189
    Middle Ages, 174
    Renaissance, 176
    Romantic, 185–86
Gregorian chants, 175
group lessons, 53, 54
gruppetto, 111
guide for parents and students, 277–84
    communication, 278

levels of parental involvement, 282–83, 285–86
    music lessons, 278–79
    practice schedules, 280
    resolving problems, 281–82
    reward good work, 280–81
guitar, 25, 46, 51, 220

Handel, George Frederic, 178–79, 282
hard work (*also see* goals):
    advice from students, 324–31
    sight-reading, 214
    and talent, 10
    work ethic, 5–6, 381
harmony, 111, 173–74
Haydn, Franz Joseph, 181–82
health (*also see* body and body language; physiology; posture):
    book list, 434–35
    calming methods, 260, 262, 269–70
    hydration, 267–68
    nutrition, 72, 262, 267–68, 391
    sleep and exercise, 99, 264, 267–68
helicopter parents, 283
hiccups, 260
hip-hop music, 18
home schooling, 360
hospitals, 255
human voice, instruments imitate, 227
hydration, 267–68

Idiot's Guide for Music (Miller), 361
immersion training, 194
Impressionist music, 187–90
independence, need for, 300–301
Inderal, 262
instruments:
    age of, 23, 30
    "authentic" instruments, 179
    casual playing, 26
    choice, 17–18, 21–27, 34, 36, 304, 309, 321–22, 360–61
    commitment to, 25–28
    design and technology, 23, 175, 177, 179
    handling, 234–35, 271, 310
    history, 177–79, 184, 188
    imitate human voice, 227
    insurance, 25, 37
    level and variations, 20, 21, 25–26, 34
    marching bands, 21–22, 26, 35, 304
    problems, 303–304
    quality, 3, 17, 20, 22–24
    simulated, 22, 24
    student questions, 309, 311, 321–22
    tone and pitch, 26, 27, 220

upgrading, 22, 24–26, 34
voice training, 70
warranties, 29
websites, 31, 436
instruments, purchasing, 29–38
advertisements and sales, 30
on approval, 35
brand names, 34
catalogs, 23, 26–27
cost and financing plans, 21, 24, 30, 33, 35, 36, 55
demonstrations, 27
fairs, 26–27
family fairness, 23, 55
as investment, 27, 34, 35
loaners, 23–24, 33
maker reputation, 21
music stores, 30, 31–32, 36
new or used, 25, 29–30, 35, 36–37
online, 30–33, 35
reasons to purchase, 20–28
rentals, 22, 25, 27, 33–34, 36
repair/trade-in policies, 36
resale, 21–22, 24, 25, 26, 29, 35
researching, 22, 30–31, 36, 37
student models, 34
when to purchase, 34–37
interactive DVDs and CDs, 44, 48, 69
internet:
instrument purchases, 30–33, 35, 37
interactive lessons, 48, 69
music stores, 198
time spent on, 92
websites, 30, 31, 32, 37, 75, 198, 384
YouTube, 198, 230, 352
interpretation, 67, 68, 225, 227–29, 345, 392
intervals, 127, 139–52, 155–56, 220, 226, 239
intonation, 108, 116, 218–22, 221
inversions, 162–64
iPods, 192

jazz, 17, 195, 303, 314, 364, 402, 435, 436
jealousy, 317, 318–19, 343
Journal of Voice (NATS), 75
judges and adjudicators, 249, 251

kettledrums, 177–78
key changes, 214, 239
key signatures, 132–38, 149–52, 188, 214
kinesthetic memory, 102

Led Zeppelin, 51, 199
Lee, Bruce, 10, 82
leitmotifs, 185

lessons (*also see* practice; singers; student–teacher relationship; teachers), 41–75
advice from students, 324–31
attendance, 59, 71, 90–91
boredom, 313
cancellation, 57
computer programs, 48
content, 294–95, 305–306, 311, 317, 321, 323
creativity, 55
electronic, 44, 48, 69
financial arrangements, 47–48, 59
group lessons, 48, 53, 54
learning pace, 302–303
length, 48
location, 47, 48, 53–54
long-term value, 6, 46–47, 55, 326–31
makeup lessons, 57
memorizing, 238, 240, 311
parents attending, 286–88, 301
preparation, 45, 47, 59–60
private lessons, 43–49, 53
recording, 71, 311
scheduling, 48, 57, 339
scholarships, 48
school programs, 44–46, 48, 54
self motivation, 48, 49
self-teaching, 43, 44, 46, 47, 48–49
trial lessons, 57, 375–77, 380, 382
libraries, 255, 370
listening:
classical music, 191–208, 361
contests and ensembles, 49, 219, 336, 339–41, 343, 390
and memorization, 239, 240
for musicality, 117, 224–25, 233
practice sessions, 5, 108, 115, 119
recordings and concerts, xviii, 48, 70, 74, 85, 172–73, 291, 315
lists:
choral music, 201, 202, 205
classical music, 199–208
composers by period, 174, 176, 180, 182, 185, 188–89, 190, 201–208
movies, 438
music books by subject, 431–35
music careers, 404–406
music magazines, 435
music professions, 404–406
music schools, 373
realities of self-employment, 408–10
references, 431–38
top 10 mistakes, 19
top U.S. colleges, 373
websites, 435–37

long-distance runners, 253
loud playing, 228

major chords, 156
major scales, 132–34
mantras, 264
marching bands (*also see* school music programs):
  instruments, 21–22, 26, 35, 304
  membership, 305, 335, 346–47, 362
  solo parts, 311–12
master classes, 52
meditation, 262
memorizing, 238–42, 311, 346
memory lapses, 241
memory test, 240–41
mentors, 398, 403–404
metal music, 195
metronomes, 104, 107, 115, 116, 119, 220
Metropolitan Opera House, 74
Middle Ages, 174, 421
minor chords, 156–57
minor scales, 148–52
mistakes:
  covering, 272
  ensembles, 344
  marking, 104–105, 110, 116, 309, 310–11, 319
  overcoming, 319
  questions from students, 309, 310–11, 319
  top beginning mistakes, 12–19
mnemonics, 134, 137, 190
mood, creating, 230
motivation:
  book list, 434
  lessons, 47
  owning your instrument, 34
  self motivation, 15–17, 48
  setting small goals, 102
  teachers' role, 50, 55
mouthpieces, 34, 289, 292
movie lists, 438
Mozart, Wolfgang Amadeus, 9–10, 101, 171, 182
music (*also see* classical music; concerts):
  choice, 305–306, 320
  commitment, 6, 324–31
  emotion, 196, 225, 227–29, 230–31
  life-lessons, 411–13
  motion, 225–27
  movie lists, 438
  and painting, 187
  value, 326–31, 335–45, 397
music, marking:
  breaths, 116

measures, 105, 116, 215, 338, 342
mistakes, 104–105, 110, 116, 309–11, 319
numbering system, 240
music associations:
  Music Teachers National Association (MTNA), 47, 56
  National Association for Music Education, 384
  National Association of Teachers of Singing (NATS), 75
  websites, 437
music careers, 396–413
  be business-minded, 398–99, 404
  book list, 433–34
  career paths, 397–401, 404–406
  finding a job, 397–99
  freelance, 184, 400
  history, 174–75
  patrons, 175, 181–82
  personal experiences, xi–xiii, 401–404, 407–10, 411–13
  reality of jobs, 396–97
  self-employment, 408–10, 413
  tips for success, 397–99, 403–404, 411–13
music collaboration websites, 437
Music for Life program, 48
music history, 171–90
  Baroque, 178–79, 421
  book list, 434
  churches, 173–74, 175, 176, 177, 192
  Classical, 181–82, 236, 421
  concerts, 181–82, 184
  Contemporary, 187–90, 422
  Gregorian chants, 173–74, 175
  Impressionist, 187–90, 421
  innovations, 176–79, 184, 188
  instruments, 177–78, 179, 184, 188
  Late Twentieth Century, 190, 422
  Middle Ages, 174, 421
  music periods, 172–73, 194
  music professions, 174–75
  nationalism, 171, 184
  neoclassical, 187
  orchestras, 177, 181–82
  patrons, 175, 181–82
  Renaissance, 175–76, 236, 421
  Romantic, 183–86, 236, 421
  string instruments, 177–78
  written music, 176
Music Link scholarship programs, 47
music magazines, 75, 352, 435
music majors (*also see* colleges/conservatories), 357–63
  auditions, 361–63

degrees offered, 358
how long to graduate, 359–60
music schools, 365–68, 373, 392
preparation, 358–61
Music Minus One CDs, 108, 119
music schools, 365–68, 373, 392
music staffs, 174, 214, 215
music stores:
    instrument purchasing, 22, 29, 31–33
    music lessons, 54, 56
    online, 198
music subscription websites, 436
Music Teachers National Association
    (MTNA), 47, 56
music theory, 125–66
    arpeggios, 3, 153–60, 216, 222, 239
    book list, 433
    cadences, 165, 234, 239
    chords, 142–44, 153–60, 162–65, 234, 239
    circle of fifths, 420
    courses in, 360
    dissonance, 147
    enharmonics, 127–30
    figured bass, 164–65
    intervals, 127, 139–52, 155–56, 220, 226, 239
    inversions, 162–64
    key signatures, 132–38, 149–52, 188
    musicality, 233–34
    review, 415–20
    scales, 3, 130–38, 148–52, 164–65, 187, 221, 228
    sharps and flats, 127, 134–38, 161
    structure, 233–34
    time signatures, 419
music video websites, 436
musical maturity, 251
musical sequences, 233
musical skills (*also see* musicality; performances; practice), 213–42
    book list, 433
    intonation, 218–22
    memorizing, 238–42
    pitch, 219–20
    sight-reading, 3, 100, 194, 213–17, 295, 346, 386
    technique and expression, 3, 223–34, 303
musical terms defined, 423–31
musicality, 223–37
    accents, 229, 230, 234
    arpeggios, 3, 153–60, 216, 222, 239
    articulation, 110, 115, 116, 229, 230, 236, 340, 345
    crescendos, 225, 226, 228–29, 233, 234
    diminuendo, 228–29

dynamics, 116, 117, 227–29, 233, 340, 345
    phrasing, 115, 116, 226–30, 233, 234, 236, 239–40, 345
    technique and expression, 3, 223–34, 303
    tips for success, 3, 224–26, 230–31
    tone color, 229, 235, 340

National Academy of Recording Arts and
    Sciences, 75
National Association for Music Education,
    384
National Association of Teachers of Singing (NATS), 75
National Center for Education Statistics, 359
nervousness, 261
New Age music, 187
niacin, 262
Nielson Media Research, 92
notes (*also see* articulation):
    accents, 229, 230, 234
    anticipating, 226
    appoggiatura, 234
    counting, 417–18
    length of, 229
    note names, 125, 126, 416–17
    notes or music, 226
    ornamentation, 108
    separating, 236
    suspensions, 234
Nussbaum, Carolyn, 35
nutrition, 72, 262, 267–68, 391

oboe, 21, 23, 25
opera, 178, 184, 185, 232, 234
Opera News, 75
Orchestra 2001, 393–94
Orchestral Musicians CD-ROM library, 389
orchestras:
    auditions, 22, 386–95
    history, 177, 181–82
    membership, 335, 344, 346–47
    school music programs, 44–46
    tuning, 221
    websites, 436
organizing (*also see* time management):
    audition preparation, 377–78
    for college, 370
    to-do lists, 84, 92–93
organs, 177, 178–79
orthodontists, 289

Palestrina, Giovanni da, 175–76
parents:
    attending lessons, 278–79, 286–88, 301, 316–17

parents *continued:*
  communicating with teens, 278, 304
  guide for, 277–84
  instrument purchase, 20–28
  levels of involvement, 282–83, 285–86
  pressure from, 294, 309, 312, 318, 321, 322
  professional musicians, 287, 306, 312, 316–17, 321
  support from, 93, 284, 288, 299, 339
  as teachers, 46
  tips for success, 278–79, 280, 284, 288
patience, 6, 17, 55, 101–102
patterns, 214, 233, 239–40
peer pressure, 299–300, 315, 317
perfect pitch, 218
perfection, 248, 257, 281, 392
performances (*also see* auditions; contests; ensembles; marching bands; orchestras), 247–73
  book list, 432
  conquering stage fright, 252–65
  cover mistakes, 272
  dress for success, 263–64, 380
  eye contact, 242, 271
  fake it, 343
  family concerts, 295, 322
  goals, 83, 86, 247, 254
  living through failures, 247, 248, 250–51, 257, 301–302, 312, 313
  nutrition, 72, 262, 267–68, 391
  opportunities for, 47, 361–62, 404
  performance day, 269, 391–92
  preparation, 253–56, 262–65
  pre-performance routines, 253, 258, 262–65, 269–70, 391
  putting into perspective, 247–51
  rewards and recognition, 248, 259
  sleep and exercise, 264, 267–68
  taking responsibility, 250–51
  training schedule, 253
  venues, 74, 255, 400
  why perform, 247–48, 251
phrasing, 115, 116, 226–30, 233, 234, 236, 239–40, 345
physiology (*also see* body and body language):
  decibel levels, 351–52
  hydration, 74
  larynxes, 70
  phlegm, 74
  sweaty hands and lips, 261
  symptoms of stage fright, 260–61
  tight throat, 261
  too much saliva, 261

voice development/protection, 70, 72–73
piano (*also see* instruments; lessons; memorizing):
  body language, 227, 230
  breathing techniques, 232–33
  electric keyboards, 22, 24
  invention of, 177
  pedaling, 116
  as tuner, 221
pitch (*also see* intonation), 116, 118, 218–22, 229, 271, 340, 389
playing by ear, 47
polyphonic music, 174, 175, 176
popular music, 196, 364
positive thinking, 257, 259
posture, 4, 116, 220, 227, 256, 271, 272
practice (*also see* goals; schedules; time management), 79–120
  audience for, 232
  braces, 290–91
  correctly, 5, 45, 60, 91, 106–107
  daily and weekly goals, 93, 96
  distractions, 257–58, 298
  how much, 91–92, 95, 108
  involving parents and teacher, 47, 93, 119–20, 282–83, 285–86
  memorizing, 119, 240, 241
  phrasing, 115, 116
  practice problems, 295, 314
  practice the performance, 117
  priorities and deadlines, 87
  problem lists, 119
  rewards for, 93, 102, 118, 314
  what to do if you're bored, 94, 102, 110–11, 114–20, 295, 300
practice agreements, 93
practice charts, 94, 99
practice content:
  daily, 105–106
  new material, 100
  repeats, 108, 118
  requirements, 301
  stretching and warm-up exercises, 99
practice methods:
  beginners, 15, 114–15
  building speed, 107–108, 115
  chunking, 106–107, 118
  do something different, 108, 117, 119
  "first chance" method, 263
  listen to yourself, 96, 108
  mark music, 116–17
  new habits, 94, 118–19
  play musically, 117
  play slowly, 115

record sessions, 108, 119, 241, 254–55, 310

rhythm and tempo, 109, 110, 115, 119

road maps, 118–19

routines, 99–100, 104, 114–20

stay on track, 93–94, 100

study, 100, 115

practice quality:

attitude and commitment, 28, 79–81, 101–103, 110, 117–19, 281, 314–15

be consistent, 93, 100

focus and concentration, 59, 60, 102–104, 116, 320

practice tips:

20 practice hints, 99–113

75 ways to practice differently every day, 115–20

daily/weekly routines and goals, 4–5, 14, 93, 95, 99–100, 114–20

hard parts, 106, 109, 110, 119

hints for success, 4–5, 60, 93–94, 99–113, 115–20, 282

mark mistakes, 104–105, 110, 116, 309, 310–11, 319

priorities and deadlines, 14–16, 87, 92–93, 314

sample goals, 95–96

take breaks, 104

pressure:

handling of, 247

from parents and teachers, 294, 309, 312, 316, 318, 321, 322

peer pressure, 299–300, 315, 317

to perform, 302

private lessons. *See* lessons

professional musicians (*also see* music careers), 174, 238, 262, 306, 312, 316–17, 321, 352

questions from students, 309–23

boredom, 311, 313

burnout, 314–15, 322–23

contests, 312, 313, 315

gossip/teasing, 316, 317–18

instrument choice, 309, 311, 321–22

jealousy, 317, 318–19

lessons, 311, 313–14, 317, 321, 323

mistakes, 309, 310–11, 319

musicians for parents, 17, 312, 316–17, 321

numbness in hands, 310

parents, 309, 312, 316, 318, 321, 322

peer pressure, 315, 317

practicing, 314, 315, 320

school music programs, 310, 311–12, 313

self-image, 309–10

solo parts, 311–12

student–teacher relationship, 312, 314–16, 318–20

students as teachers, 310

teachers, 310, 316, 317, 318, 320–21

teaching styles, 313, 317, 319–20, 321

quitting, 293–308, 314

rap music, 18

recitals, 44, 52, 57, 86

recognition, 248, 259

recordings:

auditions, 378

lessons, 311

listening to, xviii, 48, 74, 85, 108, 172–73, 291, 315

memorization aids, 239, 240–41

practice aids, 117

references, 431–38

books by subject, 431–35

magazines, 435

movies, 438

music organizations, 437

websites by subject, 435–37

rehearsal measures, 215, 338, 342

rehearsals:

audience, 231

auditions and contests, 60, 266

ensembles, 213, 337–38

mental, 258

need for, 256

schedules, 282, 338–39, 345

Renaissance, 175–76, 236, 421

repeats, 214–15, 233, 239

repertoire, 382

retirement homes, 74, 255, 267, 302

rewards, 52, 93, 102, 118, 248, 259, 280–81

rhythm:

auditions, 389

changing during practice, 110

dotted rhythms, 109

focus on, 116

musicality, 232

rhythmic patterns, 188

sight-reading, 216

talking rhythm, 114–15

rhythm and blues, 18, 435, 436

ritards, 232

Rite of Spring (Stravinsky), 172, 187–88

rock music/musicians, vi, 18, 195, 348–52, 436

role-playing, 255–56

Romantic period, 183–86, 236, 421

Rotary Club, 48, 371, 413

rubato, 111, 214

saliva, 261

xophone, 17, 22, 25

scales:

boredom with, 313

memorizing, 239, 386

music theory, 3, 130–38, 148–52, 164–65, 187, 221, 228

musicality, 224

playing with tuners, 221

practicing, 99, 117

singing, 222

scanning, 215, 226

"scat" singing, 303

scenarios, 231, 232

schedules (*also see* time management):

braces, 289

ensembles, 338–39, 345

practice, 87, 90–97, 104, 280, 282, 315, 320, 360

pre-performance, 253, 262–65

summer, 57, 298

tips for success, 270–72, 377–80

trial lessons, 57, 375–77

scholarships, 371

school music programs (*also see* ensembles; marching bands):

bands and orchestras, 44–46, 311–12, 321, 346–47, 362, 371

benefits, 328, 335–36

lessons, 54, 56

teachers, 56, 310, 313

self-confidence. *See* confidence

self-teaching, 43, 44, 46, 47, 48–49

sequences, memorizing, 239

serialism, 188

serotonin, 262

sheet music, 174, 238, 240

sibling rivalry, 298

sight-reading, 3, 100, 194, 213–17, 295, 346, 386, 432–33

silent practice, 115

singers (*also see* lessons; performances), 67–75

arias, 232

auditions, 388

book list, 432

breathing techniques, 75, 232–33

dairy products, 267

learning pace, 314

pitch, 222

voice development and potential, 55, 68, 70

voice strain and recovery, 73–74

websites, 75, 435–37

Sixth Symphony (Pastoral) (Beethoven), 184

Smart Music CDs, 119

solfegge, 361

sonatas, 178

sound:

braces, 290, 291

decibel levels, 351–52

ensembles, 236, 340–41, 345

musicality, 228, 229

orchestras, 389

soundtracks, 191, 195

stage fright, 44, 241, 252–65, 270, 315

sticky notes, 105

Strad, 352

Stravinsky, Igor, 172–73, 187–88

string instruments (*also see* instruments), 70, 116, 177–78, 220–21, 230

student loans, 371

student teachers, 56, 310

student–teacher relationship:

be a good student, 59, 60–61

changing teachers, xi–xii, 62–66, 293–94, 304, 307

choosing a teacher, 52, 55–56

colleges/conservatories, 372, 375–77

lessons, 46, 52, 71, 314, 315

singers, 71

student questions, 312, 314–16, 318, 319–20

students (*also see* lessons; practice; questions from students):

advice from, 285–88, 324–31

changing teachers, 57, 62–66

guide for, 277–84

high-school danger zones, 297

hints for success, 59–61

involving parents, 59, 65, 285–88

middle-school danger zones, 297

musicians for parents, 287, 306, 312, 316–17, 321

persistence, 10, 13, 60, 71

preparation, 59–60

as teachers, 48

when to quit, 307

studios, 52, 57

success, mind-set, 79, 80

summer music camp, 17, 24

suspensions, 234

sweat, 261

symphonies, 183–84

syncopation, 214

talent, 8–11

Tchaikovsky, Peter Ilyich, 171, 192, 282

teachers (*also see* lessons; student–teacher
   relationship), 50–58
   changing, xi–xii, 62–66, 293–94, 316,
      317, 320–21
   criteria, 50–52, 68–69, 75
   hiring, 56–57
   motivators, 6, 50, 55
   parents as, 46, 312
   professional ethics, 310
   qualities, 51, 54–56
   students as, 48, 56
   studio policies, 57
   teaching styles, 52–53, 313, 317, 319–20,
      321
teasing, 300, 316
teen radio show website, 437
telephone trees, 339
television, 92
tempo, *109*, 111, 115, 119, 214, 226, 232, 241
"The Test," 306
time management (*also see* organizing):
   contests, 247
   memorizing, 240–41
   practice sessions, 90–97, 99–100, 296–97
   quitting, 296–97
   setting priorities, 296–97, 322–23
   training schedule, 253
time signatures, 214, 419
tips for success:
   auditions, 270–72, 377–81, 386, 389–93
   basics, 3–7
   college preparation, 361–62, 363, 375–85
   conquering stage fright, 252–65, 315
   contests, 249–50
   daily practice, 4–5
   ensembles, 338–47
   memorizing, 239–41, 346
   music careers, 397–99, 403–404, 411–13
   musicality, 3, 224–26, 230–31, 234–35
   parent behavior, 278–79, 280
   phrasing, 226–27, 228, 230, 236
   playing with emotion, 230–31
   practice, 4–5, 60, 93–94, 282
   trial lessons, 375–77, 380
to-do lists, 84, 92–93

tone:
   and braces, 292
   ensembles, 340
   instruments, 26, 27
   musicality, 229, 235, 340
   non-chord tones, 234
   practicing, 116
   shaky tone, 261
   tone color, 229, 235, 340
   tone tricks, 46
   whole tone scales, 187
tonic chords, 153–56, 234
travel mishaps, 378–79
trills, 229
trombone, 14, 22, 24, 26, 43, 289
trumpet, 15, 23, 25, 26, 90, 289, 292
Tune a Day book, 12, 14, 83
tuners/tuning, 104, 119, 220–21, 337–38

vibrato, 116, 228–29, 230, 234, 235–36, 387,
   389
video cameras, 255
videogames, 94, 193
violin, 14, 21, 22, 24, 26, 184, 192
virtuosity, 10–11
visualization, 79, 258–59, 270, 309–10
vocal cords/voice box, 70, 72, 73
voice nodules, 73
voice training, 67–72, 75
volume/volume meters, 228, 229, 389

websites (*also see* internet), 30, 31, 32, 37, 75,
   198, 384, 435–37
weddings, 74
whole tone scales, 187
wind instruments, 177–78, 220–21, 229, 230,
   232–33
woodwind instruments (*also see* instruments), 34, 289
working hard (*also see* goals), 5–6, 10, 214,
   324–31, 381
world music websites, 436

YouTube, 198, 230, 352

Bonnie Blanchard is a versatile freelance musician and a dynamic instructor in the Seattle area. She holds music and teaching degrees from the University of Washington.

A flute instructor for 35 years, Bonnie has worked with many of the world's greatest flutists and teachers. Her creative ideas and unbridled enthusiasm for teaching have consistently produced students who win top awards in local and national contests and earn college and conservatory scholarships.

Bonnie is also becoming known across the country as a motivational speaker. She has shared her teaching philosophy in speeches to the National Music Teachers Association, the National Flute Association, the Washington State Music Teachers Association, and the California Association of Professional Music Teachers.

Bonnie is founder of the popular Silverwood Music Ensembles, and she plays flute on the Silverwood CD *Here Comes the Bride,* requested by brides all over the country. Silverwood ensembles have performed in the Pacific Northwest's top venues, including performances for the Boeing Company, Microsoft, the World Trade Organization delegates, and President Bill Clinton.

Bonnie lives in Seattle with her tone-deaf but supportive husband, their two sons, who each play piano and a stringed instrument, and Angie the Flute Dog.

Cynthia Blanchard Acree's memoir, *The Gulf between Us: Love and Terror in Desert Storm,* appeared in *Reader's Digest* as a "Today's Best Nonfiction" excerpt. In her 25 years as a program developer, writing consultant, and instructor, she has developed and presented scores of training programs on communication skills, business writing, motivation, and goal setting. She teaches writing at Mira Costa College in Oceanside, California.

A dynamic speaker, Cynthia has spoken to diverse groups around the country and appeared on ABC's *20/20,* NBC's *Today,* CNN, FOX, C-Span 2's *Book TV,* and National Public Radio. Cynthia sings with the North San Diego County Masterworks Chorale and plays the piano. She lives in Oceanside with her husband and their two boys, who play the trombone and violin.

record sessions, 108, 119, 241, 254–55, 310

rhythm and tempo, 109, 110, 115, 119

road maps, 118–19

routines, 99–100, 104, 114–20

stay on track, 93–94, 100

study, 100, 115

practice quality:

    attitude and commitment, 28, 79–81, 101–103, 110, 117–19, 281, 314–15

    be consistent, 93, 100

    focus and concentration, 59, 60, 102–104, 116, 320

practice tips:

    20 practice hints, 99–113

    75 ways to practice differently every day, 115–20

    daily/weekly routines and goals, 4–5, 14, 93, 95, 99–100, 114–20

    hard parts, 106, 109, 110, 119

    hints for success, 4–5, 60, 93–94, 99–113, 115–20, 282

    mark mistakes, 104–105, 110, 116, 309, 310–11, 319

    priorities and deadlines, 14–16, 87, 92–93, 314

    sample goals, 95–96

    take breaks, 104

pressure:

    handling of, 247

    from parents and teachers, 294, 309, 312, 316, 318, 321, 322

    peer pressure, 299–300, 315, 317

    to perform, 302

private lessons. See lessons

professional musicians (also see music careers), 174, 238, 262, 306, 312, 316–17, 321, 352

questions from students, 309–23

    boredom, 311, 313

    burnout, 314–15, 322–23

    contests, 312, 313, 315

    gossip/teasing, 316, 317–18

    instrument choice, 309, 311, 321–22

    jealousy, 317, 318–19

    lessons, 311, 313–14, 317, 321, 323

    mistakes, 309, 310–11, 319

    musicians for parents, 17, 312, 316–17, 321

    numbness in hands, 310

    parents, 309, 312, 316, 318, 321, 322

    peer pressure, 315, 317

    practicing, 314, 315, 320

    school music programs, 310, 311–12, 313

    self-image, 309–10

    solo parts, 311–12

    student–teacher relationship, 312, 314–16, 318–20

    students as teachers, 310

    teachers, 310, 316, 317, 318, 320–21

    teaching styles, 313, 317, 319–20, 321

quitting, 293–308, 314

rap music, 18

recitals, 44, 52, 57, 86

recognition, 248, 259

recordings:

    auditions, 378

    lessons, 311

    listening to, xviii, 48, 74, 85, 108, 172–73, 291, 315

    memorization aids, 239, 240–41

    practice aids, 117

references, 431–38

    books by subject, 431–35

    magazines, 435

    movies, 438

    music organizations, 437

    websites by subject, 435–37

rehearsal measures, 215, 338, 342

rehearsals:

    audience, 231

    auditions and contests, 60, 266

    ensembles, 213, 337–38

    mental, 258

    need for, 256

    schedules, 282, 338–39, 345

Renaissance, 175–76, 236, 421

repeats, 214–15, 233, 239

repertoire, 382

retirement homes, 74, 255, 267, 302

rewards, 52, 93, 102, 118, 248, 259, 280–81

rhythm:

    auditions, 389

    changing during practice, 110

    dotted rhythms, 109

    focus on, 116

    musicality, 232

    rhythmic patterns, 188

    sight-reading, 216

    talking rhythm, 114–15

rhythm and blues, 18, 435, 436

ritards, 232

Rite of Spring (Stravinsky), 172, 187–88

rock music/musicians, vi, 18, 195, 348–52, 436

role-playing, 255–56

Romantic period, 183–86, 236, 421

Rotary Club, 48, 371, 413

rubato, 111, 214

saliva, 261
saxophone, 17, 22, 25
scales:
    boredom with, 313
    memorizing, 239, 386
    music theory, 3, 130–38, 148–52, 164–65,
        187, 221, 228
    musicality, 224
    playing with tuners, 221
    practicing, 99, 117
    singing, 222
scanning, 215, 226
"scat" singing, 303
scenarios, 231, 232
schedules (*also see* time management):
    braces, 289
    ensembles, 338–39, 345
    practice, 87, 90–97, 104, 280, 282, 315,
        320, 360
    pre-performance, 253, 262–65
    summer, 57, 298
    tips for success, 270–72, 377–80
    trial lessons, 57, 375–77
scholarships, 371
school music programs (*also see* ensembles;
    marching bands):
    bands and orchestras, 44–46, 311–12,
        321, 346–47, 362, 371
    benefits, 328, 335–36
    lessons, 54, 56
    teachers, 56, 310, 313
self-confidence. *See* confidence
self-teaching, 43, 44, 46, 47, 48–49
sequences, memorizing, 239
serialism, 188
serotonin, 262
sheet music, 174, 238, 240
sibling rivalry, 298
sight-reading, 3, 100, 194, 213–17, 295, 346,
    386, 432–33
silent practice, 115
singers (*also see* lessons; performances),
    67–75
    arias, 232
    auditions, 388
    book list, 432
    breathing techniques, 75, 232–33
    dairy products, 267
    learning pace, 314
    pitch, 222
    voice development and potential, 55,
        68, 70
    voice strain and recovery, 73–74
    websites, 75, 435–37

Sixth Symphony (Pastoral) (Beethoven), 184
Smart Music CDs, 119
solfegge, 361
sonatas, 178
sound:
    braces, 290, 291
    decibel levels, 351–52
    ensembles, 236, 340–41, 345
    musicality, 228, 229
    orchestras, 389
soundtracks, 191, 195
stage fright, 44, 241, 252–65, 270, 315
sticky notes, 105
Strad, 352
Stravinsky, Igor, 172–73, 187–88
string instruments (*also see* instruments),
    70, 116, 177–78, 220–21, 230
student loans, 371
student teachers, 56, 310
student–teacher relationship:
    be a good student, 59, 60–61
    changing teachers, xi–xii, 62–66, 293–
        94, 304, 307
    choosing a teacher, 52, 55–56
    colleges/conservatories, 372, 375–77
    lessons, 46, 52, 71, 314, 315
    singers, 71
    student questions, 312, 314–16, 318,
        319–20
students (*also see* lessons; practice; ques-
    tions from students):
    advice from, 285–88, 324–31
    changing teachers, 57, 62–66
    guide for, 277–84
    high-school danger zones, 297
    hints for success, 59–61
    involving parents, 59, 65, 285–88
    middle-school danger zones, 297
    musicians for parents, 287, 306, 312,
        316–17, 321
    persistence, 10, 13, 60, 71
    preparation, 59–60
    as teachers, 48
    when to quit, 307
studios, 52, 57
success, mind-set, 79, 80
summer music camp, 17, 24
suspensions, 234
sweat, 261
symphonies, 183–84
syncopation, 214

talent, 8–11
Tchaikovsky, Peter Ilyich, 171, 192, 282

teachers (*also see* lessons; student–teacher relationship), 50–58
  changing, xi–xii, 62–66, 293–94, 316, 317, 320–21
  criteria, 50–52, 68–69, 75
  hiring, 56–57
  motivators, 6, 50, 55
  parents as, 46, 312
  professional ethics, 310
  qualities, 51, 54–56
  students as, 48, 56
  studio policies, 57
  teaching styles, 52–53, 313, 317, 319–20, 321
teasing, 300, 316
teen radio show website, 437
telephone trees, 339
television, 92
tempo, *109,* 111, 115, 119, 214, 226, 232, 241
"The Test," 306
time management (*also see* organizing):
  contests, 247
  memorizing, 240–41
  practice sessions, 90–97, 99–100, 296–97
  quitting, 296–97
  setting priorities, 296–97, 322–23
  training schedule, 253
time signatures, 214, 419
tips for success:
  auditions, 270–72, 377–81, 386, 389–93
  basics, 3–7
  college preparation, 361–62, 363, 375–85
  conquering stage fright, 252–65, 315
  contests, 249–50
  daily practice, 4–5
  ensembles, 338–47
  memorizing, 239–41, 346
  music careers, 397–99, 403–404, 411–13
  musicality, 3, 224–26, 230–31, 234–35
  parent behavior, 278–79, 280
  phrasing, 226–27, 228, 230, 236
  playing with emotion, 230–31
  practice, 4–5, 60, 93–94, 282
  trial lessons, 375–77, 380
to-do lists, 84, 92–93

tone:
  and braces, 292
  ensembles, 340
  instruments, 26, 27
  musicality, 229, 235, 340
  non-chord tones, 234
  practicing, 116
  shaky tone, 261
  tone color, 229, 235, 340
  tone tricks, 46
  whole tone scales, 187
tonic chords, 153–56, 234
travel mishaps, 378–79
trills, 229
trombone, 14, 22, 24, 26, 43, 289
trumpet, 15, 23, 25, 26, 90, 289, 292
Tune a Day book, 12, 14, 83
tuners/tuning, 104, 119, 220–21, 337–38

vibrato, 116, 228–29, 230, 234, 235–36, 387, 389
video cameras, 255
videogames, 94, 193
violin, 14, 21, 22, 24, 26, 184, 192
virtuosity, 10–11
visualization, 79, 258–59, 270, 309–10
vocal cords/voice box, 70, 72, 73
voice nodules, 73
voice training, 67–72, 75
volume/volume meters, 228, 229, 389

websites (*also see* internet), 30, 31, 32, 37, 75, 198, 384, 435–37
weddings, 74
whole tone scales, 187
wind instruments, 177–78, 220–21, 229, 230, 232–33
woodwind instruments (*also see* instruments), 34, 289
working hard (*also see* goals), 5–6, 10, 214, 324–31, 381
world music websites, 436

YouTube, 198, 230, 352

Bonnie Blanchard is a versatile freelance musician and a dynamic instructor in the Seattle area. She holds music and teaching degrees from the University of Washington.

A flute instructor for 35 years, Bonnie has worked with many of the world's greatest flutists and teachers. Her creative ideas and unbridled enthusiasm for teaching have consistently produced students who win top awards in local and national contests and earn college and conservatory scholarships.

Bonnie is also becoming known across the country as a motivational speaker. She has shared her teaching philosophy in speeches to the National Music Teachers Association, the National Flute Association, the Washington State Music Teachers Association, and the California Association of Professional Music Teachers.

Bonnie is founder of the popular Silverwood Music Ensembles, and she plays flute on the Silverwood CD *Here Comes the Bride,* requested by brides all over the country. Silverwood ensembles have performed in the Pacific Northwest's top venues, including performances for the Boeing Company, Microsoft, the World Trade Organization delegates, and President Bill Clinton.

Bonnie lives in Seattle with her tone-deaf but supportive husband, their two sons, who each play piano and a stringed instrument, and Angie the Flute Dog.

Cynthia Blanchard Acree's memoir, *The Gulf between Us: Love and Terror in Desert Storm,* appeared in *Reader's Digest* as a "Today's Best Nonfiction" excerpt. In her 25 years as a program developer, writing consultant, and instructor, she has developed and presented scores of training programs on communication skills, business writing, motivation, and goal setting. She teaches writing at Mira Costa College in Oceanside, California.

A dynamic speaker, Cynthia has spoken to diverse groups around the country and appeared on ABC's *20/20,* NBC's *Today,* CNN, FOX, C-Span 2's *Book TV,* and National Public Radio. Cynthia sings with the North San Diego County Masterworks Chorale and plays the piano. She lives in Oceanside with her husband and their two boys, who play the trombone and violin.